Books by Emily Hahn

Animal
Gardens

EMILY HAHN

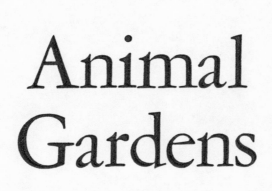

Animal Gardens

DOUBLEDAY & COMPANY, INC.
GARDEN CITY, NEW YORK
1967

Grateful acknowledgment is made for the use of the following:

Poem from *China's History of Africa* by Jan Jullus Duyvendak. Reprinted by permission of the publisher, Arthur Probsthain.

Lines from "Willy" by Richard Moore, which appeared in the August 12, 1965, issue of *The Reporter*. Copyright © 1965 by The Reporter Magazine Company. Reprinted by permission of Richard Moore and *The Reporter*.

"Invocation" from *Following the Equator* by Samuel L. Clemens. Reprinted by permission of Harper & Row, Publishers.

A substantial portion of this book
has appeared in *The New Yorker*

Contents

□

Illustrations

□

PHOTO CREDITS

New York Zoological Society – Nos. 3, 9, 12, 14, 15, 16, 17, 18, 19, 20, 21, 22, 23, 24, 25, 28, 29.
San Diego Zoo, by Ron Garrison – Nos. 1, 4, 7, 8, 31, 32.
Paul Steinemann, Zoologischer Garten, Basel – Nos. 5, 6.
Fort Worth Zoo – Nos. 2 (a & b).
United Press International – Nos. 26, 27.
Detroit Zoo – No. 10.
Henri Frenay – No. 30.
Frank Stevens – No. 11.

Introduction

□

I like zoos. I have liked them all my life, from the first time I was taken in a stroller to the St. Louis Zoo in Forest Park. Some people who visit new cities, as soon as they arrive, rush off to museums or art galleries or bookshops: I go to the zoo. Obviously there is one important distinction between these hobbies. The museum and gallery displays are of inorganic objects, while those in the zoo are living creatures. It is a difference that often lands me into argument with those many individuals who consider zoological gardens cruel and would like to put an end to them. They feel that I am contributing to the cruelty of mankind by visiting zoos, and are convinced that if only I and the thousands of others who share my enthusiasm were to see matters in the proper light, we would cut off our patronage; that the consequent loss of gate receipts or municipal appropriations would discourage zoo managers to the point of closing down. I respect the generosity of these sentiments but I don't accept the idea of a boycott, or, indeed, the concept of the zoo as a place to be eliminated. Argument on such an emotion-engendering topic is seldom of any use, but I don't like being classed with bullfight fans and the Marquis de Sade, and would like to make my position clear.

Some zoos are excellent. Some are not excellent, others are downright bad, but given education and good will, they can be reformed. It should be obvious that a capable zoo man is not cruel. For practical reasons he wants to keep his charges healthy and contented. Once in a while, though rarely, one finds the wrong type in charge, a person who actually enjoys cruelty to his animals. Zoo administrators should be vigilant against this danger. In fact, a zoo director must always be alert: his profession is full of pitfalls. In his little world he has tremendous authority, especially

nowadays when zoos have become big business. He must be able to find
assistants and keepers that he can trust. Some keepers are good all-round
animal men, others are excellent with certain species yet not with others.
Such idiosyncrasies must be taken into account. I heard the other day of a
herpetologist who had just taken his Ph.D. and got a job as curator of
reptiles in a large zoo: unfortunately he was terrified of snakes and would
not go near one. For the time being he is working with fish. Then there
is the veterinary officer: he should know how to work with wild animals—a
country veterinarian who can treat cows, or has worked only with dogs and
cats and other pets, is not the vet for a zoo. In the old, unspecialized days
a zoo vet had to cope with anything and everything that came his way,
from the impeded delivery of a pregnant anaconda to a deer's broken
leg, and most of the time he was working in the dark. Today, with preliminary training for the doctor and vastly improved equipment, things
are less rugged for the vet and animals together.

A director may have insufficient say in the housing of his animals, which
all too often falls short of the ideal. Government officials, who usually
control such matters, are apt to place zoo buildings low on the priority
list, and unless the director can prove that the expenditure he proposes
will pay off in money or prestige, he doesn't get his appropriation. When
officials do disgorge, they often want to call the tune and select the
architect. And private donors, too, must be treated with prudence.
Usually they have their own preferences regarding architects, and are apt
to select those that know little, if anything, about building for zoos.
Even in zoological societies such problems arise. The zoo director must be
a politician too.

Apologists for the zoo as an institution often speak warmly of its
contribution to education, and they are justified, but once this has been
said the matter is not closed. How can the displays be exploited to best
advantage? The signs are of utmost importance: where should they be
placed? How should they be worded? How much information can the
ordinary visitor take in, and—a more important question—does he *want*
to take it in, anyway? Signs are only the beginning of it. A city zoo is
usually called on to entertain and inform groups of schoolchildren; the
wise director encourages such a use of his domain. In the course of such
visits, children should be instilled with the correct concepts of natural resources.

A director should welcome the scientific use of his animals, as long as
this offers no harm to them. Many specimens, rare even in the wild, can
be of invaluable aid to research. Scientists need experience with living
creatures as well as dead, to observe their behavior, their physical nature,

details of parturition and lactation, a hundred branches of knowledge. In bacteriology alone zoo animals are able to bring a whole world into the laboratory.

The director's duties take him beyond rendering aid to science in this way. The conservation of species depends very much on him. A modern director will not be content to boast, as many of his predecessors did, when his zoo possesses one of a rare species. He aims to have a breeding pair. In extraordinary cases, when he can't find a mate for his animal because there are no more available in the wild, he seeks one in another zoo and arranges a match either by borrowing the other specimen or lending his own. Such co-operation is not always easy to arrange. A director might well hesitate to trust his treasure to the dangers of travel, but the feeling is growing that one rare animal is, in a way, worse than none, and zoo people are more and more inclined to take such risks. Foreign affairs sometimes complicate the problem. In 1965, the London Zoological Society suggested to the authorities of the Moscow zoo that their giant pandas ought to get together. No other giant panda than these two could be found in the non-Chinese world, all other previously exported to foreign lands having died off. There remained only the male An-An in Moscow and the female Chi-Chi in Regent's Park. [Chi-Chi's presence in London is in itself an example of the difficulties that can be caused by politics. Brought out of China by a private dealer, to fill an order hopefully made by an American zoo, her entry into the United States was sternly banned by Washington on the grounds that, according to law, no articles of Chinese origin can be imported into the United States. The British quickly bought her instead.] Grown to maturity, Chi-Chi had become irritable during her season, losing her appetite and moping generally, but at first the Russians refused to consider the marriage. A year's reflection, however, brought about a change of heart. Nobody can be sure just what prompted the alteration in Red policy, but the American anthropologist Dr. Henry Field thinks he might have the answer. He and his wife Julia, who used to be director of the Crandon Park Zoo at Miami, were on a visit to Moscow shortly after the first Russian "No" was delivered to Regent's Park. During an interview in Moscow with the Russian director of all Russian directors, Mrs. Field brought up the matter of An-An and Chi-Chi. Speaking as a woman and a mother herself, she said, it was a pity not to give the animals a chance.

Whatever brought on the decision, the Russians gave way, and at this moment of writing, in the spring of 1966, Chi-Chi is in the Moscow zoo, in a cage next door to An-An, waiting for the next auspicious time for them to meet. They have already had one at which the encounter immediately came to blows. According to the Chinese experts in Peking, where three little giant pandas have been born in captivity, this is nothing out of the ordinary: mating pandas *do* fight, often fiercely and bloodily. On the other hand, many wild animals in captivity, unlike domesticated animals, do not mate at any and every chance. If two of the opposite sex don't like each other, that is that. We can only hope for the best with the giant pandas.

Though the London-Moscow panda affair is the most spectacular example of conservational co-operation between zoos that has come to light, happily it is not unique. For example, in the Dutch publication *International Zoo News* for December 1965, a letter from Clyde Hill, associate curator at San Diego, acknowledges a helpful gesture from across the American continent: "In order further to set an example in zoo conservation practices, the Bronx Zoo recently sent its only female Gerenuk to the San Diego Zoo for breeding. This move is particularly significant because the Bronx Zoo sacrificed a prime exhibit for the single purpose of conservation, an act that is almost without precedent. Conservationists everywhere will be heartened by the news."

The ideal zoo director should have at least one more quality that is of great importance—discrimination in his relations with animal dealers. We will give more attention to this subject in the body of the book.

A person who hates zoos may well ask why such supermen, if they exist, are in the profession at all. Surely they could find something better to do with their talents than run a concentration-camp and keep wild creatures robbed of their liberty, cooped in cages with wanderlust frustrated, never again to know the fierce joy of the hunt.

> *Hush, my babe, in vain you rage.*
> *See the eagle in the cage.*
> *And his cage is strong and true,*
> *And he cries aloud like you.*

Literature is full of poems and prose about caged animals; the dissenter has a point indeed, but there are arguments for the other side as well. Dr. Heini Hediger, psychologist, animal behaviorist, and director of the Zurich Zoological Garden, has a good deal to say on the subject, as for instance that many criticisms that are made of animal captivity are results of anthropomorphism, or the attributing of human reactions to non-human beings. It was Hediger who introduced the use of the term in this connotation, but others have seized upon it—obviously it satisfied a long-felt need for a portmanteau word to describe the attitude, and the term has now become so popular that there is an adverse reaction to it: one angry writer has called "anthropomorphism" the dirty word of all dirty words in contemporary zoological circles. It is true that some scientists lean over backward to avoid interpreting animal behavior in human terms, but we can easily understand them when we examine the legacy of animal stories left us by our immediate ancestors, who discerned Christian piety in elephants, superhuman reasoning powers in dogs, and emotional refinement in horses. The attitude still persists in backwaters: a riding mistress of my acquaintance claims that one of her horses wept at being removed from her stables. "Tears rolled down his cheeks," she insisted.

Studying wild animals in captivity without admitting such weaknesses to mar his judgment, Dr. Hediger feels sure that they simply don't long for liberty in our poetic sense. Humans long for the wings of a dove, and enjoy taking to the woods, tramping, and sleeping out in what we call the natural way of life. But at such times we are relaxing, enjoying a holiday rather than going about our serious business, whereas the animal that lives in the wild is very serious about it. He's got to be. His business is just that, moving about to find food, to watch out for enemies, and, in general, to stay alive. He doesn't roam for the fun of it. His wanderings are never without a purpose. If he is not in search of food he is patrolling the boundaries of the territory to which he has staked out a claim. Within this tract he finds everything his nature demands, but he must look for it—food, a place where his mate can rear their young in safety, and so on. He must keep out dangerous intruders. This being so, he doesn't move out of his territory unless something drives him out. In his prime he is obsessed, completely taken up, by the battle to stay alive and keep his family safe, and in living thus he is merciless to weaker creatures, as other beasts would be merciless to him if he couldn't defend himself unrelentingly. In his old age—but the phrase is meaningless, since in his native habitat he is not permitted to achieve old age. In the wild, few creatures die of senility.

Not that it is a kindness to put a wild animal into captivity. There his food is supplied, relieving him of the necessity of scouring the territory for it, and he is safe from his natural enemies, but he can't be expected to realize these advantages, as some of his strongest instincts are being affronted. In time, however, most wild animals in zoos do adjust themselves to the proximity of Man and settle down. An animal's keeper knows when the change has taken place, because the animal becomes willing to eat. And a creature that can't range far afield, and doesn't have to, loses the impulse to move about. Only an animal that feels completely settled in the zoo can breed, which is one reason among many that directors take pride in a good breeding record. The greatest drawback to life for the occupants of a zoo, especially those that have been captured rather than cage-born, is not frustrated wanderlust, but boredom. Relieved of their customary preoccupations, they have nothing to do. For some species quick to learn—great apes and elephants—this boredom can be alleviated with comparative ease. To amuse less "human" animals, antelopes or wild sheep, offers more difficulty, though the problem is being studied. In the ideal zoo there would be recreation for all species, not only because it would be kind, but that the wild animal in conditions of captivity, at least captivity as it now exists, is bound to alter in nature and cease being the creature we want to see. Even physically, in spite of all the care that can be given, he alters. Animals born in captivity are often smaller and lighter than their wild brothers.

Yet we keep them in captivity, and I, for one, think that we should. Apart from their value to scientific study and as educational factors, they are the only representatives of wild life that we are likely to have at all in the near future. The wilderness is shrinking, the animals in it are on the way to extermination, and soon the only survivors will be those living in protected areas and zoos. Man increases at such a swift rate that the question of conservation will soon be purely academic. We live in an urban age. Even most of our domesticated animals, adapted and trimmed down as they have been by man, are out of sight and mind to city children, who catch glimpses of cattle, sheep, and barnyard fowls only in the "contact area" of the local children's zoo. If we permit these beasts to be crowded out of sight even though they are necessary to our daily lives, what chance has the wild animal whose material worth is not readily apparent? Most people feel a curiosity about these creatures, and if it were not for the zoo they would have no idea what a real elephant, or tiger, or wolf looks like, since no picture however vivid, no list of measurements or other description can take the place of the actual animal. Children especially should have the chance to see a zoo, if not a reserve. In some respects a child is himself a wild animal, not yet resigned to his place in that enormous zoo we call civilization. Even if it weren't for nursery-school stories about bears and lions and the fables of Aesop and La Fontaine, most children would—and should—feel kinship with creatures of the wild. But how are they to profit from such feelings without evidence of some object for them—not dry bones in a museum or pictures on a flat page, but the animal itself, alive? These days we talk and worry a lot about the detached personality, yet continue a steady process, as we bring up our children all among the glass and steel and concrete, of detachment.

Whether or not we recall it, most of us have visited a zoo at least once in childhood. I firmly believe the effects of such visits to be incalculably valuable, and the rest of the world seems to agree. At any rate the visits go on. In thousands and tens of thousands, people go to the zoo. And in most places there is a handy zoo for them to go to. In the *International Zoo Yearbook* for 1965 the world list of zoos considered by the Advisory Committee worthy of being included numbers four hundred and twenty-two, not counting aquariums. These, remember, are only the accredited institutions; there are many more that don't measure up to committee standards or have not applied for inclusion. Most nations are represented, though Norway is not, because Norwegian law forbids the keeping of wild animals in captivity.

"I still believe," says the British Leonard Williams, in *Samba and the Monkey Mind*, "that zoos are necessary institutions, and that arguments directed against them in principle are hardly worth examination. Some animals enjoy more freedom in zoos than in their wild state. Freedom is a peculiar word. Freedom from what, and to do what? Freedom for the gorilla to return to what is left of his native haunts, to catch a virus disease that often destroys whole families of them in a matter of weeks, or to be hunted and killed for its meat by natives? Freedom for a vast number of African animals to return to nature reserves determined by the needs of man, barren and infertile areas which have no economic, industrial, or agricultural value for the human invader?"

Zoos must carry on. Their abolition would mean the disappearance of the world's last vestiges of wild life.

I thought about these things for a long time, for years, until I decided to go into the subject thoroughly. I would find out what I could about zoos of the past, then investigate the institution as it exists today—which proved to be a more active pursuit altogether, and a very enjoyable one. It also led me into the further subject of zoos as they are going to be, or at least one hopes they will be. On the way, inevitably, I often found myself sidetracked on paths too fascinating not to follow—the study of dealers and how they supply animals to the zoos, owners of private zoos, past and present, and the ways of animals in captivity. These and yet other topics have so much bearing on the main subject that I feel no guilt in having spent time on them. Not surprisingly, it proved quite impossible to study all the zoos in every country, or even any zoos in some countries, and if, at the beginning, I hadn't had just enough common sense to omit aquariums from the program, it would have developed into one of those longer-than-life jobs that are never finished. As it was, I was hampered by political difficulties as well as the limitations of time. I couldn't visit China, of course, and though the Russian authorities didn't bar me from the country, they wouldn't let me go to the preserve at Askanya-Nova in the Ukraine, where I understand they are doing some of their most interesting work. Because time ran out I have neglected Latin America, Denmark, and Sweden, omissions which I regret very much, and I have touched not at all on the modern zoos of Spain, Portugal, and some other countries. The reserves of Africa, with the exception of a few glancing comments, I have not treated because I feel that they don't really come within the scope of this book.

Nevertheless, I saw a lot of zoos. While at this work I never ceased to give thanks in my mind to the admirable *International Zoo Yearbook*, published in London under the editorship of Miss Caroline Jarvis, of whose ability I would say far more in praise except that I understand the Regent's Park staff eschew the Cult of the Personality.

In 1964, carrying little but a vast ignorance of the zoo world, I was introduced to it at the AAZPA (American Association of Zoological Parks and Aquariums) spring meeting in Cincinnati, Ohio.

Animal
Gardens

CHAPTER 1

"I Went to the Animal Fair . . ."

□

To the Editor of The Times:
Sir:
The time has come to abolish the Zoo.

A letter starting this way, which appeared in *The London Times* early in 1964, set off a stream of correspondence that appeared endless. At least, it was still going on, under the daily heading "ABOLISH THE ZOO?" seven or eight weeks later, when I left England for a visit to New York. I was not surprised by such volubility; nothing stirs the British up so much, or so often, as a controversy about zoos, unless it is one about blood sports, and as a long-time resident of England, I seem to have caught some of the same feeling. At any rate, when I heard, while in New York in early 1964, that an organization called the American Association of Zoological Parks and Aquariums was about to hold a meeting in Cincinnati, I asked the proper authorities whether I might attend it as an observer. It turned out that I might, and the next Sunday afternoon there I was, at the Sheraton-Gibson Hotel, in Cincinnati, duly registered and with a name card pinned near the left shoulder of my dress. The formal meeting was to begin the next morning and to end on Wednesday, but delegates had been arriving all day, and that evening there was a cocktail party billed as an "Ice Breaker." By the time I joined the party, old friends had found each other and were standing around in little groups, talking shop. I heard tantalizing snatches of conversation: "Can you use a baby elephant, thirty-seven inches high? I ordered four, but the other three are about forty." . . . "He would like to find a female okapi." . . . "He wanted seven hundred and fifty for that Cameroonian goat."

The delegates were a varied lot, coming from all parts of the continent, and even from Europe and Africa, and representing all branches of zoo activity. Among them were zoo directors, veterinarians, keepers, curators, bird men, fish men, herpetologists, animal trainers, game-farm owners, animal dealers, zoo architects, and a man from a Nebraska horse-meat company. Costumes were mixed, some of the men affecting hairy tweed with enormous plaid designs, and others dressing as soberly as bank managers. There were women, too—not very many, but some, even apart from the Cincinnati ladies who had been invited to the Ice Breaker to help entertain the visitors. At first, I assumed the visiting women were all wives who had come along for the ride. They looked the part—quiet and smiling, with fresh hair sets, fancy hats, and fur stoles—but I soon learned that a few were there on their own, in an official capacity. Standing near me and talking to a couple of men was a tall blond girl whose name tag proclaimed her to be a keeper from Florida. (Everyone, of course was labeled, like me, with a piece of cardboard giving his name, job, and place of work. At conferences, looking at a label without obviously craning one's neck is quite an art.) I introduced myself to her, but at that moment a muscular young man in a bright-blue short-sleeved shirt approached her and asked, in a southern accent, "Just what do you do at your zoo, Ma'am?"

"I run the hospital," the girl said. "Take care of animals that get sick, and new cubs, and so on. You know."

He nodded, and said, "I don't guess you'd try handling a sick cat, though?"

"Oh no, not alone. I leave them to the men," she replied.

Someone called her away then, and the young man stared after her for a minute. "Well, why not?" he said to me. "There's plenty of jobs a woman would be right good at in a zoo. Many a keeper depends on his wife to take care of bottle feeding. You couldn't run a zoo without a woman somewhere, it seems like. Why shouldn't that little girl be a keeper?"

Without waiting for me to answer, he took off after her. Another woman, petite and vivacious, now spoke to me—Mrs. William Hoff, the wife of the executive director of the Cincinnati Zoo. She rapidly introduced me to several other women, among them Mrs. Mildred Davis, of Columbus, Ohio, who was the first person in America to raise a gorilla successfully from babyhood. "Most of her family's in zoo work," Mrs. Hoff told me. "You find quite a few families like that, where they all go in for it. Mrs. Davis' son is here, too. He's director of Cheyenne Mountain Zoo, in Colorado. Carrying on the tradition. Have you met Mr. Hermann Ruhe, Jr.? He's another case in point. I think he's a third-generation animal dealer. His father was famous, too. They were at Arusha, in Tanganyika, but Mr. Ruhe has moved to Germany now—says Arusha's all shot. Zoo people are all such nice people—I don't know any other lot of men who work together so well. They're really devoted to their work. But there's one thing you might be surprised at—they have absolutely no inhibitions." Mrs. Hoff looked at me solemnly, to make certain that I was taking in her warning. "They'll discuss simply anything, anywhere at all," she assured me. "They talk about the breeding habits of animals, and sewage disposal, and everything—it doesn't matter where they are or who's listening. They're so absorbed in their work, you see. But don't worry about it. You'll get used to it."

Her warning proved unnecessary, at least for that evening. Everyone I talked with was far more interested in snake bite than in any other topic. Not long before, Gerald de Bary, the thirty-seven-year-old director of the Hogle Zoo, in Salt Lake City, had died as a result of the bite of a puff adder. The case had been much written about at the time in newspapers and magazines, but then the general public had forgotten about it. The members of the AAZPA had not forgotten. I heard many comments on Jerry de Bary, as he was usually called, but was unable to get much information; people said they were waiting to get the true story in the course of the coming sessions. Around eight o'clock the party came to an end, and the zoo people went off about their own concerns.

We met again at nine the next morning, in a large room filled with rows of folding chairs which faced a platform with a table, a microphone, a few men in more chairs, and a white screen. As we entered, each of us was handed a large black folder containing a mimeographed program and a pad of notepaper. I studied my program, trying to match the names on it with the people on the platform. I spotted the co-chairmen for the morning, both directors of Texas zoos—Lawrence Curtis, of Fort Worth, and Pierre Fontaine, of Dallas. Mr. Carson S. Whiting, president of the Zoological Society of Cincinnati, made a welcoming speech, and afterward, though the program said he would be followed by Dr. Theodore H. Reed, president of the AAZPA, we were addressed by Walter Stone, director of the Franklin Park Zoo, in Boston, who explained the switch by saying, "Ted Reed couldn't make it. He's in Djakarta, stealing a march on us by getting a Komodo." He gave us a brief rundown on the talks we were to hear that day, and added that since the program had been printed, an additional address had been scheduled—some remarks by

Lamar Farnsworth, the director of the Hogle Zoo, on the subject of Mr. de Bary and antivenin. At this, everyone sat up straighter. Mr. Stone told us that a De Bary Memorial Fund had been set up, and that anyone wishing to contribute to it should speak to him later, and then he called on us to stand in silence for a moment in memory of the unfortunate director.

The next speaker was William G. Conway, director of the New York Zoological Park, which everyone stubbornly insists upon referring to as the Bronx Zoo. The title of his talk was given in the program as "The Seven Sins of Zoo Business," but Mr. Conway, a lean, youthful-looking man with dark hair, explained that he had changed his plans at the last minute, and now proposed to read aloud, instead of his own talk, a letter that he was sure would interest us more than anything he himself might have been able to say. "It was found by our veterinarian under the wing of a Canada goose killed by vandals in 1963 in our zoo," he explained. "The signature isn't easy to make out, but it seems to be Branta canadensis." Everyone laughed, and continued to laugh at intervals throughout the reading of the letter, into which Mr. Conway had put a good deal of telling criticism of zoo management. The goose described a long career of zoo tenancy here and there, and condemned "slum-tenement" conditions in one place, the bathroom-tile atmosphere at another, and the hugger-mugger manner in which specimens are often exhibited. "Down with representation without education!" cried Branta canadensis. The tour de force was a great success, and Mr. Conway was warmly applauded as he stepped down. "It just came to me last night at the last minute," he said modestly when a friend congratulated him. "I owe the idea—in part at least—to a piece I read a long time ago by William Morton Wheeler, the entomologist. He wrote something on that order about termites."

Next, Mr. F. Bob Truett, director of the Birmingham, Alabama, zoo, spoke to us on "Making Popular Speeches Out of Difficult Science Subjects." Certain topics, he said, were of unfailing interest to the public, two of them being "What is Evolution?" and "How Snakes Live." Snakes? I waited expectantly, but for the moment the subject was carried no further. Mr. Truett was now assuring any of us who might suffer from shyness or stage fright at the prospect of making a speech that everyone goes through a similar ordeal at one time or another. "It's normal to be scared and who wants to be abnormal?" he said. Nobody volunteered a reply, and Mr. John McKew, personnel director of the New York Zoological Park, took the floor to speak on "Wages of Menagerie Keepers and Employees' Fringe Benefits in Zoological Parks." Both wages and benefits, it appeared, were unsatisfactory.

It was time for a fifteen-minute break, and we all walked about the room, filling cups with coffee from an urn in one corner, talking, and generally relaxing. All the talk was not recreational, however. Trading seemed to be going on here and there. Just behind my chair, a pair of wild pigs was swapped for fish of a species unfamiliar to me, and a deal in lizards was put through over my head. Above the hubbub, a man on the platform shouted that Mr. Gerald Lentz, assistant curator of the St. Louis Zoo, was taking a reptile and amphibian census and would appreciate it if everyone with a collection of fifty or more reptiles would keep records of all specimens and turn them in to him at the end of every year. As a side effect, the announcer said, this would furnish a good idea of the standard collection, but Mr. Lentz's project had three main purposes—to stimulate the keeping of zoo records, to supply information on keeping difficult specimens alive, and to facilitate trading.

"That's Lentz over there—that tall young fellow," a neighbor told me. "His father is Moody Lentz, the general curator at St. Louis, and he's at the end of the row there, with his wife. We have quite a few St. Louisans here. You know Marlin Perkins from television, don't you? His program used to be called 'Zoo Parade,' but it's something else now—I forget what. That's Mrs. Perkins with him, up at the front of the room talking to Curtis."

The man on the platform was broadcasting another request, this one from the elder Lentz, who wanted information on the feeding of baby elephants and had made out a questionnaire on the subject, copies of which could be picked up at the registration desk. By the time we were full of coffee and back in our seats, Mr. Farnsworth, the director of the Hogle Zoo, was behind the mike, ready to tell us about the death of Mr. De Bary, who had been his predecessor in office. He looked pale but spoke matter-of-factly, saying that it was natural for the accident to have stimulated a good deal of comment but that the authorities had been surprised and dismayed by the mistakes in many of the printed accounts. The mistakes showed that there were still people who never let facts spoil a good story, so Mr. Farnsworth was grateful for this opportunity to set the record straight with the people who were most closely concerned. I got the impression that he really was finding it a relief to be among men who knew what he was talking about, and who wouldn't look at him with awe and terror when he spoke about the affair.

"All of you who knew Jerry know how devoted he was to his work," Mr. Farnsworth said. "That, of course, is why the accident occurred. He was cleaning out the snake cages at night. No doubt he shouldn't have been doing it—shouldn't have been there at all at that time—but it wasn't unusual for him to be working late, and this is something that's got to be done either before or after the public is on the grounds. As I needn't tell you, he was always fond of reptiles; they were his favorites. He was planning to leave about nine-thirty, when this job was finished. The only other man anywhere nearby was a keeper on night duty." Mr. Farnsworth outlined the events of the next few minutes, after explaining that the snake cages at this zoo had glass doors that opened from the front. De Bary had just opened the door of the puff adder's cage when he had a spell of vertigo and fell forward, raising his right arm to break the fall. "He'd had these spells before, but not for some time," Mr. Farnsworth said. "We can tell you exactly what happened, because Jerry told us; at intervals during the next day and a half, before his death, he was able to talk as clearly as I'm talking to you now. He saw the snake coming for his arm, but he couldn't do anything about it before it got him. Both fangs went into the lower arm, possibly into the vein, immediately."

De Bary threw the snake back into its pit, slammed the door, and called the keeper. This man, who had recently had a routine lesson in first aid for snake bite, applied a tourniquet and summoned the police, a doctor, and Mr. Farnsworth, in that order. The police arrived first, and then the doctor, and, what with all the excitement, no one on the spot at first remembered that two bottles of antivenin were kept close at hand, in a refrigerator in the office of the reptile house, for just such an emergency; instead, the police hurried over to the main refrigerator, on the other side of the zoo premises. In all, there were eighty centimeters of antivenin available in Salt Lake City, and this—if there had been no delay—might have saved De Bary, sixty cubic centimeters being the maximum advisable amount, according to a Salt Lake authority on snake bite. The victim was put in an ambulance and taken to the hospital. During the journey and in the hospital, the doctor administered antivenin at ten-minute intervals, until the sixty cubic centimeters had been given. Should more antivenin have been used? It was hard to make up one's mind, even after the event, said Mr. Farnsworth. The stuff was fresh enough—it was only six months old—but the poison worked so rapidly that the tissues in De Bary's arm and shoulder simply melted away. Apparently, the venom of the puff adder, like that of some other snakes, has much the same effect as digestive juices in breaking down body tissue. "The autopsy showed that the flesh and muscles and blood vessels in the arm had just dissolved," said Farnsworth bleakly, and paused. Then he resumed, "The fact was, after the initial bite there was very little choice except, perhaps, the alternative of immediate amputation. Jerry was the only one there who had complete knowledge of what to do in such cases, and at the important moment, Jerry . . ." Again there was a pause. "Remember, the puff adder isn't the most treacherous snake in the world, yet Jerry is dead," Farnsworth went on. "Though he had transfusion immediately, his whole system changed and he died in thirty-one hours. He'd be all right, then he'd go into complete shock. Between these intervals, he was completely lucid. He'd seem to be holding his own. Then the blood pressure would drop down to zero, and it was during one of these times that he died."

Somebody asked what was known about De Bary's earlier blackouts, and the reply was that he had suffered from one or two at a previous zoological convention, in Washington, but that a complete checkup had shown nothing wrong, and he had put them out of his mind.

"Hadn't he suffered from gastric ulcers?" asked another man.

"Yes, he had," said Mr. Farnsworth. "He'd had two sets of ulcers, but he was believed to have fully recovered." Moreover, it was not true, as some reporters had written, that De Bary was suffering from influenza at the time of the accident. A complete medical report was in the works, but Farnsworth doubted if anything new would show up. "When an incision was made near the bite, deterioration had progressed so far that fluid just poured out of the wound," he added. "There were no tissues left at all— no muscles or anything."

In the silence that followed, a man in the back row stood up to say that he had been asked by a medical officer in the United States Army to forward a request, which was that in any future case of snake bite in a zoo the people involved telephone this officer immediately, as he was doing snake venom research directed toward improving the treatment for poisonous snake bite. Later I heard more about this from the officer, who wrote that the Army is

"endeavouring to do this by investigating three different areas: improvement of commercial antivenins, the development of non-toxic chemotherapeutic agents which, if injected into the area of the bite, will neutralize the venom there, and activate immunization of man against some species of highly toxic snakes . . . Some volunteers have taken small doses of Indian cobra venom mixed with an adjuvant. The dosage was increased slowly and their immunity titer checked frequently until they could tolerate a lethal dose of cobra venom with no ill effects other than a little swelling and pain. Last year one was bitten by a small cobra and required no medical attention whatsoever. This past March he was bitten severely by a five-foot cobra. Although he lost some skin over his finger and his hand became infected, he exhibited no neurotoxic symptoms. This in their opinion demonstrated the effectiveness of the vaccine, particularly after one saw a man die from the bite of a cobra of similar size in Miami, Florida, that year. For several years, the military authorities concerned have required that all of their people who handle cobras be immunized. After a high neutralization titer has been achieved, a booster injection is given every month.

"Which reminds me," said a man across the room. "Had De Bary been tested for antivenin sensitivity as a manner of routine? Or was he perhaps sensitive to it?"

"Yes, he'd been tested, and he wasn't sensitive," Mr. Farnsworth said.

There seemed to be no more questions about De Bary, and I thought—erroneously—that the subject was closed, especially since Walter Stone, the Boston man, immediately rose to give a talk on signs in zoological parks. Mr. Stone explained that because his own zoo had just about the worst signs and labels in the world, he and his associates had conducted a survey of signs in general, which had led them to certain conclusions. He enumerated them. I had already become aware—the impression was inescapable—that the average zoo man's attitude toward the zoo-visiting public is not one of unmitigated admiration, and Mr. Stone said nothing to change my mind. He told us that signs and labels in zoos should be clear, that there should never be more than sixty characters in a line, and that the letters should be black against white. A sign should contain nothing that might strain the feeblest intelligence. The attention span of the public is limited, he declared, a period of thirty seconds being the longest that it can be expected to concentrate. Mr. Stone's peroration was "Keep it simple."

Feeling rather gloomy, I went downstairs to the dining room for lunch with Mrs. Marlin Perkins, whose husband was attending a board meeting and couldn't eat with the rest of us. Like everybody else, she was thinking more about snake bite than zoo signs. "It was so awful for that poor man this morning," she said. "It was nobody's fault that a night keeper was the only other person around when De Bary was bitten, but one naturally wonders what might have happened if he'd been incised and suction had been applied. He might have had a chance. Suction wasn't mentioned this morning, and one didn't like to ask, but I do wonder. My husband has been bitten three times and has recovered completely. It's risky handling snakes, as he does on television."

We ordered our lunch, and the subject changed with the interruption. "Are you enjoying it?" Mrs. Perkins asked. "It's great fun, isn't it? I never miss one of these meetings if I can help it. I hate not to hear every talk, because you never know when you might find out something new." She remarked that it was fortunate that she had such enthusiasm for zoos, since, of all the women in the world, a zoo man's wife is least likely to get away from her husband's work, even when she travels. "Everyone says how fascinating it must be to go all over the world with my husband, as I do, but they don't realize quite what it's like, and they might not take to it," she said. "For instance, last year we went to Europe, and I was told that we'd have a whole day in Paris. I was thrilled—I'd never been to Paris—and I made out a list of the shopping I wanted to do. I had all the addresses written down and everything mapped out. Well, as soon as we got there, one of the men from the zoo at Vincennes came to see Marlin, and nothing would do but that we go with him to look at the zoo. You can't say no, and—do you know?—we never left that zoo until we had to rush for the plane. I should have realized it would be like that, because it always is, but I wouldn't change my life for anything."

The afternoon was spent talking, or listening to talks, about children's zoos—a phenomenon that had sprung up suddenly and, as far as I could tell, simultaneously, all over the world. I first saw a children's zoo about twenty years ago, at Whipsnade, the country zoological park in England, which happens to be near my house. There, for an extra sixpence, the visitor can enter an enclosure and look the less ferocious fauna—ponies, rabbits, calves, and the like—squarely in the eye. A child not only can pet the beasts, but, if properly chaperoned by one of the girl attendants, can wear a small python as a necklace for a few minutes, or play with a woolly monkey. It gives him something to talk about when he gets back to school. There used to be a friendly llama at large in the children's zoo, but it ate a woman's hat and was removed. I often go to Whipsnade when I'm at home, especially when we have small visitors to entertain, but I had never known, until I attended the meeting in Cincinnati, that the technical name for the place where the children can pat the animals is "contact area." I heard a good deal on this subject from the zoo people.

Dr. Gordon Hubbell, veterinarian and director of the Crandon Park Zoo, in Miami, explained that contact areas perform various functions. Their principal one, I learned, is to keep children from being crowded out of the park altogether. One's mental picture of a zoo as a place enjoyed primarily by the juvenile set is not accurate. For every child who goes to the zoo in the U.S., there are two adults, and you can see what hob this plays with a child's life on a crowded day—or would play if he couldn't find refuge in a children's zoo. But even in children's zoos, it seems, adults are a nuisance. Not only do they take up too much room but they infect the children with their own fears. Dr. Hubbell said that

Crandon Park obviates this difficulty by keeping adults out of the children's zoo altogether. Inside, the children sit in a miniature stadium and observe a specimen animal while an attendant gives a little disquisition on its habitat, its nature, and its age. After the lecture, the children are permitted to touch the animal. If it is a cuddly and harmless sort—a rabbit or a mouse, for instance—they can even play with it for a short time. The adults are left to stand behind a fence, through which they can watch but not interfere. Such a contact area is beneficial to the animal world as well, said Dr. Hubbell, because the children learn how to take care of pets—how to pick up rabbits, say, or worm dogs—and because a child who has been properly informed will refuse to own an animal that has been deliberately crippled by de-fanging or de-clawing. At Crandon Park, the attendants in the children's zoo are high school girls, working part time. Girls are better than boys at handling contact-area animals, Dr. Hubbell said, but he added that it is wise to have a male attendant not far away, just in case. The exhibits in a children's zoo may vary widely. Crandon Park has used goats, pigs, turtles, monkeys, kinkajous, a brown lemur, baby coatimundis and anteaters, lion cubs, "and so on." Not far from the exhibition arena are small cages in which, for short periods, less amenable creatures are displayed—marmosets, a small hyrax, some parrots, macaws, and toucans. The problem of bites and scratches was far worse in the past, when parents came in with their children, than it is now, Dr. Hubbell said. Nowadays it doesn't amount to much.

"I disagree with the last talk," Arthur R. Watson, director of the Baltimore Zoo, said roundly. "We opened our children's zoo last year. As a result of our experiences, I don't believe in contact areas at all." This looked like civil war, but it wasn't. Mr. Watson explained the reasons for his intransigence. In his contact area, he said, a problem was created by the buzzing of hornets and bees around trash baskets near the ice cream and cotton-candy stands. The Baltimore Zoo has spent considerable sums on insecticides but hasn't got rid of the insects. An added peril to the public, it seems, is bantams, chicks, and other specimens of poultry that one might consider harmless; they have a way of stalking visitors in the hope of handouts, and frighten the timid. "Eliminate bantam roosters," said Mr. Watson passionately. "Have peacocks instead. Peacocks are fine." There is also the turnstile problem. Turnstiles are all right for admitting people of reasonably uniform size, but how can you use them to count infants in arms or tots in strollers? How, for that matter, can you keep active but small human beings from slipping underneath, thus leaving no record of their passage and making no payment? You can't.

Worse, unlucky children who do walk through properly may be hit on the head by the next arm as it swings. "We eliminated turnstiles," Mr. Watson said grimly. As a substitute for the perilous contact area, he went on, Baltimore put goats and sheep in a pen where children could reach and touch them, and found this better for all concerned. "A llama outside was O.K., because she went so fast the kids couldn't catch her," he conceded, and continued, "You can't always get the animals you want for a contact area. It isn't always the right season for baby skunks, raccoons, and so forth. The result is, the public's disappointed. I find it's better in the long run to keep your specimens in cages where the kids can reach in a single finger if they want to touch. We've had a lot of accidents with ponies and horses—kids don't know how to feed them, and get bitten. We are going to put up little poems and signs everywhere, teaching them about that."

Clearly, one section of Mr. Watson's talk found an answering echo in many hearts, and that was the section about turnstiles. A brisk discussion of these devices followed. Few of the zoo people had anything to say in favor of them, although one man maintained that the system worked all right if you had a big, strong attendant standing by. During the general discussion, Mr. Watson could be heard adding a few remarks about the injuries that his public suffered from the children's zoo: "A little nibbling. Clothing and pocketbooks. Goats sometimes steal sandwiches in the patio, or stand on the table—that sort of thing. Kids cry when their sandwiches are snatched, but I admit it's only a minor problem."

When the excitement had died down, Mr. Watson gave us the second chapter of his address, which proved to be an extract from a paper written by Walter J. Hill, the principal keeper of birds at Baltimore, on the subject of bird imprinting—taming and training birds, if anyone as ignorant as I can hazard a translation, by means of a new chemical compound. "The taming is quick and permanent, with minimum risk of injury to either bird or handler," Mr. Hill wrote, and the paper went on to describe a preparation called Fame Tame, which consists of birdseed and a secret substance, both coated with certain volatile oils. Birds like the taste and the smell, and the secret substance puts them into a receptive state for learning a new behavior pattern. Mr. Hill had watched a demonstration in Baltimore by the manufacturer of Fame Tame in which two birds were tamed—a process that took fifteen minutes per bird. "By a tame bird," he explained, "I mean one which will not fly away when approached, will allow stroking, will perch on one's hand and not bite." He had tamed a bird himself, and had taken some Fame Tame back to the zoo, where he had since tamed twelve birds with it. He went on to note that a bird, like any other animal, has a "critical distance," characteristic of its species; that is, it can be approached only up to a certain point before it flees or attacks. "It is probably a learned behavior," he said, "but whether learned or instinctive, the critical-distance factor, along with unacceptable behavior, is masked or forgotten by imprinting a new way of behaving. The birds which I tamed have undergone no personality changes . . . in their limited way, they accept people as intimates."

The zoo people showed much interest in this paper.

"What about mating behavior?" somebody asked.

Mr. Watson said that he couldn't answer that question, but that as far as he could see, Fame Tame had not affected the habits of birds known to be monogamous.

Several people asked whether the stuff had been tried on mammals.

Mr. Watson replied that the Baltimore Zoo was disinclined to try experiments on leopards or similarly intractable specimens. "We'll use it on some small cats later," he said.

"Personally, I don't think there's much that's new in it," one zoo man said to me during a lull. "Isn't catnip much the same thing? You know how catnip affects tigers."

Apologetically, I confessed that I didn't, and asked him to explain.

"Why, it works on them the way it does on house cats," he said. "If you give a tiger enough catnip, you can get in close to him and practically pull his ears, and he'll just go on purring."

The meeting returned to the subject of children's zoos. In Dallas, I gathered, the attendants are all college students, the girls in khaki culottes and tan-and-white checked blouses with their names embroidered on the pockets, and the boys, who do only the heavy work, in khaki uniforms. The girls do most of the cleaning up and feeding without objection, the speaker stated, and the room cheered lustily.

Mr. Perkins told us that he had first heard of children's zoos in the late thirties, when Roger Conant, curator of reptiles at the Philadelphia Zoo, came across an English institution called an animal bank, at which a child was permitted to borrow some small beast—a guinea pig, say, or a turtle—and later turn it in for another specimen. Many losses were incurred by the animal bank, Mr. Perkins continued, so it was shut down, but the general idea of something special for children at the zoo lived on.

In proof of this, Daniel Watson, of the Turtle Back Zoo, a children's zoo in West Orange, New Jersey, told us about the operating costs of a small place like his. He had found prairie dogs a good source of extra income, he said, because at Turtle Back the public was allowed to buy food for the prairie dogs from a slot machine, which last season netted the zoo an average of seven dollars and a quarter a day per prairie dog. Penguins, too, had done their bit for the cause, eating smelts that had cost the public a nickel apiece, and Mr. Watson said that great hopes were being entertained for the appetite of a harbor seal who was soon to be installed in his zoo.

The afternoon was drawing to a close, and I was growing drowsy. I didn't pay much attention to the plans for a new Milwaukee zoo, which were presented by its director, George Speidel. But then I saw the familiar words "Snakes and Snake Bite" on the program, and at once sat up and took notice. The afternoon speaker on that important subject was Lawrence Curtis, the co-chairman from Fort Worth, and he told us he had brought along a copy of Staff Directive No. 29 for his zoo's herpetarium and proposed to explain it to us. "Some of these points might seem to err on the side of caution, but on the whole we think it's better," he said, and no one argued as he read us the rules. In case of snake bite, the nearest attendant should switch on an emergency alarm system and then proceed with the standard three-step first-aid method— ligature, incision, and suction. Second, the attendant should notify the zoo switchboard—or, if the bite occurred at night, the city telephone system—instructing the operator to call either or both of two doctors, the hospital, the zoo director, the curator, and the herpetarium supervisor. Third, the attendant should select the proper serum in the herpetarium refrigerator—where it should be waiting, packaged and labeled, and with the type of venom specified. Finally, he should take the most readily available means of transport to the hospital. "And, as I almost forgot to say, you also take the patient," added Mr. Curtis. "You don't give him any liquor to drink, by the way. That's harmful."

Fort Worth regulations as to venomous creatures in the herpetarium were also drawn up meticulously, we learned. No poisonous snake should be handled by anyone but the supervisor or director. Cages of dangerous snakes on the "hot," or venomous, list should not be opened, ever, except by the supervisor. (This list, I learned later, is a standardized one, and is adhered to by most zoos. As Mr. Farnsworth had suggested, the puff adder does not appear on the list, because he is not aggressive, large, or flighty.) No cage of hot reptiles should be opened unless at least two people are in the building, for in the event a man is bitten he should keep as quiet as possible and not have to put the alarm system into operation by himself. No cage or container of poisonous reptiles should be opened in the presence of outsiders unless the director or some- one similarly authoritative is on hand. When venomous snakes are moved, they should be put in red sacks, which should be securely tied and then placed in a cage or container for transit. All cages holding venomous snakes should be tagged "Poisonous," and tags should also inform the reader of the number of occupants. "Otherwise, you might possibly mislay one." The Fort Worth Zoo had never yet lost a poisonous reptile, Mr. Curtis said, but on one occasion the staff thought that it had. At three o'clock on a Sunday afternoon, when the herpetarium was full of people, the keeper reported that a cobra was missing from one of the cages. In a secluded office, the authorities, sweating with worry, considered possible steps to take. Warn everybody? Out of the question. Evacuate the building without explanation? Better, but was this really necessary? The cages opened only one way, toward the back, and all the doors from the back areas leading into the public part of the building were thoroughly snakeproof; a cobra could not possibly get past. If one had got out of his cage, it must have been into the rear of the building, and he was still there. He had to be. The officials set a search in motion, wondering if they had made the right decision, while on the other side of the cages—the public side—people continued to move about innocently and lightheartedly. A child screamed. Mr. Curtis' heart, for one, jumped violently. But it was merely a child screaming. Brows were mopped, and the search went on. "All of a sudden somebody noticed that one of the remaining cobras in that cage looked larger than usual," Mr. Curtis said. "We rushed him to the vet for an X ray. Sure enough, we'd found our missing snake."

It was nearly six, and the meeting was adjourned for dinner. I could have hurried through a snack and gone to my room to watch Mr. William Hoff, the executive director of the Cincinnati Zoo, who was our host, appear on television at seven—he has a zoo program once a week—but I didn't, because I spotted Robert Bean in the crowd. It had been announced that morning that Mr. Bean was retiring from the directorship of Brookfield Zoo, near Chicago, and some of the zoo men had observed that he was about the best in the business. His retirement, which was due to health rather than age, was a great pity, they agreed, and one man told me, "He's not going to be completely absent, of course. Bob Bean couldn't exist away from a zoo. He's to be director emeritus at Brookfield, and they don't plan to put another director in his place; they're going to run the zoo with a kind of committee. It's an interesting idea, but, if you ask me, it won't work out. You need a dictatorship to run a zoo."

Now, as we all moved slowly out of the room, I waited for my chance, and when Mr. Bean had finished discussing an animal trade with somebody, I collared him. He suggested a drink in the bar, and that was where we went. He ordered orange juice for himself.

"My liquor intake's rationed, and I used up my allowance at the board meeting this noon," he said. "I'll probably keep on with animals, one way or another. I was born in the Lincoln Park Zoo, in Chicago, on May 27, 1902. My father was bird keeper there at the time. He stayed in the zoo business, of course; few people leave it once they're in. My sister married a zoo man, too. You heard him today—George Speidel, talking about the new place in Milwaukee. Not quite everybody in our family is in the zoo business, though. I've got a younger brother who's a philologist; he speaks Roman French. We're not quite sure how that happened. Well, soon after I was born, we moved from Chicago to Milwaukee; my father started the Washington Park Zoo there. If you heard George this afternoon, you know that it looks like a pretty old-fashioned place now, and it's due for a face-lifting, but I can assure you it was the last word in modernity when my father started it. Things change fast in our world. I caddied for the keepers when I was a kid, fetching their cans of beer when they were off duty, helping to mix pheasant feed and take care of setting pheasants—doing as many odd jobs as a boy can possibly squeeze in outside school hours. Then I spent a couple of summer vacations on a stock farm, at Oconomowoc, Wisconsin, owned by Fred Pabst—you know, the beer man—looking after his prize cattle. They were strenuous days. Of course, we didn't have antibiotics then, or most of the other aids, and we had to keep all the calves separate to avoid infection." He broke off and appeared to muse a little, then went on, "Come to think of it, I've been looking after other people's animals all my life. I'd like to have a few of my own for a change. Now that I'm retired, maybe I'll own a pair of guinea pigs. Well, to go on, when the First World War came along, I was about twelve, and my contribution to the cause was to paint the fencing at the zoo. That was the first year. The second year, they gave four keepers their vacations at the same time, and I took their places. When they came back, I got two weeks off myself."

Mr. Bean's parents pried him loose from the zoo long enough to send him to the University of Wisconsin, but he didn't stay the course, becoming a dropout of the twenties. ("A great mistake, and I often regret it," he said.) He moved around from one zoo to another and spent some time in Australia, from which he returned to become superintendent of the San Diego Zoo in 1926. "It's amazing to think how much the San Diego Zoo has developed since those days," he said. "It was dirt poor then. I had one can of paint the whole year and a half I was

there. That's the truth. And now look at it! The depression made San
Diego, with the PWA and the WPA and the whole shooting match of
government labor. A monument to public works, that's what it is. On
July 1, 1927, my father and I went to Brookfield to start a new zoo,
under the auspices of the Chicago Zoological Society. There was almost
nothing at Brookfield—prairie, swamp, a couple of cottages, and just one
real house. We dug a lot of ditches and planted a lot of trees, and
opened in 1934. The park was only half as big as it is today, but even
so it was pretty big. The first president of the Chicago Zoological Society
was John T. McCutcheon, the Chicago *Tribune* political cartoonist;
the second was his brother-in-law, Clay Judson; and the third—and current—president is Judson's law partner, William R. Dickinson, Jr., all
decent, generous people. They've given me my house, you know, and the
leisure to do what I want."

I asked about conservation of animal species, which I happened to
know was one of Bean's pet projects.

He shook his head in mild disgust. "It's all talk so far," he said. "People
aren't doing enough fast enough. The idea of a bank with animals from
different zoos to be borrowed when they're needed—sure, it's a nice
idea, but it's going to take fifty or sixty years before it catches on. Not
long ago, for example, there was a female Indian rhino named Bessie
in the Bronx and a male in Philadelphia. That's not very far away—
why shouldn't they have got together? But they didn't, and now Bessie's
dead. No, the bank idea hasn't got off the ground. And there's not
enough exchanging. Zoo men are too anxious about their own specimens
to let them go to other zoos, even on loan. You remember the first
giant panda ever to come to the United States? It was toward the end
of 1936. We brought that one in—got her from Ruth Harkness. Well,
way back then I had the idea of exchanging. I suggested we swap that
panda, Su-lin, to the Bronx for three months in exchange for their
okapi. They wouldn't consider it. No—people will have to loosen up a
lot more before these ideas work out. Zoo people delude themselves about
conservation. Maybe you just can't get results in a democracy—I don't
know. Royalty, though—they knew how to conserve. Almost anybody
with enough authority seems to have a taste for it. Germany had the
right idea, and the Russians, had, too, and still have. Both countries
actually kept stuff through the worst of the bombing and fighting, because
they were thinking of the future. I hear the Russians have three wild
zones fenced in, with animals from all countries. There's a Zoo Center
in Moscow, run on purely scientific lines, with one absolute authority
in charge. That's what you need for conservation." He stared ahead of

him, as if at some faraway outdoor region. "Well, maybe someday it'll happen here," he said. "In the meantime, here I am, retired. Before I get those guinea pigs, I might travel around and find out what's going on at all the other zoos. And I'd like to have another look at Australia."

After my talk with Mr. Bean, I discovered that work was not over for the day. The session carried on after dinner, when we heard more talks, most of them illustrated with slides or movies. Installing a bongo antelope in the Cleveland Zoo, trapping pygmy hippos in West Africa, collecting in Colombia—the vivid color films of sunlit foliage, corralled animals, boats gliding along shallow rivers, birds of incredible brilliance made me forget the one glimpse I'd had through my bedroom window of the Cincinnati streets shining with puddles and splashing with rain. Mohammid Hanif, of the Georgetown Zoo, in British Guiana, showed strangely peaceful slides of two-toed sloths making their leisurely way upside down along branches, and then a climbing porcupine crawling up a tree at the same rate, his limbs as bulky as a Teddy bear's. "You have all, no doubt, heard the Beatles and seen them on television," said Mr. Hanif. "This is just to show you that the Beatles didn't set the style in haircuts." The screen was filled with a closeup of the amazing red-faced spider monkey, glossy black except for his face, and with the hair of his head hanging down as straight and limp as that of an Aztec figure or, indeed, a Beatle.

Soon it was time to adjourn, but we voted to linger for a last offering— studies of an albino rattlesnake. "It's a true albino, as you can see from the pink eyes," its custodian said proudly.

The day had ended as it began, with snakes, I reflected on the way to my room. By this time, however, I was so accustomed to the subject that the chief thought I took with me was not a picture of the albino's gleaming, supple skin or traplike mouth but a recollection of the fact— for some reason very pleasing—that zoo herpetologists refer to the young of snakes as "pups."

By popular consensus, Tuesday's star turn was a talk given by Joseph P. McHale, the senior keeper of the Lincoln Park Zoo, where Mr. Bean was born. Mr. McHale imparted a rich collection of odds and ends of knowledge that he had rightly felt would not be covered by the other experts. He recommended a large number of books he had found handy, including reference books on animal care, feeding, and diseases, and even on shows and circuses—"because, after all, we're a Cadillac type of show people ourselves," he said. He mentioned the need for caution in the matter of "donations"—the monkeys, rabbits, and pet foxes that harried young members of the public often present to zoos when they find themselves unable to bear the burden of their care. "Don't take donations from anybody less than eighteen years old," Mr. McHale warned. "If a kid brings an animal in, tell him he's got to have a written certificate from an adult along with it. That's your protection from hounding afterward; otherwise they'll be along to criticize the way you're looking after it. On the other hand, it's nice to give kids a certificate of merit for donations or any other little thing they might do for the zoo. It may not mean much, but it looks impressive and they like it." Abruptly, he switched to a less pleasant topic—the hazards of a keeper's daily work. A slide appeared on the screen showing a hand with the third finger missing. "Ring-finger is what this is called," said Mr. Mc-Hale. "No keeper of experience wears a ring; rings get caught in fences or cage doors when you're closing up in a hurry. Don't wear a ring." Before I had really had time to digest this warning, we were wafted away on a surrealistic procession of more slides. A gentle little red deer behind a fence was characterized by Mr. McHale as "one of the zoo's killers," and he went on, "Always be careful handling these fellows. They kick out, a sharp hoof goes through the skin of the stomach mighty easy, and then they kick some more and churn you up pretty bad. They're dangerous, especially in the spring, when everything's jumping." Of a plain domestic broom, he said, "There are lots of uses you can put a broom to when you need a tool quick. You can even use it the way it was meant to be used. They don't want to sweep anymore—too many college graduates, I guess." Applause and laughter greeted this observation, and then we found ourselves looking at a pole. "Plain oak stick," said Mr. McHale. "One of the most useful things you can have in a zoo. You can reach things too high to get at otherwise in a cage, or put it through the bars where you have a couple of tigers fighting. Wait until one gets the other down, then hit the one underneath on the head. The one on top thinks he's killed the other one, and goes away. That way, you've saved a valuable animal. Only, try not to do it when the public's watching. People don't understand." Next, we were shown a slide of a small trap. "This is a mercy trap—a nice little trap, in case you don't want to use poison for your vermin," said Mr. McHale. "But if you do"—the slide changed to a box very clearly labelled "Rat Poison"— "this comes in handy. I don't know any zoo in the world that hasn't got a lot more rats than you'd think if you saw it only in the daytime. You ask what harm they do. Well, rats can upset a whole cage of sleeping birds. A rat or mouse running across the bottom of the cage wakes one up and it goes flying off the perch, falling down, and starts up all the others. In the morning, you find two, three birds dead on the floor, and you wonder what happened. It's a good idea to keep a light burning somewhere near your bird cage at night. You put your poisoned corn, or whatever, in this box and leave it around, and you'll get a lot of rats. Might get a squirrel or two as well, but sometimes you have too many squirrels in the zoo anyway." The screen flickered and showed a glassed-in cabinet in which were two rifles. "Better have your gun rack handy near the dangerous animals," said Mr. McHale. "Suppose you get a bear busting loose. The bear's a mean, vicious animal, and the keeper's got to break the glass quick and get up close." Flick! We were looking at a uniformed keeper on one knee and with rifle at the ready, facing some danger just outside the picture. "You've got to be careful with your shooting on account of ricocheting bullets, and that crazy public, people crowding up close," Mr. McHale went on. "Shoot the animal, but don't be satisfied if he falls down. Go up to him and shoot him again, in the head, a couple of times. Make sure. By the way, is your insurance up to date?"

The second half of the day we spent at the Cincinnati Zoo. We had lunch there, and then were told to look around the grounds until four o'clock, when we should be back in the zoo restaurant for an animal-trading session. When I returned to the restaurant, I found it full of people in holiday mood. About half the crowd had assembled at the far end of the room and was listening to speakers at a microphone— a sort of catch-as-catch-can auction, at which a man read aloud the offers of other members and pointed the members out to would-be chafferers. At the beginning, the man at the microphone was Walter Stone, but he soon yielded to a succession of people who wanted to talk for themselves.

Those who weren't interested in the auction milled around the bar, near the door, chatting.

"Aren't you trading?" I asked a man I recognized.

"I got all my trading done the first day—Sunday night. Bartender, a bourbon and water, please," he said.

Before long, I worked my way toward the other end of the room, where scattered phrases rose above the general noise.

"One female cheetah, eight years old, one thousand dollars. Anybody interested?"

"One nilgai, female—very rare. Plenty of males available."

"Three bear cubs, Japanese. Anybody looking for one for your children's zoo?"

"We've got a lot of monkeys going, interested in a trade for a male mandrill. We want a young adult."

"One pair of mute swans."

"The monkeys are taken care of. Any further discussion?"

I now saw that some very earnest discussions were taking place over at the sides of the room or in quiet corners.

More items were mentioned:

"I have innumerable spotted fallow deer and one male coati. I want a female African lion—immediately, if possible."

"A pair of yearling black buck, three hundred fifty. Say, are you just brushing your hair?"—a question addressed to a man in the front row.

Names of animals filled the air.

Three male llamas, hand-tamed, from a children's zoo. The owner would like to get two hundred apiece for them. This was intentionally funny, and everybody laughed.

One yearling mouflon, two hundred—"Yes, we'll negotiate, we'll talk to you."

Two not too young Bengal tigers, female. "We'd like to negotiate. I'll talk to you later."

"We've disposed of the bears. Any discussion on the mouflon?"

An Indian fishing cat . . . a pair of polar bears . . . a pair of koala bears . . . rhesus monkeys . . .

Someone wanted female wallaroos.

"I'm giving away black piranhas," said a harassed-sounding man. "Please take them off my hands."

I had to leave Cincinnati soon afterward, and the thought of what that man's aquarium would be like if those piranhas weren't taken off his hands worried me all the way back to New York.

CHAPTER 2

Background

□

Though this isn't a history, I must touch on the main features of the past story of zoos and how they have developed. Even curtailed it's a long one, perhaps as long as the story of mankind, for according to Dr. Hediger of Zurich, Man's efforts to tame animals, domesticate them, and keep them in captivity is as old as Man himself. It is a moot point which civilization, Chinese or Egyptian, was first to make animals captive, but both peoples certainly kept menageries from very early times. Queen Hatshepsut of Egypt owned monkeys, leopards and a giraffe: incidentally, she also imported greyhounds, the first of these dogs to be seen in her country: whereas in China, the early princes maintained "parks of intelligence" in which to keep exotic animals, as distinct from their deer parks. Mencius tells of how King Hui of Liang stood with him by a pond and said, looking around at his geese and deer, "Do wise and good princes also find pleasure in these things?" Another Mencius essay speaks of a "marvellous park" belonging to King Wan, where fat, sleek does took their ease and the pond was full of leaping fishes. The tradition of animal gardens continued unbroken in China, and Marco Polo saw a splendid menagerie belonging to Kublai Khan at Xanadu.

An obelisk set up at Nineveh by Shalmanazar II, of the ninth century B.C., depicts the paying of tribute "of the land of Musri" with dromedaries, buffaloes, elephants, and apes. The Greeks preferred pet wild birds to mammals, but when they invaded India and saw how elephants could be trained to work or fight, they promptly drafted these great beasts for war. Alexander the Great maintained stables of both African and Indian elephants, and kept bears, monkeys and whatever other strange animals he could get in tribute from the peoples his army vanquished. He was the first man in history to turn his menagerie to scientific use, enjoining his tutor, Aristotle, to study natural history by means of its captive animals.

Hannibal's famous elephants constituted a fighting force, not a menagerie, but he did put them on show from time to time between wars, tethered in an open field outside the city, where the public could see them.

In India, princes used not only elephants but cheetahs for their convenience, because these cats could be trained to hunt. Persian nobles had the same custom. The Romans, however often they may be cited as the originators of the practice, supplied merely one link—and rather a late one, at that—in a chain of considerable length. Like the Greeks they seized wild animals as spoils of war, along with human slaves and gold and jewels: at the end of a successful campaign, animals were marched in triumphal procession among the human captives. Kings and nobles everywhere regarded wild beasts as desirable, for show or as particularly honorable gifts. Nero had a pet tigress, Phoebe, who sat at table with him and was sometimes regaled with a human victim who had aroused the emperor's wrath. It is easy to understand why monarchs had such pets. To own a tigress, a lion, or an elephant was a way of showing off and vaunting one's strength. "I can command lions and elephants: see how powerful I am!" Added to which, some lords may have felt affection for these animals. Few princes could trust other humans, and one must love something. Charlemagne, for one, liked animals and took a special interest in exotic species. Once he hinted to the Caliph of Baghdad, the legendary Harun-al-Rashid, that a few characteristic animals from Mesopotamia would be very welcome. The Caliph promptly shipped off to Charlemagne a whole set of things, perfumes and spices and monkeys, with a non-Mesopotamian elephant named Abul Aba as the *pièce de résistance*. As soon as the word reached the Emir of Cairo, he too sent animals to Charlemagne—a lion, several bears, and other beasts. Charlemagne, greatly pleased, distributed the lesser animals among his various country estates, but Abul Aba was a favorite pet and went everywhere with him.

The craze for keeping wild animals grew in intensity. For William the Conqueror, who built Woodstock, the idea seems to have been a new one, but he was pleased that his eldest son, William, should have brought him a bear as a housewarming gift, and his fourth son, Henry I, amassed a great collection. The taste skipped Henry II, but Henry III liked animals and kept a great many. This Henry left Woodstock and moved into the more commodious Tower of London, a decision the inhabitants of

London soon had cause to regret, for the king's proximity ran the citizens into heavy expenditure on account of his menagerie. When he was given a polar bear by some noble friend, Henry announced that the city of London must pay for its upkeep. As chief representative of the people the sheriff had to comply, but he did so in a manner far from lavish, handing over four sous a day—about twopence—to cover the keeper's wages and the cost of the animal's food. The keeper argued that it wasn't enough. After haggling for some time he agreed to take his charge into the Thames River every day, so that it could catch its own food and he could pocket the four sous. The sheriff paid the expenses of these fishing expeditions—a rope and a chain to hold the bear with, and a warm wrapper for the keeper, because he had to go into the water along with his bear. As if this weren't bad enough for the unfortunate Londoners, in 1254 Henry received another curious animal, from Louis IX of France —an elephant, the first ever seen in England; Louis had brought it back as a souvenir of his crusade in Egypt. Henry ordered the sheriff to build a house big enough for the beast, twenty by forty feet, so designed that it could if necessary be used for other purposes. The elephant was installed, and people came from miles around to stare at it and marvel. So many of these pilgrims arrived that the citizens of London were called upon to disgorge yet more money, so that a shelter could be built for them.

What with all this hubbub about bears and elephants, the royal household in the Tower may seem to us excessively menagerie-minded, but when Henry's sister, Elizabeth, crossed the Channel in order to be married, she did not leave all talk of wild animals behind her. Her fiancé, Frederick II, Emperor of the Holy Roman Empire and the King of Sicily, was even more of a zoophile than her brother. Frederick kept a great variety of animals, including hyenas and a giraffe which he obtained from the Sultan of Egypt in exchange for a polar bear. He set up a training school for cheetahs, and when he traveled he liked to take plenty of four-footed friends with him. When he went to Worms for his wedding, his procession included elephants, camels, lions, panthers, monkeys, and cheetahs, all as splendid as ornaments could make them.

The kings who supplanted Henry III at the Tower continued to mulct the citizens for provender and care for their captive beasts. For a lion owned by Edward II the sheriff was required to supply a quarter of a sheep and three sous every day, but this was nothing to what was demanded for the falcons and lions of Edward III—two shillings and a penny for meat, and twelve sous for the attendants. At last, perhaps inevitably, something went wrong with the supply line, and all the lions died. The rest of the collection languished until, in 1445, Henry VI took a bride, Margaret of Anjou, whose father René had a famous animal collection. One of Henry's courtiers, confident that the lady would wish to carry on in her father's tradition, gave her a lion for a wedding present, and his confidence was justified, for Margaret was pleased. For her sake the old Tower enclosures were rebuilt, new animals acquired, and the royal collection grew bigger and better than it had ever been before. Under Edward IV the trend continued with yet more rebuilding. Today, visitors to the Tower are told that there used to be an edifice called the Lion Tower just where the ticket office is now, and are shown how part of its circular foundation is still visible in the road. Around the Lion Tower in those days were the cages, standing twelve feet high, where the Court could entertain honored guests with animal combats modeled on the Roman games—bears pitted against dogs, or lions against tigers. It became a state duty for a monarch to keep up the Tower menagerie, if only to be ready for such occasions, and Henry VIII, and Elizabeth after him, did not fail to do so.

On the Continent the story was much the same. As might be expected, Italy was one of the first countries to revive Roman customs: Florence in the time of Cosimo dei Medici possessed at least ten lions, and wild boars, wolves, bulls, and fierce mastiffs. One famous day all these animals were set loose together into a specially built arena, to fight for the delectation of Pope Pius and the Sforzas, over from Rome on a visit. The designers of the spectacle naturally thought there would be bloody and therefore pleasing scenes of carnage, but it didn't work out like that. The animals had taken part in a preliminary procession through the streets, and the lions, instead of killing, simply lay down and dozed. Cosimo was discouraged by this fiasco, but when his son and successor, Lorenzo, came into his inheritance, he worked hard at building up the Menagerie of Florence until it became the city's pride, sung by the poets and visited by the painters who made that age so glorious. As a result we see meticulously represented wild animals in the painting, frescoes and sculpture of the time. Some artists even kept wild-animal models themselves: Leonardo da Vinci did.

The lordly patrons of other Italian cities attempted to make collections that would vie with Florence's. Pope Alexander Borgia introduced bull-fights from his native Spain. A Medici who succeeded him, Leo X, harked back to his family's original idea and set up a menagerie in the Vatican with monkeys, civets, lions, leopards, and bears. The star of his collection was an elephant sent by King Manoel I of Portugal, which Manoel's ambassador Tristan da Cunha brought himself from India. Many cardinals, doubtless feeling that whatever the pope did must be right, tried to emulate him. One arranged a fete in honor of Eleanor of Aragon, with a pageant that featured not only Orpheus charming the wild beasts with his lute, but Bacchus sitting in his car drawn by pards. A second cardinal specialized in peacocks and Syrian goats; a third bred guinea-fowl, but it remained for yet another Medici, the cardinal Hippolyte, to outdo the lot of them by keeping a *human* menagerie filled with slaves from many countries: Moors, Tartars, Indians, Turks, and Africans.

Portugal was not as quick as Italy to take up the fashion of menageries, but the thirteenth-century king Dom Diniz made a sort of gesture toward doing so. While hunting in the mountains he had a narrow escape from a bear, and thereafter, to commemorate the incident, he always kept a captive bear at one of his country estates. It remained for a later king, Afonso V, to become a leader among royal menagerie-keepers. Afonso waged successful battles against the natives of Africa—he became known as "Afonso the African" for this reason—and his collection, therefore, was almost exclusively African in origin. He housed the beasts at his castle at Cintra, where he often staged "beast shows." More lavish in this respect than any monarch before him, he sent specimens to friends and relatives, bestowing lions and hyenas and other creatures in much the same spirit that motivates us when we send flowers. He presented a variegated lot of creatures from Guinea to Louis XI of France, all in one blow. To René of Anjou he sent an elephant, several monkeys and some marmots.

After Afonso, another Portuguese king, Manoel I—he who sent an elephant to Pope Leo X—imported the first rhinoceros to set foot in Europe since Roman days. Unfortunately, he could think of nothing more intelligent to do with it, once he had it, than pit it against an elephant in the arena. For what it is worth, the encounter proved that an elephant is afraid of a rhinoceros, or, at any rate, that that individual elephant was afraid of that particular rhinoceros. Remembering his earlier success with the pope, Manoel now sent his rhino to the Vatican, but the ship carrying it ran into a storm and sank with all hands, drowning the animal.

Like Portugal, the German states and Austria were late climbing aboard the menagerie wagon, although some thirteenth-century nobles followed the fashion of keeping a few wild animals around the house, either as a whimsy or because similar animals were depicted on their coats-of-arms. A fine menagerie existed, however, early in the fifteenth century, at Marienburg, containing such unusual beasts—unusual, that is to say, in captivity—as seals and walruses, and even five aurochs, the great wild ox that is now extinct. Other collections existed at Nuremberg and Frankfurt-on-Main. In the sixteenth century Maximilian II, Emperor of the Holy Roman Empire, who spent the greater part of his youth in Spain, returned to his native Vienna with an elephant of which he was so fond that he insisted on its attending the ceremony, in 1564, at which he was crowned Emperor of Austria. Maximilian also had a tame pelican that followed him everywhere.

In comparison with these often agreeable court pleasures, the ways of the Russians, Poles, and Swedes with animals, at least up until the seventeenth century, seem simple and brutish. There, the great show animal was the bear. Wandering bear-leaders led their charges from one settlement to another, where the bears danced or did other tricks. Bears are not very amenable, and cautious showmen kept two men in charge of each animal. In higher social circles, bears were trained to keep quiet when dressed up and set onstage as characters in "living pictures" that burlesqued the actions of human beings, rather in the same way that makers of colored postcards today portray kittens or puppies in top-hats or ruffles or baby carriages. Bears in evening dress, clutching feathered fans, sat on elegant sofas, or at pianos. Bears in funny hats and shooting-jackets posed as Nimrods. Bears wallowed around in boudoirs, presumably getting dressed to go to the ball. In more bloodthirsty mood, nobles would watch games of bull- or boar- or bear-baiting, and the insane Ivan the Terrible kept bears in dens within his castle, and fed certain of his enemies to them.

The people of the Netherlands were more advanced in their tastes. At the castle of the Hague, in the fourteenth century, was a menagerie belonging to the Count of Holland, containing lions, bears, and a camel. The dukes of Gelderland maintained two collections at different castles, hunting wolves in the surrounding woods with which to feed the captive animals. A certain nobleman of Ghent kept a lion, as we might keep a watchdog, tied to a pillar near his entrance gate. Like other lords of his time he made the townspeople maintain his pet, a policy hardly calculated, one would think, to foster a warm love of animals in the peasant heart. But a later duke of Ghent, who lived in the same château after Flanders had become the property of the Burgundians, and who kept *four* lions, evidently realized that times must change; and instead of charging the town for his lions' support he made a deal with the local butcher, who agreed to provide them with their meat and a boy to take care of them in return for a flat daily rate. The pay wasn't enough to cover expenses, but the duke explained that the butcher would be able to make a profit nevertheless, owing to his exclusive right to admit the public, at a fee, to see the animals. Both duke and butcher had no doubt that the commoners of Ghent would gladly pay a few coppers for this privilege, but they were mistaken. The people never came near the place, and a new arrangement became necessary.

One institution, which the historian Loisel calls "the last Dutch menagerie of the Middle Ages," is particularly interesting because it was *not* the private property of a nobleman. This was a lion-house in Amsterdam, a city that won its own municipal constitution—that is, its freedom—from Count William IV in 1340: its alderman kept the collection of lions as an emblem of Amsterdam's independence. Foreign merchants visiting the busy port sometimes brought or sent lions to Amsterdam as gifts.

The popes who lived in Avignon between 1309 and 1377 set up a lion house to comfort them in their exile.

If certain European dignitaries seem to have gone too far in their efforts to have and to hold captive animals, let us consider the Yung-lo Emperor of China, of the Ming dynasty, under whose reign an expedition, in 1417, sailed all the way to Africa because of a giraffe.* The voyage does not fall into the ordinary category as something that came about because of a collector's greed: rather, it was a gesture of statesmanship. It is doubtful if the emperor had much feeling, or sentiment, for animals, nor was his pride involved—after all, like generations before him he had been surrounded all his life by imperial gardens full of exotic beasts from tributary countries: one of the earlier emperors even owned a rhinoceros. Giraffes, however, were still unknown in China, perhaps because no Chinese voyager had yet sailed a ship as far as the Dark Continent. To be sure, the nation was aware that Africa existed, and other species of African beasts had been represented at court, having been passed on from one monarch to another around the world, but the Chinese, as it happened, had never seen or heard of giraffes. Then, in 1414, a number of Chinese ships, part of a large expedition, chanced to put in at Bengal and found the place in gala mood, for a new king had just been crowned. The Chinese ships' officers were cheerfully invited to join the party and inspect the coronation presents. Among the gifts were rare animals from all over the Moslem world, including several giraffes from Melinda, on the east coast of Africa, and at sight of these long-necked creatures, the officers got excited to a degree that perplexed their hosts. The reason was that they all had the same thought at the same moment—that they were looking at k'i-rins, or k'i-lins. They had always heard of k'i-rins, but had never hoped to see any. In their mythology, a k'i-rin was a magical being that brought good luck. It was described, as every Chinese scholar well knew, as having the body of a deer and the tail of an ox. It ate only

* *China's History of Africa.* J. J. L. Duyvendak, London, 1949.

herbs, and was harmless—exactly the characteristics of the giraffes before their eyes. If anything was lacking to seal their conviction that they had found the lucky omen in the flesh, it was speedily supplied when they heard that the Somali word for giraffe is *girin,* which sounds exactly like k'i-rin if you pronounce it with a Chinese accent.

The king, noticing their delight—indeed, he could hardly have missed it—graciously insisted upon sending one of his giraffes to the Emperor of China with his compliments, and the Chinese accepted the favor eagerly on behalf of their master. Then, fearing that in spite of all precautions the animal might not survive the voyage, they gave the Melindan ambassador a strong hint that a second giraffe from his country would be very well received at Peking. The ambassador sent the word to his own king, and a replacement was despatched. In the event, both giraffes arrived safe and well, the one from Bengal in 1414 and the one from Melinda a year later. In 1417, as a direct result of all this, a Chinese expedition sailed all the way to Africa and opened up one more country for their trade.

It can be imagined what a turmoil of joy Peking was thrown into when the first giraffe was brought to the city. The Board of Rites begged the emperor for permission to present a memorial of congratulations—a formality reserved for the most auspicious occasions—but the emperor was determined not to lose his balance so easily, and refused, taking the opportunity to preach: "Let the Ministers but early and late exert themselves in assisting the government for the welfare of the world. If the world is at peace, even without k'i-lins there is nothing that hinders good government. Let congratulations be omitted." But a year later, when the giraffe from Melinda was landed, His Majesty went in person to receive it at one of the city gates, accompanied by a "celestial horse," or zebra, and a "celestial stag"—which was perhaps, Duyvendak thinks, an oryx. The emperor had again insisted that congratulations be omitted, but he relaxed a little and made a few remarks when the giraffe actually walked through the gate. The happy event, said the emperor, was due to the abundant virtue of the late emperor, his father, and to the assistance rendered to him by his ministers. Everyone felt very happy.

Court painters made pictures of the giraffe, and academicians of the Han-lin wrote poems in its honor. Here is part of an inscription on one of the pictures:

. . . *In a corner of the eastern seas, in the stagnant waters of a great morass,*
Truly was produced a K'i-lin whose shape was high 15 feet,

*With the body of a deer and the tail of an ox, and a fleshy boneless
    horn,*
With luminous spots like a red cloud or a purple mist,
*Its hoofs do not tread on (living) beings and in its wanderings it
    carefully selects its ground,*
*It walks in stately fashion, and in its every motion it observes a
    rhythm . . .*

This must be as good a description of a giraffe as can be found in
literature.

Incidentally, the diplomatic, if cumbersome, tradition of shipping
animals from one country to another as pledges of respect or friendship
has not completely died out. Horses from Arab countries are sent as
pledges from the chiefs there to European dignitaries and American
officials, and kangaroos arrive by ship or plane addressed to the Queen
of England, as the gifts of some loyal Commonwealth citizen. Queen
Elizabeth II hands these animals over to various zoos in the country
rather than maintain them at Buckingham Palace or Windsor as her
early ancestors would have done, but the principle is the same. When her
daughter Anne was a child, Mr. Khrushchev sent the little princess a
Russian bear cub. Naturally. What else would one have expected a great
Russian to do for a royal infant? Mr. Nehru used to hand around
elephants to national zoos: I have seen Nehru elephants in Kumasi,
Ghana, and Ankara, and there must be many more. In Addis Ababa
there is an Imperial Collection of Abyssinian lions, the property of
Haile Selassie, Emperor of Ethiopia and Lion of Judah. It was my
privilege to make the acquaintance of two of these animals who, like me,
had come a long way from home—specifically, to Amman in Jordania,
where I saw them in the garden of the royal palace. I was being shown
around by one of King Hussein's secretaries. The lions were making a
similar excursion under the protection of a tall, attenuated Ethiopian
keeper who had come with them from Addis Ababa when the emperor
sent them as a gift to Hussein. They had been cubs then. Now they
were nearly adult, and gave the keeper a hard time, frisking and pulling
at their leads. Catching sight of the secretary and me, they grew excited
and tried to rush to us, or on us as the case might be, while the poor
keeper, nearly jerked off his feet, shouted directions now to us, now to the
lions, in a very distracted manner. My escort and I retired—not too fast, I
hope, for dignity—to a spot guarded by shrubbery and out of their sight,
though we could still hear shouting and snarling until the lions settled
down.

"Does His Majesty really like this?" I asked curiously, when I had caught my breath. "I mean, does he enjoy having lions all over the place?"

The secretary, wiping his forehead, replied, "Not really, but what can he do? The lions were a present from the Emperor *himself.*"

The evolution of the public zoo really got its start in France, under— of all people—Louis XIV, the very last monarch, one would have thought, to play such a role. He was the perfect example of self-centered overlord, yet he did lay the foundations of that thoroughly republican institution, though the deed was inadvertent. Louis made a special hobby of menageries, regarding them in the light of trimming for his favorite palaces, along with flower gardens and fountains. Loving architectural planning and grand buildings and spectacles in general, he designed the living quarters of his wild animals as part of the whole scene. He may have made pets of some of them, but the interest he and other fashionable people of the day took in captive wild beasts was rather related to a love of venery. It is a short step from stocking parks with deer, boar, and birds, and breeding them for the chase, to filling cages with such curiosities as tigers and elephants. Louis used his exotic beasts sometimes for special shows and battles, but mainly they were part of the decoration. Yet no doubt in his fashion he liked them. After all, even today we have the phenomenon of the man keen on hunting and shooting, who at the same time is sincerely fond of wild animals.

Foxes and deer are conserved for his sake so that he might hunt them down in the proper season, but the animals he has never been so keen on hunting—wolves, for example—have vanished from their old haunts, killed off by less direct methods than his. It's a puzzling subject that I can't begin to sort out, and puzzlement increases when one reads the memoirs of big-game hunters who write with admiration and affection of the beauty, gallant spirit and so forth of animals they have killed. The baffling thing to opponents of "blood sports" is that these hunters really *do* understand wild animals, divining their habits and reactions far better, usually, than those same opponents.

Both as hunter and animal-fancier, Louis XIV would have maintained menageries even if he hadn't cared much about them, because by the time he was born such a taste was a tradition in the court. For generations kings of France had built and stocked aviaries, lion houses and bear pits in the customary royal fashion. Louis XI had actually introduced the canary bird to Europe, and there is a most stimulating story about Henri III, who in 1583 had a bad dream in which he saw lions, bears, and dogs tearing themselves to pieces. That did it for Henri III, and as soon as he woke up he commanded that his entire menagerie be shot dead. However, his heirs made good the damage, and the custom carried on. Louis XIV's father, at the age of nine, had his own collection; a camel, a deer, and a few monkeys. Louis himself was too young when he succeeded to the crown even to ride a camel—he was only five—and his mother and the chief minister, Cardinal Mazarin, took care of the royal duties for the time being. Even after Louis grew to young manhood Mazarin stayed on as guardian and confidant, a fact that has some bearing on our subject, for the Cardinal thought it prudent, during political upheavals in 1654, to assure the royal household of a food supply even if Paris should be isolated from the countryside, and so set up a mixed farm outside the walls, in the park of Vincennes, where cows, chickens, and sheep were kept. The emergency passed, as did others, but Mazarin kept the farm in working order until he died in 1661, and the young king felt free to put the land to the purpose he had long planned, as the site of a menagerie. It was his first.

Later, after many other essays in the art of animal architecture, he embarked on a tremendous project at Versailles, building palace, gardens, and approaches combined with a Menagerie du Parc that surpassed any yet seen in the world. Little Vincennes was forgotten and abandoned. One of the striking features of the Versailles experiment was that the king concentrated all his animals in one place, with cages and enclosures close together. Until then, menagerie keepers had tended to scatter their collections, aviary well away from the lion house, which in turn was segregated from the bear pit or elephant stable. It used to please a host, showing visitors around his domain, to surprise them with some unexpected animal house just around the turn of the path, but for the sake of architectural design, Louis changed all that. Another of his innovations was to plant trees, bushes, and flowers around and between the caves, concealing the ugly bars and fences. Nobody before him had thought of thus combining greenery with animal exhibits; for this reason the French historian of zoos, Loisel, was of the opinion that the Versailles menagerie merits the title of the first zoological *garden* ever known. (At least in the Western world, I feel constrained to add.) Versailles' animal enclosures were wedge-shaped and radiated like the sections of a fan from the château's octagonal courtyard. A stout wall enclosed the whole *évantail*. The interior of the little palace was as pretty as the outside, with paintings of birds and beasts on the walls, and tapestries, chair covers, and porcelain carrying the same theme. It was approached by waterways where the banks were covered with flowers, arched over here and there by climbing roses. The Versailles complex, château and menagerie, became famous in the great world, and played an important part in diplomatic exchanges. Visiting monarchs toured in state to see it; ambassadors were invited out to Versailles as a special sign of royal favor. Witnessing so many processions, the captive animals must have become used to music.

With such a glittering example before them, other nobles imitated Louis. A menagerie became something every great man must have, and ladies coveted them too, the king's mistresses and female relatives pestering him for advice in their collecting and designing. The Prince de Condé, like other lords, had inherited a splendid menagerie, but an old-fashioned place like that was not good enough: he must bring it up to date, or, better, build another one, so he abandoned his family menagerie at Chantilly and set up a splendid new estate at Vineuil, plundering Chantilly for the purpose and imitating Louis's fan-shaped enclosures.

But success palled on Louis XIV, and after playing with his toy for a while he lost interest in Versailles and the animal garden. The place fell into disrepair. Streams choked up, stonework became shabby, and the animals, though they were still looked after, were not replaced as they died. Word went around that Versailles was no longer worth seeing, and it might have faded away altogether if it hadn't been for a little girl named Adelaide, Princess of Savoy. As fiancée of Louis's son the Duke of Burgundy, the eleven-year-old Adelaide came, in 1696, to stay with her future in-laws, and the king was charmed with her. One day after lunch at the duke's house, the party took a stroll through the grounds and saw the menagerie—something no child of Louis's, of course, was ever without. Adelaide was delighted with the animals, and Louis rose to the challenge. If she admired this paltry show of his son's, he said, what would she say about Versailles! He continued: all French princesses had menageries, and Adelaide should have one too, the best and most beautiful of all. He would give her Versailles.

It was a hasty promise which he would gladly have forgotten, but Adelaide kept reminding him, especially after she was married. Louis tried to fob her off with other châteaux, but it was no use, until at last he capitulated and gave orders that the places should be smartened up for its new mistress. Then, of course, his interest in his creation was rekindled, and he started to improve it, until, after seven years, he declared it ready for his daughter-in-law. A grand party celebrated the reopening.

But after the deaths of Adelaide and Louis, Versailles fell again on evil times. Louis XV, for all it was his birthplace, was not interested in wild animals, and Louis XVI cared even less for them, though he and his wife liked the palace so much that even today we think of Marie Antoinette playing there as a dairymaid, in the Laiterie. The menagerie survived only because of the inertia that keeps royal functions going: it was there and had to be maintained, but nobody made improvements. Diplomatic gifts of animals continued to trickle in, and the caretaker kept appealing to Paris for funds to keep the buildings and grounds in repair, but nobody answered. All over Europe, the whims of fashion had deserted menageries. In Florence nothing was left of the Medici collection; in Portugal the royal collection at Queluz had vanished even before its owner fled to Brazil. But in England animals still paced at the Tower, even though the royal household had moved upriver to more comfortable residences than the old stone pile. The public was permitted to view the Tower animals at a charge of threepence a head, or, failing threepence, a dog or cat to help out on the exhibits' food rations—a thrifty expedient that would find scant favor in Britain nowadays. Yet it might have been this varied diet that helped the lions, in spite of the misty Thameside climate, to breed: during the reign of Queen Anne there were eleven of these great cats at the Tower, though by George III's time the number had shrunk to two, with two tigers, two monkeys, and a few other creatures. In addition to the Tower animals, the royal house of England owned the menagerie at Windsor and two other collections at Kew and Osterley Park. It was a poor showing compared with the menageries of France, but British aristocrats didn't often go in for wild animals, because they preferred to lavish their wealth on deer parks, grouse moors, or model farms.

During eighteenth-century pre-Revolution days there was only one continental menagerie that did not belong to a nobleman, located in Amsterdam. In that city, it may be recalled, the municipality of medieval days had maintained a lion house, but the wild animals of "Blaauw-Jan" (Blue John) constituted a private collection. Blaauw-Jan was an inn that owed its strange name to the fact that in earlier days it had been a dyer's establishment. The proprietor's menagerie was housed in the garden, where guests and visitors partook of refreshment at tables among the cages, watching the birds and animals at the same time. The owner kept a good selection of wild animals, adding new ones at intervals from the Cape of Good Hope, for he functioned as dealer as well as a showman; it was a Blaauw-Jan proprietor who supplied the Emperor of the Holy Roman Empire, Francis I, with animals to stock the new menagerie His Majesty had built for his wife, Maria Theresa, at Schönbrunn, outside Vienna. Indeed, this Netherlands inn played a part in the intellectual life of the Continent. Those were days of great scientific endeavor, and men of renown in natural history liked to visit the garden, using Blue John as a kind of outdoor laboratory. Artists made themselves at home at the tables, sketching birds and animals and drinking beer. A frequent visitor to the inn was William V, Prince of Orange, who owned a pet orangutan to which he was devoted, and kept a fine menagerie at his palace at the Loo, near The Hague.

The Revolution in France put an end to the old ways and to most French menagerie fanciers as well. The court frivolities were forgotten. Never again would Marie Antoinette play dairymaid at the Laiterie. Cheering, the mob listened to proclamations telling them that all the property of the aristocrats and the king himself—their lands and all that stood on the lands—now belonged to the people, down to the very menageries. The menageries were particularly mentioned, for in the minds of the revolutionaries they symbolized all the vices of the former régime—waste, vanity, conspicuous spending on fripperies, food lavished on wild animals while their owners grudged the merest sustenance to human beings. Various famous menageries were sacked immediately after the proclamations, but the people of Paris took their time getting around to the royal Menagerie du Parc at Versailles, because they found other places to loot nearer at hand. At last, in October 1789, they arrived at its gates, full of indignation at the stories they had been telling each other of the guards who insisted on their daily allowance of six bottles of wine per man, then gave most of the liquor to the elephant and the dromedary, just for the fun of watching them drink it. And what of the antelopes, eating their heads off in useless splendor? It was time they themselves were cut up for meat. To the sound of fife and drums the citizens marched on the château and were there confronted by the director of the menagerie, who had bravely stood by his charges, though no funds had come through for months and he had no idea of what would become of the collection.

"Open the cages," commanded the mob's spokesman. They had come to liberate the animals, he announced—to liberate them so that they might serve God's will and become food for human beings. No more would these idle beasts eat the fruit of the land. "In the name of the people of France!" he added.

"Certainly," said the director. He was heavily outnumbered. "But before I begin, there is one point that should be settled. Who is going to eat which? The lion, for example, and that rhinoceros—they're both very fierce. Are you quite sure you want to liberate them?"

This was a very good question: the Parisians paused to talk it over. Finally a few cages were selected and opened, and in the ensuing rush for sport and food some of the birds and beasts escaped to the forest. (There, years later, even as late as 1840, hunters now and then came upon exotic birds from Asia and Africa, and a few puzzling species of goat.) The looters, having had their fun and grabbed trophies, went home, leaving behind, still locked up, those animals they feared—the lion and the Indian rhinoceros, and a few other beasts that had escaped slaughter for one reason or another. One of them was a Dalmatian hound. Outside the empty cages the faithful palace officials held worried conference. What was the director to do now? Who would be responsible for the animals? The estate manager said he had a vague idea and it might be helpful: hadn't there been a discussion, in fact a quarrel, about keeping live animals in the Jardin des Plantes? Someone had told him that the naturalist Buffon was in favor of this enlargement of the garden. The manager added that they, the Versailles group, should certainly investigate chances of getting the beasts into the place.

The Jardin des Plantes, originally called the Royal Garden of Medicinal Plants, had been founded before the birth of Louis XIV, in 1635, to be a useful source of material for medical students and apothecaries—who in those days, of course, were herbalists. At first it served this purpose well, but with the growth of medical and chemical knowledge its resources became insufficient until more land was taken into the boundaries, in 1732, and new plantings were made. By the time Versailles was looted it had become more than a splendid botanical garden; it was also the repository of valuable scientific collections of many kinds. It was virtually the national museum of natural history, though it had not yet been given the name; and was also the place where the country's learned professors of science did their work. The estate manager was right. Buffon *had* once suggested that a museum of natural history was incomplete without living specimens as well as the dead ones on show in the Jardin buildings, but he was shouted down by the other professors. What, sacrifice their greenhouses, surrender their precious land, hand over their Eden to ranting wild beasts? A fantastic notion. If it was carried out they would be swamped with disease and dirt. Certainly nobody would be able to work. The suggestion was laid aside. Shortly before the house fell in on him, Louis XVI had appointed a new man to head the Jardin, a scientist named Bernardin de Saint-Pierre, who wrote novels in his spare time, including the popular *Paul and Virginia*. As director, Bernardin de Saint-Pierre was very much on the side of the no-animals-in-the-garden school, which made it all the more annoying when he received a letter from the Versailles estate manager proposing that the beasts and birds still remaining at the king's menagerie be sent to him. Preposterous! Especially the last line of the letter, which the poor estate manager, in his innocence, must have thought would sweep away the last objections—"There is a superb rhinoceros."

If the letter had come without reinforcements, Bernardin de Saint-Pierre

would certainly have pulverized the writer with scorn, but the awkward
fact was that it *was* backed up, by names too powerful for even the
Jardin des Plantes director to defy. Upon due consideration, he moderated
his wrath and tried to temporize. The pro-animals group kept up its pressure, and little by little Bernardin de Saint-Pierre gave way, until the day
came when the authorities refused to wait any longer. Even before the
Versailles animals arrived, the leavings of other pillaged menageries were
dumped on the Jardin's doorstep, one shipment following another, until
the dignified savants were at their wits' end to find places to put the
beasts. Faster and faster came the animals. The whole world seemed to be
taking up the idea of snatching wild beasts from their owners and turning
them over to Bernardin de Saint-Pierre's garden. Not only menageries
were being raided. The police now concentrated on the bear leaders
and other itinerant animal-trainers who wandered through the countryside. Their kind had done this from early times, from one town to another,
following the fairs. Lately, however, some had adopted a more settled life,
putting their charges through their paces year in, year out, at permanent
stands in the streets of Paris. Now all of a sudden the police, perhaps
because of the liberation fever, perhaps because their leaders were acti-
vated by that impulse toward austerity characteristic of republican movements, began swooping on performing-animal shows and confiscating the
artistes. The beasts were carted off to the Jardin des Plantes without so
much as a warning to the professors. The savants protested furiously that
the municipality had no authority to commit these outrages, and demanded that the police take back the twenty-six trained bears, leopards,
and monkeys which Paris alone had contributed, but argument was futile,
and they were left to scrounge around for yet more space in their once
hallowed grounds. It wasn't for a long time that Bernardin de Saint-
Pierre managed to elicit from the municipality funds for cage building.
Then construction went ahead at top speed, the workers constantly
urged on by frantic gentlemen who were trying to get wild animals out
of their workrooms. Fortunately, the Versailles refugees didn't arrive
until 1794.

Contributions continued to trot in—thirty-six animals from the Duke of
Orléans' estate, a few beasts here and a few birds there from subsidiary
collections at Versailles, and some survivors from Chantilly. Two Indian
elephants had been the star attractions at William V's menagerie at the
Loo, in Holland. Most of their lives had been spent there in the care of
an English trainer named Thompson. In 1795 it became clear that the
French were on their way to the lowlands, and the prince paused in his
preparations for flight to tell Thompson that the elephants must be killed.

Otherwise, he pointed out, they would suffer torture and starvation at the hands of the soldiers. They were bound to die in any case, he declared. But Thompson didn't want to kill the beasts, being sure he could manage to take good care of them. William agreed to leave the matter to him and went away, and Thompson stayed with the elephants, Hans and Parkie, to face the victors. Events justified his judgment. The French cavalrymen, though they slaughtered most of the other creatures they found in the menageries not only spared Hans and Parkie, but helped Thompson out, giving him part of their horses' rations and fuel to keep the elephants warm and fed during the bitterly cold winter months. Later, when officials came from Paris to claim what was left in the menagerie, it proved more difficult than they had anticipated to transport two large elephants. Cages broke down and wagons crumbled under their weight, but they arrived at the Jardin des Plantes at last, in 1798.

By this time the faculty had become reconciled to their picturesque dilemma. They were used to the animals: some of the men actually enjoyed having them around. On one point, however, they were all determined: in no circumstances must this living museum be confused with ordinary frivolous menageries and trained-animal shows. Theirs was a serious collection, maintained in the cause of knowledge and progress. They could hardly prevent the citizens deriving uninitiated pleasure from gawking at the specimens, but the faculty must never miss the opportunity of impressing visitors with the fact that it was not a peepshow. In fact, learned men did use the Jardin to great effect: Lamarck, Cuvier, and Latreille worked among the animals as soberly as Buffon had done among the greenery, when the garden was really only a Jardin des Plantes. Post-Revolutionary scientists formed many of their theories there, thanks to observations they were able to make of living specimens. Chemistry, physiology, geology, physics, philosophy—all these, as well as botany and zoology, were furthered at the museum until few people could doubt that republican times were better, for science at any rate, than they had been in the old days, when dignified academicians were forced to lurk outside the walls of the king's menagerie in the hope that it might please His Majesty, after the games, to toss them a dead tiger for dissection.

CHAPTER 3

Jardin des Plantes

☐

After a quarter of a century the menagerie at the Jardin des Plantes was no longer a sore point with France's learned professors. On the contrary, it had gained such respectability that it was established as one of the most praiseworthy institutions in Paris. To be sure, members of the unenlightened public stubbornly continued to regard it as a place of amusement, and took their children to see the animals much as they took them to the carnival on holidays, but the Jardin bore a better reputation than that among intellectuals at home and abroad—so much so that a number of British gentlemen began thinking seriously of creating a similar sort of display, a non-profit-making zoological collection where Londoners, too, might look on the wonders of nature and broaden their minds. The leading spirit of this group was Sir Stamford Raffles, the founder of Singapore, who was an ardent amateur naturalist. During his years of service in India and Southeast Asia, he had made a habit of sending back to interested friends vast collections of plants and animals, and his published works are full of observations and descriptions of these species which he encountered in strange countries. He had discovered at least one new plant in the East Indies, which is named for him, and his residency when he became governor always swarmed with wild-animal pets. Now, in retirement, he was free to turn his attention to the fulfillment of what had always been a favorite dream, the building of a place in London where live animals rather than stuffed ones could be exhibited. He was immediately attracted by the reputation of the Jardin des Plantes in Paris, and made a point of visiting it, as did some of his cronies. Among those who shared his enthusiasm were the noted chemist Sir

Humphry Davy and Sir Joseph Banks the botanist, who had outfitted Cook's ship *Endeavour* and accompanied Cook on his first voyage. Both men had served a term as president of the Royal Society.

Early in May 1826, these gentlemen and others of the same ideas held a meeting and resolved to publish their intentions, as a group they called the Zoological Society. Their aim, they announced, was to encourage the study of zoology and animal physiology, to introduce "new and curious objects of the Animal Kingdom" into England, and to put these creatures on permanent display somewhere in London. Such members of the public as heard of these plans for their educational benefit hardly appreciated them. They knew all about performing-animal shows and Mr. Cross's menagerie at Exeter Exchange, though, and there was an uneasy feeling among the middle classes that men of such eminence as Raffles and Davy ought not to associate themselves with vulgar, childish amusements. Here and there an eyebrow was raised, but for the most part the announcement was received with indifference. Little comment was made on it in print, though the weekly journal *The Literary Gazette* of May 6 published an article of a facetious nature that was disapproving:

"King Henry the First enclosed the park at Wodestoc with a wall . . . for all foreign wild beasts such as lions, leopards, camels, linxes, which he procured abroad of other princes. . . . This is the first British National Menagerie that we have read of; the Romans were much addicted to wild beast shows. Considering the advanced state of knowledge it is to be expected that the new Zoological Association will beat both the Romans and King Henry: though we do not know how the inhabitants of the Regent's Park will like the lions, leopards, and linxes so near their neighborhood."

Such scoffing did not last long—at least not for more than a few years. In 1829 the Society received its charter from George IV, and people began to take it seriously. Many still disapproved—many still do—but nobody dismissed the proposed park any more as a mere crackpot scheme, for the beginning was there in full view. Besides, the climate of thought was changing.

It was a time when the Western world appears to have been waiting for a sign or a prophet, someone with the vision to sum up the wonder and curiosity and misgivings that were besetting serious thinkers. In the mass of data scientists were collecting there was much that troubled people, for it seemed impossible to reconcile some of that information with the laws of nature. The anonymous writer of an article published in 1838* was obviously struggling with questions aroused in his mind by the study of a chimpanzee. Worriedly, he thought of Cuvier's fossils and the conclusions one must draw from them. "Ignorant and bigoted men, who are either too illiterate to appreciate truth, or too indolent to be at the trouble of investigating it, may declaim, as they have invariably done in all ages and all countries, against the innovations of science: they may hold up to popular odium now the great truths of zoology and geology, as heretical and anti-religious, in the same manner that they formerly reviled the sublime discoveries of Galileo, of Locke, and of Newton . . ." The writer pointed out that when zoology and geology proved our present creation only the last of a series of similar epochs through which the planet has already passed, "prejudicial and ignorant men immediately raised the cry of irreligion and infidelity, because the new doctrines appeared to contradict their own interpretation of the Mosaic cosmogony . . ." Of course, one could go too far in the other direction, too, as witness the eccentric Lord Monboddo, who, like Rousseau, "strenuously maintained that men were but monkeys or orangs, which by accidental circumstances, succeeded in emancipating themselves from the original debasement of their nature, and, by the gradual development of their mental faculties and physical structure, at length reached the high degree of perfection which they at present enjoy." This was so ridiculous as scarcely to call for comment. The only thing resembling fact that theorists who agree with Monboddo could present was that there is actually "an uninterrupted graduation of mental and physical qualities in a kingdom, also modifications occur under our own eyes, in domestic animals . . ." but does one of these facts necessarily connect up with the other? Need we assume that each link in the chain necessarily sprung from that which preceded it, rather than that it had a separate and independent origin . . . "and that all were equally due to distinct acts of creative power?" After all, though varieties occur, they are nevertheless confined within certain strictly prescribed limits. "Who has ever seen a dog produced from a horse, or a monkey from a dog? Yet this is just as probable as that man could have originally derived his origin from the orangutan, or this from any of the inferior monkeys."

Darwin's *Origin of Species* was not to appear for another twenty-one years, but the yeast was working.

The founders of the Zoological Society were necessarily on the defensive. They expected, and got, opposition, not only from those citizens

* *The Menageries: The Library of Entertaining Knowledge*, Vol. 1. London, 1838, page 2 et seq.

who condemned menageries as mere purveyors of amusement for gin-drinking, winkle-eating people of the lower classes, but also from church-goers. The Society had to make its members' position clear and assure the critics that they were not pandering to depraved instincts, or attacking organized religion. The animals exhibited in London, they re-peated, were to be objects of scientific research, and this introduction of living species was only a part of the Society's plans. It also hoped to provide material for museums and anatomists by forming a comprehen-sive collection of zoological books, by publishing the results of zoological research, and by maintaining and assisting research in anatomy and taxonomy. Prudently, even before announcing the birth of the Society they had acquired permission to use government land in Regent's Park, after a protracted and difficult struggle with the Commissioners of Woods and Forests. A lot of strings had to be pulled before they were permitted to put up cages on this tract of five acres: they had originally requested twenty, but five was what they got. Here Decimus Burton the architect hurriedly constructed housing for the two hundred specimens already ac-quired—monkeys, llamas, birds, bears, and a number of ungulates, in-cluding a giraffe that was presented to them by King George as soon as he received it as a gift from Mohammed Ali, the ruler of Egypt. Soon the area was so crowded that the Society bought a piece of property out in the country, near Kingston, where they kept superfluous animals and breeding females.

From the start, however, the zoological garden was such a success that the commissioners could not hold out, and soon they had granted more park land. The respectable middle classes took the garden to its heart, looking on it as a place where they could take the children and their country cousins without themselves suffering boredom. It was more amus-ing than the museum and nothing like so offensive or dangerous as the theatre. Moreover, the king obviously approved of it. Even after his death he proved helpful, because half of his private royal menagerie at Windsor was handed over to Regent's Park as a legacy. The other half went to Dublin, where a zoological garden had recently been established in frank imitation of London's.

Soon other imitations were springing up everywhere, on the Conti-nent as well as in Britain. The idea had caught on, and so had the new slang name for a zoological garden, "zoo." It owes its origin to the British love of nicknames, but it was exported along with the whole conception, until the word "zoo" appeared everywhere a zoological garden was to be seen. Finally it achieved the dignity of inclusion in the dictionary: the Oxford English Dictionary gives 1847 as the date of its first appearance in print. By that time, public zoos were so much a pattern of civilized life that people had forgotten there was ever a time when they did not exist.

CHAPTER 4

Britain

☐

In England, as often as I am near a TV set on Wednesday afternoon, I watch "Zoo Time" from five in the afternoon to five twenty-five, then turn to the other main channel for the other animal series. "Zoo Time" represents the Zoological Society of London, whereas the later program emanates from Bristol and other West Country places. In England the five-to-six TV period is a kind of sacrosanct children's hour, and these programs are excellent for the purpose, but I hope Bristol will forgive me for saying that I prefer London's. My reason for doing so casts no aspersions on the Bristol series. It is simply that Desmond Morris, curator of mammals at Regent's Park, who presides over "Zoo Time," has a more adult approach, and, after all, I am an adult so its suits me better. When Bristol's Johnny Morris talks in a babyish falsetto through the mouths of ringtail lemurs or okapis, something inside of me snaps. If you come right down to it, I have no business watching television at all during the children's hour, but I do enjoy "Zoo Time." Even without it, the London Zoological Society's attitude toward children is generally good. They have—or, rather, their Miss Jarvis has—organized a junior association called the Young Zoologists' Club which attracts more than four thousand enthusiastic members from Greater London: an eleven-year-old boy of my acquaintance is a star member of the Herpetologists' Section of the club, and he never misses a lecture or field trip. Moreover, the girl next door shares his enthusiasm, and they attend the affairs together. Sometimes on special days the club goes far afield to visit other zoos. In addition there are courses organized by the Society in London's schools, when classes of children attend "lecture-demonstrations" at Regent's Park and Whipsnade. Often I see them swarming through the

Whipsnade lanes, overcrowding the miniature railway, shouting and fighting and behaving generally like supers onstage in a production of *Aida*. Of course they are unruly, but they know their animals, and each is a little zoo public-relations official in himself.

Ultimately, they grow up into big zoo public-relations officials—but then the British are naturally zoo-minded. It is doubtful if any other thirty-six acres in the world has ever meant so much to its public as Regent's Park, though as far as plant goes, one must admit it isn't the most modern zoo in the world. Probably it won't ever be. It will never catch up. Things move fast in the zoo world but slowly in England. Money for such purposes, as for all purposes, is usually scarce, and they've had the war, *both* wars . . . I repeat, it takes the British a long time to recover. But Regent's Park, with Whipsnade, nevertheless has a tremendous collection of animals, more than fifteen hundred species, which record alone places it among the top four.

In a newspaper article in 1963, James Fisher listed the growth of what he called Regent's Park's higgledy-piggledy architecture. The first design for the grounds, made by Decimus Burton in 1827, was not fully carried out—what zoo design ever is?—but before the axe fell, Burton managed at least to build a giraffe house that still serves the zoo well. Another plan was drawn up in 1909, but the First World War settled that, though the architect succeeded in putting up some things, among them the still-extant Mappin Terraces and a few barless pits designed in emulation of Hagenbeck's at Hamburg. There was a third plan duly frustrated when the Second World War interrupted the building of an elephant house and condemned Regent's Park pachyderms to a long, long term of existence in makeshift surroundings underground. At last, in 1963, things actually did begin to progress, and when Mr. Fisher reported on conditions there was a new footbridge over the canal, a walk-through aviary designed by Lord Snowdon, nearly finished, and, as a climax, a genuine, fully built elephant house. At the beginning I didn't care for that last structure. I said so to one of the officials, who replied, "All right, but say what you will, it's nice to get our elephants above ground after all those years." I had to admit that he was right. Furthermore, I like it now—I like it a lot. And I am trying to get fond of Lord Snowdon's aviary too, but that's going to take longer. The real point is, it's there, and so are new cattle and zebra and antelope and deer houses, and a gibbon cage, all of them badly needed for a long time.

Though London has all those species, the curators can tell you that the acquisition of animals, even rare ones, is less than half the problem. The real test comes in maintaining them after you've got them. Of course this means proper housing, but it also calls for a good deal more in the way of personal care—superintendents, keepers, vets. To learn the technique of maintenance in zoos has taken years of wasteful trial and error. To be good with wild animals a person must have what amounts to an extra sense. It is more than empathy. There is something of maternal feeling in it (though the right approach is not necessarily sentimental), and something else that corresponds to the green thumb of the good gardener. A lot of zoo people will tell you that a good animal man is born, not made, but that doesn't mean that training is not useful too. It seems true to say that some people from their earliest youth are suited to work with animals, whereas others never acquire the knack no matter how hard they may try. Civilization being what it is, many a good animal man may go through life without realizing his hidden talent, but fortunately for everybody, one of these gifted people, Abraham Dee Bartlett, happened by chance to hobnob with captive wild animals from the time he was five years old. From then on his mission was plain, to himself if not to his family.

He was born in London in 1812, the son of a barber, John Bartlett. John had learned his trade as apprentice to a master barber named Turner, and still worked for him when Abraham was an infant, at Turner's place in Exeter Street, the Strand. (Incidentally, Turner's son became the famous painter.) In a collection of pieces entitled *Wild Animals in Captivity*, which a son published in 1899, A. D. Barlett tells how John used to take him along when he went to work and leave him with a friend close by in Exeter 'Change. This friend was none other than Mr. Cross, proprietor of the popular menagerie. The little boy was allowed, as he says, "to crawl about in the beast-room of that menagerie, playing with young lions and other animals that were not likely to harm me." As a result he didn't have the remotest recollection of the first time he ever saw lions, tigers, elephants or other beasts of foreign origin. The happy acquaintanceship with nature seemed doomed when John insisted that his son at the age of fourteen become apprenticed to himself, putting away childish things to learn hairdressing and brush-making. For seven or eight miserable years the boy dutifully toiled in the shop in Drury Lane, his only relief a hobby he had learned from Mr. Cross, preserving the skins and feathers of dead birds that the menagerie-proprietor had passed on to him. "Somewhere about 1833 or 1834," he recalls, "I determined again to seek the society of wild animals, but as I could not offer myself as a keeper, and as I had no means of becoming a proprietor, what was I to do? It then occurred to me that I could become a taxidermist . . . I gradually became an expert in skinning and preparing . . . and in the course of time I succeeded in mounting, or, as it is commonly called, stuffing, various specimens."

Bartlett became so adept at taxidermy that he found it possible to make a satisfactory living at the art, even, he says, beyond his expectations. Naturally he was patronized by the new Zoological Society, and the members felt a personal gratification in his triumph when, in the International Exhibition of 1851, he won the taxidermy competition with an imaginative reconstruction of an extinct bird, the Dodo of Mauritius. The last living specimen of the Dodo had been seen at the beginning of the eighteenth century. "An ingenious example of the art," was the judges' verdict. When the Exhibition ended, Bartlett stayed on with the Crystal Palace Company. He was supposed to be their naturalist, but the work disappointed and offended him and he was unhappy. He had thought the business would be "devoted to educational greatness," and as one who shared the Zoological Society's ideals this attracted him, but it proved to be merely a glorified amusement center like those found at seaside resorts—"Punch and Judy, tight-rope dancing, roundabouts, etc.," he wrote scornfully. The Zoological Society saved him. In 1859 it offered him the post of superintendent of Regent's Park, with the added inducement of a house within the zoo confines. For thirty-eight years thereafter, Bartlett reigned over his kingdom of beasts, becoming a familiar figure to the public with his beard, top hat and tails.

Zoo keeping was still a new profession, and a superintendent was much on his own, feeling his way in the care and tending of wild animals. Nowadays he would have the help of a long list of specialists—the vet, the pathologist, the gardener, the dietitian; as for the business side of it, that would be another department entirely, and so would the consultant architect's work. Bartlett had to do all these things himself. He had keepers for the dirtier work and to help with the handling of difficult beasts, but it was up to him to make decisions when a rhino's horn, for example, needed attention, and to do the necessary surgery. He did remarkably well at all of it. He worked out his own methods of keeping animals warm or cool, and formed some sound theories about their temperaments and reactions. He answered the public's questions, which poured in. It was of course his duty to sequestrate such animals as in his opinion were unsafe, and such a decision led to one of the stormiest periods of his long career, precipitated by Jumbo, a great African bull elephant.

Jumbo, who had come to London as a small beast shaky on his pins, grew up to a splendid specimen weighing about six tons: the Society's council claimed he was the largest elephant in captivity. Everybody knew Jumbo. Children rode on his back, until as the years went on the public got used to him and assumed that he was always benevolent. Behind the scenes, however, the staff knew better, because—after seventeen years' residence in the zoo—Jumbo showed disturbing signs of maturity, becoming subject to attacks of *musth*, as Indians call the periodic madness that affects elephants. During a frenzy he attacked an iron door with such force as to break off both tusks. Afterward the jagged ends grew upward, curved back, and irritated the insides of his cheeks, causing painful abscesses. Naturally, the beast's temper grew worse with the pain, until Superintendent Bartlett contrived a long-handled spear with which he managed to lance one of these blisters. Jumbo made little fuss about what must have been an agonizing operation. More; having once experienced relief, he quietly allowed Bartlett to lance the other side. He then remained calm for a time, but the Superintendent felt that the respite was only temporary, and warned the council that Jumbo might have to be shot. Not relishing the prospect of telling the public the news, the members put it off.

Soon afterward came a most timely offer from Mr. P. T. Barnum of Barnum and Bailey's Circus in America. Mr. Barnum said that he would like to buy Jumbo, and the council welcomed the suggestion, especially when the showman agreed to pay two thousand pounds, but as soon as the news came out, the British public, or at least the newspapers, raised a noisy outcry. What, sell their Jumbo to the barbarians? Never! The council was nothing but a money-grubbing body, they said, and the Society was outraging every law of decency. One paper printed drawings of Jumbo leaning lovingly against a reciprocating female elephant—by this time the zoo did own a female elephant, as a matter of fact—with captions addressed to the wicked councilmen in the elephants' names, begging them not to separate two such affectionate mates, to which Bartlett scornfully retorted that the animals had never even met; Jumbo was a confirmed bachelor. He was sure that Barnum had stirred up the hullaballoo for publicity's sake, and he may well have been right. Anyway the council did not revoke its decision, and Jumbo sailed West. In America he was a circus star, traveling about in pursuit of his new career for three years, until a Canadian freight train accidentally ran into and killed him.

Bartlett died at an advanced age. His son, who succeeded him, was nothing like so good a superintendent as his father had been, and was soon released.

After trying out several replacements, the council reluctantly concluded that *nobody* was likely to be as satisfactory as A. D. Bartlett, at least not all in one person, and in 1902 they nominated a committee to reorganize the whole administration. Dr. Peter Chalmers Mitchell, appointed Secretary of the Society at the same time, changed the aspect of his appointment, so that the secretaryship ceased to be a mere honorary post: he and the superintendent worked together, sharing the responsibility. As a medical man, Chalmers Mitchell had certain ideas that startled and alarmed his contemporaries. In one important respect he anticipated Dr. Clarke of Bristol, and insisted that the animals be given fresh air, even those from tropical climates, which until then had been carefully and lovingly smothered in hermetically sealed rooms. Until 1902 no lion, tiger, parrot or monkey in Regent's Park was permitted fresh oxygen, and when one quickly died, as such animals usually did, it was assumed that somehow in spite of all precautions it had been subjected to a fatal draft. Chalmers Mitchell insisted that these animals had simply been stifled. "I do not suggest that the provision of heat is in itself an evil," he argued. " . . . The first requisite is free access to the open air, the rest is light, space and cleanliness; these things having been secured, any form of heating that may be thought advisable may be added, in so far as it does not in any way interfere with the primary considerations." It was to take him twenty years to reorganize Regent's Park buildings, but during the very first year he managed to get his way in one particular: he moved the baboons into unheated outdoor cages, and they not only survived but flourished. This was several years before Carl Hagenbeck opened his park; Chalmers Mitchell stood alone in his battle to let animals adapt themselves to climate. The rest had to come later, but it came. As time went on the secretary continued to hammer away at a few pet ideas including open-air cages or enclosures, preferably barless like those in Hagenbeck's new park. He even suggested a place in the country where exhibition specimens from Regent's Park might rest up from their arduous town duties. This latter notion seemed fantastic to most of the council, but Chalmers Mitchell proposed it again and again, and finally convinced the important majority. They may have remained skeptical as to an animal's psychological need of peace and quiet, but the thought of having more space was attractive. From the beginning Regent's Park Zoo had been cramped, and the more the animals prospered the more young they produced, so a breeding farm was a tempting idea. In 1928 the plan was approved and elaborated. A summer rest home, good. A breeding farm, better. Why not also open it to the public as a country zoo? People might be willing to journey a long way to see animals in a "natural" setting, and pay for the privilege. Chalmers Mitchell and the superintendent, Dr. G. M. Vevers, found a place called

Hill Farm at the village of Whipsnade near Dunstable, Bedfordshire, only thirty miles from London comprising something more than five hundred fifty acres of rolling land high on chalk. The Society bought it, and Whipsnade Zoo was opened in May 1931.

"The whole concept was experimental," says the Society's *Zoo Newsletter* for autumn, 1965, "but many developments which were planned were interrupted by the outbreak of war in 1939." Nevertheless Whipsnade history in those early days makes good reading if only because of the experiments that were tried and abandoned. In an old number of *Zoo Life*, for instance, I found mention of Whipsnade's Chimpanzee Island, which puzzled me because to the best of my knowledge—and I know Whipsnade very well—there is no such place. There aren't even any chimpanzees. But later in another article I discovered that the chimps on that island had adapted a fallen tree and floated themselves across the moat on an improvised raft to what might be called the mainland. No doubt they were ultimately rounded up and sent back to London, but things must have been lively around Whipsnade for a while.

"In the limited area of the London Zoo"—I am quoting the *Newsletter* again—"it is the Council's policy to exhibit pairs or small groups of a wide and representative range of species, but the aim at Whipsnade . . . is to establish and build up large groups and herds of animals in surroundings which are as natural as possible. Buildings and heated houses are kept to a minimum, fences are replaced by sunken ditches, and always the Council and its architects have in mind the importance of maintaining the park-like atmosphere where the undulating landscape, the woods and avenues of trees, the bushes and wild flowers form a natural background to the animals in their paddocks."

Well, yes and no. The background is natural to England. The park is an English park, but most of the animals are not English and have had to get used to all that unfamiliar green lushness. Whipsnade's designers eschewed the Hagenbeck pattern of make-believe background; you will see no concrete caves or artificial mountains there, only the gentle Bedfordshire countryside. Bison roam the meadows, lions sun themselves on greensward never seen in Africa, and tigers loll under oak and beech trees. Yet they flourish. Bennett's wallabies never had it any better in Australia; like the peacocks they wander the terrain at will, and they have so many babies that Whipsnade's director sells at least a hundred surplus every year. A nine-foot fence surrounds the entire tract, made of steel bars each of which turns at the top and points down in a graceful curve that ends in a sharp point. The curve is outward, not inward as it was originally, when the fence was designed to keep the zoo animals from escaping. Almost immediately after it was put up it became painfully apparent that these foreign wild beasts offered no problem about crossing it, but British wild animals did. Foxes, especially, learned to get across the barrier, and once inside they destroyed rare birds and eggs, and carried off exotic small mammals until the fence-bars were swung around.

To date, Whipsnade's breeding successes include an increasing group of Thomson's gazelle from East Africa, polar bears, Indian rhinos (three), more than a few hippos, pygmy hippos and three onagers. Musk oxen, usually difficult to keep, do well here, and the staff can boast one of the finest deer collections in the world. Chinese water deer are said to share the freedom of the place with the wallabies and peafowl, but they do their wandering during "closed" hours, cannily staying in one paddock or another by daylight. In sum, Whipsnade has proved itself adequate as a breeding center, but the public knows and enjoys it better as a zoo, the pleasant object of a drive into the country and a place where children may ride on a camel or a pony. Elephant rides have recently been discontinued: the constant flight overhead of jet planes has ruined the nerves of the great beasts until they can't be trusted.

Most foreign visitors to Britain don't know that in the north of England near the west coast, at Upton-by-Chester, is a jewel of a zoo. If they are zoo-conscious they do know about Regent's Park, Whipsnade, Bristol, and Peter Scott's Wildfowl Trust at Slimbridge, and they must have heard of Gerald Durrell's zoo in Jersey, to see which many of Mr. Durrell's readers actually brave the crossing by ship. But Chester Zoo, though it is the pride of northerners, hasn't received the attention outside the country that it merits. Like Regent's Park and others, it is maintained by a zoological society, in this case the North of England, but unlike the London Zoo it started out as a private collection, the property of the man who is now its director-secretary, Mr. G. S. Mottershead. If I am asked why Chester is my favorite, I can only say that it's the prettiest zoo I ever saw. Yes, I know: flowers and plants should be of only secondary importance in an animal collection, and, admittedly, Mr. Mottershead's flowers and plants are beautiful. But that isn't what I mean when I say "pretty": I mean the paddocks, the elephant house, and the moats protecting some of the displays, on which you can travel by water-bus. Not even the Tropical House would tip the scale all by itself, wonder though it is. It's the aggregate of all these features that makes Chester outstanding.

Mr. Mottershead said that he can't recall a time when he was not

fascinated by wild animals. He used to be a farmer not far from Upton—
that is, in theory he was a farmer, but he kept buying animals, giving
up more and more of his land to them, until he capitulated and admitted
to himself that what he had was a zoo, not a farm. More space was
needed, however, before he could open his gates to the public, and he
bought the tract on which the zoo now stands, a well-wooded, hilly
piece of West Country where breezes from the sea keep the air temperate,
as they do down the coast at Bristol. What was originally the farmhouse
of this land stands more or less in the middle of a triangular park, a
vast rambling structure with the famous Rose Garden outside its entrance
and a garden of other flowers to one side. Mr. and Mrs. Mottershead,
who live in the house, can look out at the colors whenever they like.
On the day I saw the rose garden in spring it was like a great round
cushion of blooms—a mountain.

"Our gardener used to work for the royal family," said Mr. Mottershead.
"This is a zoo first and foremost, but in this part of the country we
like our flowers, and I understand that some visitors come to the park
just to look at them rather than at the animals. Myself, of course, I'm
an animal man. The zoo opened in 1931, in the spring, about the
same time as Whipsnade, and it was immediately popular, but after a
while I realized that I couldn't handle it alone financially. I thought of
closing down, but the city didn't want that; it was bringing people in,
you see, and generally putting us on the map. Some of the leading
citizens and the council got together and formed the Society, since when
we've done very well. We don't have to depend on donations or municipal
handouts. We've shown a profit ever since '42."

"Forty-two?" I repeated, surprised. "But, surely, that was right slambang
in the middle of the war—how could you have started doing well then?
I thought zoos everywhere were getting rid of their animals and closing
down just about '42."

He nodded. "Perfectly true, but the zoos that dispersed their stock
were those near London or other important towns, like industrial centers
or ports—places that expected bombing, and got it, for that matter.
Knowing that there would be no object in the Germans' bombing us—
after all, what have we here of military significance?—zoo directors all
over the country dumped their animals on us. Those were busy days.
We had to improvise all kinds of things. Almost overwhelmed, we were."
He chuckled mildly and looked around at his quiet, well-run domain.
"We learned a lot from it," he added.

I followed Mr. Mottershead first to the Pachyderm House, thinking
as I went of what William Conway of the Bronx Zoo told me about

Chester one day when we were talking. He spoke warmly of it, mentioning the elephant house in particular as a perfect example of what can be done when zoo directors don't waste money on frills that are appreciated only by human beings. "They built it during the worst of England's austerity time, just after the war. They used whatever they could get—army surplus, old concrete road blocks, and even flattened tin cans, and it was the best house for elephants I've ever seen in my life. If I were an elephant and were given my choice of where to live, I'd go to Chester."

I reflected that I must pass on this compliment to Mr. Mottershead, but before I could say anything we arrived, and I saw at once that this wasn't the building Bill had talked about, even though it, too, seemed highly desirable from an elephant's point of view. This edifice was soberly handsome, and there wasn't a tin can to be seen. Indoors, in the vast resounding dusk that evidently suits these animals, were two of the great beasts, and beyond a large barn door I saw others in a paddock, sporting in a roomy pool that the director told me was six feet deep. Hippos lived to one side in their own paddock, and tapirs occupied stalls at the other end.

"This place is one of the newer additions," said Mr. Mottershead. I spoke of Conway's report on the old house, and he said, "Oh yes. Well, that's a thing of the past, though we spent only twelve thousand pounds even on this one . . . I believe it cost Regent's Park half a million to build theirs. Mr. Conway—yes. It wasn't long after his visit that we had a horrible experience in that same old house. Anthrax. We had a fine herd of elephants at the time and it was almost wiped out. Have you seen anthrax? Until that day I never had. I was up at the office and the head keeper telephoned to tell me that two of the animals were acting odd and refusing to feed. He said they were just standing there. I hurried down, but before we could begin to wonder what to do for them, before we could even guess what was the matter, two fell down dead, right before our eyes. Then another showed the same symptoms, and another. In spite of anything the vet could do we lost them—four altogether. I never saw anything so sudden. It was terrible, especially afterward, because according to the law we had to destroy the bodies then and there, by fire. Well, as you might guess, it's not so easy to destroy an elephant's corpse by burning, and we had four of them; the necessity had never arisen before in Chester, and there were a lot of arguments, especially with the sanitation people. Then when that was settled we had to trace the infection, or at least do everything we could to try to trace it. The inspectors concluded at last that it

[1]

BONOBO, OR PYGMY CHIMP

Bred in San Diego Zoo in 1966.

[2]

FRESH-WATER DOLPHIN FROM THE AMAZON

[3]

GIRAFFES

[4]

KOALA

[5]

ACHILLA, A GORILLA IN THE BASEL ZOO

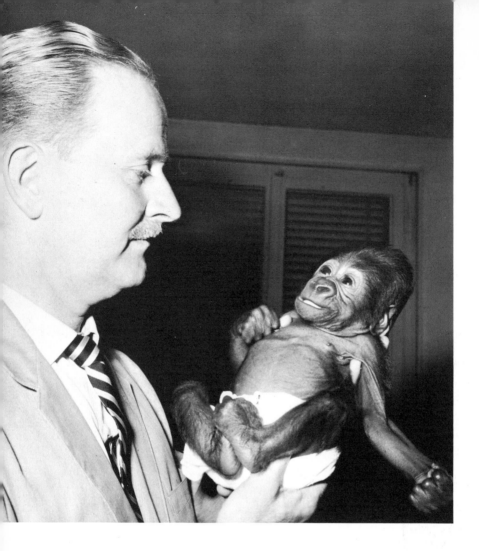

[6]

DR. ERNST LANG OF BASEL WITH ONE OF ACHILLA'S BABIES

[7]

OKAPI

[8]

INDIAN RHINO

Rare, not to be confused with African rhino.

had come in a load of hay. They couldn't find any here in the ground, so it had to be like that. They also decided that it couldn't have been prevented, but—" He shook his head with renewed sorrow. "Still, if you're especially interested in how we constructed buildings with salvage, we still have some, though we've replaced the elephant house. A den over there was built out of road blocks, that was just after the war, and the polar bear's place is made completely of pillboxes, and looks well enough. Sometimes even now we have to improvise when things happen unexpectedly. Speaking of which, come and see the rhino house. My daughter was recently traveling with her husband in Africa, and suddenly we got a cable that they'd acquired a female white rhino—we already had a male—and it was on its way. Well, I'd asked her to look out for one, but I hadn't expected her to be successful so soon, and we had nowhere to put it." He stepped out toward the new house and I ran to keep up. "We got to work immediately and constructed this house," he went on. "Everybody worked at top speed, and do you know, it was more or less ready in time?" We entered the building, a long row of moated pens, and paused to gaze admiringly at a white rhino, which gazed back admiringly at us. "If you look carefully you'll detect a few rough edges, perhaps," said the director. "We still have a lot of finishing to do, but for the time being, it serves. You'll want to see the aquarium; my daughter manages that. Next, though, I think we'll look at the Tropical House. It's our latest."

He explained further that it had been open less than a year at the time, early in 1965, but that certain of its inhabitants had long been a feature of Chester before that. "It's a unique establishment, we think, in that it contains so many separate features."

He preceded me through a rubber curtain which acts, he explained, as an insulator between outdoors and the much higher temperature inside. While he talked about the reptile section off the main hall, crocodiles and alligators and snakes and lizards, and the nocturnal house in yet another wing; while he talked of great apes and the wonderful heating system that could be adjusted to different temperatures in different compartments, I gave him only half my attention. I was busy gawking up and around at the Main Hall. We stood among great and small tropical plants—palms, lianas, elephant-ear, and related plants in great bushes, orchids and blossoms I'd never seen before, some rooted in shallow water, others high and dry. A stream trickled here, a waterfall sounded its cool, silvery note there. The brilliant flowers were outshone by the birds that flew about from tree to tree—purple birds, or green or yellow or iridescent, tiny sunbirds, parrots, and a trumpeter bird that walked after our feet wherever we went. Mr. Mottershead took me upstairs to a gallery that ran around the walls, from where we were level with yet more of the flying birds. He explained that each male bird staked out its own territory, so that the keepers knew just where to find each one, resting or on the wing. "See these little fellows; they're always here," he said, indicating some small yellow creatures that swooped about in a well-defined area of space. "They catch midges that play in this ray of light," said the director. "A few of my birds are nesting, and some should soon be laying, but it will take others a longer time to settle down. Our chief enemy here is the rat. We've done a lot of ratproofing, but still one has to keep constant watch. They hide out at the bases of the plants, or in corners."

The great apes live in conditions I should like to see copied in all zoos. Each family, including a pair of the rare mountain gorillas, has two portions of territory: a sleeping or resting place in the Tropical House complete with bars and ledges, and an outside bit of field or meadow—a tongue of land surrounded on its free sides by the waters of the moat. Just as I came out to see these front yards the sun broke through the thin covering of clouds that had kept the day rather gloomy until then, and a chimpanzee strolled from her house to lie on the grass and enjoy the warmth, arms outstretched in complete relaxation. Beyond her on their ground the mountain gorillas sat close together, one grooming the other. On a peninsula between them an orangutan moved out of his front door to look around, then went back in.

"They don't mind cold weather when they can go into the warm again whenever they like," said Mr. Mottershead. "All winter they come and go like that, taking sun-baths from time to time." The chimpanzee spotted him and turned her head in absent-minded, careless greeting. Then she pulled up a stalk of grass and nibbled it.

CHAPTER 5

Feeding: The Little Zoo

□

It is surprising, says Hediger sadly in his *Psychology of Animals in Zoos and Circuses*, how people fail to understand the ways of animals, the outward signs of their reactions. An incident at Basel impressed him profoundly with this truth, when with a number of zoo attendants he was trying to move an African Barbary wild sheep from one enclosure to another. The animal panicked, jumped at the head keeper's face and knocked him down, then began dashing up and down the enclosure with nostrils fully distended, foaming mouth open as it gasped, tongue hanging out, eyes staring and starting from their sockets. It panted hoarsely, its flanks heaved, the hair along the back was bristling, the tail stuck up stiffly—in short, the sheep was so clearly in a state of extreme distress and excitement that only a blind person, one would have thought, could fail to understand the situation. Yet, "At that moment," says Hediger, "a lady with a large party of children came on the scene, rummaged around in a paper bag, and, blissfully ignorant of what was going on, cheerfully held out a piece of bread to the foam-flecked maned sheep, as it dashed by her."

The incident may have staggered Hediger and his helpers, but it wouldn't have surprised me at all. People who visit zoos, especially with food for the animals, see *nothing*. You can hang bright red danger-signs at eye level or any level you like: they won't read them. They wouldn't read them if they were in red, white, and blue, or flashing neon. Some years ago, at Whipsnade, a Boy Scout went too close to the fence around the lions' enclosure and teased a reclining lioness until she whirled around and grabbed him. He died of the encounter, and in the ensuing outcry the staff showed how carefully and thoroughly the place was placarded with danger signs. But, just to make sure, extra fencing was put up around the enclosures and new rules were passed: nowadays children less than twelve years old can't go into Whipsnade unaccompanied by adults. At Regent's Park not long afterward there was a slight contretemps involving Guy, London's great gorilla, when another boy got inside the railings around Guy's cage, and the ape put his hands through the bars and grabbed him. Guy was persuaded to let go his prize before anything serious happened, but everybody got nervous all over again, so the authorities erected a glass wall between the cage and the railings to supplement the warning signs that already bristled all over the bars to tell the public that the animal was dangerous and must not be fed. Of course, questions were asked in the House of Commons—all that. Well, a few days later in Regent's Park I strolled around to see Guy's glass shield. It stood about six feet high, but that didn't foil the woman I saw there, smilingly boosting her small child up until it cleared the barrier, leaned across to the naked bars, and held out a peanut to the gorilla.

You've got to accept it: regardless of signs and all the rest of it, visitors *will* feed animals peanuts, candy, paper bags, coins, and sometimes more sinister gifts like poison and razor blades. A few zoos allow no feeding, but too many take halfway measures and permit the feeding of all but their valuable and delicate specimens. In private, zoo men admit that this is a risky procedure and their charges would be better off without it, but the custom persists, because, as the directors argue, people like to feed the animals and a ban would cut the gate receipts. Besides, say some of them, the sale of suitable food on the premises cuts down the risk and brings in extra money. It is an attitude that hangs over from the bad old days when public feeding lessened outlay for the zoo proprietor, but this is specious reasoning, since one loses far more from death than one gains in this way. Little by little, most directors are coming around to a more sensible point of view; I have seen the change taking place. More than thirty years ago, at a small English zoo on a Sunday afternoon, I saw a woman in a hat and coat—a visitor, that is to say—carrying a large basket from cage to cage and handing out to the animals broken hunks of bread, gnawed bones, cooked greens, and potatoes. A large hyena apparently recognized her and came slinkingly to the bars to receive its ration. Even after getting it the beast remained pressed to the bars while she caressed its head and murmured endearments—not an ordinary sight. The woman must have been a regular visitor with her table scraps, who was allowed to feed the animals anything she liked. I doubt if anybody could do that today in a reputable zoo, but the situation is still confused, which is unfortunate. A lot of people believe that wild animals have an instinct that protects them against harmful food, but it isn't true. A wild animal may know enough to avoid familiar dangers, but anything outside his frame of reference is as mysterious to him as it would be to a human being. And zoo visitors are not all well-meaning: among them are neurotics and psychopaths who try deliberately to do harm.

In permissive zoos there is no objection to feeding the tougher monkeys such as the rhesus macaque, or most ungulates and elephants. Whipsnade and Regent's Park sell sixpenny bags of "Animal Snacks" guaranteed not to harm anybody. At other zoos visitors may buy fish (usually at exorbitant rates) and throw them to sea lions or penguins. It is possible sometimes to buy peanuts, grapes, bananas and oranges inside the zoo and hand them on to the exhibits. But of course it is also possible to buy, not for animals but for the visitors, cartons of ice cream with little plastic spoons, and Coca-Cola, and tinfoil-wrapped bars of confectionery, and in spite of signs and warnings a lot of cartons and spoons and bottles and so on end up where they shouldn't be, in the cages or the animals themselves. In a zoo where all feeding is forbidden it is not easy for a visitor to get away with breaking the rules in this way, but where permission is granted at all, especially on a busy day, the keepers can't handle the situation. Not long ago I visited a zoo that is the proud possessor of a pair of the rare Indian rhino. Signs are hung all over their bars forbidding the public to feed these animals, but on that holiday afternoon a family party was gathered around cheerfully handing various things to one of the rhinos. In zoos I am an unabashed tattle-tale, and when I saw a keeper standing near the scene with his back turned, I said, "Somebody's giving food to that rhino."

He didn't move: he only smiled wearily and said, "Goes on all the time, madam. I can't stop it."

When making an autopsy of a suddenly dead zoo animal the vet looks first for poison administered, innocently or not, by some member of the public. Next he examines it for mistakes in feeding. No animal is absolutely immune, and there are limits to what even a rhesus monkey can digest. More or less at random I pick out from the autumn number, 1951, of *Zoo Life*—formerly published by the London Zoological Society—the superintendent's regular report. "It is distressing to have to conclude my article . . . with a note about the recent deaths of the two elephants . . . Ranee was found dead in her den in the early morning, after having seemed perfectly well the previous evening. The post-mortem examination revealed an acute gastro-enteritis. As further investigations suggested that she may have been poisoned, the police were consulted but inquiries produced no additional information."

Frankfurt's zoological garden takes no risks. To be sure about this I wrote to Dr. Grzimek the director, who replied that the feeding of the animals there is strictly forbidden: "We do not believe there is any good in the animals being fed by the public. We have had too many losses due to this feeding." He adds that though there may be some animals such feeding would not harm, the visitors can't know and will not learn which species these are. They don't approve of "a partial feeding permission" as this would induce people not to take the warnings on other cages seriously, and skeptics would escape notice when they disobeyed. Posters and signs are hung all over the zoo, declaring that people who offend against this rule will be ejected and fined twenty-five deutschmarks. "Our system works fairly well," wrote Dr. Grzimek. "There are only a few visitors whom we ever have banished from the zoo." He enclosed a little throwaway in English on bright magenta paper, which is handed out to first offenders by the keeper:

"You have just been seen feeding animals! If you are again found violating the regulations we shall be under the necessity to impose a fine and request you to leave the Zoological Gardens. Please, be kind to our animals. Even if you consider the feed alright, cases of serious disease and death may occur when many people feed the animals at the same time. An animal, living on a hay and oat diet all through the week, may come down with a serious disease if it is, all of a sudden, fed bread by hundredweights on a day with a high attendance figure. We in the Zoo must know why an animal refuses to accept its feed—is it ill or has it been overfed by visitors? If we do not know that, many cases of disease are being treated too late and may lead to the animal's death. Please do not cause harm to our animals, be considerate and kind to them!"

This policy doesn't seem to have had a discouraging effect on attendance: the 1965 figures for Frankfurt are 1,773,443.

The larger the city, the more problems for the zoo. It is not that such places are neglected. On the contrary, people flock to them in ever-increasing numbers. A director of my acquaintance believes that the ordinary city dweller makes a subconscious identification with captive wild animals. "They come out of their bed-sitting rooms and go straight to look at creatures leading even more circumscribed lives than theirs. It's a kind of catharsis," he says. Perhaps it is, but I suspect he is over-elaborating. It is more reasonable, surely, to conclude that townspeople outnumber their rural neighbors at the zoo for the same simple reason that they go to shops and theatres—because the places are conveniently near at hand.

In any case this very popularity confronts the bigtown zoo with a problem: the more flourishing the city the higher the value of real estate, and the zoo, though it ought to be enlarged to meet a constantly increasing demand, can't easily afford to do so. The established zoo parks that boast the longest histories are particularly unlucky in this respect. In the spacious days of private menageries, a rich man with a taste for collecting animals had what he considered plenty of land for the purpose. For one thing, he was blissfully ignorant of many of the animals' needs. Louis XIV could play with cages like so many building-blocks, arranging them in any design that suited his aesthetic sense. The pioneers of public zoo building who came in the wake of private owners followed their example in this respect and laid the foundations of amusement parks rather than zoological gardens—parks that happened to possess the added attraction of animals in cages, and were as often as not squeezed into the middle of town where the public could more easily see them. Some are built inflexibly around concert-halls, restaurants, or playgrounds, with no land nearby that can possibly be added. Even those that were originally of more forward-looking design have difficulty nowadays. The garden in Regent's Park is jealously kept within limits—thirty-six acres for a collection the size of London's is not very much. Antwerp's zoo, managed by the Société Royale de Zoologie d'Anvers, has a fine record, all the more admirable when one considers how they are squeezed into a corner in the center of town, up against the main railway station, with only twenty-four acres' breathing space. Of course a large zoo is not to everyone's taste. Children, old people, and invalids don't want to walk long distances. A zoo like San Diego's must offer some form of transportation. It boils down to the old conflict of interests, Man's versus captive animals, and the problem has reached the point where some authorities ask themselves if a highly diversified collection is really such a good thing when zoos can't properly accommodate all the specimens they have. These people declare that wide-ranging species like wolves ought not to be kept where they are subjected to close confinement, though many other animals don't need so much space. In rebuttal, the small zoo's director says that he owes it to the community to give them everything he can: if a zoo is to be educational, it must exhibit representative birds and mammals from the far reaches of the earth, and the more exotic they are, the better. He can rightfully argue that size is certainly not the most important factor in a zoo's success. A number of small collections have excellent breeding and longevity records, maintaining in good health many a species formerly believed impossible to keep in such conditions.

Zoo people know that we, the laymen, are lamentably prone to measure zoos by the same yardstick that we use on human habitations, condemning one or another in disgust because it is small and smelly and the cages are dark. Yet often the very place we disapprove of most strongly has healthy animals that breed regularly and live more than their natural span of years. Some animals are ill at ease when their living quarters don't smell; they do their best to repair the deficiency as soon as possible after their cages have been cleaned out. Some prefer half-darkness to airy light. This is not to say that every small, smelly, ill-lit zoo is better than every large, odorless, bright one, but only that we still don't always know what is best, and should not allow prejudice without knowledge to sway us. I remember the attendant who showed me around the Mysore Zoo in 1950, who was himself as fascinating as any of the animals. A Negro dwarf in a red fez, he had been a favorite of the Maharaja before Independence came to India, and showed such aptitude for taking care of the animals that he was put in charge of them. He was clearly proud of the zoo and kept up with developments in zoo keeping all over the world: it was through him I first heard of the trade publications that keep his colleagues in communication between widely separate places, so that animals can be swapped between, for example, Czechoslovakia and Argentina. Showing me a particularly beautiful Bengal tiger, he said, "Do you notice anything special about this place?" I made a couple of guesses —landscaping? size?—to which he shook his head. He answered himself, exploding with enthusiasm: "No *smell*, madam!" and more explicitly held his nose. It was true, I admitted: I didn't get the slightest whiff of cat.

"It's the way our cages are placed," he explained. "They catch every draft of air—you won't find another zoo in the country like it."

Now when I think back, I believe that his tiger was better served in another way than by ventilation; in having a large apartment walled off from the public gaze. Tigers want privacy—at least, so it is thought; it is one of the rules of thumb men have adopted after years of trial and error in tiger keeping. But one can't be sure even of this: some tigers don't seem to care whether or not they have privacy. The only really safe dogmatic statement to make is that zoos need more room generally. It is not a new complaint: in *The Times* of London for Tuesday, May 22, 1866, after the Whit Monday Bank Holiday, a reporter wrote,

". . . As the day advanced the crowd at both the entrance gates became very great, and in spite of the excellent arrangements made to prevent confusion, the society's officers and the attendant policemen had no little difficulty in keeping order among the throngs of applicants for admission. Inside the gardens appeared a perfect sea of heads, and round the enclosures of all the more favorite animals such large bodies of sightseers were congregated that the walks in the neighborhood of these spots became quite impassable. It became evident, in fact, that the ground allotted to the society for the exhibition of their large series of animals is no longer sufficient on these crowded days . . ."

My mind was full of this subject on the day I went to Schönbrunn, the zoo just outside Vienna. Schloss Schönbrunn and its gardens were once surrounded by the quiet woods and fields of the emperor's estate. Now it is the center of a bustling town among others of Vienna's suburbs, an easy ride by tram from the Ringstrasse. The castle rises proudly over its paths and lawns, a tourists' Mecca. I walked among a whole troop of other visitors, most of them laden with cameras. A wide approach led us through gateways decorated with marble statues of allegorical figures or nymphs or animals, toward the castle and its graceful stairway and wide arch. On the other side of the curiously flat building are wide lawns, their limits marked by hedges which hide formal gardens and avenues shaded by tall, aged trees. Tucked into this marginal and carefully tamed wilderness, between empty lawns and public road, is the Tiergarten. It is cunningly hidden, and none of the Schloss tourists accompanied me when I sought it out. Within the zoo, every square inch of ground counts. It's got to. Schönbrunn pays with cramped quarters for its proud record as the oldest zoo in the world still in operation.

"Yes, it has lasted longer than any of the others in continuity," said the zoological director carefully. He is Dr. Walter Fiedler, zoologist and anthropologist, a disciple of his famous compatriot Konrad Lorenz. "Strictly speaking we date from 1751, but the tradition of keeping animals, as you know, is far older, and the Hapsburg family bought all this area four hundred years ago to use for a deer park. They kept peafowl here as well, and lots of other ornamental and game birds: probably they preserved wild boar. Then the Emperor Francis I got the idea of setting up a formal zoo as a present to his wife, Maria Theresa. He planned the architecture and the landscaping. It was a kind of private playground of a menagerie. You can see that it's just a pleasant walk from the Schloss, but so cleverly arranged that until we recently started enlarging and cutting down some of the trees, one couldn't see the building at all. The emperor wanted it to break on the observer suddenly. Judged as an architectural feature it's a gem, but as for keeping animals seriously—" He broke off and shook his head. "We had to enlarge. There was no other way."

The original garden inherited by Dr. Fiedler and his staff is perfectly circular, the plan like a wheel complete with radiating spokes, the hub a charming pavilion of orange plaster, a hexagon standing on an elevated lawned terrace, surrounded by a circular gravel walk. Beyond the walk are the wedge-shaped enclosures, each with its curved section of orange wall on the near side decorated with white plaster baskets and vases of fruit and flowers. Each wedge contains within its barred confines an orange house at the wider end of the ground, to accommodate the inhabitants; all are alike. The original idea was to observe the animals as one sat at ease on the terrace or strolled along the walk, and this can still be done as you drink your syrup or chocolate under a bright parasol outside the pavilion, now a cafe. Within view are giraffes, zebras, antelopes, elephants, hippos, and bears, but the old-time symmetry has been blurred. Prettiness remains, but a large area outside the circle has become more important than the enclosures between the wheel-spokes.

"We started the alterations by tucking in the odd space here and there," explained Dr. Fiedler. "Wherever possible we use the barless method. Outside the perimeter we have these kangaroos, and over there is a pond for diving-birds, and an otter pool and a small bird cage. We had to squeeze in rhinos and bears around the corner. We had considerable overflow from the original enclosures, because they aren't anything like large enough for some of the animals, and the single barrier they used to have between compartments didn't prevent some of the species from fighting and hurting each other through the bars. Then most of those houses, though they're pretty, aren't fit for their purpose. Ultimately we hope to run some of the enclosures together to make them larger, and separate others with trenches and double fencing, or even pathways between. Each alteration has helped a little, but never enough; we couldn't get caught up with ourselves, and finally the moment came when we'd used up the last bit of space available. Then the Federal Ministry of Reconstruction and Commerce found us twelve more hectares—that's about twenty-eight acres—and we're all much more cheerful now. It may not seem a lot compared with a big place; Munich, for instance, has fifty acres. But it's a great relief to us, especially as one of our specialties is mountain ruminants, and they've simply got to have a bit of room. We're having luck with those."

On the plan I examined before doing the rounds on foot, the new territory jutted straight out from the wheel like a stumpy jackknife blade, narrowing to a point where a gate opened onto a Schönbrunn street. When I looked through this gate, I was surprised to see an ordinary city scene, with a line of buildings across the road and a busy stream of traffic between. Yet behind me was a silent stretch of trees that appeared to go on forever. Concealment was accomplished by various features; a penguin pool, a large enclosure for elks, the reaches of a bird sanctuary, and a cleverly constructed path that twisted and turned at all the right places through a landscape of miniature mountains and valleys where sheep, goats, deer, and antelope grazed, each on his proper terrain, with climbing beasts on steep slopes and others in the valley bottoms. We strolled through this countryside, back toward the old zoo, and Dr. Fiedler at my request recounted outstanding triumphs: the female ibex pregnant once more, an aoudad that had borne eight young, a large, flourishing flock of mouflon. For some time we watched the reindeer. A moss they are very fond of is imported for them from Yugoslavia. An old man doled out pieces of the stuff, hand-feeding a reindeer, exchanging shouted comments the while with the director. "He's been with us for years," said Dr. Fiedler as we moved off. "A wonderful old man, especially with those deer. I don't know how we're ever to replace him when he retires. Good keepers are hard to find. Now, as you may have noticed, we've had to keep these new enclosures as small as possible without defeating our purposes, but we've tried to make up for it vertically, using a good deal of up-and-down. Scientifically, we would be perfectly happy to concentrate on our ruminants, but a zoo can't depend completely on one specialty, and we *have* had our triumphs among other animals too. We've bred orangutans. The climate here is mild and that might play its part, but diet is important as well. Here's something you might like— many people admire it." A mosaic on an outdoor wall that overlooked the wading-bird pool depicted St. Francis surrounded by cranes, geese, and ducks in a round design of glowing colors. Dr. Fiedler assured me that all the species in it were faultlessly portrayed. "Now let's see," he went on, thoughtfully. "We have a famous male hippo that was born at the Budapest zoo. He came here in 1926 and is possibly our oldest inhabitant; he's fathered many babies, fourteen from one female alone. Unfortunately she's dead now. We have a replacement that hasn't turned out satisfactorily at all. She has the babies all right, plenty of them, but she kills them. Not one has survived. We'll have to get rid of her. Possibly some small zoo could make room for her—a zoo that isn't ambitious to breed young hippos. But the male still breeds. It's wonderful, really."

Neither hippo was visible. The light rain that had been falling for an hour now ceased, and the zoo was suddenly noisy with a very different kind of visitor than those I had left on the other side of the woods photographing the Schloss. These were mainly children, schoolchildren and babies with their elder relatives. Obvious habitués, they knew their way around, from food-dispensing machine to lavatory, from chimpanzee to aquarium. Dr. Fiedler led the way along a forbidden path to the back door of the elephant house, and into a large office opening directly on to a place like a barn, with windows high enough to be out of reach of the longest trunk. A richly cowlike smell filled the air. Two Asian elephants were shuffling about the barn floor, directed by a man in blue jeans who, in turn, took advice from another man standing over to one side. The latter man behaved like the director of a play, waving his hands as he told the blue-jeaned man where to lead the animals and what to make them do. We two standing in the doorway were the only audience, but the elephants performed as if to a full house, solemnly standing on their hind legs for a moment, sitting down at command, and revolving. Finally the men, apparently satisfied with the rehearsal, opened a great door into an open yard and the pachyderms marched out.

"Will there be a regular public show this afternoon?" I asked Dr. Fiedler, who said, "No, not today—it's not an everyday affair, but we have the training period every day no matter if we put on the show or not. You're probably familiar with Hediger's theory that elephants need something like this; the therapy of movement is most important. We believe that here. These gentlemen can tell you more about it."

The trainers, wiping their faces, came into the office. Both were elephant men with plenty of experience. One, an Englishman, had gone on the Hannibal expedition of 1959 arranged by a few devoted historians and naturalists as a practical reconstruction of the Carthaginian general's feat of 219 B.C. According to history, in his campaign against Rome Hannibal marched an army of fifteen thousand men and thirty-seven elephants across the Alps. The experiment was designed to answer a question that had often been asked by modern students: could such great beasts from the tropics really make the journey described, across high, cold mountains, canyons, and rushing streams? Though the 1959 expedition didn't go the whole way, it was admitted that their elephants covered the most difficult terrain. Most of the doubters are now convinced that Hannibal and his forces, both biped and quadruped, really did it.

"Hannibal's elephants were African, weren't they?" I asked. Oh yes, said the trainer—African, not Asian, and they'd answered the purpose perfectly well. He spoke emphatically, because another old controversy has recently cropped up again—an almost perennial one about the African elephant. Every so often somebody states that African elephants can't be trained: that if you need a performing or working animal you must get an Asian one. It is true that most zoo and circus elephants, at least since the early nineteenth century, have been of Asian origin, but even so some well-known beasts have come from Africa: Jumbo, the London Zoo's first elephant, bought by Barnum from Regent's Park and taken to America, was an African. India has a long tradition of training elephants to the point of domestication, whereas Africans have done very little to adapt any animals to domestic use. They used the elephant only as a source of meat. It was the white man who introduced the idea of training them, and he started late, so it has always been easier for dealers to procure tame beasts in the East than to get them in Africa. Yet in 1932 I visited a government elephant-training farm at Gangala in the Belgian Congo, and saw a number of the great creatures working to clear forest from a tract of ground, rooting up tree stumps and pulling heavily laden vehicles. The manager told me that they took experienced tame animals on annual hunting trips and collected wild elephants with their help. The various training techniques had been brought over from India by imported mahouts who, accompanied by their Indian mounts, lived in the Congo a full year and taught African apprentices the fine points of the business before they went home. Thus the methods of capturing and training elephants in Africa have a distinctly Indian flavor. That afternoon, watching a procession of Congo elephants coming back from the river after a bath, I heard the Zanda riders singing a chant they had learned from their Indian teachers, which in its beat imitated the measured pace of the pachyderms. The Zandes didn't know what the words meant and the Indian had deteriorated into gibberish, but the air remained:

"How stupid can people be!" said Dr. Fiedler, his usually gentle voice angry. He stepped inside the railing around the alligators' pool, leaned over, and picked up a paper bag which he brought out with him to show me. It contained cookies. "Giving food like this to saurians," he said. "The *ignorance* . . ."

The sun was stronger; it shone down with late-afternoon gusto on the lawns and paths littered with peanut shells and bits of pasteboard. Boys crowded around the monkey-cage were handing pieces of orange peel to the animals. "I regret the feeding," said Dr. Fiedler suddenly. "I regret it deeply, but we ourselves sell the food: it is claimed that we need the money. For myself I would like to do as Frankfurt does: there, feeding is absolutely forbidden. But . . ." He shrugged.

The remarkable Bristol, Clifton and West of England Zoological Society sponsors a garden known to most people, naturally enough, as the Bristol Zoo, in spite of persistent efforts on the part of Society members to make it known as the *Clifton* Zoo. It is a convenient one to contrast with Schönbrunn, since it too can claim a respectable age—though nothing like so advanced a one as Schönbrunn's—and is even smaller; twelve acres, to be exact. Though the area is soon to be immensely enlarged, it should be remembered that Bristol has won its reputation in cramped conditions. There was an advantage in its location, but this was not evident at the beginning when Clifton Downs was an all-but-empty waste area high over wooded hills and the river valley. In time to come Clifton was to be a smart residential suburb, but in 1835 nobody wanted to live there, and land was cheap. Even then, however, the surroundings were beautiful, like all the countryside that makes Bristol a gem among cities. The soft air of the West Country, combined with the Bristol people's keen enthusiasm for horticulture, resulted in prize gardens. There were nurseries everywhere. The zoo itself has always been a botanical center as well as an animal collection; indeed, it is the only zoological garden listed in the IZY that has an official mycologist on the staff. Incidentally, against considerable odds it has always been kept independent of financial aid from local or national governments, but the chief distinction between Schönbrunn (first opened in 1752) and Bristol, where the gates swung wide in 1836, is that Schönbrunn was an emperor's private plaything, and Bristol was founded by commoners for commoners. They represent entirely separate ages.

In a short history of Bristol Zoo by Dr. A. H. N. Green-Armytage, published by the Society in 1965, we learn that it was founded by a group of leading citizens who had noticed and admired the new London Society under Sir Stamford Raffles' leadership, and wanted to match it in their own city. The fortunes of this prosperous seaport had been made through shipping, sugar, and the slave trade. Now, secure and content, the heirs were ready to do good in the sight of the Lord: as the historian says, the nonconformist conscience was strong in Bristol. At a general meeting the customary resolution declared that a Zoological Society like that one would tend to "promote the diffusion of local knowledge by facilitating observation of the habits, form and structure of the animal kingdom, as well as affording rational amusement and recreation to the visitors of

the neighbourhood." But what neighborhood? For a while it looked as
if the Society might take over part of a local nursery garden for their
purpose, but in the end they changed their minds. Instead, the group of
two hundred and twenty men, which included the famous engineer-
designer I. K. Brunel, invested something under four thousand pounds in
a piece of farmland on the Downs, complete with cottage, lime-kiln,
and garden. The money came from the sale of shares in the Society,
valued at twenty-five pounds each and limited to five hundred. There was
to be no dividend on this investment: the only benefit a shareholder gained
was free admission to the zoo for himself, and reduced subscriptions for
members of his family. "An eminent landscape gardener" was engaged to
landscape the property. It was shaped like a shallow saucer, with the deep-
est depression not far off the center, so he put in a lake at the low point.
He kept as many of the original trees as he could, and more were donated
by friends of the Society, who through their shipping interests could
easily import rare exotics. Like practically all vegetation in the Bristol
area, the trees flourished; many are still there. The landscape artist tried
to design the cages so that they would merge, as far as was practicable,
into the background. That was the fashion of the day among enlightened
architects, but their modern successors feel that the idea has perhaps been
overdone; that cage-builders, in their anxiety to present a tactful "natural"
appearance to such premises, have sacrificed an inordinate amount of
space actually needed by the inhabitants. A bear or a lion can hardly be
expected to appreciate the general effect of which he is a part: his
aesthetic sensibilities are limited, and a cramped cage, even if it be over-
hung by the rockiest-looking rock the synthetics manufacturer can supply,
is still cramped. Still, the builders meant well, and these are only the
afterthoughts of a later age. According to the standards of the day, Bristol
cages were good. They were too good: in spite of the fact that many of
the animals were gifts, the Society ran into debt. It was found necessary
to borrow funds, and eke out the ordinary revenue from annual subscriptions and gate money—a shilling per adult—by renting the zoo grounds
to various clubs and firms, for fetes, concerts, croquet tournaments, tennis
parties and archery contests, all held on the splendid lawns that are still
one of the Society's prides.

As Dr. Green-Armytage says, this sort of thing was not quite what the
founders had intended. He adds, "(it) cannot have been much to the
taste of the animals, especially when the festivities involved fire-works,
as they often did . . . But fetes there had to be. By 1849 they were ac-
counting for more than half the Society's total income." To be sure,
there was another way out if only the shareholders could have been per-

suaded to take it. If they had consented to open the zoo's doors on Sunday, they would have made a lot more money, but they didn't want to do that. They kept talking about keeping the Sabbath holy for the working man. In actual fact they liked having the zoo to themselves on Sunday: it was nice for the children. So the fetes went on, and, inevitably, became more important than the zoo itself, until the animal collection dwindled to insignificance, and Bristol Zoo was more an amusement park than a respectable zoological garden. By 1850, nobody with intellectual pretensions took it seriously. Fortunately, just before it was too late, the Society got a grip on itself and appointed officers who pulled the place out of the doldrums. The grounds were improved, new stock was acquired, and the bank balance began telling a more cheerful story. It helped that Clifton was growing up around the park, with new houses everywhere and more subscribers appearing on the register. Clifton College opened in 1862, just across the road from the zoo: the boys and their parents became regular visitors. In 1871 the Bank Holiday Act came into force, and at last the working-class population, who until then had only had Sundays off, got their chance to come and look at the animals. True, on such holidays "it was always necessary to mobilise additional police," but even though the behavior of some of these newcomers gave added determination to the shareholders who vetoed Sunday opening, Bank Holidays helped the coffers. And the barricades were falling. In 1886, for the first time, subscribers and their families were permitted to join the shareholder groups on Sundays at the zoo.

An enterprising treasurer—as the Society called the director—did a good deal during his term of office, from 1886 to 1908, to improve the zoo's different departments, adding to both the zoological and botanical collections and building a new restaurant. Nevertheless the fetes continued, because they were still necessary. In fact, they were more necessary than ever as the century ended. "The Zoo," wrote its historian, "was moving further into the Amusement Park business and away from the sphere of Useful Knowledge and Rational Recreation as envisaged by the founders." To show how much was now entailed in the fete business he lists the program for 1899: band concerts every Monday and Saturday afternoon and every Wednesday and Saturday evening; school sports; a stretcher competition held by the St. John's Ambulance Association; a carnival in aid of a nurses' home; three performances of "Pastoral Plays" by Ben Greet's Woodland Players; the Salvation Army annual demonstration; a number of "grand fetes and galas," and five firework displays. There were bank holiday fetes on six occasions, and tennis parties, and skating parties, and boat trips on the lake. Never a dull moment for the animals.

"The Zoo is many things at once," wrote Dr. Green-Armytage. "It is a business, with shareholders, balance sheet and profit-and-loss; it is a collection of animals requiring keepers and administrators and partaking, to some extent, in the nature of a stud; and it is a botanical collection requiring gardeners, nurseries and potting-sheds. It is also a scientific institution, requiring the services of and rendering opportunities to professional students of zoology." That all this can be true of one twelve-acre plot of land is an imposing fact, and another fact even more imposing is that in spite of all the fetes and fireworks, the Bristol animals did well. Once established, says the historian, the menagerie in the nineteenth century was largely self-financing. Bristol lions, tigers, and leopards bred freely. Their famous lion Jupiter lived many years, and a Ceylon elephant, Zebi, presented by the Maharaja of Mysore in 1868, survived until 1909.

Bristol kept going through World War One, though the collections, both animals and plants, suffered badly before the armistice was signed. Attendance figures actually rose during those troubled years, but after peace was declared the council was plagued with fresh misfortunes. The British government levied heavy taxes on entertainment and amusement places. Claiming to be educational institutions, the zoos of London and Edinburgh were exempted from the tax, but Bristol Zoo couldn't get away with that. The revenue officials said flatly that it was an amusement park, not an educational institution, and so was ineligible for tax relief. It was a shameful manifestation of how far things had slid at Bristol, a zoo founded with the highest principles, because the revenuers were absolutely right. During those abased days, one of the Bristol lions was even hired out to a road show, just for the money. The blunt truth was that the place was dowdy. Most members of the younger generation ignored it. And then, just when one would have said that things couldn't get any worse, the Georgian poets took up the cause of the animal kingdom, decrying not only hunting and trapping but the caging of wild beasts. A large number of the British became anti-zoo, a sentiment which has survived until the present.

In 1922, the gates were at last opened to everybody on Sunday, but it seemed to make very little difference after all. Gate receipts were disappointing, Sunday or no Sunday, until a few years later when two able men, cousins named W. Sefton Clarke and Dr. Richard C. Clarke, became committee members and interested themselves in improving the zoo. Already the entertainment tax had been reduced, and soon would be lifted altogether, but there were many other defects crying out for remedy. As the new secretary, Dr. Clarke decided that one of their most pressing needs was an intelligent, educated man to take charge of the keepers. To this end a very young man, R. E. Greed, who had been with the zoo for some years, even though he was only twenty-three, was elevated to the post of superintendent. Next, the gardens and the animal collection, which had begun to deteriorate again, were built up. Then one of Bristol's most prized animal groups, the orangutan Rudolph and his mate and baby, suddenly died, and Dr. Clarke did some hard thinking as to the causes of the catastrophe. It seemed to him that animals prone to certain diseases common to human beings—primates, for example—were endangered every day by being exposed to the public. The zoo had just acquired an even bigger attraction than Rudolph, a young gorilla that at the time was the only one of his species in Europe. Putting this animal, Alfred, on display in an open cage would be signing his death warrant, thought Dr. Clarke. He subscribed to the newfangled theory that zoo people pampered animals from tropical countries to their detriment. It seemed to him that these animals would be better off with less stuffiness and more fresh air, and plenty of vitamins in their diet. Accordingly, Alfred's cage was moved eight feet back from the railings, and his diet and regime were adjusted. Alfred lived, and in a healthy state, until 1928.

The zoo's gate receipts improved, and nobody minded that fetes weren't paying so well any more. In his heart, Dr. Clarke probably rejoiced that matters were at last appearing in their proper proportions. Now, scientific studies and research were encouraged, with much benefit to the animals as well as the students. The zoo succeeded in keeping penguins, which had always been difficult, and even breeding them. Dr. Clarke saved the lives of moribund lion cubs by including Vitamin B in their diet. He added to the staff an anatomist, a dental surgeon, a veterinary surgeon, a biologist. Bristol University scientists were made welcome, and permitted to use the zoo animals for research. Xenopus frogs were bred there in such numbers that their tadpoles were supplied to universities abroad. Zoologists everywhere sent their congratulations when a chimpanzee baby was born and successfully reared at Bristol; this was the first time such a thing had happened in captivity. Scientific work in such close connection with the university of Bristol was not only valuable in itself, says Dr. Green-Armytage: "but also benefited the Zoo more indirectly. It improved what is nowadays called its 'image' and helped to allay those guilt-feelings about the imprisonment of noble animals. Science was a sacred cow, and if she allowed the Zoo both to feed and milk her it could not be an Untouchable." Besides, he points out, all the new homes provided for the animals were obviously more comfortable than their former quarters: a prison that doesn't look like a prison has lost all its grimness.

Nineteen thirty-eight is marked as the first year in its history that the zoo got no revenue whatever from fetes. "The Zoo had at last ceased to lead a double life," says the historian triumphantly, and the pattern was set, to endure through the war. And the zoo's excellence has increased: long before I went to Bristol I heard of it. Bristol had bred okapis, Bristol's black rhinos bred regularly, Bristol had a pair of those white tigers from Rewa—it was enough to make anyone think. On top of all this, it seemed that Bristol was beautiful. A German told me, "On a summer's day, when ladies in bright dresses are walking around that lake, there's nothing prettier in the world than Bristol Zoo."

It was a summer's day when I went, and even before I reached the zoo gates I had capitulated. The road wound upward between trees and hedges bursting with green of every shade, which now and then gave way to afford a glimpse of far blue distances, or the sparkle of river-water below. As I passed through the gate, I thought for a moment that I had stumbled on one of the old-time fetes, but it wasn't a fete, only the public enjoying the zoo in the ordinary way. Dozens of them were sitting around on the vivid grass, the grown-ups sunning themselves, the children tottering about or chasing each other. One got the impression that this wasn't a zoo at all, but a park, since what met the eye first was a broad expanse of lawns. Over to one side the grass was broken here and there by flower beds, and a flower border ran along the outer edge. Everyone in the sunlight looked young and rosy.

Then I saw other details; the lake in the middle, with ducks and geese at liberty on the water or waddling over the grass, and other birds paddling lazily in the shade of willow trees. A small copse, more trees, showed over the slow rise of land beyond the lake. Evidently the zoo was not round like Schönbrunn, but four-sided; not a square, however, unless you can imagine a square that has melted and been pulled out at one corner. Finally I located the animal enclosures, which in other zoos would have been the first things that leap to the eye. These were for the most part against the walls, or as paddocks were placed so naturally near the lake that they might have grown there. Near a concentration of trees, a platoon of gardeners were at their mysterious work, moving between a grassy bank and a vehicle loaded with potted plants.

"You come at an unfortunate time," said Mr. Greed, whom I found in the offices, upstairs over a cafe. "The flowers are just being changed. You should have seen it last week."

There spoke the true gardener, I reflected. Mr. Greed was just as I'd seen him the preceding week on a TV program—white-haired and gently-spoken. His son Geoffrey was with him. Geoffrey had just returned from some years away at other zoos, learning the game at Chester and Munich. "He was trained as a chartered accountant," said Mr. Greed, "because I didn't want to force him into anything just because his father's in it. But, as you see, here he is."

"Here I am," said the son. "After all, when one's practically born within zoo limits . . . I even went to school across the road there, at Clifton College."

Geoffrey was to take me around and show me the finer points of the place. As we paused at the foot of the outside stairs to survey the picture-postcard scene spread out before us, he said, "I'm afraid it won't take you very long to see the whole thing, but I can tell you which are the more recent developments and what we plan for the future. We've got hold of some new land, as I believe my father told you—a hundred and ninety-four acres all told, about five miles from here in the country."

"But surely you don't mean to move out of here?"

"Oh no. They'd never stand for that—the Society, I mean. I wouldn't care for it myself, if it comes to that. No, we mean to use the new land for overflow, keep breeding animals there, for instance, and perhaps a larger hospital, and, of course, there'll be an exhibition section as well. I believe Lindemann has the same arrangement at the Catskill Game Farms in America. I'd like to see this as a sort of game farm. We've got some Manchurian cranes there already; they've just arrived, and we thought we'd keep them quiet and see if they'll start laying. They've nested already, but there aren't any eggs as yet. Too soon to expect them, perhaps. Well now, here." He paused to recover from his dreams for the future. "Our latest important acquisition is here." He led the way into a passage. "These gorillas," he said, stepping back. In a dimly lit cage, two young gorillas were slowly wrestling with each other in their solemn way, as if carrying out a ritual. "They're a terrible price," said Geoffrey. "One resents the outlay, but that's how it is. A zoo's got to have gorillas: the public demands it. Still, these are in good condition and they ought to be all right. There should be a keeper playing with them just about this time, and usually there is, but we're short-handed this week. Still, they're keeping each other toned up."

Outside again, I had the opportunity to approve of the gibbon house, a tall structure surrounded up to the middle by glass. Visitors, even those who follow the staircase that winds around the cage, can't hand food to the animals. Inside is plenty of gymnastic equipment where the gibbons can leap and brachiate for considerable distances. "Yes, it's not bad," admitted Geoffrey modestly. "It's one of our later developments. I must apologize for that awful little cage over there where we've got two other gibbons, though."

"I noticed it."

"We can't do everything all at once, unfortunately, but we're going to scrap that whole row of old cages as soon as we've got the money."

The elephant house was another thing to be proud of, with its deep pool. Two young females, one Asian and the other African, were all but submerged in the water, while an attendant in black oilskins scrubbed them with a long-handled brush. While we watched, he too went into the pool. "It's not perfect yet," said young Mr. Greed. "We've got a tree coming, thirty feet high, which we're going to plant in the yard. They need the shade, and we've got to start out with a tall tree or it's no good; they'd kill it off. It's costing a packet, but it'll be worth it. That house itself cost thirty thousand pounds when it was built; God knows what it would be now. Around here is the rhino house; doesn't look much, I'm afraid. I'd like to have it a lot bigger." The rhino's yard was not all that small, however, space having been saved by an ingenious arrangement of walkways around it, one high up, the other low. We looked down on a large and a small animal. "Rhona was the first black rhino ever bred in Great Britain. She's had three children, and all five are still living. We're getting another male soon from Hanover for the young female; she's more than two years old now. Planning to put them into the new place, possibly in seclusion until they get used to each other. One of our unusual problems here is that the old rhinos don't die off, so we're a bit pushed. And here are the giraffes—they've had two and she's expecting another now. We might put some into the new zoo. As a matter of fact, the new place is going to *have* to be a game-farm for a while, until we get full possession, which isn't to happen until the owner dies. She's an old lady, and that was one of the terms of the sale. Speaking for myself, I don't care how long it takes—it's wonderful to have that land, the run of it, for uninterrupted programs. We can keep whole herds out there if we like."

He talked of the quarantine laws of Great Britain. Zoos that have special facilities because they are near seaports, like his own, are fortunate. "The animals can be quarantined right here. We often help other zoos board theirs, too," he said.

Resuming the tour, he called my attention to a herbaceous border: "It's said to be the best in England; I don't know. You'd have to ask my father about that. But it ought to be; do you realize that we have so many gardeners it amounts to half a man per acre? And the lawns are done by yet another team. Here's our nocturnal house, converted in '55;

I think it's the first nocturnal house in this country, but it's not a tunnel like the ones the Americans are putting in everywhere." Steps led up to a circular stone wall around a pit, past a bust of a gorilla labeled "Alfred." In the center stood a structure of stucco or stone, like an Indian temple, swarming with rhesus monkeys. Geoffrey frowned as he regarded it. "This eyesore is doomed, I'm glad to say. Ridiculous, isn't it? They put it up way back in the early days of the century when everybody was reading the *Jungle Books*, and it was quite celebrated at the time. You wouldn't believe it, but a lot of people around here still love that thing."

"But so do I," I protested. "It has great charm."

He looked at me as if I'd taken leave of my senses. "It's horrible. Look at the space it takes up, too. I'll be glad to see the last of it—I'm *ashamed* of it." He didn't cheer up until we reached the next port of call, the penguin enclosure, where he told me that the Blackfoot species of these birds had been for a long time a self-perpetuating colony at Bristol. He was also reasonably pleased with the aviary collection: "It does well, considering how far north we are in England. The cattle egrets do all right, and so do a lot of other tropical birds. Through the winter we protect them with glass, and all year round they're sheltered from the worst of the wind; at night they go indoors to sleep there—an all-glass house. Naturally, being on show interferes with their breeding, though. In a small zoo especially you always have the decision to make; to breed or to show. So we've worked out a combination arrangement—six cages for display and two behind the scenes for the breeding birds. We shift them around when the time comes. Secretary birds tend to be nervous; they need a lot of privacy, so the new place will be better for them. With birds you've always got to be on guard against rodents, you know. I wish you could see how well they manage birds on the Continent, especially Stuttgart. Their scarlet ibis breeds, for instance—we couldn't manage that here. It's because some of their birds are always inside, where the climate can be controlled. Well, here we have several sorts of flamingos. It's generally thought that they segregate according to subspecies, but these have been known to crossbreed." As we passed a cage of macaws and parrots, one of the birds said in a low, insinuating voice, "He*llo*." "He's a character," said Geoffrey, absently. "I want to show you the cage where our old gorilla lives. He's a widower, recently bereaved, which is the reason we got the young pair. I must say he doesn't seem to be brooding too much over his late wife." The gorilla, Congo, was a beautiful silverback, pacing with dignified steps from one end of his domain to the other behind elaborate ironwork, the pattern of it much too varied to look like bars. The cage was set a good way back from the railing, in accordance with Dr. Clarke's ideas. "It's a handsome place," said my guide, "and Congo looks well, doesn't he?" The great animal sat down and stared out at us with sprightly interest. "He weighs more than five hundred pounds, but he's not too fat," said Geoffrey. "You'll want to see the Tropical House: it's one of our features."

In a dark passage behind a glass window gleamed a bank of bewilderingly bright flowers, orchids and other fleshy blooms. "Fantastic, isn't it?" said Geoffrey. "It gets plenty of attention; they change that display completely about three times a week. To begin with they tried keeping hummingbirds in the same place, but it didn't work and they had to give up the idea. All these plants and things, the ones outside as well as here, can't be looked after in the zoo: we've got a lot of hothouses just across the road. Over here are the cats, especially the white tigers—the only pair outside India just now. They've got a white female in the United States, at the National Zoo; she bred, but I believe the only white cub of the litter died. These cost a fortune. Still, they *are* beautiful." Through one-way glass at the back of the cage we watched the animals. One was pacing, the other lay stretched on the ground and surveyed the scene quietly. A nearby yellow tiger roared, and both the white ones leaped to attention, frozen except for their slowly flicking tails. "And that's the lot until I drive you over to see the new land," said Geoffrey. "Oh no, we mustn't forget the bears. This row of bear pits is one of the oldest structures we have, and they'll have to be replaced. The polar bears have always done well, but we've lost the old female, who made history in her time, and we can't seem to find a replacement as yet. She bred and raised a cub back in the days when that seldom happened in a zoo. The famous Brumas of London, born just after the war if you remember, was a lucky accident, and I'll tell you why. Until we tried our new system polar bears didn't breed in captivity, or, if they did, the cubs didn't live more than a day or so. The fact is, a polar bear needs a warm, dark, dry cave. You wouldn't think so, but that's the truth; furthermore, the female ought to have her warm cave to retire to a whole month before things start. We gave our animals a place where the floor was electrically warmed, and it worked immediately. Nowadays all the zoos do the same and polar-bear cubs have become commonplace. Let's look at the okapis."

"You've had an unlucky time with those, haven't you?" As most zoo men will tell you, the okapis of the Belgian Congo were completely unknown to the outside world until 1900, and it took years of argument after that before zoologists decided where to class them. They now share the Giraffidae family with the giraffes; no other species are admitted. All zoo specimens are still watched with fascinated interest, so I was well aware that Bristol's female okapi had twice produced young but lost each one at an early age.

"That's right. The young ones died of aspergillosis," said Geoffrey.

"But that's a bird disease, isn't it? Penguins?"

"Not exclusively. It's a lung infection, a sort of fungus that lots of animals succumb to. We figured that the foals may have got it from the lucerne we give the adults. We've had all that hay very carefully analyzed, but this time—she's expecting again—we aren't taking chances: they're going on evergreen oak and elm from now on, and absolutely no lucerne. We also plan to remove the mother and disinfect the baby. It's awfully difficult to handrear stock, but it's worth a try in this case. We figure that the infant might get something the adults can withstand but a weak newborn one can't." The strange beasts, with bold stripes on their long necks, legs, and hindquarters blending off into the rich chestnut glossiness of their bodies, regarded us patiently with great dark eyes. I saw a red-lettered sign on the bars, warning the public against feeding them, and wondered how effective it was. We turned away. Axis deer browsed in a hilly meadow not far from a number of kangaroos reclining in the sun. "Oh yes, they get on well together," Geoffrey assured me when I commented on the unusual combination. "There, can you see them?—two pairs of red kangaroos; in another enclosure there are more. We have wallabies as well, and other roos." Sprawling in the grass near a water trough, a male red scratched himself. Two others lay closely entwined, one curled about the other, watching with amiable indifference as a large axis doe tittupped along with her fawn to drink from the trough. In the background a fine peacock displayed with fully extended tail. It was altogether a pretty picture, but one calculated to give nightmares to any serious ecologist.

Mr. Greed had time when we returned to show me the greenhouses across the road just outside the zoo precincts. "We managed to acquire this whole piece of property with three houses and garden space," he said. "It was a good stroke; we let the houses to people who like the quiet of the neighborhood, and still we have all the space we need for our flowers. It helps with the budget. I ought to cross my fingers as I say this, but we're managing very nicely. That doesn't mean one doesn't have to work, of course—one's got a good deal on the plate."

"You got home awfully late last night," said his son accusingly.

"Yes, I'm afraid I did. I had to inspect the lavatories after closing time: it's astonishing how dirty people can be. We had a general cleanup."

It was about six-thirty when Geoffrey Greed drove me into the country to see the new territory, but the zoo stays open late on long summer days, and the crowd had not thinned out very much. Slanting rays of sunlight fell on babies still walking uncertainly on the close-mown turf. Studying my guidebook, I said, "You make it very plain, I see, about the feeding rules. You don't trust the public's ability to read. Pictures in color of the food they can give them, pictures of the animals they're allowed to feed—"

"Well, wouldn't *you* make it plain?" he retorted. "You know what it's like."

"You sell animal food at the stalls, though."

"Yes. You'll be glad to know that we're stopping that at the end of the season."

After the buzz of the zoo, the countryside seemed strangely hushed as we drove between well-grown fields of grain and woods. The car turned into a tree-lined driveway, followed it a long distance, and drew to a halt at last in a brick courtyard, surrounded by sturdy old stalls. When Geoffrey turned off the motor, sound again filled the air, the chirping of birds before they settled down for the night and a far-off lowing of cattle. It was somehow quieter than absolute stillness. He drew a deep breath.

"Nice, isn't it? And one never sees a soul. The old lady has her own drive and we have the rest of it. The place was almost a jungle when we started, but some of the zoo men have got a few corners into shape. As much as we need for the present, at any rate." I walked after him through a lush, overgrown path, plentifully shaded with trees, to a series of simple roofed enclosures. In two of these Manchurian cranes stalked about; other birds occupied the others. Geoffrey indicated the stretches of rolling, wooded country that was to be the home of herds, and indicated where places had been earmarked for rhinos. "It's too much land," he said. "No zoo could cover all that ground without buses or a small railway, and we don't want to go in for those. But we had to buy the whole ground or none, so we'll probably farm part of it, raising our own fodder and some of the fruit. You saw those stables and the dairy-room; lovely, aren't they? Strong as the day they were built. We can use all that." He smiled in anticipation, and stared across a clump of flowering shrubs. All gold and green, the trees stirred in the breeze and sent pieces of broken shadow scuttering across the grass.

CHAPTER 6

North Europe

□

Newspapers run animal stories three or four times a week. Some keep a permanent space for this feature and manage to publish something in it every day. The item might be of local interest only—"High Street Traffic Stops For Swan Mother," or a good old reliable such as "Long Trek: Johnnie's Dog Goes 200 Miles to Find Home." But there are times when the editor gets a longer story which is sure to interest everybody. The courtship of the giant pandas Chi-Chi and An-An is a case in point, or Jane Goodall's discovery that wild chimpanzees make tools, or Dr. Lilly's loquacious bottlenose dolphins. These, the temporary sensations of the second section's front page, are still fresh, but in due course they too will be forgotten, like the tale of Achilles the gorilla. Achilles made the front page all over the reading world, but where is he now? Well, it just so happens that I can tell you.

The first part of the story is recounted by Hediger, but I'll condense it. The Zoologischer Garten of Basel acquired Achilles as a very young animal, little more than a baby, and kept him in a cage adjoining a storeroom, through which was the only access to the cage door. Like other children, Achilles was avid for company and amusement, and he worked out a way to get both. Every time a keeper came into the storeroom for something, he hung near the top of his cage with one arm between the bars, crying piteously to show that he was stuck there. The unwary keeper would come into the cage to rescue him, upon which Achilles dropped on him and grabbed him so firmly that the keeper could extricate himself only with the utmost effort. It was lots of fun for the gorilla while it lasted, especially as he grew stronger every day, but word got around and soon nobody was falling for the trick any more—until a new girl joined the staff. Achilles' joke was old history by then, and nobody thought to warn her. On the evening of one of her first days, after the zoo closed and everybody else was gone, she went into the storeroom to put something away and noticed the poor little gorilla stuck up there between bars, crying. Naturally, she rushed in to help him and was immediately imprisoned. She couldn't get Achilles off. Hours went by. Now and then Achilles dropped off to sleep, but every time she tried to disengage his clutching hands and feet, no matter how gently, he woke up and hugged even tighter. She wasn't released until morning, when her colleagues found her there soaked to the skin and very tired, but unhurt.

The newspapers had a wonderful time with the story, and Basel Zoo had a record attendance for almost a week. The incident became a saga in which little Achilles was portrayed as something between Androm-eda's dragon and King Kong, while the buxom Swiss girl shrank to the more appealing dimensions of a fairy-tale princess. No sexual con-notation was ignored in the hints, until, at the height of the clamor, it was discovered that Achilles was, in fact, a *female* gorilla. At once, recalls Dr. Hediger, the story was dropped and left not a wrack behind. But Achilla has hit the headlines again since then. She has given birth to three children, and raised them all herself, very successfully. After all, she has always been a resourceful gorilla.

"Most unusual," agreed the Basel director, Dr. Ernst M. Lang. "We were not the first zoo to breed gorillas in captivity, but Achilla has accounted for half of the six born in zoos." (Since this interview, two more zoo-bred gorillas have been launched into life. All of them, like Achilla, are of the lowland subspecies; at this writing, no mountain gorilla has been born in a zoo.) Dr. Lang is both director and veterinarian of Basel, a relatively small—twenty-seven acres—garden which has never-theless made history with its breeding records. At the time I met him he was chairman of the Zoo Liaison Committee formed at the "Symposium on Conservation" held in London shortly before, where he read a paper on breeding: seventy-five percent of the animals at Basel produce offspring.

Among the photographs thick on his office wall I noticed one that was strikingly unusual—a young gorilla riding a scooter. I asked about this, and told Dr. Lang about the performing gorillas I saw at Nagoya. He was not surprised. "We had performing gorillas here, too," he said. "It was a mixed-ape act with four gorillas, a chimpanzee and an orangutan: we believe in the Therapy of Movement theory, and encourage training for animal acts. There is a circus ring here. For the ape act one gorilla played the drum and two danced with tambourines. But I noticed that they weren't developing at the rate they should have done, in physical growth: they didn't gain weight properly, and I came to the conclusion that they were fretting about their performance, taking it too hard. They are highly organized animals, you know. Very sensitive. I put a stop to the performances, and they recovered their calm."

Like Bristol's, the zoo is a private society in which the shareholders' only privilege is the right of free entry. It is self-supporting, and pays no taxes because the government considers it an educational and charitable body: with an attendance that now tops a million annually, the books balance satisfactorily. Achilla's family is only one of the reasons Basel is so well-known among zoo buffs: another is that theirs is the first breeding colony of flamingos to be established in Europe, where the birds have hatched Chilean flamingos and some hybrid Cuban and African. Another rarity is the breeding group of Colobus monkeys. These beautiful black-and-white animals seldom adapt themselves to captivity well enough to produce young, but it happens at Basel. Dr. Lang took me to see them. "This one is a Western subspecies," he said, indicating a large female. "We bought her in New York. She's an interesting case—won't mate but loves babies: she's always trying to take away other females' babies. Over here are the Java macaques, which do so well that we take out about ten every year. The sacred ibis are a productive colony too—"

"What are those birds perching on top of the cage?"

"Oh, that's a pair of gray herons that always sit up there. They seem to like it, and the ibis don't mind. On the whole, however, we haven't a large collection of birds: we'd be happy with only a few breeding pairs, if I could have a good enough aviary. When I took over the zoo it was mostly birds; hundreds of birds. I sold more than half the collection. Of those we kept, nearly all nest and lay eggs. Dr. Wackernagel interests himself in them particularly, and can tell you more than I can. We have Rothschild's mynahs—a very rare species discovered in Bali in 1931: we've got two pairs, and between them they've raised a dozen young."

It was a pleasant day, overcast but mild considering how alpinely chilly the preceding night had been. For Switzerland the land at Basel is reasonably flat, though mountains are close at hand. At that season everything was fresh and green. "We're doing a lot of new landscaping," said Dr. Lang. "When this zoo first opened, in 1874, it was laid out in the approved way of those days, with straight walls and many barred cages. Now we must change all that. It's rather a long, thin tract; you can't see where it ends now—at least I hope you can't—up at that end, because we've been busy planting cleverly to hide the fence. Beyond that we have breeding grounds for our rare birds; I'll get Hans Wackernagel to take you. Here's something we find very useful." He pointed to the line of hedge surrounding a bird cage ahead of us, and I bent over for a closer look. It was stiff, unyielding, prickly evergreen. "It has a discouraging effect on trespassers," he said dryly, "prettier than barbed wire and even more effective."

Moats instead of thorn, camouflaged with vegetation, surrounded a large enclosure where four okapis grazed. "Two pairs," said the director proudly. "Up until now we've had three calves. One of the pairs came direct from the Congo: the export was carefully controlled before the revolution, and we hope whoever's in charge there now will go on conserving, though nobody can tell nowadays. One of our babies has gone to Rotterdam, another to Vincennes, and the third to Copenhagen. I think the moats are pretty well concealed, don't you? But there's one place where photographers can get a little closer; I'll show you." He took me around to a corner where the bushes gave way, and I could look at the okapis at close quarters. "We provide one photo-point like this at all the outside enclosures. Otherwise the animals are far off from the public, which is excellent from the standpoint of hygiene. This concealment is important: I think that people who live in big towns like to see natural green when they come here. And it's nice to make the asphalt disappear. You wouldn't be able to guess that we use concrete in these moats, would you?"

Basel's Indian rhinos have produced five young, easily the record for such animals in captivity: they have had two generations at the zoo. The Père David's deer have more than replaced themselves, and the pygmy hippo group of one male and five females, even though one of the females is past the age for childbearing, have rolled up the awesome record of thirty-one children. These little creatures are listed by the IZY as rare, but when they are at ease in their surroundings, as they clearly are at Basel, they produce with heartening regularity. Though at first glance they much resemble their relatives the large hippos, this separate genus is dissimilar in bone structure as well as size, and their habits differ as well: pygmy hippos, unlike the bigger animals, are not addicted to submerging and spending long periods under water.

As we passed by a stadium somewhat reminiscent of the elephant arena at Colombo, Dr. Lang said that it was the elephants' stage for their daily performance, and repeated his firm opinion that for elephants to give a rehearsal and performance every day was an excellent thing for their health. "By coincidence, this very ground was used before our time, before the war, for side shows," he added. "There used to be exhibitions here of Eskimos, African people and other races."

"Like Hagenbeck's."

"The same thing, yes. It was a good idea—I'd like to have kept it going if it had been possible. You'll be able to see the elephant show this afternoon."

I said, "I've heard about your elephants. Aren't they African? A lot of people say that Africans are untamable."

He rose to this: "One hears that often, but it's nonsense; the theory's been disproved right here. Mind you, African elephants do need a different approach. They're more susceptible than Indians; they hate being whipped even more than Indians do; they're more sensitive. Why, our elephants are so tame that children ride them just as they ride the Indian elephant you have at Regent's Park. We even send them into the city on special occasions to give the children rides. Let me show you something." He gave directions to a keeper, and in a few minutes another attendant approached, leading one of the largest bull elephants I had ever seen. If you are used to Asian elephants the long legs of these relatives are startling. The bull, Omari, came to a halt beside an outsize mounting-block, and I climbed up and sat on the benchlike contraption he wore on his back, accompanied by three small giggling children. Omari stepped out, and we went at a good clip down the avenue.

"You see?" shouted Dr. Lang, trotting along behind. "How do you like it?"

I yelled back, "Fine, only it's an awfully long way down."

"But quiet and gentle, no?"

Omari went once around the square and returned to his starting point, and we all slid off. Dr. Lang said, "Tell that to people outside Switzerland and they won't believe it."

Now that it was over I hardly believed it myself, any more than I did the performance when I saw it, with an African and an Asian elephant blowing giant mouth organs in a weird duet. The troop of five Africans and the one Asian went through more paces than I'd seen at Colombo, Omari at the end snitching a large spotted handkerchief from the trainer's pocket and waving good-by to the audience. It is sad to think that Omari is gone now. He became dangerous, as elephants occasionally do, whether in captivity or in the wild, and they didn't think he was of an age to recover. Up to now, the cause of these mental attacks is not thoroughly understood.

Dr. Hans Wackernagel is the young man who spent so much time in Philadelphia learning the principles of the Ratcliffe diet. He was taking me to see his special charges in the breeding grounds, telling me on the way about the adaptation of the diet they use at Basel—carnivores won't touch it, but the other animals flourish on it—when there was an interruption. A girl zoo worker in breeches came down the road followed by a little mouflon, with long legs and clattering hoofs, which stuck close to her heels. Wackernagel laughed, and said that the mouflon was so tame it was becoming a nuisance. Certainly it did its best to follow us through the gate, but he was firm and we left it behind to enter a field full of pens, where the grass had been cut down to about four inches.

"This was a flower garden, but we're changing it around," he said. "The grass mustn't get much longer than this, or we wouldn't be able to see the small ducklings and goslings." Walking slowly past the pens he named off some of the rarer occupants: a number of little Laysan teal hatched in the incubator—"We started out with a pair, now we have two pairs, both breeding"—the Hawaiian goose, and others. He suggested that we look into one of the buildings, where in a large room, opening out into the grass, a number of tiny birds scuttled about in the wake of a slightly older fledgling, and pecked at the ground. "That bigger one serves as mother for the newly hatched ones," explained Dr. Wackernagel. "We always put one or two older ones in with an incubator batch, to show them the ropes; they know where the food is and so on. Though we use setting birds too, when it can be done. Here's a turkey hen looking after a clutch of eiderdown eggs. We use her a lot. First we put her onto china eggs to get her into the mood, and now she's a good nurse; comes out only once a day to eat and drink, then goes right back to the job. Over there are Carolina ducks; here's a funny one, black mallard crossed with domestic duck, and there's another rare one, a maned goose."

On the way back to the public zoo we stopped to look at the animals' commissary, and Dr. Wackernagel showed how the food concentrates for one day are lined up in pails, complete with their complements of fruit and oats. "Here's something we're working on, a synthesized pigment to keep the red color in flamingos and scarlet ibis. Nobody understands just why they sometimes fade in captivity. For a while everyone thought it was because they needed carotin in their food, but that doesn't always work either. And not every zoo has the same problem. It's confusing. We're waiting to see if this does the trick."

Soon the afternoon would draw in dramatically, as it does in the north. In zoos, as in nature, animals grow drowsy when the sun gets near the horizon; the last part of the visit must be speeded up. Dr.

Lang took over the tour again, and in his company I surveyed a select group of pumas in which every one in the family was coal-black, a number of servals that represent two generations in Basel, and a newborn litter of leopards. Dr. Lang said, "As you may have noticed, we keep all our families together; give them plenty of social life. It's a good thing. Here, for instance, are a family of lions—two cubs, an older sister, and the parents all living together without friction. And now we come to our outstanding example of domesticity: Achilla and her children."

They were all there in one big cage—Goma, born in '59, Jumbo, two years younger, and the infant Michael, whose birthday was in '64. Their father, an enormous animal that weighs something like six hundred pounds, has a sweet, kind nature and likes to play with humans—I quote from Dr. Lang. A number of photographs of Achilla with her babies, taken shortly after these infants were born, never fail to elicit gasps of wonder from people who see them, for they depict the new baby being held, even dandled in the air, by Dr. Lang or the gorilla's keeper, while Achilla sits there proudly looking on, and shows not the slightest sign of anxiety or ferocity. It has been explained that in gorilla communities, as in some other primate groups, it is customary for the mother who has just given birth to hand her baby around in order that the rest of the animals can examine it. In Achilla's world the keepers and Dr. Lang are her nearest relations, and so she shows off her baby to them.

A large crowd stood packed around the railing, as it always does when there is a great ape to look at. To get a clear view of the gorillas, Dr. Lang and I stood on a slight eminence some distance off, and looked at them over the heads of the crowd. Achilla saw us in return. At the sight of Dr. Lang she straightened up, and her face changed animatedly. She bounced with joy, bobbing her head and bowing in welcome. Gravely and courteously, Dr. Lang bowed back. As for me, I just stared. In that dignified, motherly creature I could see no trace whatever of the impish little gorilla who kept a girl prisoner all night, and, worse than that, masqueraded as one of the opposite sex.

On my way through Zurich, a charming city, to the Zoologischer Garten, I reflected that my trip was a sort of pilgrimage to pay homage, for Zurich's zoo director is Professor Dr. H. Hediger himself, who is to zoo people what Konrad Lorenz is to other naturalists. Moreover, he is the man who introduced the word "anthropomorphic" to this particular aspect of zoology. But once I had met him, it was impossible to think of him as a sage. For one thing he is too young; for another, he is clean-shaven. Sages should be elderly and bearded.

The garden is high in the mountain—something, admittedly, that can be said of every locality in Zurich, but the zoo is even more elevated than the town. One can look out while on the way from the bears to the reindeer, or from the reindeer to the ape house, over considerable depths, straight into an ice-blue sky. Dr. Hediger's office, at the top of a stony staircase leading from the entrance-gate, is full of books and pictures and autographs and small pieces of sculpture, as well as—on that day—a number of copies of his latest book, just off the press, *Mensch und Tier Im Zoo*.

"To begin with, I wasn't an animal psychiatrist," he said. "I was a zoologist who studied psychiatry and ethnology merely as part of the whole subject. It was only later that I began to apply the principles of psychiatry to other animals. My wife, on the other hand, did start out as an animal psychologist, but after a time she grew tired of the animals and turned to human studies. We have simply exchanged fields. But I always had a desire to be a zoo director, or, at least, to work in zoos, though it didn't look as if I'd ever have the opportunity. Then I got the chance when I joined the staff at Berne. In 1944, during the war, I moved on from Berne to Basel, where I remained for nine years, coming here to Zurich in '54. This zoo is a private enterprise, helped financially—and occasionally—by donations, as well as contributions from the canton and municipality. It dates back to 1929, and through the years it became badly neglected. When I arrived I had a lot of clearing to do—we really haven't finished it yet, but then, when is a zoo ever finished? Besides, I haven't been at it all that time: in '59 I was fired by the board of governors because, as they said, I worked too hard. Actually they resented the fact that I had taken on a task they considered outside the limits of my duties, at the university where I give two lectures a week. Naturally, I consider this connection with the chief educational institution of Zurich an important part of a zoo director's work, but they objected and pushed me out. Well, this brought on quite a storm. There was a revolution among the students; many of the public who weren't students protested as well, and in the end I was reinstated. It was the board that was fired." As I learned later, Dr. Hediger's lectures drew such a crowd of students that the audiences have had to be split, so that the time he spends at the university is doubled. Nobody objects now, however. "Because of that interruption," he continued, "some years' work was lost, and we had to start over again in '59. Then there is the money factor. We're given enough funds regularly for general maintenance, but for new construction we have to scrimp and save and plan, and only one important innovation a year can be accomplished, according to what extra contributions we can get. In this way, we got the new ape house. Last year the Africa house was completed, and so on.

"In addition, I've had some opportunity to study the natural parks of Africa. I've made two visits twelve years apart. Spacing them gave me the chance to observe some rather dramatic developments in conservation, which on the whole are not encouraging. For example, the first time I was there white rhinos had been placed under protection, because their numbers were dropping dramatically. After the protection order went into effect the known number increased by about one thousand, and everybody was happy. But on my second visit, twelve years and the Liberation later, rhinos were being slaughtered again, by the thousands. There were many other examples of what's been happening to the animals of Africa. Take the white giraffe I saw at the border of the Karamba National Park, where it marches with the Sudan: a few months later I was told that it had been killed. People had hoped it would be protected by superstition, but that didn't work." He looked sad.

But Zurich itself possesses a pair of white rhinos, which had arrived just before I paid my visit, and was already possessed of a pair of black rhinos, as well as some hippos. These animals live in a place built according to the director's specifications; he pointed out to me that he had provided the pool with a very short staircase, because in nature such approaches are not long or steep, like many one sees in other zoos. "I call those 'official stairs' because they're like staircases in palaces or houses of parliament," he said. On the way to the ape house Dr. Hediger spoke further of zoo architecture. "It was here that I could first realize one of my ideas. I hate the cube. Zoos always keep their animals in cubic compartments: why? Because we ourselves live in rooms, cubicles. But just because we do, why should wild animals? I persuaded the architect to forget the human point of view, because to keep animals like that simply humanizes them, and the whole point of having wild animals vanishes."

Like every other building here, the ape house was constructed, perforce, on several levels. To get into it we humans came down flights of stairs, but the enclosures were not bound by such dimensions, and the apes had vast heights in which to disport. Two lowland gorillas, one unusually fair in color, shared a cage with a chimpanzee: Dr. Hediger believed, he said, that another gorilla was on the way to Zurich, courtesy of the late Dr. Schweitzer. "We have put that chimpanzee in with them because he's only six years old and very lively," he said. "It keeps the gorillas more active. Notice that we don't use bars, but twisted chrome steel wire that gives a better view, and the glass is welded in a curved shape. We have glasses everywhere in this house to seal off possible infection. Do you see what a wide space we have out between the people and the glass? Now, up here, we keep many other chimps; we have twenty in all. One old male—there he is—has fathered five little apes. He's prone to sudden bursts of temper, like all chimps; odd, how they go into these bursts of hysteria, but according to observers it's not cage behavior, as they do the same in the wild. I'd hoped we could have screens of climbing plants between the railings and the glass, but the lighting here proved to be too weak for plant life, and if the architect had depended on direct lighting, reflections from the glass would have made the apes invisible. Here we have lar gibbons. We've had four young from them—see the baby in that female's arms? You can just see it . . . There!"

On the glass of the chimps' cage were four round spots of color: red, yellow, green, and blue respectively. Dr. Hediger said that these were a part of experiments he was making in comparative behavior. "At first we painted them inside the glass," he went on, "but the apes scratched them away. Now we paint them outside and Homo sapiens scratches them away. We are always repainting them. We keep a repairman handy just to do this . . . The architect who designed this house was given an award for it by the Society of Architects."

In the Zurich zoo, though it is barely more than twenty acres in extent, Hediger has accomplished a widely varied number of experiments, and the breeding record is remarkable. He is interested in the ostrich's relatives found in other continents. Zurich's rheas, the great birds of South America, have produced many chicks, of which the zoo has sent seven to Whipsnade in exchange for a Père David's deer. We climbed a little hill to see a brood of five-day-old rhea chicks, and I learned some interesting, if unedifying, facts about this bird's home life. "The father does all the incubating," Dr. Hediger told me. "All the hen does is lay the eggs, then the male takes over. He sits for forty days, turning the eggs every day, while the hen simply goes off and lives her own life. We must remove her from the vicinity altogether once the eggs have hatched, or she would kill the chicks. And the hens of the Australian emus over there in this next field have even worse habits—last year a female emu killed her chicks before we could get to her. Emu fathers incubate for sixty days—they're more long-suffering than rheas, because they never leave the nest. The male rhea does leave his eggs for twenty-five minutes every day, to eat and drink, but a broody emu father doesn't eat at all." He broke off to chase away a female emu over on the other side of the fence. She looked like a cartoonist's drawing, all legs, with odd tufts of feathers sticking out around her head and a squinty, bad-natured expression. She had obviously been trying to administer a vicious peck to a chick straying close to the wire. "The chicks must be protected at all times against the hen's aggressiveness," said Dr. Hediger.

Wherever we went, whatever we saw, Dr. Hediger had some anecdote about the animal's species or its individuality. Of the immense lammergeier, or bearded vulture: "It is said that this bird carries away young children, and the story is possibly true." "Our tigress; she is expecting children today. It's her first time." "The mother of this leopard family is a pet, raised by a woman in her house." "The civet cat came from South Africa, where they still use civet musk for making scent. It's a demarcation odor, quite a nice smell in fact." "That female lion is quite tame. She was found as an abandoned baby in the Kruger National Park, by tourists who brought her in to the Johannesburg SPCA. She stayed there until she was half-grown, and then the police said she must be removed. They were going to shoot her, but a South African lady told me about it and I got possession of her. Some benefactor paid the air freight to bring her to Switzerland. That happened years ago, but she remains quite tame. So do our hyenas. Hyenas are very intelligent animals. I once sold a cub to a friend who runs a circus, and a year went by before I saw either of them again, but then when I visited the circus and called her, she came straight over to the bars to be stroked just as she'd always done. That's a long time for a wild animal to remember a human being. Yet there's a strong prejudice against hyenas. I wonder why."

He remained in a thoughtful mood until we got to the zebras, which share their enclosure with ostriches in the amicable manner of the Hagenbeck animals. They have an artificial termite nest to rub against, copied from the great red iron-hard columns characteristic of East Africa. Zebras need such a rubbing post, and Dr. Hediger is much in favor of such artifices. He spoke with admiration of an arrangement he saw at Regent's Park, where London's one tickbird was supplied with an imitation rhino's back to sit on. He would like to have tickbirds in Zurich, but for the moment must content himself with cattle herons. In one of his books he tells how he introduced these foreign creatures to a herd of Swiss cattle, and the herons immediately flew to the cattle and perched on their backs. This, of course, was not surprising. What was extraordinary was that the

Swiss cattle accepted their outlandish guests as if they had known and appreciated cattle herons all their lives.

We visited the beaver colony. Not that I saw the beavers—I never do—but I have Dr. Hediger's word for it that a family lived there, near a waterfall—Canadian beavers that had raised eighteen young. Dr. Hediger, who *has* seen the animals, said that the adults carry the young on their forepaws, or keep an anxious eye on the little ones when they are swimming, in case the infants stay in the water too long. If this does happen, a parent beaver will haul the baby out by the scruff of the neck, using his teeth to do it, and carries him off in—I almost said, in his arms.

"This is the first open aviary to be constructed in Europe," said the director as we entered another building. "We made it out of the old birdhouse, which was full of little cages. This was opened after I returned from exile. It isn't the first one in the world, though: that one was in St. Louis, and the second was Philadelphia's. This is the third." As open aviaries are not so rare nowadays, most zoo visitors know the principle on which they operate without bars or wire or any other physical restraint: diurnal birds remain where it is light and avoid the dark, so it is all a matter of lighting. Next came lizards and the aquarium, with a lungfish from Australia. "You know the story, perhaps? About a hundred years ago a Queensland farmer, William Foster, found one of these fish wrapped in dried mud, which is how they weather the dry season. Because it was the first connecting link ever found between water life and land life, there was tremendous excitement in the scientific world and people came from everywhere to study it. Today the existence of such a creature is well known, but the fish itself is still not very common in captivity."

Outside again, we paused to look over the valley far below, and Dr. Hediger said, "We have very long winters here, and snow makes a lot of trouble for us. Often we use the Bactrian camel to pull the snowplow."

No Swiss zoo could function without bears. Berne has the most, but all have some, and though Zurich's polar bears have had their moment when the female became a mother, the brown bear is the favorite. Dr. Hediger showed me a brown female in an enclosure just beneath us, backed by sheer cliff and furnished with a high tree. "She's had two families of three cubs each. Brown bears are kept in the nest the first three months—they're very small at birth, and the eyes don't open until the cubs begin to walk. Then they're all over the place, very likely, too adventurous for their own good. On the day her first cubs started to climb that tree without permission, the mother managed to pull two of them off before they got out of reach, but the third kept going until it reached the top. Little bears can climb up, you know, before they know how to climb down—they're always getting stuck that way—and this one finally fell off, and broke a leg. With her second lot the mother bear wasn't going to take any chances, and when one of the cubs climbed all the way up the tree she followed and showed it how to descend . . . I don't like to say that she showed it, but I don't know how else to express it."

"Why don't you like to say it?" I asked.

"Because it sounds anthropomorphic." The great Dr. Hediger actually blushed.

One July day in 1966 the news bulletins of press, radio, and television all featured a story bound to attract attention: LIONS AT LARGE IN PLANE. The incident came about because Lord Bath, owner of a large Wiltshire country seat called Longleat, had recently opened a lion park in his grounds to boost the estate's takings from paying visitors. The exhibit, much on the order of Japan's "Kenya" at Tama Park, proved a great attraction, and Lord Bath, encouraged, sent for three more lions from Abyssinia, where the splendid, black-maned cats come from. It was this shipment, traveling by chartered plane, that caused the excitement when the lions got out of their cage and started exploring the vehicle, somewhere over northern Europe. Wandering about, sniffing here and there, they strayed at length into the pilot's cabin and scared the daylights out of the crew. Over the communications system the pilot appealed to the nearest big airfield, Schiphol, near Amsterdam, to let him land because there were lions all over the plane. Not unnaturally, the man who received the message replied, "Go and sleep it off," or words to that effect. Ultimately, however, the Dutch were convinced of the unlikely story and everything was ready for the plane when it landed. Grim-faced police were there with machine-guns, and they quickly formed a ring about the craft. There was an ambulance too, and a cage on wheels, and perhaps, though I am not sure about this, a fire engine.

The plane landed, taxied, and stopped, but its door did not open. Shouting, the pilot explained why: the lions were between the crew and the door, he said. Nobody outside liked to open up, either, and that was how matters stood when my television set took up the tale. Another car now drove onto the tarmac and stopped near the plane, and two people got out, a man in uniform and a woman I couldn't see very well because the man was between her and the camera. But as she strode toward the plane, something about those purposeful feet was familiar, and when the announcer spoke, I knew. "And then," he said, "up stepped a woman of no more than five feet two in height . . ."

"Agatha Gijzen," I said aloud to the empty living room.

It was, too. Dr. Gijzen doesn't work in Holland, though she is Dutch-born—she is biologist at the Société Royale de Zoologie d'Anvers—but Antwerp isn't all that far from Amsterdam, and she got to Schiphol just in time to save the poor lions' lives. First she peeked into the window, and sniffed scornfully. "Mere babies," she said to the crowd. "Little ones!" She whipped the door open, said, "Here, pussy, *nice* pussy," and stepped back with a small lion held firmly back of the ears. She shoved it into the cage on wheels, and stepped into the plane with a stick of some sort in her hand. In no time at all she had shooed the two elder beasts, too, into the cage, and the incident was over. Afterward, I have no doubt, she went back to Antwerp, fuming about time wasted on foolishness.

When I made her acquaintance at the Antwerp Zoo she did the honors of the place for me because the director was away. If I should forget what sort of day it was, my blistered, splotched notebook reminds me that it was a filthy one of dismal clouds and persistent torrents. I said to myself as I waited to get in, in company with a line of schoolgirls in uniform and their chaperone nuns, that the Belgians are a hardy race. Inside the gate were more schoolchildren, a seething, scampering, splashing mass of them. The zoo is immutably fixed near the center of town, hemmed in by the main railway station and ancient buildings that mark out its twenty-four acres with a skyline that makes one think of battlements, courtyards, and cobbled streets. What has such an atmosphere to do with the wild animals of forest and plain? Yet somehow an illusion is created and persists; thanks to growing plants wherever they can be squeezed in, green shadows of the Congo hang over Antwerp's zoo.

The absent director, Walter K. van den Bergh, published an article about the zoo in the IZY for 1966, setting forth the Society's point of view as to a zoo's functions. "Every zoo man," he said in part, "would agree that the majority of public visitors to a zoo have not come for the sole purpose of learning something. People mostly go to the zoo to seek distraction, in order just to be out." This is quite all right, he continues, but a zoo's cultural value is much greater if education can enter into the recreation. The ghosts of Sir Stamford Raffles, Sir Humphry Davy, and the worthies of nineteenth-century Bristol seem to have blessed his pen as he wrote, "The exhibition of rare animals is only justified when it does not take place merely to be spectacular, but above all for scientific and educational purposes." People must be familiar with an animal before they interest themselves in protecting and conserving its species. In Belgium, a heavily industrialized country, most visitors are not acquainted with the animal world, and one must stimulate their interest "so as to awake the concept and love of nature." But this teaching must take place inconspicuously, almost incidentally. So much for the average Belgian. The zoo must also, however, take care of naturalists, students, and conservationists who have another purpose in coming, and the Royal Society, according to this article, takes on a considerable responsibility for education. Zoo visits are a part of the syllabus in the Antwerp schools for all pupils between and including the ages of twelve and fourteen. The schools are given free material from the zoo and the Museum of Natural History that is a part of it, and before their visits are told what particular things to observe, since afterward they are given tests about them. Dr. Gijzen told me something about this ambitious program, and I began to understand why so many juveniles thronged the pathways on a regular, heavily-rainy school morning. "We get five or six schools visiting every day," she said.

At Paris' Jardin des Plantes, the national museum stands close to the zoo. But in Antwerp the museum is an intrinsic part of the garden, as well as an important place for the town's cultural life. Within its dark, solid walls is an assembly-room that holds two thousand people, in which concerts and movies and lectures and expositions take their turn. The assembly room is on the ground floor: so is another chamber Dr. Gijzen led me into, twice as high-ceilinged as any ordinary room, containing a number of flourishing palm trees of the very tall kind known to me as "royal." "We are preparing this for a bird of paradise display," she said, indicating workmen chipping at the wall. "They are being sent by Sir Edward Hallstrom in New Guinea. We'll have some small mammals too; there's one here already—a kinkajou. This room can be heated, so it's convenient. The palms were planted in the time of Napoleon, by his command."

"They were lucky to have a place that could accommodate trees of such a size," I said, and Dr. Gijzen gave me an odd look. "The place was built around them," she replied briefly.

I asked how things had fared for the zoo during the latest war, and learned that conditions were much as they had been in other continental zoos. "When hostilities broke out, by order of the government all the dangerous carnivores were immediately put to death," she said. "Later the flying bombs destroyed practically all the other animals, and we had to start all over again when the war was over. The first two new animals we got—I remember it well—both came from a circus in Luxembourg, a lion and a polar bear. That was 1945. There were great celebrations in Antwerp over their arrival. The lion was already old and exhausted, but after we got our first lioness—from London—he bred a lot of cubs from her, and didn't die until 1958."

As soon as we went upstairs into the museum's main hall I felt at home.

Here was the pure essence of museum, that good old familiar haunt of all our childhoods, smelling faintly of formaldehyde and camphor, full of cases of stuffed animals, and cabinets, and mounted skeletons. I love museums. Happily I followed Dr. Gijzen as she pointed out insect specimens filed in drawers, stuffed birds, and a collection of Belgian and Congolese fauna—two okapi calves born here in the zoo but killed by their aberrant mother, two Cuban flamingo chicks born here, a stuffed Komodo dragon that lived here for a space before dying. One case held a large bird that I first took for a peacock, then, hesitating, decided was a pheasant. Dr. Gijzen waited patiently while I wavered, and finally came to the rescue. "You're not the first to be puzzled by that bird. It's most unusual—a Congo peacock, something halfway between peacock and pheasant but of more primitive form. Not many zoologists have studied it—it's rarely seen, even in the wild. But"—her color heightened with pride—"*we* have them in the zoo, three breeding pairs. It is most unusual. We were the first, as we have been with the Cuban flamingo and the okapi. . . . Over in that room is the Henri van Hueck collection of historical microscopes. One may have been made by Leeuwenhoek himself."

As one would expect, the living collection is strong in the African department. But there is also a briskly breeding colony of marmosets, all born in Antwerp; some ringtail and other lemurs; five species of kangaroo. They have one of the only three bongo antelopes in captivity, a male who, lacking a female of his own species, has consorted with female marsh buck and produced interesting hybrids. Antwerp has an outstanding collection of birds of prey, and has built up a good colony of gorillas including *two* pairs of the rare mountain species as well as two lowland animals. It was here that I learned the difference easiest to spot between the two: the lowland gorilla has a smaller nose than the mountain. "They say that the mountain gorilla has a tomato-nose," said Dr. Gijzen. "We opened this ape house in '58, so it's quite modern. Do you see how we weigh the animals?" Something shaped like a mushroom sticks up from the floor inside the cage, and whenever a gorilla sits down on it the weight is registered on a scale set in the wall outside the bars.

Antwerp has a pair of Bonobo chimps, too.

Dr. Gijzen, who has written a number of papers on widely differing subjects, is an authority on pinnipeds—seals, walruses, and the like—so I was able to ask her about the attractive Baikal seals, those little animals that float on their backs and look exactly like Li'l Abner's schmoos. It turned out that Antwerp has owned a pair of these, and still has the female, but Agatha had something new to show. We went into a cage where the floor was almost entirely occupied by a round pool. "This is something you won't see very often," she said. A ghostly white creature reared itself from the water, swam over to us, and propped itself up on its front limbs—flippers?—to look yearningly at Dr. Gijzen. She patted its head affectionately. "This is a manatee. I don't know of any other zoo that has one; this one's been here for ten years. Manatees can't come out of the water at all, though they're mammals. Sometimes they bask on shore, half in, half out, in the position this one's taken. Look at that upper lip, cleft in the middle like a caterpillar's. It munches with a caterpillar's movements. The nearest relative it has in the animal world is the elephant."

She reached into her pocket, and I expected her to bring out—after all, one thought of seals, and walruses, and other sea animals—a fish. Instead, she took a lump of sugar from her pocket, and the manatee accepted it eagerly. Dr. Gijzen was quite right. If you can imagine a caterpillar eating a lump of sugar, that's the way it looked.

CHAPTER 7

Paris and Rotterdam

□

It is impossible without a careful definition of terms to generalize about zoos, and of defining there is no end. I am stuck for a reply, therefore, when people ask me what, in my opinion, is the best zoo I've ever seen. What does "best" mean? Largest number of animals, or architectural beauty, or longevity records, or breeding, or scientific research facilities, or gate receipts? They are only a few of the things that count in a summing up. But if you want to know which zoo is the most popular, you are on ground more solid. For one thing, zoo attendance depends somewhat on nationality: the peoples of southern Europe—Italy, Spain, and Portugal—are not as fond of zoos as the peoples of the north. I do not speak of Greece because her only zoo, in Athens, is still being constructed. This is not the same thing as saying that the directors and zoologists of the southern countries are laggard. On the contrary, Italian ornithologists have done outstanding work, and at a small private zoo near Rome, in January 1966, a cheetah cub was born. The birth of a cheetah in captivity is a sufficiently rare occurrence in itself, but this one is even more remarkable than that: its mother is rearing it. The very few cheetahs hitherto born in captivity have failed to survive or were hand-reared.

What I'm getting at is that in spite of having these excellent men at work on their captive wild animals, the public in Italy, like that in Spain and Portugal, remains more or less indifferent to zoos, whereas in Germany, Switzerland, Belgium, Holland and France, people flood in to look at the animals, quite as eagerly as do the denizens of the British Isles. So do Swedes and Danes, though Norwegians can't, because they haven't any zoos. I am not able to account for this difference in national tastes, and I'm not going to try. Presumably there are many reasons, both psychological and economic. The British would say, "Those people are no good at all with animals—look at the way they treat horses," but I am sure it is more complicated than that.

I thought it logical to start my tour of the Continent in France, specifically at the Ménagerie du Jardin des Plantes in Paris, because that is where the first public zoo in the Western world was opened, you will remember, in 1793. But as things turned out, I went to Vincennes instead because the director of both these institutions, Professor Jacques Nouvel, wanted it that way. On the telephone he explained that he did most of his work at the Parc Zoologique de Paris, in other words at Vincennes. The whole public park—Vincennes Woods—still seems a fairly long way from the city center, though it isn't segregated any more by the walls of Paris, and a constant stream of traffic rolls past all day on its way to more residences beyond the limits of the forest. As the taxi approached these tree-shaded reaches I did the proper thing and reflected that here too was a part of zoo history, for the kings of France used to keep collections of wild animals in these groves, and entertained visiting potentates with Roman games. The modern planners have retained as many trees as possible, so that when I came through the gates and found my way to the administration offices I walked in shade nearly up to the door. But there was no truckling to historical sentiment in the architecture; all was pure early-twentieth-century public school, outside and in. As I walked carefully down the echoing corridor on what looked like brown polished lino but seemed slippier, I reminded myself that the zoos of Paris are, as a matter of fact, supported by the Ministry of Education.

Professor Nouvel talked to me in a brown waiting-room. "As the oldest modern zoo anywhere in the world," he said, "the Jardin des Plantes, surrounded as it is on all sides by city buildings, became too small for the national collection many years ago. The authorities were overtaken by an embarrassment of supply, if you like. In 1934, therefore, this zoo was opened. It was not intended to take the place of the Ménagerie du Jardin; some smaller animals are still kept there, but here it is possible to spread out and accommodate large groups and herds." The difference in size is considerable: the Parc Zoologique covers forty-two acres, whereas the Jardin has only nine. Even with their forty-two acres, said Monsieur Nouvel, the Vincennes staff would like more space, and are hoping to get permission soon to use some of the surrounding land.

"I see that you and all the assistant directors are veterinarians," I remarked.

He nodded. "We find it more satisfactory: the veterinary doctors manage the zoos, and the zoologists and other scientists work under our scrutiny. A considerable amount of research goes on here. The buildings that occupy the rest of this clearing are all laboratories." Botany, with emphasis on tree culture, is also studied at Vincennes, which seems a fair-play turnabout considering that it was the botanists who had to make way for all those zoological specimens back in the Revolution at the Jardin des Plantes.

I was ushered about the zoo by an assistant director in a white coat like a television doctor's. On our way to the first exhibit he told me that the Parisian zoo people, in feeding their animals, use the diet system of Professor Herbert L. Ratcliffe, of the Penrose Research Laboratory which is connected with the Philadelphia Zoo. "Professor Ratcliffe himself was here last year," he said, so enthusiastically that I refrained from asking if there were any dissenting opinions held by staff members. Yet the Ratcliffe diet, which can be loosely described as a system of instant feeding, is not universally approved, though nobody denies its convenience and the chances it offers to make economies. In a bulletin published in October 1958, Dr. Ratcliffe writes that he evolved the diet to obviate the results of malnutrition in zoos—breeding failures, rickets and cage paralysis, poorly formed and maloccluded teeth, intestinal disorders, reduced life spans, low resistance to infection, poor quality of offspring, obesity, and/or poor hair coats or plumage. "Since 1935 we (in Philadelphia) have used controlled diet mixtures to meet the needs of a great majority of our animals," he continues. "These mixtures are prepared in a central location, then distributed in predetermined quantities each day to the exhibition buildings. Their actual preparation requires not more than 40 hours of semi-skilled labor each week. Thus, these diets are not expensive to prepare and may readily be fitted into a daily routine." He lists five basic diets: Diet A, "for omniverous mammals and birds," is broken down into three subdivisions—one for debilitated monkeys, one for cage birds, one for flamingos: Diet B is for herbivores: Diet C for carnivorous mammals, birds, and reptiles: D for anteaters and aardvarks: E for all the cats. No diet has been found for fish-eating animals, he confesses, better than fish itself.

Probably the most outstanding opponent to the Ratcliffe diet is Dr. Hediger of Zurich, and he feels strongly about it. He maintains that a wild animal in a zoo must not be treated and fed like a domestic animal—a battery hen or calf—or the whole point of keeping it disappears. At best, he says, a captive animal is beset with boredom, and the only highlight of his day is his relief from routine. The instant diet recommended by Ratcliffe destroys this mitigation and also spoils the relationship between keeper and kept.

On the other hand, the temptation to make work easier in a zoo is great. As Ratcliffe says, "This system . . . relieves the keepers of preparing foods, except the fruits and vegetables for small birds, and so reduces kitchen space in exhibition buildings. And finally, the system eliminates much of the labor of feeding the animals. For example, at one time our apes and monkeys were fed no less than six times each day. We have reduced feeding to twice each day and, should the need arise as it sometimes does, all food—mixed ration as well as fruits and vegetables—may all be given at one time." Those of my readers who have tried the Metrecal diet will have an inkling of what Hediger means when he objects to the Ratcliffe system. Mrs. Julia Field, formerly director of Crandon Park Zoo at Miami and a lion tamer in her own right, is emphatically on Hediger's side in this controversy. In a conversation with me she explained why, at least as far as lions are concerned:

"A lion ought to have bones," she said firmly. "Of course you can't let the cats have everything they would in nature; they can't be permitted to kill their own food in zoos, for instance—it wouldn't be practical. But as it is, in many zoos they're given ground bones; they don't even have a chance to chew. Preparing bones for cats is a special thing, but it can be done, if you have experts. What a lion likes is not so much the kill anyway; he likes the tearing and clawing. He can spend two hours with his meat, getting his face all bloody; then he feels as if he's been doing something."

Ratcliffe argues in rebuttal that this is an old-fashioned attitude: "The introduction of a system such as this (his diet) into a zoo demands a willingness to break completely with the past." Two men who have adopted his ideas wholeheartedly are Dr. Ernst Lang, the director of the zoo at Basel, and his assistant, Dr. Hans Wackernagel. Wackernagel even spent some time at Philadelphia, working at the Penrose laboratory, and has written several articles since on the application of Ratcliffe principles to the working of Basel Zoo. He and Lang both reported to Ratcliffe that they found most opposition from their keepers, not the animals, most of which accepted the diet readily.

"And, of course, the men who feed the animals have every right to explanations," says Ratcliffe, ". . . for this may disrupt relationships with certain animals and visitors. The need for change rarely is evident to them and we must admit that occasional animals do live amazingly well on what seem to be very poor diets. In fact, our record for gibbons, about thirty-two years, was established by an animal on a diet of bananas, rice, and bread. It is beside the point to show that he died of osteomalacia, which could have been corrected easily. He was a keeper's pet and shared his keeper's lunch, which is a major source of opposition to the controlled feeding."

Reading this, I had to admit that Dr. Ratcliffe had lost me. Does he mean to say that the gibbon would have lived longer than his record thirty-two years if he'd been given the Ratcliffe diet, and hadn't been a pet of the keeper? I'm afraid so.

But I didn't mention the Philadelphia gibbon to Dr. Rinjard. He told me proudly of their herd of okapi, seven at one time, including three babies born there. They still had five, and eight giraffes, and a collection of bears representing every species in the world. I thought the landscaping very pleasant, and he assured me that this aspect of zoo keeping was of first importance with the French, or at any rate the Parisian, public. People wouldn't come, he said, if the Parc wasn't pretty. We paused to look at an "island," or moated enclosure, where lived a troop of spider monkeys, and then surveyed a genuine island in a little lake, where five chimpanzees disported. "In all, we have fifteen chimps in this zoo," said my guide. "Here on the island they are all about five years old at least, but we also have a new baby at the ape house. Let's see how it's getting on." Like so many ape babies born in captivity, this one had been deserted by its mother. We found it taking the air like a British baby, outside the house, in a basket at the back door. Its black hair stood up on its head like a mop. It was timid, and screamed at Dr. Rinjard, so we went away.

"Here we have a pair of Indian rhinos," said the doctor. "Male born at Basel, female from Assam. Here's a baby yak. And there ahead of us, the Grand Rocher, the center of the zoo."

One sees the Rocher a long way off, so it didn't burst on me as a complete surprise: nevertheless, close up it was enough of a novelty to stop me in my tracks—an artificial mountain rising more than forty yards into the air, all white, with paths winding around it to the peak. Mountain goats played on these man-made trails. Around the base were pools and penguins, each species to its own pool. These were outfitted with fountains or sprays from above that operated at intervals to keep the birds cool. "We have many kinds—Kings for one, and, naturally, Humboldts," said Dr. Rinjard. "You see those caves behind the pools—they lead into chambers that are air-conditioned for hot weather; we can vary the temperature from five to eight degrees Centigrade." Some of the penguins breed—no doubt as a reward to the authorities who have made them so comfortable, far from home. But goats and penguins are not all that the Rocher has to offer. There is a master cave in the middle of the rock, between the honeycombed walls with their penguin inhabitants, which contains the base of an elevator shaft, featuring a ride so popular that we had to wait in a long line for our turn to go up to the top. When we got there and stepped out on a little balcony—higher, I was glad to note, than the highest point on the goats' path—the view was well worth waiting for. Paris seemed far off, calm and blue on the horizon as a cardboard cutout, and from where we stood even the Vincennes trees were small, like thick dark green rushes that held the zoo with its tiny grazing beasts and our pretty, artificial mountain as if in a pond among them. Or perhaps, I thought, the Parc Zoologique was like a neat flower bed set in the middle of an untrimmed, grassy lawn.

Next morning I thought without eagerness of my planned visit to the Ménagerie du Jardin des Plantes. For one thing, I'd been there many years before and remembered only a kind of shabby sparseness. Mainly, however, I had been put off by several casual remarks made by the Vincennes doctors: I'd got the impression that the Jardin was merely a repository for leftovers from Vincennes, smaller animals and so on. It seemed a waste, taking a whole day just to look at rabbits and mice. But it had been arranged, and I went. Past the gate and into the grounds I went, casually reflecting that the terrain was much prettier than I remembered, with its eighteenth-century formality—and found myself looking straight into the enormous tawny face of a European bison. I actually stepped back, but I need not have been cautious: he was a peaceful animal enough, and a stout fence separated us. He had a lot of family connections with him, too. I was still wondering pensively what the Vincennes idea of a bigger animal might be when I found three Przewalski horses—not as large as the wisents, but still hardly as small as rabbits. Silently I apologized to the National Museum of Natural History and all its works. If, when you are strolling in the menagerie part of the Jardin, you are troubled as I was by little flashes of that *déjà vu* feeling, there is no cause for alarm: what you are recognizing is the background of many a Delacroix painting. That artist of wild animals often used Jardin inhabitants as models, and saw no harm in brushing in as well the very rocks they reposed on, just as they were and still are. The Rotonde, in what approximates the Ménagerie's center, built in 1802 with some of the first money extracted from the Revolution's government in Paris for the upkeep of the new public collection, stands as it used to, an impressive red bulk that gives weight and authority to all the grounds. Its five entrances lead into animal houses that must be as blank and dark as medieval prison cells, but there are outside paddocks now, and most of the Rotonde is used for storage. The guidebook serves for the whole museum, botanical and geological displays as well as zoological, but it pays its due respects to the zoo's early days, when "Certain beasts of the Jardin des Plantes were celebrated all over Paris, like the lion from the Royal Menagerie at Versailles whose inseparable companion was a dog, and that other who, in friendly spirit, used to rub himself tenderly against his keeper."

Animals apart, the Jardin is still what it has been since 1635—a botanical museum. Moreover, ever since the Revolution it has been, as it is now, the National Museum of Natural History. It has extensive laboratories, library and galleries, and serves as center and clearinghouse for the work of all French natural scientists. In short, the professors, in spite of the affront to their dignity that the Republic administered back in the seventeen-nineties, have held their own. I found an interesting item in one of their library books: in 1793 the king, Louis XV, maintained in the Jardin des Plantes a small collection of living animals—peacocks, coypus, monkeys. So there was precedent, after all, for that intrusion on the hallowed precincts of the botanical gardens.

Outside Rotterdam on the broad flat fertile plains of Holland, Dr. A. C. van Bemmel reigns over more than thirty acres of zoo land. Life there is peaceful, but it wasn't always. In 1940 the Stichting Koninklijke Rotterdamse Diergaarde (called the Blijdorp Zoo if you are in a hurry) was brand-new, and opened its doors to the public only to close them again immediately, when the Germans came.

"That wasn't its real beginning, however," said Dr. Van Bemmel. We were in his sunlit office, surrounded by books and papers on zoo subjects. "The ancestor of Blijdorp as it is now opened in 1857, close to the railway station in town. I suppose our story really starts with this fellow." He turned his chair around and pointed to a framed engraving hanging on the wall at his right hand, one of those romanticized likenesses beloved by actors and other entertainers of a century ago. The subject of this one stood between the conventional open curtains of a stage, a muscular man, heavily mustached and scantily clothed in a loincloth and short toga against the background of what looked like a circus ring. He stood with legs wide apart, supporting the weight of a tiger as tall as himself that was reared on its hind legs, leaning on the man's shoulder in what might have been affection, though its tail was evidently waving fiercely. Under this pair, in flowing script, was the title: "Mr. Martin et Son Tigre Ater."

I didn't recognize it, and said so. Dr. Van Bemmel said impressively, "That's Henri Martin, the first man to train lions and tigers for carnival appearances. He was a famous performer in circuses and carnivals, and is still the patron saint of all animal trainers. I believe he started out in his career with hyenas, but he soon went on to the big cats. He fell in love with a Miss Van Hagen of a famous zoo family, and after they married he brought all his animals to the Van Hagen Zoo and worked with them there. This was just before the eighteen-fifties, I believe. Then Martin's wife died and he hadn't the heart to go on with the animals, so he retired—as he thought—and settled down near here, outside Rotterdam, to grow roses. A young lady artist who specialized in flower paintings came to see his roses and paint them. Ultimately, she became his second wife.

"Now it happened that the stationmaster of the Rotterdam railway station was very fond of animals. He kept a few around as a hobby—some ducks and geese, things like that, and a few small animals as well; rabbits perhaps, and foxes. In those days the train services were a new thing, not well developed. There were few trains, and passengers used to have to wait a long time between connections. So at Rotterdam, to kill the time, they would look around the stationmaster's little zoo, and this attention encouraged him to enlarge his collection, until finally he opened a regular zoo on the spot, and charged a small admission fee. As you may know, this wasn't the only railway zoo in Europe. Antwerp's grew up by the railway station and is still there, but ours at Rotterdam preceded it. The Rotterdam zoo grew with the railway, and had become quite a respectable affair by 1857, when Henri Martin was asked to be the first director. He was probably glad to get back into his old game, and he readily gave up his roses and accepted the offer. So that was the way it all started. As zoos do, this one got too large for its original premises, and in 1939 it was decided by the society that ran it to move out of town to where we are now. Money was collected from the municipality and the province, as well as a private fund: plans were made, building began, the animals were moved to their new quarters, and in 1940 the zoo was opened to the public—just in time to be closed again by the bombing."

Dr. Van Bemmel trained as a zoologist at Amsterdam University and worked as an assistant at the Artist Zoo of Amsterdam for some years. He told me that opportunities for zoo men were few in Holland, in spite of the high standards maintained by the national authorities, because of the restricted size of the country. "In the whole land there are only five trained zoologists in the zoos, so you can see what I mean. I went out to the Indies and worked at Buitenzorg there, now called Bogor, but after the Indonesians got their independence, like other Dutchmen I wasn't made to feel very happy under Sukarno, and in '51 I came back. I worked with Nature Protection for a while, and came here in '57."

As we made a tour of inspection, Dr. Van Bemmel said that the zoo had one quality that might be considered an advantage from the artistic point of view, but he found it hard, as a director, to appreciate it: this was its architectural unity. "The entire garden was planned before any building was started, and what you see now is very much as it was on opening day —including several places that were unfinished then and are still unfinished. One architect planned the whole layout, houses and gardens together. As a result, it's difficult to fit in anything new, especially because it's all such an irregular shape. We've adapted buildings and use them for purposes the architect hadn't provided for; even so, the place is filled to the limits. Take this, for instance—" He led the way past a children's playground, with slides and swings and jungle gyms, swarming with screaming infants. At one side their elders sat at little outdoor tables, eating and drinking. Looming over the scene was a kind of pavilion with boarded-up windows. Dr. Van Bemmel pointed to it and said, "Before the war, that was a winter garden. It came into its own after the hostilities, when the entire center of Rotterdam had been destroyed by bombs and there were no big rooms left there. Then the townspeople thought of this winter garden and used it for all their social gatherings until new places were built in town. 'Riviera Hall' is what it was called. But its day of glory is over now. We use it for storage, and hope that in a few years' time we can have a new winter garden."

He spoke as if any self-respecting zoo would want a winter garden, and the attitude interested me, as did the children's playground, for "winter garden" and "playground" are words that evoke—to me, at least—the old idea of the zoo as one section of the important whole, the pleasure park. I thought of Sunday evenings in such a park, of ladies in summer dresses and flowered hats, and men with straw boaters, sitting on iron benches with pretty scrollwork backs to enjoy the band-concert: *The Chocolate Soldier* or *Il Trovatore* played by musicians in uniform on a platform under a wooden canopy. It was all a far cry from the science-laboratory atmosphere of the modern zoo, but perhaps I was judging only by American standards. I said tentatively,

"At any rate you have a fine playground. Tell me, is that the usual thing for zoos on the Continent?"

He looked startled. "Oh, one must have a playground! How else are you to keep the children from teasing the animals?"

How indeed? I was about to ask what rules they had at Blijdorp about feeding, when he stopped at a sign and translated it for me: " 'A real lover of animals doesn't feed them.' Not that it really stops people who insist on feeding," he continued sadly, "but the signs help a bit and so make a difference. It would be splendid if we could stamp it out completely. Did you ever hear of the keeper who kept count, just for an experiment, of what one elephant was fed during one Sunday by the public? Just one Sunday, mind you. It was *fifty-two kilos* of food. The wonder is that they survive at all." Sadly we plodded on. "I've explained that some of the old original plans were never carried out. One result is that we have no aquarium and very little storage space, and the only way we ever got a reptile-house, a thing the architect hadn't allowed for, was by using what was originally planned as a cafeteria. But we have it. We have it. Specialties? I would say our apes"—a shadow crossed his face—"and carnivores. In ten years the zoo's tigers, both Sumatran and Siberian, have bred a hundred and fifty cubs. Here's the tiger house." It was in fact a series of cages, smaller than many I have seen but not small. Each was supplied with trees and bushes or tropical plants. The director said, "The secret of breeding is to keep your animals close together, and let them have places where they can feel hidden."

Next, as one of his *pièces de résistance*, we visited a fine herd of Przewalski horses, two stallions and four females. It was the first time I had seen so many specimens of this beautiful animal in one place, and Dr. Van Bemmel took me inside the enclosure that held the older stallion. The horse knew him, and nuzzled his arm softly with its soft nose. "He's sired ten foals, this fellow," said the director proudly. "I wouldn't say it on my own authority, because I've never claimed to be an expert on Przewalskis, but Mrs. Moore—do you know her? She *is* an expert, and she said he's the finest stallion of the breed she's ever seen. And she's seen them all."

Przewalskis, or wild Mongolian horses, are light in color, with—but let's let Lee Crandall, General Curator Emeritus of the Bronx, speak on the subject. In his "Management of Wild Animals in Captivity" he says the horse is "a small, chunky animal, light bay or 'yellow dun' in color, with a narrow dark stripe down the back and occasionally with faint leg stripes. Lower legs, mane, and tail are black and large, with Roman nose, while the ears are small and neat. The mane is short, stiff, and upright, there is no forelock, the tail is fairly full except at the base, which is thinly haired." The Western world first heard of this horse when N. M. Przewalski, late in the last century, came back from an expedition in central Asia bringing with him a skin and a skull of the animal. In 1900 it became known that Falz-Fein, a Russian private collector, had a few living animals of the same sort on his estate, and then other reports began coming in to England of Mongolian horses in captivity elsewhere, until that indefatigable collector the Duke of Bedford asked Carl Hagenback to get *him* some. (It was this same impulse that led the Duke to gather in specimens of Père David's deer, now famous as ancestors of the only surviving animals of this species.) Accordingly, Hagenbeck sent an expedition to Mongolia, where the horse was already thin on the ground; it returned with twenty-eight animals, almost as many more having died on the way. The Duke of Bedford got only some of them. Others went to various zoos. But zoo people were more careless then than they are now, and the Przewalski horses in captivity were allowed to slip from public notice. Nobody kept track of their offspring; some must have been crossbred with other equids: some changed hands and were lost. Only two zoos, Munich and Prague, maintained their herds and kept track, until Volf of Prague, in 1958, called attention of the zoo world to the problem. People were now presumably more enlightened on such matters, and they listened. At Volf's suggestion, all Przewalski horses known to be living in captivity were listed and observed in consistent fashion. A stud book is kept, the animals are counted every year, and all known facts about them are published. The IZY for 1966 reports a minimum of one hundred and twenty-one horses distributed among twenty-nine zoos: this is called the minimum, because not all zoos with such animals have imparted their statistics, even though the information was requested. Askaniya Nova in the Ukraine is one of these secretive groups, but it is known that they have Przewalskis, probably a flourishing herd at that. The picture, then, is more cheerful than it was in 1958, when Volf estimated that there were only fifty specimens in the world. In the wild, it has been years since any Przewalskis have been seen. They are almost certainly extinct.

The Blijdorp reptile house installed in the old cafeteria proved to be a combination herpetarium and greenhouse. Plants grew around the inside walls in profusion, their roots in unpaved strips of ground. The place was kept warm, and two marmosets living among the plants seemed to find everything much like home. "Do they always live free like this?" I asked.

"Oh yes. They were in a cage originally and escaped, but they were all right the way they are, so we've left them. But here's another kind of fauna that shouldn't be here." He looked down with distaste at two mice running among the twisted roots, and called a keeper over to point them out and give stern directions. We looked over the reptiles, especially a huge king cobra, which Dr. Van Bemmel said was the most expensive animal in the zoo. "He eats only snakes, which we have to import, deep-frozen, from Italy. We've tried everything else we can think of that looks like a snake—eels and even sausages—but no, he won't touch substitutes. Last year the supply from Italy failed, and we had to import five hundred all the way from Singapore. It cost a lot."

Another problem faced by the Rotterdam Zoo and others in the same country is that of foundations. We were looking at a herd of mouflon in a pit that was surrounded by a wall, and Dr. Van Bemmel said, "The difficulty is that we're on reclaimed land, fourteen feet below sea level.

It's all peat soil—peat fifteen or sixteen feet thick. Everything you build on this stuff, unless it's built on poles, sinks away sooner or later, and that has happened with the bottom of this pit. If you'll notice, the wall now seems too high, but we didn't build it that way. It will have to be constructed all over again. . . . These brown bears have a Bohemian background: they used to be with a circus, a group of three. One night they attacked the lady singer, and one of them had to be shot. I couldn't blame them for doing it, you know: she couldn't sing at all: they were quite right. I took the other two, because I knew it would be safe. We have no music here. Now, over here, is an exhibit that isn't quite orthodox. Do you see what I mean?" I saw what he meant, and knew where I'd seen it before—in Ueno Zoo, Tokyo.

"Did Mr. Hayashi ever visit here?" I asked abruptly.

He thought I was changing the subject. "Yes, I think so," he said. "Some Japanese did, at any rate."

"I'm sorry, I just wondered. These are Barbary sheep and baboons, aren't they? They seem to get on all right."

"Yes, they do. We tried chacma baboons first, but it didn't work. Chacmas can jump so high that ours got out and were all over the zoo for a good hour before we could round them up—it was quite a mess. Now we have gelada baboons, which can't jump so well. Ecologically speaking, I think it's justifiable to put these species together in an exhibit. They both come from Ethiopia."

We approached the monkey house, but before we got there, Dr. Van Bemmel said, "I suppose you heard about our disaster? No? It was the orangs. We had a fine group of ten. We'd bred nine ourselves—a record: no other zoo has ever produced so many of this rare animal—and of those nine we successfully raised seven. Of the two failures, one died of pneumonia while still a small baby, and the other was born abnormal and never had a chance. Still, to keep seven! Then, out of that generation, a pair produced another baby. In other words, we'd bred two generations, the first and only zoo to have done this in all zoological history. The second-generation baby—three generations in all, you understand—had reached the age of two by last December, and was well grown.

"Well, in December we received a pair of giant armadillos; they come from South America, but these had been bought from a Belgian dealer, and had been in his shop for some months before coming on. They seemed quite healthy on arrival. We put them into a cage in the monkey house, glassed in like all the cages there. A few weeks later they showed signs of some disorder. Their noses and eyes were running, and they broke out in vesicles. Nobody knew what they had, and before it could be diagnosed by laboratory tests, our young orang, the two-year-old, sickened and was dead within three days. Three days! Then the others came down with the same thing, one after another. Too late we found that it was monkey pox that had been carried in by the armadillos, and orangs are peculiarly susceptible to this complaint. Some of the monkeys and chimps caught it, but they recovered: a few, even, were only lightly affected, but the orangs died—six of them. Gone, like that, in a few days: the patient work of years snuffed out."

There was nothing to say. I saw tears in his eyes. For weeks afterward I couldn't forget those orangs. And I was not the only one to remember them. Seven months later, in December 1966, I came across the following item in a zoo trade magazine:

"On the 20th September, 1965, the Blijdorp Zoo received a valuable gift from a Dutch firm: a couple of fully grown Orangs, from the Yokohama Zoo, and a young Orang, which was born at the Hagenbeck Zoo at Hamburg. On 14th October the Director of the Artis Zoo, Amsterdam, presented a 5-year-old male Orang Utan. With these very fine presents the Blijdorp Zoo can again start their well known Orang breeding."

CHAPTER 8

Contrasts in Germany

□

"There is a unique feature about this place," said Dr. Wilhelm Windecker, director of the Aktiengesellschaft Zoologischer Garten, Köln. "Cologne is a very Catholic town and nearly all the children here take first communion, at a little ceremony you know, for a batch of them at one time. Well, on that day of communion, as soon as the ceremony is over they are brought straight over here to the zoo to celebrate, to make a little party of it. I don't know how the custom started; I only know it's very old, and it serves to show you how the public regards the garden—with full approval. I think it began because the church authorities said that it was a good thing to give young people a harmless view of the lives of animals. To start them off right in life."

In spite of the ravages of war, Cologne is still a beautiful city, which in rebuilding has retained her old character. Naturally the zoo is not as old as all that: no zoo is, even in Germany; but there was a spic-and-span look about it that fitted in well with the rest of the city. It's at the edge of the town's boundaries, or seems to be, situated over the river on an isthmus. The administration building was new, and so were most of the houses I could see from the glassed-in lobby as Dr. Windecker led me through the door and the gate beside them. It was a fine bright day. There was a high wind, but the thick border of trees that surround the grounds acted as a kind of shelter, and a number of people strolled about or sat on benches in the sun as if they were on a Riviera beach. They seemed to use the zoological garden as we in America use our ordinary parks—a place to take a walk or think quietly, as well as to look at animals.

"Another distinctive thing about this garden is that it's built next to a fort," Dr. Windecker was saying. "It might sound like an odd place to keep animals, but this zoo—or in any case *a* zoo—was here before it was ever thought that the fort would matter. Still, the fact that the fort was here, sharing the spot, has always had an inhibiting effect on the growth of the collection, especially since the war. It's awkward, I admit. Not that we're inaccessible, because we aren't. You can get here by car, boat or air. But we're on a military site, one can't deny it, so directors have always reasoned that no big houses could be built, nothing like elephant houses, for example: the authorities were afraid they might only have to pull them down again as soon as they'd been set up. Now, you are going to ask what is the use of a zoo if you can't have big houses in it." I hadn't been going to ask it—he was way ahead of me—but he swept on, regardless. "The answer is *birds*. They built birdhouses—dozens of them. Cologne is still primarily a bird zoo. In such a position, awkward situations arrive. Suppose someone offers you an elephant: what are you to do about it? It so happens that I myself like elephants very much. I would like to have fourteen, even sixteen elephants, but"—he shrugged—"we have birds."

He laughed then, cheerfully. In fact he was exaggerating, as I was soon to find out.

"Ah well, it will be changed in good time," he continued. "What has held us back since the war was not the fort, not any more; we had to put up a completely new zoo, you see, on the old ground. Almost nothing was left—certainly there was nothing very useful. And it soon became apparent that we no longer have enough room. There are only twenty acres here. However, seventy acres more have been put at our disposal close by. It was impossible to enlarge this piece: the other land is over there beyond that busy street, but we are working out the best way to make connections. It will either be by bridges arching over the road, or by tunnel: perhaps both, like the arrangement at Regent's Park. There was some talk of giving up this ground altogether and starting in a new part of the city, perhaps on the other side of town where it would be easier to expand, but what would be the good? I've discovered that wherever you start, any zoo is bound to be too small after a while. . . . Here are some of our birds; more birds, as you see, are going about more or less free. Over there is the pool for water birds. But you must not think that Cologne was always a mere aviary. The first American tapir was bred here—not in my time, exactly; it was back in 1868, but it shows that we have taken some interest in mammals from time to time." He paused thoughtfully. "You may have heard that Frankfurt bred the first American tapir, but that's not the case. Look closely at the report and you'll see that what they claim as a record is the first *Hessian* American tapir." He broke off and shook his head in mock sorrow.

Because Cologne has adopted the moat-enclosure system, walking there is something like strolling in an English meadow, an illusion only slightly impaired by the sight of camels in a paddock, since, grazing side by side with them, are a few tiny horses. They didn't look like Shetlands, but like true horses in miniature, and I asked if they came of the Argentine stock that has lately been featured in the news.

"I don't think so," he replied. "We find them here in Germany, or in Britain. They pull carts over at the playground; they're very popular with the children. Aren't you surprised to see them with the camels? It was an experiment that has turned out to be successful, because the two species don't compete: they eat different sorts of grass and you can see that they pay no attention to one another."

In spite of Dr. Windecker's deprecatory remarks, it was obvious that he has no need to be ashamed of the mammal collection, which contains a large number of comparatively rare animals and several that are very rare. Cologne has a pair of wolverines, several polar bears, some Kodiaks and a grizzly. It has a pair of black-striped wallabies. It has one of the very rare Javan tigers, and a cheetah, as well as a hooded seal, an elephant seal, and a pair of Przewalski horses. There is a group of ringtailed lemurs, and Cologne's tigers have successfully produced young almost every year for a long period. A white puma is exhibited next door to a black panther. There is a recently opened deer park, admirably landscaped with water and woods: Cologne owns a pair of Dybowski's deer, two pairs of Beisa oryx and a pair of European ibex, as well as commoner stock. The gibbon island evoked my admiration, though Dr. Windecker said that there was a disadvantage in keeping the little apes in such freedom, because nearby residents of the zoo complain that their calls early in the morning are earsplitting.

Inevitably, however, we returned to the subject of birds. Birds were on his mind. During a trip he'd just made to Australasia he acquired a number of new species, including birds of paradise. The bird collection already has a number of rare specimens that he could have boasted of: a pair of the Hawaiian nei-nei goose, some Cuban whistling ducks, seven Laysan teal, a bald eagle, two horned coot, two giant coot, seven Rothschild's mynah, and a variety of unusual pheasants. We paid a visit to the pool, which shares about half the space of an enclosure surrounded only by a low fence, the rest of which is greensward. Here a number of large birds sunned themselves.

"Last year the black-and-white storks bred for the first time," said Dr.

Windecker, "and this year some of the whites have begun nesting. There's our marabou, who's been around a long time." The large, heavy-set stork stood near the railing in a sulk, his beak nestled into the strange red pouch hanging from his throat. "I think he'd better be moved to a quieter place," said the director thoughtfully. "He's getting too old to be bothered by people; some day he might attack a child while it's offering him food."

"Oh, do you permit feeding?"

"No, we don't, but people feed all the same, and resent you when you tell them to stop. We have signs everywhere, but—there, do you see that?" As if on cue, a pretty girl with an elaborate pile of blond hair approached the marabou and leaned over the rail, offering him a piece of bread. When he raised his beak to take it, she teasingly withdrew it a bit.

Dr. Windecker went over and spoke to her in a low tone; I couldn't hear what he said. The girl gave a little shriek, turned around, and hurried off.

"What did you tell her?" I asked when he came back.

He smiled. "Oh, I didn't scold. I merely said that the bird might peck out an eye."

Dr. Bernhard Grzimek, director of the zoo at Frankfurt-am-Main, has long worked for the cause of nature conservation, and spends much time in East Africa, where he keeps an eye on the various animal reserves in the national parks. The eagerness with which his public-relations department seizes on every possible way to get publicity is often the subject of wryly humorous comment among the staffs of other zoos, but to speak fairly, it has a purpose beyond that of mere advertisement. It is part of a carefully planned campaign by which Dr. Grzimek and the Frankfurt Zoological Society educate the public in conservation. Close relations between the Garden and the city schools are fostered. In the Society's annual report for 1964—the 106th since the Society was founded—is the following passage: "Cooperation between the Education Officer (i.e., the zoo's) and the municipal education authorities is becoming closer each year. The number of school classes which receive instruction in biology in the Zoo . . . is constantly increasing and in the year 1964 reached a total of 664 classes. . . . In addition to this the Education Officer gave courses of lectures for the instruction of teachers so that they would be in the position to undertake modern teaching in biology in the school and to prepare the children for their lessons at the Zoo. In addition, a monthly circular is sent to all the Frankfurt schools and three times a year to all the schools in Hessen, Rheinland-Pfalz and Unterfranken."

Every attendant at the zoo is sent to spend several weeks in East Africa, observing wild animals at large. "In order to interest . . . Hessian Youth for the fauna," says the report for 1963, "we arranged a large handicraft competition where the children were asked to make animals. Prizes were given to the best works, the first prize: a photo safari to the Serengeti/Tanganyika, free of charge." In addition, Frankfurt's Zoological Society collects and sends to Africa funds for "Aid for the threatened animal world," which are distributed between Tanzania and the Cameroons, earmarked for various conservational institutions. Dr. Grzimek is adviser to the government of Tanganyika "on questions of nature conservation," and is honorary curator of the national park there. Added to all this the director, who is also a professor, gives a course of lectures in biology at the University of Giessen.

So, everything considered, I was not surprised to find that Dr. Grzimek was not in Frankfurt at the time of my visit, but in East Africa. As the only day I could go happened to be a Sunday, nobody else on the staff was there, either, but the public-relations man had sent me a sheaf of literature, and I knew what the highlights were. The Garden was full of visitors who had stood in line to get their admission tickets in spite of the fact that it was raining briskly. Nearly one and three-quarter million people clocked in at Frankfurt Zoo that year, and I think Sunday's crowds must have made up a considerable proportion of the figure. The zoo was founded in 1858, but was so badly bombed in the war that it had to be built again from scratch. This is a costly business, but otherwise it is not as dismaying as it appears; many a director of my acquaintance would rejoice at the opportunity to modernize his zoo so drastically. I knew from my printed aids that the most recent display is the birdhouse, including a pheasantry of the sort young Mr. Greed at Bristol pined for, with outdoor enclosures and indoor flight rooms planted with tropical vegetation. The list of Frankfurt's rare birds, like that of its rare animals, is long and includes Hume's pheasant, Blyth's tragopan, kagu, and Rothschild's mynah, but I had another goal in mind and only glanced at these creatures before going on to follow a large crowd that I hoped would lead me to the ape house. Instead I found myself going into a building labeled EXOTARIUM—a useful word that was new to me. All sorts of things were to be seen there: penguins in a huge refrigerated room, one Komodo dragon, three Galapagos land iguanas . . . To be sure, the throng was so thick I could hardly do more than check up on these before leaving the Exotarium and continuing my search.

Outside, reflecting with vexation that I hadn't even peeped at the two echidna listed among Frankfurt's specialties, I toyed with temptation.

Should I put off the ape house again, and try to find the tailless tenrec? I had never seen a tenrec at all that I knew of—a hedgehog-looking animal from Madagascar. Or the very rare white-tailed gnu? Or the only Mindanao tarsiers in captivity? Or the only zebra duikers, likewise? Wondering how the staff managed to get so much into a plot of ground that measures less than fifty acres, I detoured into the carnivore house to admire a progression of pictures above the cages, illustrating the family tree of carnivore evolution. Then I aimed once more for the ape house.

My dizzy head told me that one cannot go on a straight line at Frankfurt Zoo—one is led round and round; it is like moving in a gigantic hedged maze. Then, unexpectedly, there I was in the ape house. There, over the heads of the rain-soaked multitude, I was able at last to see what I had been seeking, the family of four Bonobo chimpanzees. If you aren't particularly interested in chimpanzees you won't understand why I was so fascinated by these animals, but I defy you to look into the matter without being caught up in the subject like me. This Bonobo, or *Pan paniscus*, is a separate species of chimpanzee, a dwarf ape first spotted and named in 1954, by Dr. Heinz Heck of Munich. Any chimp fancier learns early that all chimps don't look alike, even when they are all of the familiar species of *Pan satyrus*, or *Pan troglodytes*, as the usual species is also called. Some have lighter complexions than others. The facial expressions vary. The body-hair may be sparse or thick. The build may be heavy or light. Chimps aren't always black-haired: there are quite a few with reddish hair. But the Bonobo is more different than this. It has been aptly observed that he's like a cross between a chimpanzee and a gibbon, because he walks upright with a lithe, supple pace, he is smaller and lighter than *Pan satyrus*, and where *Pan satyrus*' ears are large and stick out, Bonobo's are small and lie neatly back against his head. Bonobo's face is light in color, and the teeth are not so prominent. When a dwarf chimp grimaces, pulling back his dark red lips from his teeth, the effect is startlingly like that of a human smile.

Not everyone can make these observations for himself, since at the moment there are only twenty-two Bonobo chimps known to exist in captivity, and they are distributed among only four zoos—Antwerp, Elizabethville, Frankfurt, and San Diego. There may be more, unrecognized as the special creatures they are, just as there must have been others made captive in the past before the species was identified. But these are all that are known about, and Frankfurt is the only place where a baby has been bred: the birth took place in 1963. I saw the young one frisking about; at the age of two it was still apt to cling to its mother. However, San Diego has hopes of breeding more dwarf chimps. It was there that I saw my first *Pan paniscus,* a frisky little character named Kakowet. At that time, early in '65, he was living in a large enclosure with a number of the bigger *Pan satyrus.* Dr. Schroeder, the director of San Diego, was walking with me, and when Kakowet saw him, though we were on the other side of a large trench at considerable distance from the chimp pit, he grinned and scampered along to keep up with us, running upright like a human child. The keeper smiled, too: "That's a character, that Kakowet," he said.

"Everybody around here feels that way," commented Dr. Schroeder. "I don't think we've ever had a more engaging animal. We suspect we've got another Bonobo, though we aren't sure yet if she really is. I think so, though. We're keeping them apart just now because they've almost reached mating age, and it works better if they meet as strangers. As you may know, animals brought up together sometimes get a kind of sibling complex, or are too used to each other or something—anyway, they lose interest."

A year later, when I returned to San Diego, the first animal I asked about was Kakowet. Dr. Schroeder said, "Yes, they're together now," so as soon as I got a chance I went to look at them. I found them in a cage of their own, with a tree growing in the center. The two little apes were going through an elaborate mating ritual, something that *Pan satyrus* never does. Kakowet's lady danced. She didn't dance like the big chimps, stamping on the ground, but stretched out her arms like a ballerina— or a gibbon—and whirled around in accomplished pirouettes, one after another, at the same time covering the ground in a circle around the tree. Kakowet watched her for a few minutes and then stretched out his arms in the same way and whirled after her. They were as graceful as birds.

I have been told that when the ritual is consummated, something I didn't have time to wait and see, the sexual embrace, like the dance, is unlike that of the big chimpanzees. *Pan satyrus* mate in the posture we call dogfashion, but *Pan paniscus* embrace face to face.

Dr. Heinz Heck of Hellabrun Zoo outside Munich is a member of a family that has been interested in zoological gardens for several generations. His father was a famous zoo man, his brother is a zoo man, and a nephew works in America with Roland Lindemann at the Catskill Game Farms. Dr. Heck himself has been with the zoo at Hellabrun ever since it was founded in 1930. He is a big man, tall and broad, with one overriding interest described in the International Zoo Yearbook as "breeding species that are threatened with extinction and back-breeding to species that are already extinct." The animals that interest him most are ungulates, which need a lot of grazing ground. Hellabrun meets this need—it extends for one hundred and eighty acres. But the staff can point with pride to triumphs in other fields as well. For one thing they have bred chimpanzees to the fourth generation. Moreover, "The first African elephant bred in Europe was ours," said Dr. Heck. "However, we don't go in deliberately for such records. We don't try to acquire rare animals. That's merely a question of money—you pay enough and you get the animal. Such rarities as we have are of purely scientific interest. Most of our species are well-known." He added with significant emphasis, that Hellabrun was not like certain other zoos he wouldn't name, and didn't pander to the public desire for sensation. "We have two aims," he said. "To awaken a love of animals in the public by broadening their knowledge, and to breed for conservation. We have been doing that for years, long before so many other zoos adopted the same ambition."

When Dr. Heck says "conservation," however, he means more than the mere preservation of species. For nearly forty years he has been working to restore—his own word—two species that have disappeared comparatively recently, within the time of man. One is the aurochs, forerunner of domestic cattle, the horned animal often seen in cave paintings. The other is the tarpan, a little wild horse even more recently extinct: it was in existence until a hundred years ago. Dr. Heck had only the cave paintings to use as model for his prehistoric cattle, but for the tarpan he had a couple of skins of the actual beast, and the head of one. He softened and stretched the hides, taking exquisite care in the process, and measured them, and made notes of the color of the hair. He then set to work breeding and cross-breeding in two lines, using modern cattle of many sorts for the aurochs and both domestic and wild horses for the tarpan. Now he has a true-breeding line of each which he is satisfied reproduces the two original species. At least, as Conway of the Bronx reported after seeing them, Heck's aurochs and tarpan constitute "a most fascinating and educated guess as to the appearance of these extinct animals."

In a stinging rain we paddled along soaked pathways. Like most herd zoos, Hellabrun is more like a farm than a garden, with great fields and paddocks dwarfing the buildings. On the way Dr. Heck talked of other conservational projects: tapirs breed at Hellabrun, as do chamois from the Alps and Siberian reindeer. He spoke admiringly of what Sweden has done for the capercaillie, the great Scottish bird that had nearly disappeared from its native country until Swedish zoologists took over the problem of protecting and breeding it. They have been so successful that they are beginning to restock Scotland with the capercaillie. Such work is obviously the stuff of Dr. Heck's life. He showed me wild goats from the Mediterranean, ancestor of the domestic goat and now existing in a wild state only in Crete and a few other Greek islands. "Here is the Alpine ibex, a breeding group," he continued; "it's quite prolific now. In one year I put out twenty in the mountains, and tomorrow we are sending more to the Alps, but we are still experimenting with what food is best for them, and what conditions of warmth."

He led me into a building, an Antler Museum he called it, which reminded me of certain great halls in English country houses. Antlers and other deer horns and heads of all sizes and shapes hung on the walls or were arrayed in cases, an oddly inappropriate display, I thought, in a place devoted to conservation, but Dr. Heck clearly saw nothing incongruous about it. "This is good for public instruction," he explained. "You see we have every kind of antler here, and pictures of the antler-bearing animals as well. That moose head comes from the Bronx, a present from Dr. Conway. Here we have pictures of the Asiatic and European mouflon and bighorn, and here's a white sheep from Alaska. An elk over there. There's another Alaskan animal, the snow goat we call it, but we shouldn't—it's a goat-antelope really." He looked proudly around the bristling walls. "We have other museums," he assured me. "They hold similar collections of red deer and sheep."

Back in the open, we resumed the rounds, looking at living beasts. "There are Nubian ibex, a species nearly killed off in Egypt," he said. "This is one of the last families in captivity, or in the wild either, for that matter. We're hoping to preserve them. Here are Arabian ibex. We started with two: now there are nine. Roe deer—it's very important to have roe deer in Bavaria, but they were deteriorating before we got to work, I got some from Lord Lucas of Wadham Court in England—a wonderful man. Those English roe deer are doing very well here: they grow bigger, and we're working to improve the breed altogether. Przewalskis? We have a few; we bred one only recently. The story of our herd is interesting. They had a stallion in London Zoo before the war, and they didn't want it: they consented to swap it with us for a big orang. The horse arrived here on the same day Neville Chamberlain came to Munich. Because that was a day of hope for Germans, I named the animal 'Neville.' Later Neville was the main stallion of our herd. When the war came, I put the horses into various different zoos, splitting them up in the hope that some, at least, might be saved. Then the Russians came into Germany; they took some back to Russia and put them into Askaniya-Nova, where they were joined by others from Turkestan Arabia. After the war they sent me one in exchange for one of ours here. . . . Lots of the so-called Przewalskis that you see in zoos are not purebred. You can tell from the mouth and the tail: the tail should have long hair. We don't keep many Przewalskis—four mares and one stallion is enough; that's the herd we have now. We've sent some to other zoos—Copenhagen, Berlin. . . . Here are my tarpans."

They were grazing in the field, small horses of strange and beautiful color, like slate or gunmetal, depending on the way the light struck them. The leader caught sight of Dr. Heck and trotted over to the fence to greet him. Others followed, to nuzzle our hands with their soft noses. Each had a dark stripe down the back, reminding me of Przewalskis or our own Western mustangs. The manes were short and stubby like those of zebras. They crowded up to be patted.

"Very tame," said Dr. Heck fondly, and then we moved on to view his other creations, the aurochs—huge creatures with just the same wide, curved horns I've seen in cave paintings. The males are nearly black. Young cows have a reddish color, but Dr. Heck said they darken as they grow older. "The public used to be confused about these animals, considering them to be the same sort of thing as the wisent. Of course they are not: they are of entirely different lines. The wisent is like your bison, and easily cross-breeds with the bison: he has nothing to do with the evolution of the common cow. The aurochs is progenitor of all domestic cattle. Today, now that we have these animals to show them, people can see the difference for themselves. They are convinced. They have learned."

CHAPTER 9

Hagenbeck's

□

One day in 1857, on Luneburger Heath between Bremen and Hamburg, a raccoon was shot. The affair caused much excited speculation among naturalists, for raccoons had always been considered strictly New World animals, but no explanation was forthcoming for half a century. Then Carl Hagenbeck, in his autobiography *Beasts and Men*, explained the mystery: that year of 1857, when he was eleven years old, he went by diligence with his father from St. Pauli in Hamburg, where they lived, to Bremen, where they picked up a small menagerie of American animals bought unseen by the elder Hagenbeck—an assortment of possums, monkeys, parrots, and a raccoon. Halfway back on the ride across country the raccoon escaped, but the Hagenbecks did not dare advertise for their lost animal: "We should have had the authorities down on us for letting loose wild beasts in the heart of Germany," confessed the writer.

Actually Carl's father, Gottfried Claas Carl Hagenbeck, was a fishmonger, but he was fond of animals, and became an animal dealer in addition, more or less by accident. For his own pleasure he usually kept at home a few pets—some goats, a cow, a few barnyard fowls, a monkey and a parrot, these last two exotic items obtained from the sailors who frequented St. Pauli. Like other fishmongers, Claas had a regular arrangement with certain fishermen who were pledged to bring him everything they caught, and one day these men, fulfilling their contract to the letter, brought in, in addition to the customary catch, six young seals that had been caught in the nets. Claas was pleased. He filled a couple of his wife's big laundry tubs with water, put the seals in, and placed them on show, charging his neighbors a Hamburg shilling—a penny or two—apiece for a look at the animals. A lot of people paid their way, and Claas was encouraged to take his seals to Berlin and exhibit them there. It was 1848, and the political situation grew so unsettled that he cut short the visit, but he had made a profit on the venture, and show business had him firmly in its toils. He enlarged the St. Pauli menagerie, procuring new seals—he had sold off the first ones in Berlin—and adding a polar bear, a few hyenas and some other animals, for which augmented show the public paid *four* shillings.

But it was a chancy way to make a living, and Claas was never able to relinquish his fish business. As Carl grew up he learned how to help in both trades, "a ceaseless round," he remembers, "of very hard, and not over-profitable, work." Fish money went into the animal-trade coffers more often than animals helped out with fish. When Carl was twelve, his father had a serious talk with him about plans for the future. Claas said the boy had better choose between the two businesses, and strongly urged him to opt for fish, which were safer. Carl voted for the animals anyway—a fortunate choice, as things were to turn out, for he had been born at the beginning of the great zoo boom, when cities all over Europe were trying to catch up with London's Zoological Gardens. Moreover, the race into Africa was beginning. Though it was fundamentally a political scramble, African animals were peripherally involved: the adventurers who flocked into the new territory learned that they could defray the expenses of their trips and make handsome profits by killing or capturing lions, hippos, giraffes and other creatures which they could sell dead or alive. Carl, son of a Hamburg fishmonger, stepped straight into a brisk new trade. He moved from one city to another, taking orders from zoo directors and circus managers, or investigating the reports of African hunters. Soon he was finding it more satisfactory to hire hunters of his own. Still in his twenties, he was known as the top animal dealer of Europe: he was only twenty-eight when he sold £3000 worth of animals to Barnum, and afterward Barnum bought exclusively from Hagenbeck's.

It was not long before Carl was intimately connected with the mechanics of hunting and collecting. Casanova, his best hunter in Africa, a man who had many feats to his credit, was on his way home with a large consignment when Carl got word that the Italian was lying very ill in Suez and couldn't proceed further. Carl therefore set out with a younger brother to take over. As was necessary in those pre-Canal days, the Hagenbecks disembarked at Alexandria and continued by train. Puffing into Suez station they had their first glimpse of the results of Casanova's enterprise when elephants and giraffes pushed their heads out of the windows of the next train where they were being lodged.

But this was only a small part of the collection, as the men realized
when they reached the hotel and found the courtyard chockablock with
animals. "Elephants, giraffes, antelopes and buffalo were tethered to
the palms; sixteen great ostriches were strolling about loose; and in addition there were no fewer than sixty large cages containing a rhinoceros,
lions, panthers, cheetahs, hyenas, jackals, civets, caracals, monkeys, and
many kinds of birds."

Casanova died almost immediately after they arrived, and the Hagenbecks had to take over the whole affair. Even for men without encum-
brances, travel was a long, weary process, and with Casanova's creatures
the train trip back to Alexandria was a nightmare for all concerned.
It was necessary to add to the caravan a hundred goats to supply milk
for the youngest animals and meat for the carnivores, along with tons
of hay, bread, and vegetables. On the way to the station the ostriches
got loose and had to be recaptured. Then one of the railway trucks
caught fire. Still, they got to the ship and sailed off to Trieste, where
all the beasts were unloaded, and the Hagenbecks took them away by
train, going to Hamburg by way of Vienna, Dresden and Berlin, at
each of which cities they unloaded a number of animals for the local
zoo. Even so, with what they had left when they got home the old
house in St. Pauli could hardly accommodate them, and it was not
long before the Hagenbecks moved to bigger premises, a house with a
two-acre garden attached.

The boom in animal importing started to decline in the 1870s. Too
many hunters had moved in on the act, and supply exceeded demand.
Carl looked around for some way to extend operations. Though his
attention had long been engrossed in trade, he still hankered after that
other branch of work that had also fascinated his father; showmanship.
Now, through a friend, he stumbled on his chance to get back in it.
The friend, an animal painter, was at the house looking at some reindeer that Carl had just imported. He remarked that Hagenbeck should
have brought in some of the human beings that lived in reindeer country,
along with the deer: a family of Lapps would be very picturesque.
He spoke half in jest, but Carl eagerly seized on the idea. In those
simple days, when frontier regulations hardly existed, it was easy to
find a Norwegian willing to bring over to Hamburg a group of Lapps,
and soon there they were, complete with skis, sledge and reindeer, "three
little men dressed in skins, . . . a mother with a tiny infant in her
arms and a dainty little maiden about four years old, standing shyly
by her side." The human curiosities calmly put up their tent in the
Hagenbecks' back yard and settled down. Carl was in business. "All

Hamburg came to see this genuine 'Lapland' in miniature," he reported contentedly. The specimens were equally content, and very obliging. For each performance they would catch their reindeer with lassos and milk them, or drive the sledge around like Father Nicholas, while the Germans looked on.

After the Lapps were repatriated, Hagenbeck brought in real live Nubians: they were supplanted in their turn by Eskimos from Greenland, who brought with them a kayak in which their leader paddled around in the sea, now and then rolling completely over to give the spectators a special thrill. The Eskimos proved such a success that Carl took them touring to Berlin and Dresden and Paris. From that time on, he was almost never without an "ethnographical show," as he called these exhibitions—Somalis, Indians, Kalmucks, and many others. Without realizing it, he was following in the footsteps of Hippolyte, the Medici cardinal of an earlier century who maintained a human zoo. One of the largest Hagenbeck ethnographical shows was that of the Ceylonese in 1884. There were sixty-seven of these people, and Carl took them "all over Germany and Austria" along with twenty-five elephants and a number of cattle.

Back in triumph from the Ceylonese tour, Hagenbeck reflected that the public had probably had enough of ethnology for a while. At any rate he had a new venture in mind: animal training. At that time, trainers' methods were harsh and cruel. They whipped their beasts to make them go through their paces, and chastised them with red-hot irons. Carl had always been distressed by these practices, and felt that they should not be necessary. In 1887, with the Ceylonese safely repatriated, he set up a circus in the garden of the Hamburg house, hired a trainer who agreed to work according to his employer's newfangled notions, and started trying out these notions on dogs and cats, training them to do tricks without the use of force—"except in cases of gross disobedience." It worked quite as well as, if not better than, the usual whips-and-hot-irons routine, and the trainer was convinced. Now Carl was ready to try out his system on big cats. He selected twenty-one possible lions, then sifted the candidates and discarded from the program every animal that did not respond properly: slow or intractable lions were dropped. Only four passed all tests, but their success was "astounding." "They carried out all sorts of tricks," he reported proudly, "the climax of the performance coming when the trainer harnessed three of the mighty carnivores to a chariot and drove triumphantly around the cage." Hagenbeck first produced his wonderful act at the Cirque d'Hiver in Paris in 1889, and followed up this show with a lengthy and profitable tour. Soon animal acts trained according to the Hagenbeck method were much in demand at world fairs and expositions, especially in America.

Carl was also getting interested in breeding experiments. What with this, and his new researches into acclimatization of wild animals, and the circus and the numerous cages, he was feeling restricted, and so were the animals. Resolved to leave the city's limits altogether and move into open country, he bought land near a village, Stellingen. He was somewhat worried at the prospect of being such a long distance from Hamburg, especially as at Stellingen there was very limited communication with that city, but it was comforting to know that at last he would be in a position where he could put a number of theories into practice. The zoological garden that he was planning would be different from any other in the world. "I desired, above all things, to give the animals the maximum of liberty," he wrote. "I wished to exhibit them not as captives, confined within narrow spaces, and looked at between bars, but as free to wander from place to place within as large limits as possible . . . I desired to refute the prevailing notion that luxurious and expensive houses with complicated heating apparatus were necessary for keeping wild animals alive and healthy . . . I wished my new park to be a great and enduring example of the benefits that can be wrought by giving the animals as much freedom and placing them in as natural an environment as possible. A certain point must be fixed in the garden from which might be seen every kind of animal moving about in apparent freedom and in an environment which bore a close resemblance to its own native haunts."

He planned artificial mountains for chamois and wild sheep and ibex, wide commons for the plains animals, glens for carnivores that would not be railed or barred but separated from the public by deep trenches. He would need room, too, for the other animals, those not part of his zoo but destined to go on to customers—for Hagenbeck's had never abandoned the animal trade, and was now dealing in hundreds every year. In 1904 he had to accommodate forty-three elephants at the same time. He was well out of the St. Pauli house. Even now, before the park opened, he wanted more space: after much business activity, which entailed disposing of his Hamburg land and buying more acreage in Stellingen, he was ready to start construction. This was in 1902.

Hagenbeck employed engineers, architects, and sculptors. They built backgrounds in accordance with his vision—a "mountain landscape" for African animals, a "Polar Panorama" for animals of the frozen spaces, and a number of "glens," separated from the public by ditches, for the carnivores. The ditches, or moats, were designed as carefully as possible, according to knowledge Hagenbeck had gained while training animals. Each species has a maximum leap, he learned—the highest possible point up, and another maximum distance across land. He had measured them all. The moat for the lions must be not narrower than a certain distance. Another distance was needed for tigers, and yet another for bears. As an added precaution, Carl saw to it that there was never an open path in the enclosure leading easily to the ditch—in other words, an animal could not work up the speed to make a running jump across.

The park, opened in 1907, was immediately successful, even famous. Zoos far and wide adopted moated enclosures in frank imitation of Stellingen, and Hagenbeck's went from triumph to triumph. A list recently published at the zoo lists some outstanding events in the firm's subsequent history:

1909: The Empress of Germany opened the first German ostrich-farm in Stellingen.

1910: Elephant seals and rare species of penguin first introduced to Germany by Lorenz Hagenbeck.

1911: Opening of the Rome Zoo, built and equipped by Carl Hagenbeck and his son Heinrich. This is one of the five zoos in Europe and the U.S.A. built on the Hagenbeck model.

1913: 60 species of mammals, brought back alive for the first time by the firm of Carl Hagenbeck, who died at the age of 69. . . .

1931: Zoo equipment and animals supplied to the Colonial Exhibition in Paris.

1933: The first Far Eastern tour of a German circus. The HAPAG liner *Saarland* carried Carl Hagenbeck's Circus to Yokohama. Opening in Tokyo. Followed by a world tour.

1936: Extension of the Zoo with new open-air enclosures for elephants and rhinos, pony-stud, Indian jungle etc. Work has been going on since 1927, under the direction of Heinrich Hagenbeck. The Circus is on its third South American tour (Uruguay and Argentina.)

1943: 80% of the Stellingen Zoo and the winter quarters of the Circus destroyed in 90 minutes in an air-raid. 8 people and 450 animals killed. After the death of his father Heinrich Hagenbeck in 1945, Carl-Heinrich Hagenbeck took charge of the reconstruction of the Zoo.

1948: Centenary. Clearing-up operations more or less completed. Gifts of animals arrive from abroad. . . .

1950: Hagenbeck's animal-collectors again go overseas and return with a wide range of specimens. . . .

In 1960, the historian was able to report that with the finishing off of the "Troparium" the reconstruction of the zoo following wartime devastation was complete.

Hagenbecks almost automatically go in for zoo work. Cousins, uncles, and, most of all, direct descendants of Carl find it perfectly natural that they should tie themselves to the Hagenbeck Zoo and its subsidiary activities. The distant relative of Ceylon who planned and made Colombo's zoo was simply obeying the family code, as are Carl's grandchildren, Carl-Heinrich and Dietrich Hagenbeck, the sons of Heinrich, co-owners and directors today at Stellingen. It was Carl-Heinrich I met the day I went to see the zoo—making the trip, incidentally, with the greatest of ease straight from Hamburg's airport. Carl Hagenbeck need not have worried about communication with the big city when he moved to Stellingen. Stellingen is part of Hamburg now, and soon a Hamburg citizen can go to the zoo from any part of town by subway. A new station is being built just outside the park gates for this particular purpose.

Mr. Hagenbeck's office is in one of the pre-war buildings a good walk from the entrance, nestled in a copse. Well-grown trees and hedges of rhododendron hem it in.

"It's important to remember that this is a completely private affair," he began. "Never since the zoo was first opened have we had the help of government or municipal funds of any sort: nobody has ever subsidized us. For this reason we place limits on what we try to do. We can't afford and don't want big modern houses or laboratories like those you may have seen in some other places. Our idea is still what it was originally when Carl Hagenbeck built the place—we want a park with invisible barriers to hold the animals, and animals that can live best in this climate. It's not a collection of rarities, but of the simple, expected animals that most visitors look for: lions and zebras, the expected things. Our animals are healthy and they breed well—we like to think we take good care of them. As far as the permanent collection is concerned, that is the whole story of Hagenbeck's, but we are collectors for other zoos as well, and, of course, we also sell our own surplus." Mr. Hagenbeck was showing a modesty rare in some of his contemporaries, I reflected, and wasn't proffering information on features he could well have boasted about. I had to ask questions to discover that they were in fact pretty proud of one rarity at least. "We have a breeding herd of onagers, the Persian wild ass, you know," he admitted. "We have sold quite a few of those. They are almost extinct now in Persia, in the wild state." Przewalskis? No, Hagenbeck's kept none, though, as he reminded me, his grandfather had brought back the first of these Mongolian horses ever seen in Western Europe.

The famous Hagenbeck Circus is a thing of the past. One of Hagenbeck's uncles used to run it, and when this uncle died in 1953, the circus was closed down altogether. The only remaining bit of the setup is a little animal show that is given daily at the "Training School," that building in which Carl Hagenbeck developed his theories of how to train animals without cruelty. Later in the day I attended the performance, sitting with a number of families and small children around a little circus ring in which a monkey walked a tightrope, clutching a frilly doll's parasol in one hand, a baboon rode a pony around the arena, jumping on and off in approved equestrian fashion and leaping through paper-covered hoops, a young elephant balanced on a rolling barrel, and sea lions went through their paces. There was an old-world touch to these acts: the troupe of monkeys, for example, was pulled around the ring in a tiny carriage of a design reminiscent of Queen Victoria's days—but then, there is much in Germany generally that reminds one of Queen Victoria. I felt that the show existed chiefly because of the proprietors' filial piety, but I might have been wrong; it was obviously a great attraction as well. On that rainy weekday, scarcely a seat went unoccupied.

The morning, however, was given over to sight-seeing with the director. From the moment we left the office I was on guard, determined not to be startled or fooled by any optical illusions. After all, in the nearly sixty years that have elapsed since Hagenbeck's park opened, a lot of other zoos—all of them that matter, in fact—have adopted the hidden-barrier scheme, and I've seen dozens of such enclosures. I'd already had a taste of Hagenbeck's original technique when I entered the main gate. There, as one steps inside, Kodiak bears loom up on the right, sauntering about a clearing that looks for all the world like part of the ground on which one is standing. Carl called this display his shop window. But now as I walked along the winding path with Mr. Hagenbeck and a strange-looking hare with exceedingly long legs lolloped across the path directly ahead of us, I could not accept the idea of optical illusion.

"It is no use telling me that that animal is in an enclosure," I said firmly.

Mr. Hagenbeck laughed. "Of course it isn't. We let our Patagonian cavies free to roam about, like the birds. You'll see a lot of free-ranging demoiselle cranes and jungle fowl and sacred ibis and cavies."

A lot of trees and tall hedges shaded much of the path system. I spoke of this, and Mr. Hagenbeck said, "Yes, you will notice how all our paths are marked with arrows and numbered, so the visitor can't get lost or double on his tracks. It's necessary because the woods are so dense. Yet all this vegetation, every tree and bush, was brought in, you know—planted. When my grandfather bought the land it was just a potato patch. A *flat* potato patch, at that." The path, with a final bend, brought us out into the open and we paused. "Here," he said, gesturing ahead. "This is one of the original panoramas, the African Plains."

A stream separated us, as if by nature, from a meadow where zebras and ostriches grazed peacefully together. Back of them was a range of striated rocks and boulders, closed in on either side by trees; the whole thing a cunning stage set, though a stage set with unusual depths. Between these tree-banks, and looking a long way off, reared the head of a mountain, steep as the hills in traditional Chinese paintings.

"It's all artificial," Mr. Hagenbeck said, "mountain, rocks, everything, in fact, but the animals and vegetation. As I said, this was a part of the earliest zoo, and for the most part it survived the bombing, though we had to rebuild the mountain. It's convincing, isn't it?"

He led the way beyond to another original exhibit, the epoch-making lion pit, or glen, without bars. "My grandfather called it the Carnivore Glen, and there are some photographs of him surrounded by lions and tigers there in the middle," Mr. Hagenbeck said. "All the rock is made of the same concrete composition as the mountain you saw, and in the rear where they can't be seen are rooms where the lions go at night. When necessary we can heat those rooms, but we don't keep the animals warm except in unusually bitter weather. Over here"—he walked on as he spoke, around a sharp bend in the road—"we have elands (we are still in the African section, you understand)—it is a breeding group. Nice beasts, elands. Then come the giraffes, and beyond them are smaller ungulates, and—here we are, right at the foot of the mountain. Barbary sheep: they have the freedom of the mountain." We rounded the structure until we found some bright reddish-brown animals of familiar shape. "What are those?" asked Mr. Hagenbeck, like a schoolteacher.

Feeling rather foolish, I gave the obvious answer, "Goats."

"Yes, but goats with a difference," he said. "They come from Robinson

Crusoe's island, San Fernando. In the days of sail, sailors left the ancestors of these goats on the island to assure themselves of a meat supply when they might come again. Then they stopped coming and the goats simply ran wild. Originally domesticated, they became wild animals, a kind of reverse process that often happens to domestic animals when they get the chance. But this lot, being isolated, remained absolutely characteristic of the old stock. After hundreds of years on San Fernando, they are invariably of that unusual color, reddish-brown."

We had turned and turned again until I'd lost my sense of direction. Now the path branched away from the mountain, and he said, "We have left the African section of the zoo. It is all geographically divided, you know—the four corners of the earth. Here we have South American animals, and next we'll see Australian. Actually we've crossed most of the old park and from here on, until we turn back across the top, we'll be in what's called the new portion. When my grandfather moved out here, a road ran straight across what is now the estate. It was one of the zoo boundaries. Then the city of Hamburg made new plans and altered some of the roads outside, and my father arranged to take over the entire street and some of the area beyond. He filled in the street, raising it to park level, but he left that stretch unplanted with trees, thus keeping a ready-made avenue or *allée*. Can you see what I mean?" We stopped at the edge of a greensward, or ride, that swept between trees all the way up to the horizon—or seemed to. "You can't see them, but there are many pathways crossing this allée. From where we are standing we are quite close to one busy path with people on it, but you can't see a thing." It was true. The green avenue seemed quite unbroken, and nobody was in sight for a long way around.

An enormous jardiniere of blue-and-white porcelain stood in the meadow to our left, incongruously, like one of those irrelevant objects in a Dali landscape. It must have been at least seven feet high. The meadow also held a number of cranes, stalking about and scratching at the grass. In the distance I could see what looked very much like, and indeed was, a Japanese arch, or *torii*, and beyond its red-lacquer glitter, surely there was another one? Mr. Hagenbeck shrugged it off when I asked about these objects, muttering something about the oriental section; and I gathered that I was anticipating things. The Far East came later. For the moment I was to be shown India: another glen, this time for tigers, which had stone caves, an overhanging ledge, and a wide pool. I recognized the glen immediately: I had seen it copied half-a-dozen times. Mr. Hagenbeck called my attention to the pool, a section of filled moat, saying, "Tigers like to swim. They should always have water."

Temporarily we had been in another part of the forest. Now the trees gave way again to a clearing where we stood on a gently arched bridge over a stretch of ground that gave way to a lake. (That landscape gardener employed by Carl must have been a brilliant designer. Today I still have the impression that the lake was enormous, stretching off for miles, though it couldn't have been.) On the low ground, scattered over the grass or half-immersed in the shallows, were great motionless figures of prehistoric lizards. There was an Iguanodon, and that dinosaur often pictured in comic strips, and the sort with frills down its back. An alligatorlike creature was crawling out of the water, jaws agape. Though these were indubitably the figures I had seen copied in Japanese zoos, they were immeasurably better and far more cunningly placed.

"The man who made them was Josef Pallenberg, the best sculptor of his time," said Mr. Hagenbeck, pleased by my admiration. "My father got him to do them. He went to immense trouble to have them just right, going to La Plata to measure the bones that have been unearthed there. They're beautifully done. Look at the way he hinted at the muscles beneath the skin . . . These figures are fifty years old. Some were destroyed by bombs, but the model of every one made by Pallenberg still exists in the museum at La Plata, and we've been able to repair some of the damage."

Across the bridge we were in Far East country. One knew it from the Burmese temple on the lake, where ornate lions, one at each corner, guarded two staircases that led down to a platform standing on short pillars over the water, and grotesque animals guarded the walls everywhere. This place was built by Burmese wood carvers who came over in the old days as part of one of Carl Hagenbeck's ethnological exhibits. Like many of the surrounding objects it was badly damaged during the bombing, but has been restored. In this portion of the park Heinrich Hagenbeck had placed a number of other objects not usually seen in zoos—large Japanese bronzes. One of them was sheared off near the base by a bomb. The present generation of Hagenbecks have left the base there, with a plaque to explain the circumstances: what with one thing and another, it was with a slight sense of dislocation that I found myself back in a zoo when we arrived at the pachyderm house.

To one side of the shelter an Indian rhino stood reflectively, after the manner of his kind. His mate had produced a calf and was soon expecting another—one of the out-of-the-way records that Mr. Hagenbeck was modest about. A group of children were feeding a row of elephants, African and Asian together: "Yes, we allow an amount of feeding," said Mr. Hagenbeck, "within reason, of course. Nobody can feed our meat-eating or fish-eating animals, nor giraffes, nor apes, but elephants, antelopes and deer can have bread and fruit. We sell little cakes for that purpose. We don't like any feeding, but the public do, and—"

We had arrived at a large paddock, well fenced. Inside the onagers were frisking, pale gold in color, smaller than most horses but larger than domestic donkeys. Indeed, it was difficult to think of them as related to donkeys at all, they were so lithe and graceful and lively. One recognized Mr. Hagenbeck and came up to have his nose rubbed. Then he turned to inspect me, did not approve, laid back his long ears and bared his teeth, and leaped into the air, kicking out his rear hoofs. Mr. Hagenbeck chuckled and said proudly that they could be very fierce. He added as we departed, "At sunset when the rays catch them in just the right light, those coats turn a strange color, almost lavender." I looked back for a last glimpse of the golden beasts. Another one frisked and kicked at nothing, out in the middle of the field.

We passed by a herd of zebu cattle, the humped animals of India, and I said something about having seen the same sort in Brazil. "Brazilian cattle breeders like them best," I said, "and try to get cattle with some zebu blood at any rate, because they can walk long distances without losing much weight. Herders have to take their stock for miles in Brazil."

"Yes, I know. My grandfather introduced those cattle to South America, and most of them today—like the ones you saw—are descended from his stock."

Carl Hagenbeck believed in mixing up his animals if they got on together and were accustomed to similar conditions. Sometimes he even sacrificed his customary adherence to geographical boundaries when making these experiments, and to some extent his grandsons do the same thing. At least they mix up the anthropoid apes. In a sort of kindergarten cage, among seesaws and climbing apparatus, a number of young chimpanzees and orangutans played together. One thing struck me immediately about this group—the unusual liveliness of the little orangs. In the ordinary way these red-headed apes are comparatively quiet and slow-moving even while young; as they grow older they slow down even more. But these children were as lively as their companions, the chimpanzees. One orang, walking upright, carried a rubber tire across the cage floor with the solitary single-mindedness of a three-year-old human, until he came to a bench with projecting seat slats. On one set of these slats he carefully hung the tire and stepped back to admire the effect. Along came a chimp who pushed the tire off. Then the little apes went into a wrestling match.

"That's the idea," said Mr. Hagenbeck when I spoke of what I had noticed. "Our orangs don't get a chance to be lazy—the chimps keep them too busy." He looked reflectively at another orang in the cage next door, an older animal that was presumably free to be as lethargic as he wanted, since no chimpanzees were with him. He wasn't lethargic, though. He moved about at quite a brisk pace. "Orangs are very intelligent," the director said. "Probably they are cleverer than chimps, but they can't be bothered to prove it."

He showed me into the children's playground close by, saying, "This has been built all over again since the bombing, and it's bigger and better than it used to be. Most children prefer playing here than looking at animals; many parents bring them here just for the sake of the playground. Still, we've put their special collection next door—here they are; rabbits, guinea pigs, small beasts generally, because children like little animals, not big ones. We are now entering the old zoo again. I want to show you another original display that dates from my grandfather's time."

It was the Polar Panorama. Polar bears walked around a rocky hillside, and just as we got there one dived into the water beneath. It all looked craggy and very cold. To the left, in what I would have sworn was the same water, seals were diving after fish a keeper threw for them. And at this point, in spite of my resolution earlier in the day, I blotted my copybook and was caught. Earnestly I said, "But you can't keep those animals all together in one place, Mr. Hagenbeck! Don't the bears eat the seals?"

He smiled triumphantly. "Of course they would if they could get across, but they can't. Clever, isn't it?"

It made things no better to reflect that the trick is as old as the park itself. Still, I'm in good company: even Thomas Edison was once a victim of Hagenbeck's optical illusions. Visiting the zoo in 1911, he rounded a clump of trees and found himself staring into the eyes of a large lion only a few feet away. Nothing seemed to separate them, not so much as a bush. Thomas Edison was scared stiff.

CHAPTER 10

Russia

☐

In honesty this chapter should be headed "Russia, a Small Part Of." I tried to see more of it than I did, but as anybody with experience in these matters can testify, it is impossible to break the pattern of Russian tourism. I started trying well ahead of time, writing from home to a man high up in Zoocentre Moskva, the government department that manages all zoological gardens in the country. Dr. Henry Field and his wife Julia had given me his name. The official actually replied—not exactly eagerly, I admit—to say that I should look him up when I reached Moscow and he would see what he could do then, but it was a pity, he added, that I couldn't arrange to come on a regular exchange, as then everything would be much easier. It hardly needs saying that I couldn't begin to fix up such an exchange. How does one go about finding a Russian who wants to visit American zoos in order to write about them? Even if I found him, could he get permission from his government and mine to do it? One way and another, my desire to see places off the regular Intourist beat was doomed from the start, but I thought I ought to go on trying, so I took a list of the zoos I wanted to see, headed by Askaniya-Nova in the Ukraine, and visited the Intourist office in London, where I was to apply for my ticket. There, as soon as I showed it to the girl in charge she went into a terrible dither. She stammered for a while, then told me to go away, please, and come back later. When I had done this I found another woman in her place, an older one, who read the list without flinching and looked up the places on an enormous map. I didn't take much heart, however, from this sign of interest, because she kept shaking her head as she did so. Finally she gave her answer: Intourist took people to *none* of those places, and that settled it. But it didn't matter, she said:

Moscow and Leningrad both have zoos, and I would find them most interesting.

She wasn't close-mouthed. At mention of Suchumi, for instance, she said sharply, "That is where scientists torture monkeys," with a look on her face indicating that even in scientifically minded Russia there are a few adherents of the anti-vivisectionist school. As for my chief aim, Askaniya-Nova, I gathered from what she said that unless I worked a few miracles in Moscow I would never in the world get there—and she was right. I haven't been able to find out why this place is so shrouded in secrecy. It sounds as if it were nothing more nor less than an admirable game farm, with its special interests, to quote the *Yearbook*, "acclimatisation, hybridisation and breeding of exotic animals." It has plenty of land—about twenty-four hundred acres—and I've seen photographs of some of the animals, including an eland being milked. Eland's milk is believed, in Russia, to be very good for invalids. The man who took the pictures is a Canadian. I would like to know how he arranged his exchange, but I've never found out.

In Moscow it went on being no use. The official who had answered my letter was harder, now, to get in touch with, and Intourist people kept saying that it was all very difficult, so finally I gave up, as they'd known I would, and we all relaxed. Still, fair is fair. Certainly I was shown the zoos of Moscow and Leningrad very thoroughly, with special guides and everything.

Officially, Moscow Zoo claims an annual attendance of three million, and Leningrad is awarded a million and a half, a division calculated in density, one might think, down to the last bit of ground, since Moscow extends for just under forty acres and Leningrad's size is exactly half that. Obviously an approximation, it is probably not far out: Moskovskii Zoologichesski Park was pretty well crowded the day I was taken to see it, and they told me that even more people come on Sundays. A large, pretty lake was the first feature that leaped to the eye. Unlike other zoo lakes I've seen, it was fenced. Beyond were the cages and enclosures. This zoo was opened in 1864, in the days when most large European cities were hurrying to catch up with England's Regent's Park, and I doubt if it has changed much since then. Like so many other edifices in Russia, these buildings give a strong impression of pure nineteenth century. What was good enough for Czarist animals is good enough for USSR fauna, and no newfangled, corrupt, decadent modern architect has been permitted to spoil things. At least that was my first interpretation, but later I noticed a few details that may be put down to more enlightened ideas. The distance between cage and railing is admirably wide, even though the cages are still lined up in straight rows, like showcases in a school museum, and there was no easily perceptible scheme of arrangement. I looked for something Julia Field had mentioned, and saw it immediately—the close-meshed wire that covers a number of the cage bars, like reinforcements. She was told when she asked about it that the wire is there to prevent people from throwing stones at the animals, but I found it hard to believe that any members of the Russian public would dare to do such a thing, even though they might want to. According to *my* guide the wire is to keep people from feeding the animals. There was no way of knowing which version is correct.

The guide, a young female biologist from the staff, conversed with me through my Intourist interpreter, so our chances of getting intimate were limited. Nevertheless I thought I had a reasonable notion of what she was like; there seemed to be little difference between her and a number of other zoo people I've encountered who live a long way from Moscow. She seemed just as keen on her job, asking a number of questions about developments abroad, on which she was well informed. Of course the first important exhibit she showed me was An-An the giant panda, whose betrothal had not yet been arranged. The girl said proudly that many delegations came from all over the world to look at him. He was housed in unusual grandeur, in a special large cage with an enclosed space in the back. A tree, a swing, a rubber tire and various other playthings were disposed around his front yard, and among these the black-and-white animal, like a live Teddy bear, turned somersaults or rolled over on his back with all the ebullience of youth. He is younger than Chi-Chi, who had already outgrown that playful stage, but the biologist told me that he had been in Moscow for more than eight years, and was still in re-markably good health. This was a triumph, considering how often zoos in other countries, especially the United States, have tried to acclimatize giant pandas and failed in the attempt.

"We keep the house artificially warm for him in the winter," said the girl, "but he seems to prefer staying outdoors most of the time. He doesn't mind the cold."

No, he wouldn't, I reflected: it can get pretty cold in the mountains of his native country. But what about his food? The reason given when pandas died in America, I recalled, was that it was impossible to give them the right kind of bamboo, which they simply had to have. "No, we don't worry about bamboo," said the biologist. "He gets birch twigs to eat, and likes them. You see, we haven't got any bamboo."

"And he takes birch twigs without any trouble?"

"Oh yes, he likes birch. He has a very good appetite. He likes lots of tea, too, with plenty of sugar."

When Chi-Chi got to Moscow later, she too took to birch twigs without the slightest difficulty.

After An-An, the rest of the zoo seemed to merit little more than a cursory glance, but I looked at everything. Their black Australian swans, she told me, live in the open the year round, even when the thermometer drops to twenty below freezing. What's more, they nest and lay eggs every spring. Then there's an orangutan from Borneo, which has lived in Russia in good health for thirteen years. Some of the animals had labels on their cages to say that they were gifts to the zoo from this or that general on his return from service abroad: a lion, a group of trained bears. Three newly arrived Père David's deer—sent, perhaps, by the Duke of Bedford, who was soon to visit Russia—and a kulan, or wild ass; a Przewalski horse from Askaniya-Nova: a rhino: a hippo which was, she said, a "good hooligan" because he liked to splash people. Raccoon dogs, native to the eastern regions of the USSR, offer no problem and breed in the zoo. Two Indian elephants were living in separate quarters because they fight each other. "They like vodka," she said.

Like other tourists I had been much struck by the number of women in Russia who do jobs I'd always thought of as man's work, such as cleaning the floors of airport buildings, mending roads and carrying things. Women take tickets at the opera and on the subway. The surprising thing is not so much that they are women, I suppose, as that they're such *old* women. After a few days of watching them tottering about their tasks, I came to the conclusion that the entire system depends on them, and the government would have a grave crisis on its hands if they were suddenly withdrawn from circulation. I was more than ever impressed by this state of affairs when I got to the zoo, where the Russian female really comes into her own. There old women are the keepers and the cleaners, bossing all the animals around. When, showing me the chimpanzee collection in an unusually good and modern group of cages, the biologist wanted to take me inside the railing where we could be at closer quarters, she couldn't do it because the necessary old lady was missing. We had to go and look for her, finding her at last with another old crone on a park bench, having a pleasant gossip—both, of course, wearing caps and aprons over their black dresses. Russia's workwomen always wear that outfit, no matter what the job—swabbing out lavatories, running elevators, or sitting guard over the room keys on hotel floors. I thought this particular keeper, annoyed at being interrupted, was going to refuse to help us out, but I misjudged her: that peevish expression was just her usual one. She did grumble a little, but she searched under the apron, through voluminous folds of rusty black, and came up with what was wanted, a key of Gargantuan size. Leading us back to the chimpanzees, she unlocked a padlock of equally impressive dimensions and let us in, afterward standing like a sentinel to watch and make sure we didn't steal one of the great apes. While this went on, across the pathway another crone was cleaning out a bear cage with a broom—just the right appliance for her, come to think of it—while the bears cowered in the furthest possible corner.

So that was Moscow. Leningradskii Zoologichesskii Park was prettier, and I thought seemed fresher, though I don't know why it should be. It was opened in 1867, not long after Moscow's, and according to my guides, a young man and a girl from the staff, was founded by one Gebhardt of Holland. Perhaps they meant "designed" rather than "founded," or perhaps Mr. Gebhardt was a wealthy resident of St. Petersburg, fond of animals. I found it difficult to pursue such questions through an interpreter—no matter how intelligent the interpreter may be (and Olga was a bright girl), the subject finally becomes too much trouble, and one drops it. Instead, we worked up a lot of steam on elephants. Elephants were the first animals ever kept at the Leningrad Zoo, they told me—perhaps the millionaire Gebhardt had a fixation on them—and ever since its inception the park has never been without at least a few of them, mostly Asian. One of their bull elephants, now sixty years old, has had a checkered career: before going into show business he was an honest working animal in Vietnam. "At a match factory," added the youth. I suppose it's logical enough: elephants haul timber. Another elephant, a cow named Betty, was a victim of the siege of Leningrad, killed at the age of forty by a stray shell. Obviously the thought of this outrage still rankled in my guides' breasts, and it is true that the war record of the zoo lives up to Leningrad's proudest principles, for while the town's humans were withstanding the siege, which lasted nearly two and a half years and cost them almost a million lives, a school for workers' children was living in the zoo park, taking care of a hippo cow, Beauty by name. Every day the children carried water to Beauty and scrounged for her fodder. Like everybody else in Leningrad, Beauty went hungry more often than not, but she came out of the ordeal and lived a long time afterwards.

The guides enjoyed showing their birds, some in a pleasant and large aviary, others at large on the lake. Penguins do well there: I could hardly believe it on that torrid August day, though the heavy boots I'd seen for sale in shop windows kept me reminded of the region's bitter winters.

Soon we ran into trouble on names, which Olga's dictionary didn't always include. What species, for example, are the penguins the Russians call by the lovely name of Gold-hairs? Other birds were unmistakable—the cassowary, for instance—but I concentrated on Russian specimens: two kinds of pelican, cranes, a number of native geese and ducks, a "Sultan fowl," like a jungle fowl, from Baku, Russian skylarks, and such game birds as grouse and partridge.

The zoo's emblem is the polar bear, and there is a flourishing family on show, with a recently born pair of young ones. Not unnaturally in a Russian zoo, there were many other bears as well. A brown one shares his cage with a dog, and I was assured that neither of these animals will suffer his friend to be threatened. The guides made a big production of showing me Grisha, a brown bear that has lived at Leningrad since 1941, thus taking his place as one of the oldest inhabitants. During the war, they said, Grisha did his bit, performing in hospitals and camps, but they must have been afraid that I would immediately ask for a performance, and headed it off, saying, "Of course he's old now, and very cross."

They were pleasant people and I'm sure they are good zoologists. But it was depressing that so many of Leningrad's animals, even a favorite like Grisha, should spend their lives in such bare little boxes of concrete and iron. They are used to it, of course—some must have been born in just the same kind of box, and have never known anything better, but it seemed a sheer, stupid waste of the beauty of animals and a blind disregard of much that can be learned about them to house them like that. As for the public, I don't see how anyone could profit from the sight of a bear or a raccoon just sitting in a dark cell or pacing back and forth between dingy walls. Admittedly some enclosures were better than that, but still there were far too many straight rows of dull little cages. Some of the rows were actually double, one on top of the other. It was in such a one, on the lower level, that I saw an animal whose English name none of us could work out. The Russians knew it, of course, in their own language, but Olga's dictionary didn't give the translation. She wrote it in my notebook in Russian: rossomaha. Though it was difficult to see it in the gloom of its kennel, I made it out—a black, shiny, long-haired animal about as big as a fox-hound and restless as a stoat, leaping and rolling over on the cement floor in a self-manufactured struggle with a log of wood. It wrestled with the log, kicked it into the air, gnawed at it, threw it away and grabbed it again.

"I think it's a wolverine," I decided at last. "The nose looks a little too sharp, and I've never seen one quite so black, but what else could it be?"

Olga looked through the English half of the dictionary for "wolverine," but it wasn't there. "Not wolverine," she said flatly, tired of the whole thing. "*Rossomaha.*"

The zoologists in eager chorus described the habits of the *rossomaha*; how it lives on the tundra and is very cunning, evading traps with easy contempt. It follows predators, like the jackal. When hunters with dogs chase it, it can roll itself into a tight ball that defeats the dogs. In summary, Olga translated, "It is very dangerous to human beings." We all looked with new respect at the *rossomaha*. Just then along came an old woman with bucket and broom and started to clean out the animal's cage, shooing him into a corner.

Here I must anticipate. It took several months of searching before I was able to get *rossomaha* translated. Most Russian experts seem to be better at political vocabulary than natural history terms, but a Yale undergraduate finally managed to track it down for me. A *rossomaha* is a wolverine.

We finished the tour and made for the main entrance where I could thank the zoologists, shake hands with them, get into the Intourist car with Olga, and leave Leningrad's zoo, very likely forever. I was thinking as we walked that I come to conclusions too hastily, as I'd done in Moscow when I decided that Russian zoo people are just like their colleagues in countries on the other side of the curtain. I now told myself that there's a big difference, and I should have sensed it earlier. It's because of the way Russian lives are organized. Russian zoologists are interested in the same things, of course, but their enthusiasm is stunted. A nation whose people were forced to swallow one man's wild theories on the inheritance of acquired characteristics just because their Prime Minister believed him is hardly likely to produce much in the way of independent thought. The most a zoo man can feel for his work is a dutiful, patriotic pride. He can do it, obey the rules, follow the pattern. He can hope for advancement, but he can't alter or improve anything in his own zoo without the blessing of Moskov Zoocentre . . .

But again I was being hasty and found that I must change my mind. My last glimpse of Leningradskii Zoologichesskii Park was of one of the old women holding up a pail from which a tiger lapped through the bars of his cage. As the liquid's level sank, she tipped the vessel accordingly. I wouldn't have been at all surprised to learn that the stuff in the pail was vodka, but I was too busy to wonder: I was coming to another conclusion. There it was, I said to myself. Moscow or no Moscow, *that* was the person who really ran the place.

CHAPTER 11

Subcontinent

□

I

Because I remembered the Mysore Zoo I felt that I knew something about the zoological gardens of India. It was a confidence without foundation—a person might as well say the same about American zoos after visiting the Bronx—but I had it, and Mysore was in my mind as I rode in a taxi, out of the capital, toward the Delhi Zoological Park. That visit had been in 1950, only a bit more than a year after independence and the partition. The Sri Chamarajendra Zoological Gardens had recently been handed over to the State of Mysore by their owner the Maharaja. It was all a part of the general relinquishing of the Indian princes' possessions and powers. This Maharaja was a popular one, and his people, by themselves, would never have wanted to reduce his stature, but that was the way things were.

It was obvious that His Highness had lavished money and care on his animal collection. The well-housed elephants were trained to salaam to visitors on order from the mahouts. The tigers' quarters were airy and large. The lovely white horses that had drawn the royal carriage on state occasions were still in their elaborate stables, with jeweled harness on display and glass cabinets full of rosettes and trophy cups from races other horses of the Prince's had won. In fact, on all sides the influence of His Highness lingered, to such an extent that I felt uncomfortably like an intruder in a country house, and, if I understood the behavior of the other visitors, I was not alone in this reaction. There were only a few, all but tiptoeing around, the women hushing their children and giggling behind their hands, the men very silent.

Near the middle of the grounds, on an open grassy plot, a little lion cub stood tethered to a stake. A few members of the public stood around at considerable distance to look at him, while a keeper fondled the little animal and now and then beckoned to the onlookers to come closer. Nobody accepted, those the keeper selected merely hanging back and smiling sheepishly. Eventually the man spotted me, the only foreigner, and gestured invitingly. Because everybody was looking, I went over to the little cat, but I admit that I felt uneasy at first, until I heard him purring. I stroked his head and he batted at me with soft paws, like any kitten. Playing with him was pleasant after that. He rolled over so that I could tickle his stomach. He stood on his hind legs and wrestled with me, and pretended to chew at my arms, and the onlookers laughed appreciatively, but still nobody else dared to come closer. The little cat was alone again when I left, sitting on his haunches, head cocked wistfully to one side.

Now, in 1965 in the taxi, I reflected that one should understand this attitude. In a country full of animals in the wild, a zoo merely carries coals to Newcastle. No doubt this zoo and the one in Calcutta would prove to be as empty as the Mysore Zoo I remembered from fifteen years earlier.

The car turned off the main road before it came to the entrance to the Old Fort, an imposing red bastion that dominates the country outside Delhi. It has stood on guard for centuries, foundations deep in the arid land of northern India. I stared at it as I always do, and didn't notice that we were slowing down until the car stopped in front of the zoo gates. Then I looked around and found the pavement crowded with people waiting to buy tickets and get in. They didn't behave at all like that Mysore group in 1950: here they were animated and eager, families that included babies in arms to old crones and all ages between, happy at the prospect of spending the day among the animals. Through the gates I could see spic-and-span grounds with shrubs, some in flower, and winding pathways and hilly distances. When I passed through the gate at last I found the red wall of the Fort away to the left—otherwise there seemed no boundary at all, and I was struck by the feeling of space.

The director, Mr. N. D. Bachkheti, was in his office. I introduced myself and congratulated him on what must be a high regular attendance. He said, "Oh yes, we are fortunate in that respect, and in others as well. You see, we have no history—we are really new on this ground. People who run other zoos often have to cope with inherited disadvantages, in buildings that date back to less enlightened times, but this park was created only in 1959; that year saw the beginning of construction. For some years earlier the government had cherished the idea of having a park and zoological collection for the people of Delhi, but until then the times were not right. We made many plans before we began the actual work, and we've had the benefit of advice from experienced people. I doubt if you would find more experienced men than Major Weinman of Ceylon and Mr. Hagenbeck of Hamburg." At the name "Hagenbeck," glorious in zoo annals, I raised my eyebrows admiringly, and Mr. Bachkheti nodded. I said,

"In that case, of course you have the moat system."

"Of course." Mr. Bachkheti, a grave, stocky, spectacled gentleman with a soft voice, handed me a bottle of iced Coca-Cola and sat down to imbibe his own. "We don't claim to be specialists here. The aim is to give people an idea of animals from all over the world. But naturally, inevitably, our collection tends to be more Indian in character than anything else, since it's easier and cheaper to get specimens of Indian animals, and the climate suits them. If it comes to that, however, the climate suits many of the exotics as well. Like most zoo people these days we concentrate on breeding, and we've had a fair number of successes, notably with the brow-antlered deer—so far, one pair of these deer have bred four times. In this respect the climate is *most* advantageous. As you have seen, the park is popular, which is gratifying, especially considering how short a life it has had, and how unfinished it still is. I haven't the exact figures in my head, but you can see from the *Yearbook* statistics that during the last year we had nearly a million visitors, and there will be a larger figure quoted in our next report. At the moment the greatest draw is the white tigers. You've heard of them? It's a strain that first appeared, I believe, in the private menageries of the Maharaja of Rewa."

"A long time ago?"

"Oh no, quite recently. His Highness recognized that he had something special in this breed, and he immediately notified a number of zoologists who came to examine them. For several years now the tigers have been breeding. Some of them have been sent out of the country, but not many. The authorities keep an eye on them, of course, and the records are complete."

"Are they albinos?"

"No, not albinos. There's no sign of a lack of pigmentation, weak eyes, or anything like that. No, it's simply a color mutation. They're normal otherwise and the stripes are like those ordinary tigers, but the background skin color is not yellow, it's nearly white. I'll show you later, when we're in the grounds. We've had three litters out of our pair —not all white ones, you understand, just the occasional ones that Mendel would have prophesied. It's all most interesting, and we're proud of having had such success at breeding them. After all, we're a young zoo in a country where some of the zoos are fairly old. Madras, for example, recently celebrated their centenary. Calcutta's quite old, and there's Trivandrum. Not that we can claim to be the newest, either. One has just been opened, I understand, at Darjeeling."

I said, "Isn't there a zoo at Katmandu in Nepal? I've just seen a write-up in some magazine that doesn't give a very good report of it."

Mr. Bachkheti looked distressed. "Oh, it's going to be a good zoo, a very good zoo," he assured me earnestly. "They're working hard on it, and they've got a lot of plans in mind. The director, I believe, is in Calcutta at this moment, studying modern methods. I am quite sure that you'll be favorably impressed if you pay a visit to Katmandu in a year or two."

As for himself, he said, he was not a zoologist, but a tree man. Before taking this post he had worked for years in the forestry department, and thus had many dealings with wild animals. Wild life had always interested him. "So I was very glad when this chance came, to serve in such a capacity," he went on. "It's a privilege to help to build a zoo: I find it fascinating. Do you like the site? Major Weinman and Mr. Hagenbeck were asked to decide between several potential places, and with hardly any hesitation they agreed that this was the best. I consider it a happy choice. No doubt you saw that it abuts the wall of the Old Fort over there—the Fort, four hundred years old, used to be living-quarters for kings and emperors, and the wall's masonry is magnificent, but we needed more length along the side of our zoo, so we built an addition to it, using exactly the same material. Did you realize that it had been elongated?" He was pleased that I shook my head. "No," he agreed, "I don't think it's possible to tell where old and new are joined." He put down his Coke bottle and rose to his feet. I followed him out.

A Land-Rover, with a uniformed man at the wheel, was waiting for us at the door and we set off at a slow rate, three in the front seat, privileged creatures among the throng who had to walk. The land's gentle rolling slopes lent themselves to the Hagenbeck plan of hiding the enclosure limits. Some ditches were dry and hidden by cleverly placed shrubs, but most of the animals lived behind water moats. The vegetation was young—saplings, small bushes, and new-looking flower gardens. Men in loincloths and turbans were directing irrigation streams, or dug the ground, or piled rocks, or loaded carts. "We are enlarging the moat system," explained Mr. Bachkheti, and he pointed out how the channels here and there had been widened to accommodate ponds, or marshy

stretches where rhinos and water birds spent their time. We climbed out
of the car to stand on the bank of a large, dark lake where we stared
down, past shrubs and reeds, to shade-streaked water thick with floating
birds. It was difficult to believe that the lake had been made by zoo labor-
ers. It looked as if it had been there for many years.

"And so many birds," I commented. "You couldn't squeeze in one
more duck if you tried to, could you?"

"But we didn't put most of them there," replied the director. "When
we'd finished constructing the lake we put in a few of our birds, of
course, but the others simply came and joined them. I suppose you recognize all the species?"

"I don't recognize any," I admitted, so he named off a few—Indian
swan, night heron, painted stork, white ibis, Sarus crane, and any number
of different ducks. He pointed to a small island standing near one end
of the lake basin, and said, "That was left there more or less by accident,
but it's given me an idea. I'd like to put a platform or even a small
house over on the island among the trees, in the largest one, and people
from the New Delhi Bird-Watching Society, or visitors like you, would
be able to watch things at your ease—get into the blind before dawn
so the birds wouldn't know you were there, and stay all day." He smiled
at the prospect. "Then I'd like to do the same sort of thing in one or
two of the big deer enclosures, and even with a monkey colony. We'll
have to see how well it works with the birds first." He added that one
of the biggest maintenance problems with this lake was that it kept
silting up. Men were always dredging it, and he hoped that in future
the zoo might acquire another, deeper lake.

We moved on to look at the white-tiger exhibit. The mother was a
fine specimen of ordinary yellow, but two of the cubs were a pale off-
white between their dark stripes. At that time, said Mr. Bachkheti, there
were only fourteen captive white tigers in the world; eight in India and
the other six distributed among foreign zoos. The National Zoo in Washington had a breeding pair, he said. "This mother, as you see, looks
like an ordinary yellow tiger, but she carries the genes of the white," he
explained. "Do you see something special about this cage? It's the cave
there on the right. Tigers like a good deal of privacy, and we are giving
all their cages similar caves."

We looked at large paddocks for deer and antelope, and for some
time I watched a young Indian rhino from Assam that looked as if it
were encased in armor plate. Mr. Bachkheti was hoping to be supplied
with a mate for it, but he would have to get government permission,
because the rhinos, which come only from Assam, are rare and under

special protection. Some of the lower-lying enclosures of the streams were the homes of saurians: muggers, alligators, crocodiles. The Land-Rover passed groups of monkeys in cages, several fine leopards, mountain goats, a great brown bear from Japan, some American bison, elephants . . .

"You may have observed a plan in the placing of our animals," said Mr. Bachkheti. "It's another of Mr. Hagenbeck's suggestions—the park is divided into four areas, representing Asia, Africa, Australia, and America. It's not easy to distinguish the arrangement now, but it will be clear when the construction is further along. Have you noticed the plants? It seemed such a pity not to take advantage of the warm climate that we grow rare plants as well as animals. Over there is a plantation of young gold mohur trees, lovely things when they reach their full height, which will be in another three or four years. We'll use them here and there for shade. There's what used to be a rather ugly building that we've got to keep for maintenance purposes. For a long time it was an eyesore, until I thought of covering the hillock with century plants, and now I think it looks quite nice."

The Land-Rover, at quicker tempo, took us through the backstage area garages, where workingmen, extra animals, and idle vehicles seemed all mixed up together. Work crews with horses and camels were busily razing a hill. Mr. Bachkheti talked statistics. The park held, for the moment, two hundred and forty acres; one hundred and fifty had been built up and the rest would soon be ready, but zoos have a way of demanding more space however much they possess. Often this can't be supplied, because the zoo is within city limits or for some other reason land costs more than its budget will stand. Smiling happily, the director said that this emergency was unlikely to face the Delhi park. "The river flows close by," he explained. "We draw all our water from it, which saves money. But better still is that across the river on the other side we have more land that we can use when we're ready. For us, space is no problem. Incidentally we grow all our own fodder, including sugar cane for the elephants."

It was past noon when we came back to the office—lunchtime. Groups of people, sitting on the ground in whatever shade they could find, were picnicking. I started to thank Mr. Bachkheti and leave, but he said, "Just a minute." He gestured toward the land lying between us and the Fort wall, and asked, rather like a teacher of a pupil, "What do you see there?"

I wondered what he could mean. Ahead of us was only the usual reddish sand of undisturbed land in that part of India, with scrub and a wilderness of young trees. At last I said, "Well, nothing. Why?"

"Aha!" He seemed triumphant. "You see nothing. That's very good because you *shouldn't* see anything. But it is there, I assure you, something is there—an enclosure, almost completed, with adequate safeguards against escape. It is for lions that we are going to keep there. Aren't the boundaries cleverly hidden?"

Every zoo director has a pet project, and it was clear that this was Mr. Bachkheti's. His eyes shone. "When our lions are in that enclosure they will feel completely at home, because it's like their own native bush. We've planted the thicket you see there so that an animal may feel hidden among the trees, but we can't let it grow too thick, because it will then be too effective a hiding place, and the public wants to *see* the animals." His brow clouded slightly at the thought. The zoo man's besetting problem is just that, the question of which comes first, public or animal. "The trick will be to keep the woods thinned out," he continued. "Observe how the ground rises in the center. Such a height is most important when one is looking at animals—not too low, not too high, but just at eye level." Following his example, I held my hand horizontally below my eyes and looked straight ahead. The terrain passed his test. Mr. Bachkheti went on excitedly: "Now look there. At that particular place the Fort wall is not visible. All within view is land against sky, isn't it? Thus when our lions walk across the mound on their way to be fed, or to rest in the trees, you will see them"—he made an eloquent gesture, as if painting with wide strokes—"against the sky, all black against the sky. Think of it at sunset. Beautiful!"

II.

After Delhi, any old-fashioned zoo was bound to be a comedown. The Alipore Zoological Gardens outside Calcutta are as flat as the palm of your hand, but the situation has one thing at least to be said for it: whereas in the park at Delhi every tree looked like what it was, the triumphant outcome of laborious irrigation, the Alipore gardens are heavily wooded by nature unassisted. In a shady office the deputy president, Mr. Chatterjee, looked at me with frightened eyes, because although his English was quite good, he wouldn't believe it. He sent for the veterinary officer, Dr. Dutta, and was not at ease until the doctor had arrived to interpret. Between them they told me that the zoo, founded in 1875, is one of the oldest in India. I must say that it looked it—not that it was particularly run-down or shabby, because it wasn't, but the animals were starkly presented, one after another in cage after cage that were lined up in rows like articles for sale at Woolworth's. There was no imagination at work, and one saw nothing to stir the feelings, nothing to hint of where such animals live in freedom. Creatures of a variety of species, from widely different parts of the world, were reduced to a common, dull level. Presumably they were adequately fed, and Dr. Dutta took good care of their health, but what then? Perhaps, I reflected, the zoo was disappointing because no one mind guided it—Alipore Gardens were managed not by a director but by a committee of leading citizens who served in an honorary capacity. On the other hand, I have seen many zoos that lack character just as much, though they *are* managed by directors. Alipore isn't a bad zoo. It is just a zoo. And it's popular. The yearly attendance is a staggering two million, and though the entry charge is small, the gate receipts provide the zoo's financial mainstay.

"We also make an extra charge for a special exhibit nowadays," said Dr. Dutta. "Those who want to pay another five pice may see the white tigers that the government has lent to us to encourage zoo attendance. There are two white cubs that come from—"

"Rewa."

"From Rewa, yes. In the old days entrance to the zoo was quite free, and when the government decided on a change of policy and we began charging for admission, some of us feared that the public would stop coming. It is true that for a little while there *was* a falling off in attendance, but then the people got used to the idea, and with the extra we now have a much better zoo. During the day we are never closed: no matter what the date might be—a special holiday or whatever—the gates open at six-thirty in the morning and close at five-thirty in the evening. And every month on one day, with the date announced in the papers in advance, everybody may come in without paying at all. Students never have to pay. Our zoo has a good reputation: scientists come to work here, making observations of the animals. A man from Katmandu is working with us at present to learn our methods, because the zoological garden of Nepal is going to enlarge and improve its grounds. He came by arrangement through the Colombo Plan."

I asked if they were doing anything particular in the way of conservation methods, mainly in breeding, but Mr. Chatterjee, who understood the question, said firmly in reply that they weren't interesting themselves in conservation. "Our purpose is to exhibit," he said. This seeming lack of enterprise, I realized, was to be understood considering that their area consisted of only fifty acres. Not even the most ambitious breeder would want to increase his stock within such limits, and I ad-

mitted to myself, when Dr. Dutta took me through the grounds, that
the place somehow succeeded in avoiding a cluttered or cramped look—
a praiseworthy result. The doctor led the way through a dense crowd of
visitors, all evidently bent on getting to the reptile house. I commented
on this.

"Yes, they like snakes," he said. "Only a few pause on the way to the
reptile house, to look at the tigers and elephants and so on. They like to
look at the king cobras and banded kraits. Dangerous animals fascinate
the public. Yet they are neglecting some really good specimens. We have
Indian rhinos and clouded leopards from the Himalayas. Foreigners appreciate these." He was mollified that I, too, appreciated them, and he
really cheered up when I expressed admiration of the langurs, India's
most beautiful monkeys. He said,

"If you like monkeys, you must meet another scientist from abroad
who is working here—a young lady from Johns Hopkins in America.
Come this way, please."

Unlocking a gate, he walked through the fence with me close at his
heels. On the other side the ground had been cleared of trees, and
everything was quiet—no public chattering around the animals and the
food stalls. Dr. Dutta led the way to a group of large cages, near one of
which stood a fair-haired girl making notes about the monkeys in it.
Dr. Dutta introduced her as Miss Mireille Bertrand. She confirmed the
fact that she had come from Johns Hopkins: "I am French, but I work
there—I've been there for some time. I am in India to make a study of
the behavior of two kinds of monkeys, pigtail macaques like these in
the cage—and lion-tail macaques. There is plenty of subject material in
Alipore."

From the ground came an indignant squeal. Looking down, I saw
two very small baby monkeys scrabbling around Miss Bertrand's feet. They
seemed to resent my presence. She laughed. "These babies have adopted
me and follow me everywhere. That bold one is female. The boy is much
more timid. Here in the cage I have a group that has been artificially
selected—that is, they're all more or less of the same age, adolescent.
I am trying to observe their behavior with their own peers; who becomes
dominant and so on." For a while we watched together as the monkeys,
heavy-set, short-haired animals of a yellowish color, scampered about
their affairs, struggling with each other like sparring partners, or picking
at edible leaves, or playing follow-the-leader. Dr. Dutta got bored and
went off to talk to a man sweeping the ground. "I take photographs
and make cinemas," went on Miss Bertrand. "The idea is to work out
the inter-relationships of individuals in the group. But these animals

don't live in segregated age-groups, so in this next cage I have made other arrangements—two ordinary family groups with members of all ages. Over there in that cage are a pair of lion-tailed monkeys." She was pointing at two black-and-white monkeys with heavy manes of fur around their necks and long, tufted tails. Miss Bertrand said, "They are interesting because of the morphology; it's hard to distinguish male from female without close examination, but they aren't anything like as adaptable as the pigtails. They don't tame easily. I helped collect this pair myself in Assam, on the reserve. The guide and I had a permit to take these monkeys, otherwise we couldn't have done it." Her voice trailed away and she hesitated, then, inpulsively, she went on: "That is the theory of the reserve. But to be perfectly honest, I'm afraid it's only theory. Poaching goes on more or less openly. It's bad, you know— it's very bad. That is where the Indian rhinos are, at least the few that are still living in the wild. There are so few left that they're all numbered. And yet—because these people haven't the first idea of what conservation really means—poaching of rhinos still goes on. It's terrible."

"But isn't the place policed?"

Miss Bertrand shrugged off the police. "And it's not only the rhinoceros that must be protected. There are other rare species that are supposed to be safe there, but they aren't safe, not at all. They never will be as long as men who make their living out of them are still around to catch and sell them. Those people will never take conservation laws seriously, and plenty of others, non-dealers, are just as bad. One of the inspectors at our camp—an inspector, mind you—shot a bird that's on the protected list and had it for dinner. When officials behave like that, what can you expect of the others? If I knew where to start, I think I'd organize a kind of Peace Corps for conservation. Do you think it might work?"

CHAPTER 12

Elephant Land

□

In India, no matter how lazy one may be physically, the mind works reasonably well. In Ceylon, however, I felt my thoughts flounder in a medium of gluelike consistency, and after twenty-four hours of encasement in this glue I didn't mind. Green countryside, flower scents, the unhurried, majestic booming of the sea lulled and kept me in a half-sleep that was the right tempo for Ceylon. When little things went wrong, as things are apt to in a hot climate, I didn't mind. Nothing mattered. It was in such a state of euphoria that I went to the Zoological Gardens, in a suburb of Colombo called Dehiwala.

I have never, before or since, seen another zoo that so well deserves the title of garden. In the Colombo area everything grows well in any case: behind the neat little fences of houses around town there was always a riot of green and flower colors against the red soil. This lushness was delightfully exaggerated at Dehiwala. At the ornate gateway, where I stopped to buy a ticket, I felt rather as if I were perching on the edge of a huge soup plate full of watercress. On the rim, crisscrossed with pathways, girls in saris and men in white clothes ambled about or sat in the shade, drinking orange pop through straws. Babies toddled or nodded over their mothers' shoulders. Everything was shaded, soft, and good-natured. From where I stood the rim curved away on either hand, where through leaves in the distance I saw buildings and cages; ahead of me was a large well-marked map illustrated with pictures of animals, annotated both in Ceylonese script and English. I had to go straight ahead, along the main road, to find the director's office. The way led down in groups of stairs toward the center, through several semicircular rows of animal enclosures and little garden plots, to Mr. De Alwis's gate.

[9]

INDIAN ELEPHANT KICKING AT AFRICAN ELEPHANT

She had been pushed away from her begging area by the African elephant.

[10]
TIGERS

[11]
TIGER CUB

[12]

ORANGUTAN

AUTHOR WITH BABY ORANGUTAN

The baby is in Nagoya.

[15]

THREE-TOED SLOTH

[16]

CAPE LONG-EARED FOX, SOUTH AFRICA

His office is in his house, so well surrounded by trees and bushes that I felt as I walked up the driveway that I was paying an afternoon call at a farmhouse far removed from the jungle. In the office a huge old dog was sleeping on the floor. Somewhere in the house, behind Mr. De Alwis's back, a baby cried.

Mr. W. L. E. de Alwis, B.Sc., was tall, good-looking, and youthful: he was also—unlike many other people I had met in Ceylon—crisp and alert. "I can't imagine working anywhere but in a zoo," he said. "Ever since I can remember I've wanted and intended to get some job connected with a zoological garden."

I learned that this zoo is run by the government, who support it without trying to equate the expenses with the take at the gate. This must amount to more than a pittance, though the entrance fee is small, because more than half a million people visit the place every year. "You see, it's one of the regular things tourists do," explained Mr. De Alwis. "This is a crossroads of maritime travel, and hardly anybody from abroad drops in at Colombo without coming to see us here. It's a useful talking-point whenever there are arguments about the ethics of maintaining a zoo."

"Ethics?" The word hit close to the uneasy thoughts I had been entertaining ever since my talk with Miss Bertrand. "You mean there's discussion about them?"

"Why, it's our biggest problem—at least that's how I often feel," he said. "You couldn't know about that, of course, because it's a peculiarly local question. The majority of the people here are Buddhist, which means they're strongly opposed to any form of violence or cruelty. They assume that zoos are cruel *per se*, and so they're against us as an institution—that is to say they're against us until they get better acquainted with our methods. Admittedly, when they take the trouble to come and look around the place, they find that we treat our animals well, and then they stop opposing. Incidentally I shouldn't blame it all on the Buddhists. In this matter the Hindus line up with them."

"But Hindus haven't much influence in Ceylon, have they?"

"It adds up," said Mr. De Alwis, rather gloomily. "Still, here we are, as you can see. And we make progress. A lot of erstwhile enemies have changed their minds and give us support; it happens less and less often that one sees a letter in the papers denouncing the zoo. Sooner or later, we hope, the whole country will learn that we have a good effect on children, not a bad one. If children can learn the right way to treat animals from our example, well, that's a positive virtue."

I said, "You might do what they're doing lately in London—tie up with the schools. On certain days there the teachers bring their classes to Regent's Park, where the zoo people have fixed up some special exhibit just for them—a raccoon, for instance—in a cage kept for the purpose, one that's especially easy to see into. The kids take a good look at it, and there may be a lecture about the animal from the curator or a keeper, and there's literature for them to carry home and study. Afterward, at school, they discuss the raccoon and the kind of country he comes from, the geography and vegetation and general ecology, even the people of that country, all kinds of peripheral subjects. They get a lot out of it, I believe."

Mr. De Alwis shook his head decidedly. "It wouldn't work, not here. I don't know much about English children, but ours would be too easily distracted—they wouldn't pay attention to the lecture, to begin with, and then some parents would certainly object on the usual grounds that zoos are cruel and shouldn't be encouraged. Well, let's have a look at things. I've got a few theories of my own on educating the public. Come and see."

As we walked back to the main path I reflected that the terrain resembled a Greek theatre as much as anything, but it was hard to get an all-over view between the shrubbery and trees. No two lines of cages seemed to be on exactly the same level. Soon, as we walked, the resemblance to a theatre faded out in a maze of construction. The clusters of cages and enclosures and pits were so cleverly plotted that an impression of space triumphed. I was surprised to learn that the gardens cover only forty-two acres.

"As far as the zoo in its present form is concerned, it dates back only to 1936," Mr. De Alwis said. He was interrupted by a keeper with a question that evidently took a long time to answer. After the pause, we walked on. "But it was already here, in another form. A Mr. Hagenbeck settled in Colombo in 1928. You've heard of the Hagenbecks, of course—*the* family in zoos and circuses? Well, this member of the family was in animal dealing, too; he collected them here and there and used Dehiwala as a center, keeping the stock here between shipments. It was the logical place, outside town but near enough to the port: he must have done pretty well." He broke off to speak affectionately to an antelope that trotted eagerly behind a fence to exchange greetings. Then he resumed: "I'm not sure just when he started letting the public in to look at the animals. Probably it didn't happen all at once—people started coming, and then, no doubt, he decided to charge them for the privilege, but by the time he left the scene he was making more money out of exhibiting his animals than exporting them. He went out of business, though, in '36. Being a German and all that in a British colony, he probably saw the writing on the wall. I believe he was actually interned in Ceylon later on, as an enemy alien: in any case when the war ended, he vanished from the scene. This place was confiscated as enemy property, and the government's been running it ever since. I'm the third director since it began under the new management. It goes without saying that we've all made alterations—there's always some construction or other going on in a zoo. But the original pattern is here, as Mr. Hagenbeck laid it down, and in my opinion he knew how to plan." Again we paused, this time to look at men working on the foundations for a new cage to be placed on high ground. "I've done a good deal of moving the exhibits around," said Mr. De Alwis. "I don't like the common method of putting related species all together in a group. You know, lions and tigers and leopards, all the cats, in one house or section: primates jumbled together in another, all that sort of thing. People get bored. Children, especially, will stop looking after they've seen only one or two cages. I want to hold their interest. If you don't know what you might see next, you keep on going. I like to show a few birds, then a couple of cats, then small mammals—in other words, anything as long as it isn't the same kind of thing in one cage after another. I haven't finished my arrangements of course, it all takes time, but we'll get there. And signs, or labels, on cages—they're very important. You can do an immense amount with labels. I go in for long ones, because a name isn't going to mean much to the ordinary child. Suppose we have a—let me see—a spotted genet, for instance; what's the use of telling a person totally unlearned in zoology that it's a spotted genet, and letting it go at that? He'll forget the name in another minute. I would add to the label the explanatory words, "African civet." That *is* what it is, and the name means something to a Ceylon child because we have civets of our own. In some cases I go farther. On the lesser panda's cage I've put a sign explaining that it's distantly related to the bear—we have bears in Ceylon—and I go on to say that due to climatic conditions and other factors the lesser panda adapted to its environment, thus looks different. This teaches the reader something important. Another thing about labels is that they break the monotony. Just looking into one cage after another, without knowing anything about the occupants, is bound to be tiresome. If you're used to the other sort of zoo our arrangement may seem illogical, but there *is* logic behind it: no matter how odd it may seem, it's intended to be that way. Over there, next to the elephant shed, I've put a few monkeys for a little surprise, and next to them I mean to have a cockatoo, just for contrast. People in a zoo get tired of the same thing. In fact, people get tired. I've got benches here and there in the little gardens. We like to have displays and rest places all in one. Here are some rather nice birds." He checked his long stride and wheeled into a curving path before a row of cages.

"What's that marvelous colored one?"

"That's just a purple coot: haven't you ever seen one before? We have a good many in Ceylon." He glanced at his watch. "I'm aiming to get you to the arena just in time for the elephant show, our great pride, but we still have long enough to see the reptiles first."

Among the snakes was a large placard lettered boldly, with a message composed, like all the zoo's signs, by Mr. De Alwis:

"Poisonous SNAKES of Ceylon. (Only 5 here carry poison lethal to man: Cobra, Russell's Viper or Tic-Polonga, Saw-Scaled Viper, Ceylon Krait, Indian Krait.)

"It is estimated that nearly 300 people die of snakebite annually in Ceylon, but we should not be unduly perturbed by this figure as a good number of victims die, not so much as a result of the venom, but through shock and near-hysterical fright.

"Perhaps it is true to say that there is no specific cure for snake bite, but it is now established by Western medicine that anti-venin has proved most efficacious being effective even in later stages if injected intra-venously."

I moved on in Mr. De Alwis's tracks, and we stopped at one of a series of pits that marked an arc of the zoo limits. He looked fondly down on a huge coil of patterned snake labeled: RETICULATED PYTHON: MALAYA. "How long would you say that animal is?" he asked. "Guess . . . about thirty feet. We haven't been able to measure him for several years—measuring a python is quite a job—but it must be about that, one of the greatest lengths recorded for the species. He's an awfully big snake, awfully old as well. A few months ago we had a scare; he got some sort of fungus on one spot of his skin. How is one going to treat a thirty-foot python? It would have to be at long distance, and we figured out a way. We put planks across the pit and walked out over him and lowered a lump of wadding covered with medicine on a pole. It wasn't too hard to manipulate the pole, after a little practice, and we managed to smear the infection. As you can see it's cleared up—it reacted immediately. The skin's in fine shape now. He's so old he hardly ever moves except at feeding time, and that doesn't happen very often. Pythons take a long time to digest their food."

Discussing the inevitable subject of breeding in zoos, Mr. De Alwis spoke of the secondary difficulty of bringing up the young born in captivity. Animal mothers in these conditions have been known to kill their young, and I asked if he thought these females would have done the same in the wild. He didn't. "I think it's captivity behavior, it's aberrant. But remember that an animal may be a bad mother, as we call it, at the first birth, and yet she'll be perfectly all right the next time. We've had an example of what I mean recently, a guanaco who was terrified of her first-born—acted as if she didn't know what it was, and we had to take it out of the enclosure before she killed it. Yet when the second came along, she was an excellent mother."

Hediger discusses this point in *Psychology and Behavior of Animals in Captivity*. He says that there are two forms of failure that might over-take a zoo animal giving birth. In one it is due to overexaggerated care. The mother, lacking a feeling of security, tries to hide her young in safer and yet safer places, perhaps dragging an infant about the cage by the scruff of the neck until it dies or she eats it. The other type of malfunction occurs when the mother is not yet mature, and the birth might be considered in the light of a dress rehearsal: either the infant is too weak to live or the mother, finding it a threatening mystery, abandons or kills it. He quotes Director Heck of the Hellabrun Zoo, Munich, who believes that in the wild a female elephant's first baby is always stillborn—a theory not yet verified—and also cites the testimony of Yerkes, the great-ape expert, who reported that the chimpanzee mothers at his farm at Orange Park, Florida, seemed afraid of their first babies and didn't dare to touch them.

The elephant arena at the Dehiwala Garden is about the size of a large circus-ring and is surrounded by rising tiers of grassy terraces. Some hundred people were sitting on these natural benches when we arrived, waiting for the daily show: others stood on the surrounding road or perched on the low containing-wall. As in the city, most men and chil-dren were dressed in Western style, but the women favored saris, and their colors vied with those of the brightest caged birds. It was mid-afternoon. The sunlight that filtered through tall trees surrounding us had taken on a faintly greenish tint in passing. Next to the entrance into the performing area was another of Mr. De Alwis's signs, painted in blue on the whitewashed wall:

> *East is East and West is West,*
> *Though this may not seem relevant.*
> *We all know how to milk a cow,*
> *But you can't muck about with an elephant.*

"I think this performance will surprise you," said Mr. De Alwis, a trace of pride in his soft voice. "I doubt very much if you've seen anything to approach it in any other zoo. Here our elephants actually dance. Lang at Basel has quite an elaborate elephant act. He approves of that sort of thing, you know; it's got something to do with the exercise and variety working as a kind of therapy. But he was struck by our setup here all the same. At the moment the cast is made up of six Ceylon elephants, including one young learner. Ceylon elephants are not exactly the same as Indian elephants—it's a subspecies and there are some distinctions: Ceylon elephants are usually slightly smaller, for one thing. They're supposed to be more intelligent, too, and because of that they used to be very much in demand in foreign countries. Even Indian rulers used to import a great many for that reason. Incidentally, we also own two African elephants. We haven't had them very long."

I said, "You'll never put them in the show, of course; they're untrainable, aren't they?"

"No," said Mr. De Alwis. "It just takes a different approach, to train an African animal. We're going to try to do it with ours when we get around to it . . . Here they come."

A jingling of bells, a shouting and scampering of children toward the source of the noise, and they were there, their massive footsteps making no noise in the wooded path. The procession plodded around the outside road of the arena and then down to the entrance, one by one, second holding the tail of first with his trunk, third the tail of second and so on, down to the sixth and last, a baby so small that she had to reach her trunk full length to grasp the tail ahead of her. I remembered reading that elephant groups in the wild often walk in the same manner, for which reason the trunks of baby elephants are disproportionately long. The parade was now in the arena, rounding the circle once and then releasing their grasps, to fall out of formation. Two attendants helped them line up and back off to face the audience. The leader stepped out, holding a sign high with his trunk and turning slowly so that all might read. It was a request to the visitors not to use flashlights until after the performance. He put the sign away, drums struck up, and the five big elephants rose to their hind legs and began to turn round and round.

"Ever seen anything like that?" demanded Mr. De Alwis, and I shook my head.

They stood on circus-kegs. They sat down like bipeds on the arena's ridge, front feet in the air. Then, at a roll of drums, all but one stepped back. The remaining elephant was led forward by an attendant who then lay down on the ground before it. It stepped delicately over him with its front feet and lay down on top of him. We in the audience gasped, though we were confident the attendant wasn't being squashed—all were confident, that is, except one small boy, who began to cry at the top of his voice. Standing up, the elephant waited until the attendant in turn stood up. Then it wrapped its trunk around him, lifted him, took part of the man's clothing in its teeth—though most of the weight was supported by the tusks—and carried him around the arena, the keeper remaining rigid. The little boy continued to howl. Loping like a setter bringing a shot bird to his master, the elephant trotted with its burden in a circle. The little boy shrieked so loud that at last his embarrassed mother led him away.

"When that child grows up he will oppose zoos," said Mr. De Alwis plaintively.

CHAPTER 13

Concrete in Sydney

☐

Before I went to Australia I knew nothing about Sir Edward Hallstrom of the Taronga Zoological Park Trust. Looking back, I realize that he was the most memorable director I met on the round-the-world journey. I'm not saying that he was the best. There are no bests or worsts in zoo work, generally speaking—no absolutes at all. What was impressive about Sir Edward was his original mind. Unlike many other directors he has no hereditary connection with zoos, and he wasn't educated as a zoologist, biologist, or veterinarian. He was an engineer when he started, but he has always had an inquiring habit of mind and a keen interest in wild life. And he has made his mark: few comprehensive summaries of captive wild animals do not mention his name in connection with Australian specimens. Zoo people outside Australasia depend heavily on Hallstrom for supplies from that region.

To be sure, his is a unique position geographically. Australia, along with Tasmania, New Guinea, and related islands, because it has been out of touch with other continental masses for geological ages, is the home of an astonishingly distinctive group of animals. Some of these creatures are so "far out" that for a long time zoologists couldn't classify them because the ordinary rules of definition didn't apply. These are the monotremes— the duckbilled platypus, or ornithorhyncus, and the spiny anteater, or echidna. It has at last been decided that they must be considered mammals because the females produce milk for their young. On the other hand, they lay eggs—other mammals are viviparous—which they incubate and hatch in the manner of lizards or birds. Walker comments that they are more closely related to the reptiles than are any other recent mammals: "They are not the ancestors of the marsupials and placental mammals, but they represent rather a distinct line of mammalian evolution."

Even without the complication of defining monotremes, the wild life of Australasia is bewilderingly unfamiliar to non-natives. Mark Twain, after listening to story after story of kangaroos and the others, wrote a poem on the subject:

INVOCATION

Come forth from thy cozy couch,
O Ornithorhyncus dear!
And greet with a cordial claw
The stranger that longs to hear

From thy own own lips the tale
Of thy origin all unknown;
Thy misplaced bone where flesh should be,
And flesh where should be bone.

And fishy fin where should be paw,
And beaver-trowel tail,
And snout of beast equip'd with teeth
Where gills ought to prevail.

Come, Kangaroo, the good and true!
Foreshortened as to legs,
And body tapered like a churn,
And sack marsupial, i' fegs,

And tell us why you linger here,
Thou relic of a vanished time,
When all your friends as fossils sleep,
Immortalized in lime!

To most outsiders mention of Australian wild life immediately brings to mind the kangaroo. But kangaroos and their close relatives the wallabies and wallaroos are only a part of a far wider order of marsupials. The Australian pouched animals are not the only marsupials in the world— in the Americas, for instance, we have many different varieties of opossum. But the opossum represents only a small proportion of American fauna, whereas in Australia nearly all animals are marsupial. Strangely enough, many of them bear an uncanny resemblance to certain non-marsupial mammals familiar to the rest of the world, as if evolution were bound to repeat the outward appearance of nature's creatures. The

early settlers of Australia, no doubt because of homesickness, identified
the strange animals they found there with creatures of similar appearance
at home, and named them accordingly. The names, inevitably, have
stuck. A marsupial that looks like a rat is known to Australians as a rat:
they ignore the fact that the marsupial carries its young in a pouch, in
most unratlike fashion. There are many sorts of marsupial "mice"—from
now on I propose to drop the quotation marks used by more careful
writers—of which the smallest is the tiny planigale. This animal is rarely
seen, being very quick and clever at hiding. Of the planigales examined,
the largest measured less than two inches in length, tail included, but a
female may have as many as twelve babies at a time, all firmly attached
to her teats, all dragged about by their minuscule mother until they are
ready to fend for themselves. Other marsupials include the jumping
mouse or jerboa, four genera of spotted cat, the Tasmanian devil, which
resembles a small bear, and the Tasmanian wolf, or thylacine, with dark
bands running transversely across its back. The thylacine really does look
canine, especially in front—or perhaps we must say that it did look
canine: it hasn't been seen for a long time and has been nearly exterminated by man and his accomplice, the true dog. The numbat, or
marsupial anteater, is also in danger of extermination. There are marsupial
moles, and bandicoots of various kinds. The Phalangeridae, or climbing
marsupials, are the koala, the cuscus, and the possum—not identical
with American opossums, though some are outwardly similar. Among
these is the "pygmy acrobat," a possum whose front and hind legs on
each side are connected by a membrane so that it can glide in the air.
Others are the pygmy possum, the dormouse possum, and many more.
Walker lists seventeen genera and approximately fifty-two species of
kangaroo and related animals, which come in many sizes and occupy
"nearly all types of terrestrial habitats" to be found in their country.
One genus is arboreal.

The directors I consulted before I set out didn't do more than mention
Sir Edward in passing. Perhaps this was deliberate—he would be sure it
was—but I think that the Sydney Zoo and its director simply didn't occur
to them because it was so remote. In any case I, as a greenhorn, was
puzzled when I came on the entry about Taronga Park during some
preliminary homework with the *International Zoo Yearbook*, because it
was so terse. Most write-ups of the zoos included in the reference section
are fairly informative, each giving the names of the director of the place,
the assistant director if any, the veterinary doctor, and the different
curators. For Taronga Park there were only three names supplied—Sir

Edward Hallstrom the Honorary Director, a supervisor, and a secretary.
Yet the zoo was apparently a big organization, with a staff numbering
one hundred and ten, with more than a thousand mammals and nearly
three thousand birds. And where most zoos state their sources of financial
support (usually the state, national, or municipal government) Taronga
Park listed only "Financial support from Gvt. for capital expenditure."
No government grant? No public relations officer? No veterinarian? Just
what sort of a zoo was this, anyway? Determined to find out, I wrote to
Sir Edward and said I would like to call on him and look at his park.

He replied that he would be glad to show me what they were doing
and why they were doing it. "Our breeding of wild animals has been
tremendously successful," he added. "At the moment we are embarrassed
with the numbers that we have bred over the last two years. I am offering
our surplus to other zoos."

I arrived at dawn by night plane from Singapore, and kicked my heels
for hours waiting for what I considered a reasonable time to telephone,
thus committing an error of judgment, as I discovered when at last I did
ring up. "We've been waiting for your call," said the secretary with a
slight touch of reproach in her voice. "Sir Edward has been here for the
past hour. He has a very full day. He must get ready to go to his place
in New Guinea in a few days, and what with the Duke of Edinburgh—"

"I understand. I'll come now," I said hastily. But I didn't understand,
not quite, and while she gave me directions on how to get to suburban
Mosman and the Park, my mind scurried around the subject of the Duke.
I'd been out of touch with newspapers for some time, but I finally did
recall something I'd read before I left England, about Prince Philip's
approaching visit to Australia. Now, what did this have to do with Sir
Edward? Philip is President of the Zoological Society of London, I
reminded myself, but—then I remembered clearly: he was doing this on
behalf of the IUCN, the International Union for the Conservation of
Nature and Natural Resources. He was going to give a talk in Australia,
perhaps several talks, on conservation. It seemed unfortunate for me that
our visits should coincide, but I reflected philosophically that no matter
where one goes nowadays in the Commonwealth, some member or other
of the British royal family is likely to be near.

Behind the zoo's pleasingly wacky entrance, as brightly colored as if
Disney had designed it, in the administration building, I found Sir
Edward—a thickset, medium-tall, white-haired man, who acted as if he
were packed with springs and as if every moment might be his last
chance to do something of importance. At his suggestion we sat in the

corner of a big room, in two leather chairs that shared space with a huge
board-table. We had just started to talk when his secretary called him to
take a long-distance call in his office, and I heard his voice booming
away for a time. Bouncing back, he apologized, saying, "I'm organizing a
dolphin show like the one they have in America on the California coast,
and that fellow on the telephone wants to catch some for me. I've told
him to come down to see me about it. Do you mind sitting in the other
chair? Otherwise you'll have to shout—that's my bad ear on your side.
It hasn't been much good since I was knocked over by a lion. Mind you,
he meant no harm—I knew him well, we were the best of friends, and
that was the trouble; he used to get up on his hind legs to greet me, a sort
of a game, you know, and this time I didn't brace myself at the right
moment and he pushed me over. Cracked my head against the concrete
floor. That wasn't the time my eyes were damaged—you'll notice that I'm
wearing very thick lenses? That was because of a giraffe. She was newly
arrived, not used to the surroundings, and just as I came in to have a look
at her she was startled by something outside, and jerked up one leg,
and the knee caught me in the head. I was unconscious for weeks; they
thought I was dying . . . Well now. You're interested in the zoo. It's
been my life"—here he spoke more slowly, looking hard at me to lend
emphasis to his words—"for thirty years. My life." He paused briefly.
"I'd always been interested in natural history, but as a young man I didn't
have time to do anything about it. I had a living to get, for myself and
the family, and I tried my hand at a lot of things before I hit my stride
with the paraffin—or kerosene—refrigerator. In those days kerosene was
the main fuel used by people in Australia, especially those who lived
out in the bush. Nobody had any idea that it would ever be possible to
supply electricity to the whole country, and food preservation was a
grave problem. So I designed this refrigerator, and it went like wildfire.
I was a businessman: I was a salesman. I drove miles in the bush, up
and down the country, selling refrigerators, making plenty of money.
But I had this interest in zoos, I never forgot them, and in the end I got
into zoo-keeping and learned a good deal." Certainly he learned, I
reflected: today he has a formidable list of honors—Knight, FRZS, Knight
Commander North Star, Honorary Fellow of the Zoological Society of
London.

"We were settled here at Sydney," continued Sir Edward. "Taronga
Park was opened because Sydney people were agitating for an amusement
place of some sort, and the government bought this land for a song, and
also bought up a few animals from an unsuccessful zoo—a privately
owned one—that had gone broke and was closing down. The new zoo

wasn't much, but I got interested, and I started buying animals for them, building it up, getting into it deeper and deeper, until—here it is, and not a bad place at all, as you'll see in a minute." We looked out of the window. The view was obscured by part of our building, but I could see a pleasant stretch of rolling land, and beyond it the sea. Here and there, in hollows or on built-up hills, enclosures were marked by ditches or fences. A high wall ran along the street side. Ornamental lakes looked blue in the sun.

"This isn't as far as my interest took me," continued the director. "In New Guinea I have a farm, or private zoo, where I can experiment and explore. That's a wonderful country, New Guinea; I've made studies of the animals and birds there, and collected beautiful birds of paradise. When we go around I'll show you a bird I discovered. Did you ever hear of the Glossy Black Cockatoo? You may not have in your part of the world, because he can't live anywhere but here. And do you know why? Because he's got to have one special sort of food, the berry that grows on one special tree that grows here. It's because of his peculiar digestive system. I was working on one that died, trying to find out what ailed him, and something I've always thought a bird ought to have was missing from the body. As you know, birds—most birds—have gizzards, or crops, whichever you call it. When a chicken eats gravel or an ostrich swallows foreign objects—and birds do, you know, to help digest their food—the hard gravel and so on is shoved into the crop where it can't do any harm. Now this Glossy Black Cockatoo *has no gizzard*. I couldn't believe it, but it's the truth, and that's why he can't eat anything but one kind of oily berry. If he swallows anything else, anything at all, it kills him. I keep a pair of the birds here. We grow the plant in rotation so they'll have the fruit the year round. In the wild, of course, they can follow the seasons if necessary.

"Naturally, we specialize in Australian animals. We have the best collection of marsupials in the world. I have a private preserve at Mona Vale, near here, for koalas—you may have seen some of my koalas in California: I sent some to San Francisco and to San Diego. There were a few false starts and I had to send two more lots to replace them, but they're pretty well established now—California has all the eucalyptus they need to feed on. In the ordinary way the export of native animals from Australia is prohibited by the government, and I have to get a special permit whenever I send any specimens out. They're a nuisance, all those regulations. It works the other way as well. Last year I bought some zebras I'm still waiting for: they've been stopped at the border, still in quarantine. It's the foot-and-mouth disease that makes the authorities so careful—they've got a special down on ungulates.

"Nevertheless we have a great number of exotics here, doing nicely—we aren't restricted to native fauna. It's a wonderful climate for most animals, and we have special methods to encourage breeding." He added, impressively, "Our black rhinos have bred three times. Successfully." I *was* impressed. The captive black rhino has not often been persuaded to reproduce, and the species is far from plentiful even in the wild. It is on the IUCN list of animals distinguished as RARE.

Suddenly, as he often did, Sir Edward changed the subject. "I'm widely criticized because I believe in concrete flooring for pens. People say it's ugly, doesn't give a natural look and all that. But what you've got to consider, I tell them, is that a wild animal in a zoo enclosure isn't in its natural surroundings no matter how the place may be trimmed with pretty paint and all that. You pay a high price for natural beauty when you insist on keeping animals on soil. Take a red kangaroo or an antelope; in the wild he has a wide range to graze, but you can't give him the space in a zoo no matter how big it is. Now every wild beast is preyed on by intestinal parasites—that's a natural state. In the wild, healthy animals are those that have built up an immunity to such parasites: those that didn't died off early. But even the healthy ones are still hosts. In the wild they move around, get away from their own droppings—another factor that plays to their advantage. But a captive animal can't get away from his excrement, and reinfects himself again and again from always being on contaminated soil. For an immune animal it doesn't matter, but the newborn young hasn't had a chance to build up resistance and he's killed off. It's obvious why so many animals born in captivity die within the first few weeks. Unless you put concrete or some other easily-washed substance underfoot, you get the same diseases repeatedly. It stands to reason. Ask any stockbreeder. I don't care how unbeautiful it may be, I swear by concrete. Of course I don't leave it bare. For one thing, it would be too hard for a lot of species' feet, though some ungulates do need to walk on something hard now and again to keep their hoofs ground down—I leave bare spaces for that, here and there. Otherwise we put down wood shavings or herbage of some kind, straw or fresh branches, that can be swept out every night. Then the concrete floor is washed down and clean cover is scattered on top of it. I know a lot of other directors don't see it my way and laugh at me. Only the other day I was talking to a fellow, I won't name him, but he's a well-known zoo man. The minute I mentioned concrete he said, 'Oh, everybody knows that about you—you've got a concrete obsession.'

Obsession! That was his word." Sir Edward snorted and paused for a moment, looking like an aggrieved bull. "So I said to him, 'That's all right, but let's see you match my records on breeding and longevity.' Well, of course he couldn't, and he knew it. Charley Schroeder of San Diego was here not long ago, and after he'd had a look round he said quite frankly, 'I can't say I admire the looks of your zoo, but I'll admit you've got the animals.' And I do. That's the main thing, isn't it? Because that's what zoos are for, or ought to be for—conservation. It's all in that word: the true end of zoo planning and zoo keeping is conservation. Putting on a show for the public is important, but it comes second, and so does research. How are you going to do research on a species or look at it, when it's extinct? Tell me that." With another of his sudden switches he broke off and pointed to a shadowy shape, a prowling skeleton of considerable size, on top of a sideboard against the opposite wall. "Do you know what that is?" he demanded.

"No, I don't. Could it be one of the big cats?"

"Not far off. That's a saber-tooth, and most of it is authentic. Naturally some of the bones are missing; they had to be faked, but most of it's real. I've had plenty of offers for that animal, but I wouldn't let it go. There's not another like it in the world. Nobody can look at a saber-tooth in a zoo cage, or analyze its blood samples. It died out, just what's going to happen to many of today's species unless we take care."

"Those methods you spoke of," I said. "The ones you use to maintain your breeding. Is it feeding in some special way, or what?"

"It depends on a variety of things," he said, and added nothing more to the subject at the time. I had to wait a year for more information, when Sir Edward attended an AAZPA meeting in San Diego to which he had been especially invited because the zoo people of America wanted to bestow another honor on him. In an address to the assembly he told us what his methods are. "I use Rober's Mixture. You can buy it at any chemist's, and the way you administer it is as simple as it can be. Suppose you want your black rhinos to breed: this is what you do. Take an ordinary scone—" He pronounced the word in the British way, "scahn," and left his American audience mystified. There followed much agitated whispering and questioning from chair to chair, while pencils were suspended in air above notebooks. In the meantime Sir Edward, oblivious of the consternation he had caused, pressed on. "—an ordinary scone, slice it in half in the usual way, and spread one half with good butter. Then you take a tablespoonful of your Rober's Mixture, sprinkle it on the butter, clap the scone together, and give it to your rhino. Give one to the male, one to the female. They'll love it. Do this three times a week, and soon you'll see results. The first time I tried it, within a few weeks my keeper told me that there were marks on the female's back. A short time later they were copulating—I had the good fortune to be there and I snapped a photo of them in the act which I'd have brought along to show you today, if somebody hadn't decided to appropriate it and took it out of my office when nobody was looking. That's friendship for you, and I've lost the negative, unfortunately, but don't forget what I've told you—Rober's Mixture. You can get it here. I made inquiries at the chemist's near the hotel this very morning."

At Taronga Zoological Park I tried deliberately to look at things from the point of view of the critics whose adverse comments so irritated my host. I thought that some of their unfavorable impressions might be laid at the door of climatic differences. People accustomed to British landscape or Ceylonese countryside might well be startled and dismayed at the stark aspect of Sydney's suburbia, with its unfamiliar trees thin on the ground. South Africans would be less adversely affected—they have stretches that might be called similar—but even for them most things in Australia are *different*: the very wood used in building is not what one is used to. The hues of nature, too, are departures from the norm of non-Australians. At the zoo the stranger is surrounded by new textures, sounds, vegetation: if his reaction is to resent these differences, and condemn Taronga's appearance, it should be no cause for wonder. To be sure, the controversial concrete pens didn't offend *my* eye, but then I had been warned. And aesthetics or no, there was no denying Sir Edward's claim that he had the animals, for the zoo swarmed with inhabitants everywhere—marsupials, big cats, birds of paradise, the famous rhinos, and something that made me stare in awe: a whole kindergarten of young orangutans. Some of these were old enough to play with each other, some still clung to their mothers. The birth in captivity of an orangutan, another IUCN "RARE," is usually hailed with great excitement at any zoo.

"Oh yes, six youngsters have been born here," said the director, offhand as could be. "We get a lot of chimps born too, so many now that the committee keeps after me to sell some. I'll have to do it soon, too, for reasons of space. We have a nice lot of gorillas; those that you see and two I haven't put on exhibition as yet. None of them has bred so far, but I have every expectation that they'll show some activity before long. I've got a very good man. It's not always that a director can depend on a man like him." He introduced me to his young assistant, Bill, and we all went backstage to look at two nearly grown gorillas there. I asked Bill if his experience bore out Schaller's in Africa. Schaller, studying gorillas in the wild, had found them uneasy when looked straight in the eye, and thought this might be because two gorillas, when putting on a show of hostility, try to stare each other down. Bill said that his experience with the Taronga gorillas didn't bear out the theory. "We communicate with our eyes even more than with gestures," he said. The apes regarded us with patient forbearance and, it is true, did not seem to resent it when we gazed into their big brown eyes.

Moving me on to the reptile house, Sir Edward took me on a circuit so that I could admire the new structure from all angles. He indicated a snake behind one of the glasses and said, "Do you remember poor De Bary, the Salt Lake City director who died of snake bite? There's the adder that bit him. I happened to be in touch with the Hogle Zoo people just when they were wondering what to do with the animal, and I said I'd take it off their hands, so here it is. Of course I haven't let the story out, for fear we'd be flooded with morbid sightseers. Some of the public's difficult enough as it is—zoos attract some crazy types. So for all the people know, that's a plain and simple puff adder. Now we're going to view the prize exhibit."

Following in his steps, I wondered if it would be a baby black rhino, but we were still close to the reptile house when he unlocked a door and beckoned me to come into the place with him. "Don't be afraid," he said as I obeyed. "They're very gentle—Bill can tell you that." Bill was there before us, replenishing the water in a shallow indoor pool of considerable size. We stood in a brightly sunlit room with a sanded floor. Both men looked fondly down at two enormous lizards that stood on bandy legs, turning their heads inquiringly from side to side, flicking long, red, ribbonlike tongues. "The male's quite friendly now," said Bill.

I said, "No, are they really what I think? Komodo dragons?" The men nodded proudly. "I didn't know you had any," I said. "I didn't know anybody had." What I meant was that I didn't know anybody outside the Communist zone had any, but Sir Edward understood. These great monitor lizards have in their time stirred up a lot of excitement, as have giant pandas, gorillas, and Galapagos tortoises, all one time curiosities. The lizards aren't unknown in Europe and America: several zoos have owned them, but with indifferent success in keeping them alive. In the wild they occur only in Flores, one of the Lesser Sunda Islands of Indonesia between Java and Timor. In 1965, the strained relations existing between Sukarno and most countries of the Western world made it unlikely that any of our zoos would be able to get more Komodo "dragons," as newspapermen usually refer to them. I recollected a conversation on this point that I'd had with Caroline Jarvis at Regent's Park a few days before I took the plane to New Delhi.

CAROLINE: As you're going to Australia and Malaya, why not stop off at Indonesia? They have Komodos at Surabaja.

ME: I'm not going to Indonesia. I've been there, and once was enough. I wouldn't be able to get permission to go to Surabaja.

CAROLINE: It would be worth a try, to see the Komodos.

ME: No, you don't know what it's like. They'd keep me hanging around for weeks and then say no.

CAROLINE: It seems such a waste, considering that it's the only chance you'll have to see a Komodo.

ME: It's not a chance, I tell you. It's no use going. I'm not going to Indonesia.

CAROLINE (unmoved): But they have Komodos at Surabaja.

Well, now they had Komodos at Sydney too. I wondered if I ought to cable Caroline to say so: probably not. The bigger lizard spotted me across the floor and came toward me at a surprisingly swift pace. He looked about six feet long, and his tongue, flicking out and in faster than the eye could follow, was long in proportion. Near to me he stopped, and the tongue explored my ankles, flick, flick, so lightly that it felt more like a quick little breeze than a touch. The blunt-snouted face, far from being dragonish, was so amiable that I patted the lizard's head. "That's right," said Sir Edward approvingly. "Very gentle." He went on to tell how he had acquired the lizards. In happier days he'd had some dealings with Sukarno, and a shred of friendly feeling must have remained in the old dictator's heart, for he didn't forget a promise he had made to relinquish a pair of the animals to Hallstrom. Only a few months earlier, word had arrived from New Guinea that the lizards were at last available. Sir Edward described his incredulous delight at the news, followed by worried wondering as to how to collect them. Komodos sent by ship to distant parts of the world have more often than not died on the way. On the other hand, the employees of commercial airlines knew nothing of the care of these rare, valuable beasts, and there was a question of what air pressure at high altitudes might do to them. And the temperature change—inevitable at such height—wasn't that apt to wreak harm on them? Besides, there was no direct commercial air route that could be used. The director therefore chartered a plane and himself went to fetch his prizes, taking along plenty of hot-water bottles. "I packed them in and covered them over with blankets, hot-water bottles and all," he said. "I had a thermometer in with them, so I could tell if the temperature underwent any big changes, but it didn't. The pool here was ready for them with the water heated to the exact degree of their native pools, and the minute they were turned out they were as lively as you like. We haven't had any trouble. They can move around here indoors, and when they feel like basking outdoors, if it's warm enough, we open up that courtyard and they go out. Of course we watch their diet scrupulously. That's something a lot of zoo people neglect, in my opinion."

He elaborated on this subject as we returned to the administration building. "A large percentage of zoo losses, in my opinion, are due purely and simply to malnutrition. It used to be even worse than it is now, but it's still far from good. An undernourished animal is an easy prey to any bug that happens to come along—he can't throw off the disease. The disease is what kills him, according to the post mortem, whereas in reality it's only a secondary cause. Read any zoo's post-mortem reports and you'll see, very often, the phrase, under 'Cause of Death,' 'Heavy infestation of internal parasites.' What I ask is, how did those parasites get such a strong hold on the subject in the first place? It must have been weak—underfed."

It was well past noon when I took my leave. "It was very good of you to give me so much time, especially as you must be busy with the Duke of Edinburgh's visit," I said. He waved it off, saying that he and the Duke had already met on more than one occasion, and held conversations about saving wild life. "A very sound man on the subject," added Sir Edward. "But I'm not doing much about him this time. I'll drop in tomorrow at the luncheon they're holding for him, but I don't plan to sit through it from the start, I'll get there only in time for this talk. Too much to do around here." He invited me to come up to dinner that evening and meet his wife.

The Hallstroms' house is perched on a ridge between two inlets from the sea. Dusk was falling as I walked up a paved path that wound between trees to the door. Just outside the porch were two cages on high stands, with parrots in them: another cage under the eaves held a smaller white bird. To show me these creatures and a hyacinthine macaw he was proud of, Sir Edward pressed a button that lit fairy lights in the trees. Indoors the walls were covered with paintings, many of them done by Lady Hallstrom. A married daughter of the couple came in for dinner with us, and other relatives of various ages joined us later. Perhaps because of the young people, Sir Edward fell into a reminiscent mood. He said to his wife, "Remember the time I tried to make pearls?" She laughed and nodded. He explained to me: "I was trying to make out how the oysters do it. This was just about the same time that fellow Mikimoto in Japan was doing his early experiments, but I'd never heard of his work any more than he'd heard of mine. He put small irritants inside oysters' shells. We don't have oysters on this beach, so I tried to work with a different kind of shellfish. Unfortunately it isn't a bivalve; I had to bore a hole in the shell from the top to get to the inside, and introduce my foreign object through that hole. It didn't distress the animals to any noticeable extent. The headache was to keep them happy in fresh sea water, which meant changing the water at short intervals all day. I had the children, my wife, everybody in the house carrying pails of water from the sea, all day long. And I did get pearls, you know; the trouble with them was that they didn't turn out spherical—they grew like blisters on the nacre surface, so each one was a half-sphere instead of a ball. I was just working on that problem when the world started buzzing with excitement about Mikimoto's cultured pearls, so I dropped the whole idea. Years later I met Mikimoto—not the old man; he was no longer of this world: it was his son I met, and I told him about those experiments of mine. He was interested and asked if I'd let him have one of my half-pearls for a historical museum they were setting up. When I got back here I looked high and low and couldn't find any until at last my wife dredged one up out of her workbox. I sent that one to him."

Another man arrived and was introduced as the dolphin-catcher who was to supply the animals for Sir Edward's Marineland. "I'm interested in how he plans to go about it," said my host eagerly. "The Americans wouldn't tell me how they round up theirs, so we're going to work out a method for ourselves." He and the dolphin expert went into another room to talk it over, and Lady Hallstrom smiled as she watched them go. "I do hope he can get those dolphins," she said gently. "He wants them so much. Always so enthusiastic. And he's eighty, you know."

Next morning the papers were full of Prince Philip. At twelve o'clock, coming back to the hotel after doing several errands, I discovered that the much-discussed luncheon honoring him was taking place in the same hotel. What seemed like half the town had gathered on the sidewalks on both sides of the street outside the main door, to watch the Duke's arrival. Many of the women were dressed up for the vigil, splendid in hats and fur stoles and white gloves. Policemen guarded the door, so I joined the crowd and waited. At twelve sharp the official car rolled up and stopped, and the Duke made his little journey up the stairs, shook hands with the welcoming committee at the top and vanished into the doorway, but the watchers lingered still. After a good deal of pushing and shoving I made it to the door and went to have my lunch in the cafeteria, reflecting indulgently as I ate that a good many members of the Commonwealth, to all appearances, still belong to a royalty cult.

I was genuinely surprised, therefore, by the *Daily Mirror,* a local afternoon paper, when I bought a "Late Final Extra" edition and read it. On the front page, which was headed in enormous letters DRESSED TO KILL, was a full-length photograph of Prince Philip. At first glance it appeared to be the usual thing about his clothes and what tailors thought of them, especially as there were little placards drawn in here and there on the figure—"Colored Shirt," "Two Buttons," and "Hat Carried." A smaller photograph, however, carried the bite: in this Philip was standing in the background, and the foreground displayed a number of dead foxes neatly laid in a row, the whole labeled "THE HUNTING DUKE in Denmark, wears plus-fours and tweeds, surveying the day's bag of foxes. He shot four of them, earning criticism from animal-lovers." The accompanying column elaborated: "The Duke of Edinburgh today received wide support for his appeal to preserve Australian wild life. But in Europe and Britain, he has often been criticised for his own hunting activities. The Duke and Prince Bernhard of the Netherlands in 1962 made a joint appeal for the preservation of wild life. It was noted at the time that between them they had shot an elephant, a crocodile, a lion, a tiger, Indian mountain goats, a giraffe-headed antelope, deer, wild boar and thousands of partridges, pheasants, wild duck and wood pigeons. In 1963 the Duke headed a pheasant shoot by the royal family at Sandringham. . . ."

Two paragraphs later, well down at the bottom of the page, was a quotation from a Brisbane naturalist: "Game birds in England do not enter the same category as the wild life of Australia. Many animals are being destroyed in Australia. No effort is being made to bring them along as is the case with the game birds. Criticism of the Duke has gone too far. He has the interests of the wild life at heart." A zoologist added stoutly that as far as he was aware the Duke had never shot any animal considered rare.

Clearly, in spite of the crowd, the ladies' white gloves, and all the rest of it, colonial resentment still smoldered in independent Australia. Besides, we cannot wonder if men whose sporting-life mores do indeed lead to widespread destruction among wild animals spring to self-defense when they are criticized. It remained for Sir Edward Hallstrom to bring the discussion back to the point of Philip's talk. He was quoted as saying,

"Zoos have now changed their major role of exhibiting animals to one of preservation. The name zoo should now be dropped and preservation substituted for it."

No more was said about the Duke of Edinburgh.

CHAPTER 14

Zoos in Japan

□

We shall do in this book what I didn't do in fact, and skip lightly over the next two zoos I visited. Outside Singapore, in Johore Bahru, is a zoo, or menagerie, that was formerly the private property of the late Sultan of Johore. He handed it over to the state, and for a long time after that nothing much was done about it. They were enlarging the grounds when I saw it in 1966, but I've never cared for the place, and this visit did nothing to alter my feelings. Nor was I attracted by the Manila Zoological Gardens. Like the municipality that supports them, the staff no doubt have financial troubles, which explains why they seem stagnant. Still, Manila taught me something by introducing me to the raccoon dog. I'd never seen one before and I was puzzled by the label on the cage: if it hadn't been for that I would have dismissed the creature as a raccoon. In fact, as I've since discovered, in spite of appearances it's not even a close relation of the raccoon: it's a kind of fox. Raccoon dogs are found in the wild all the way down the eastern part of Asia, from Siberia to Vietnam, and in Japan as well, though there they have almost been exterminated by hunters who sell the fur and eat the flesh. The bones are used in the manufacture of medicine.

One raccoon dog, however—not even a pair, let alone a group—is not enough to make a zoo, and I was in a cautious, curmudgeonly state of mind when I arrived in Japan. If the Ueno Zoological Gardens of Tokyo were no better than the zoos I had lately seen, I decided, I would leave the country within the next day or so, and aim for America. This would have been a great mistake. The director of Ueno, Dr. Juro Hayashi, was shocked when I gave him a rather censored version of these intentions. "But there is very much here for you to see," he said. "There is much that is interesting. Ueno Zoo isn't the only collection in Japan, you know—it's not even the largest, though of course I like to think it numbers among the best. We have fifty-two zoos in Japan, and eighty marine aquariums. It would be nice if you could visit all of them, but if that's quite out of the question you should at least see Tama Park and Osaka and the deer at Nara, and Kobe. Certainly you shouldn't leave Japan without visiting Kyoto, where there's a good zoo. For that matter, why restrict yourself to Honshu island? Hokkaido has interesting zoos, and as for Kyushu—"

That day, at any rate, I saw Ueno Zoo and forgot the disgruntlement with which I'd arrived. It was a happy, busy, growing place. After a few minutes I even got used to the constant crackle of the loudspeaker, with its verbal announcements and music. The noise seemed a part of the general gaiety, along with scampering children or sober school croco-diles, and pram-pushing mothers, and fathers taking photographs, and women carrying lunch wrapped in colored cloth bundles.

Dr. Hayashi's entrance into the world of zoology was somewhat un-usual, since he was educated as an entomologist. After the war Ueno Zoo was in a bad way, and he joined the staff to assist in rebuilding and re-stocking it, since when he has become too much a part of things to think of leaving. Ueno Zoo has a long history: when it first opened in 1882 it was tiny, comprising less than five acres. Four years later it was transferred to the management of the imperial household, which doesn't mean that it was closed to the public, but that the Emperor's representative was re-sponsible for running it. But in 1924, in a gesture calculated to suit the rejoicings of the Crown Prince's wedding, the zoo, now larger by another four acres, was formally presented to Tokyo City, under the control of which it has remained ever since.

During the Second World War, when American planes began bombing Japanese cities, the elephants and other large animals of Ueno Zoo were destroyed by municipal order. "All Japanese zoos had to do the same," Dr. Hayashi said. "In some cases, the bombings added to deliberate destruction. At the Oshima Island Zoo, for instance, a lot of monkeys and deer and squirrels escaped from broken cages and fences, and have been living and breeding in the wild ever since."

After the war, as the nation recovered, so did the zoos. By 1952 Ueno Zoo was outgrowing her limited territory, and the municipality bought more land, a fifteen-acre tract just across a road to the west. A year before my visit, in 1964, they had celebrated the zoo's eighty-second birthday, in honor of which the Tokyo Zoological Park Society's maga-

zine quoted, in English translation as well as the original, a *haiku* by
the seventeenth-century poet Basho:

> *Clouds of cherry-blossoms:*
> *The temple bell. Is it Ueno*
> *Or Asakusa?*

The new tract, called the West Zoo, brought into the limits of the
grounds a fairly large body of water, Shimobazu Pond. This has been
landscaped down to the last square inch, with a monkey island and two
other bits of land, each holding at least one nicely shaped tree, but
when I saw it these features were all but obliterated by the birds, of
which thousands swam on the water. "Wild ducks. We have a lot of
trouble with this pond," Dr. Hayashi said. "It silts up, and we have to
dredge it every year. The bottom should be covered with concrete.
Sooner or later this has got to be done, and I hope to utilize the space
at the same time. Why shouldn't we have a marine zoo beneath the
pond? An underground zoo." I looked startled. He went on, "The roof
would be the bottom of the pond, do you see? Under it could be polar
animals, bears perhaps, certainly penguins, and reindeer pulling sleds for
children to ride on." He was alive with enthusiasm. I murmured that it
sounded awfully *dark* . . . "That's a part of my idea," he said. "Lights!
We would have lights everywhere, including an aurora borealis shining
on the ceiling. Think how good it would be for the penguins. We do well
with penguins here." He broke off, and after a pause murmured dreamily,
"And walruses . . ."

At the African section I learned that the war had not wiped out
every single one of the zoo's animals, after all. The giraffe dynasty had
survived, and for that Ueno Zoo can claim a sort of longevity record.
Japan's first home-produced giraffe, a reticulated member of the family,
was born at Ueno Park in 1937, and a present representative of the third
generation was born, also at Ueno, in 1957. There are now forty-three
giraffes in Japan. This may sound like quite a few, but the government felt itself unable to give up any of them in response to a proposition suggested some years ago by Peking, when the Chinese zoo department offered to swap a breeding pair of giant pandas for some
giraffes. "They wanted a whole lot of giraffes—twenty-five, I think, or
was it twenty?" said Dr. Hayashi. "In any case, our people decided we
couldn't spare that many. Moreover, our people wouldn't consider spending foreign currency to acquire giraffes for the purpose, in Africa or
anywhere else. It would have been wonderful to get those pandas, but

the government thought that other things had to come first. Besides, suppose the breeding pair didn't breed! The Chinese might accuse us of not feeding them properly, or they might give any number of other reasons for the failure." He shook his head and turned to a happier subject: "Here we have a baby hippo. We've had quite a lot of hippo births at Ueno—one of our females has produced six calves. But the sixth one was weak, and died almost immediately, so we kept watch on the mother. She didn't seem well—wasn't eating much, and seemed tired. After making the usual tests we decided that she had diabetes. It turned out that this diagnosis was correct, because she reacted well to treatment. I don't know that diabetes had ever been found in a hippo before. Certainly she improved remarkably after we started giving her daily shots of insulin. In fact, she seemed quite well. As long as we kept up the treatment she ate a normal amount, and was reasonably energetic. Then one day, after about a year of treatment, quite unexpectedly she fell into a coma, and died without ever coming out of it. Do you know what we found in the autopsy? Some of the insulin shots hadn't gone right into the bloodstream, because a hippo has so much fat: the needle didn't always penetrate. This might have been all right if the arrested insulin had remained where it was, in the blubber, but it didn't: in time it was released, and then, of course, what with the daily shot and this much added to it, she got an overdose and died of it.

"Here are our cranes—Sarus, Australian, and so on; there's a pair of Japanese cranes. When they're nesting, you know, you can take away an egg as soon as it is laid, and the female crane, who can't count or remember, immediately lays another. Then we put our stolen eggs into an incubator and hatch them out. We get quite a lot of birds that way. Here we're rebuilding some cages. Now, look at this: do you see anything unusual about it?" We had halted at a combination pit and moat, where low ground surrounded a plaster or cement mountain full of crags, one of those arrangements made in zoos for mountain sheep or monkeys. But here in one enclosure were both these species—sheep and baboons. I looked inquiringly at Dr. Hayashi, and he grinned.

"They get on well together," he said. "They're not from the same part of the world at all; the sheep are from the Middle East and the baboons from Abyssinia, but they get on well. You can see for yourself." Sure enough, a baboon was lying unconcernedly on one of the larger ledges, his head pillowed on a reclining sheep, and on the ground below us another baboon was industriously grooming a big-horned animal that seemed to enjoy the attention.

Suddenly the loudspeaker braved out "Auld Lang Syne." This was apparently the signal for closing time, and the mothers started wheeling or leading their infants toward the exit. It was only four o'clock, but in northern latitudes animals like to get to sleep early. Dr. Hayashi said, "No hurry; we can go after the crowd has left. Have you ever eaten raw fish?" I explained that I *had* eaten raw fish, as a matter of fact, more than once. He did not seem to be listening, but he must have been, because after he had driven to another section of town and we were settled down in a tiny bar-restaurant, he ordered a number of snacks that did not include *sushini*. They were all quite unfamiliar to me, and if it hadn't been for Dr. Hayashi they would have remained so. As it was, I didn't like to refuse anything, so I swallowed some of every dish, including briny shellfish of peculiar shape, dried black objects in oil that could have been grasshoppers, and thin white ribbonlike things that he told me, falsely, were bamboo shoots. I say "falsely" because I am practically certain that bamboo shoots never have eyes. I think now, in retrospect, that it would have given Dr. Hayashi pleasure if I'd balked at some of the things: it is a national sport to dismay tourists in this manner, but at the time I didn't think, and I was hungry after so much fresh air. My unflagging appetite gave Dr. Hayashi a new idea. Calling the waitress, he demanded half a dozen little polythene bags, and into these he collected samples of all the varieties of food I had eaten, one to each bag. Pocketing the collection, he led me to another bar, where he was happily greeted by a number of cronies. There he brought out his little bags and put them down, looking around proudly. "Just see what she's been eating!" he said. I was toasted in cups of *sake*, which meant, of course, that I toasted the party in return.

Regardless of my rather sensitive head next morning, I was up early, because Dr. Hayashi and his wife were motoring to Tama Zoological Park, and I was to accompany them. While waiting to be called, I read mail from England and noticed that the new *International Zoo Yearbook* had appeared. My husband had sent along a review of it with some excerpts dealing with developments in Japanese zoos, and I put it into my handbag. Dr. Hayashi was late, and explained on the way out to the car that his wife was not with him, but would meet us at the zoo at Tama Park. "She had to go and pick up another lady who is also coming with us, the wife of a government minister, so we thought that this was better. The other lady has a special reason for wanting to come to Tama. Next month at the town near the zoo, Hino-machi, there is to be a dedication ceremony for a new building, and this minister's wife is going to write a poem of commemoration, which she will read aloud. She wants to prepare for it today by finding a temple where she can retire to write her poem."

"Oh yes." I got into the car. "You mean she'll stay there when we've found it, and write her poem between now and then?"

"No, not at all. She will write the poem during the ceremony, not ahead of time. But of course she would like to make sure that her surroundings are going to be right, and that is why we are helping her today. I am confident that she'll like the temple we intend to show her: it's a celebrated one. We will see it after lunch."

"But what if she doesn't approve of it when she sees it?"

"There are plenty of other temples," said Dr. Hayashi.

We whizzed along one of the splendid new roads that were made to take care of extra traffic during the Olympic Games of 1964. Unconsciously, I stepped hard on imaginary brakes whenever we rounded a curve, until Dr. Hayashi said cheerfully, "Do not be afraid. I have never had an accident. Arrested for speeding, yes, many times, but never an accident."

I remembered the book-review in my handbag, and brought it out to read a portion aloud: " 'A thirty-year-old donkey in a Tokyo Zoo has been fitted with false teeth with the help of which it now makes hearty meals of green grass, having previously been in pretty poor shape.' That must be your zoo, Dr. Hayashi. Did it really happen?"

He nodded. "Oh yes, quite true. It's a very old donkey, brought back by our soldiers from China at the end of the war. We did have teeth made and they work well, but the newspapers in Tokyo got the story a little wrong. The reporters said that when the teeth had been finished and put into the donkey's mouth, he immediately started cropping grass. As a matter of fact, eating grass was *not* the first thing the donkey did."

"What did he do, then?"

"Bit the dentist," said Dr. Hayashi, and doubled over the steering-wheel with mirth.

By the time we reached Tama, undisturbed by any policeman, I had learned that the zoo there was a sort of country cousin to Ueno in that it, too, is under the management of the Tokyo Zoological Park Society. The Zoological Society of London has two zoos in its care in somewhat the same way—Regent's Park and Whipsnade. But Whipsnade started out as a sanitarium and overflow reservoir for the town zoo, only later becoming a zoological garden, whereas Tama Park was created from the beginning as a zoo in its own right. It is quite new. More than ninety acres, spread over wooded hills and ravines, were set aside for it, and Dr. Hayashi came out from Tokyo to live on the spot and superintend the

construction. He was Tama Park's first director, but was replaced by another man when he was appointed to head Ueno Zoo. "At Ueno I took
over the post from Dr. Tadamichi Koga, who wished to retire," he explained, "but as it has turned out, he wasn't permitted to retire, after all.
He is now head of the whole Society. Everybody in the zoo world knows
Dr. Koga; people call him 'Elephant Koga' because he is big."

The country was unusually wild and unsettled for that populous part
of Japan: even the entrance to Tama was strikingly bare of the houses
and shops that I had learned to expect around the entrance to a park.
"It's a long way from Tokyo as we count distance," said Dr. Hayashi.
"Because it's so far away, we didn't expect a great crowd on the day we
had our opening celebrations, but more than a hundred thousand turned
up, and we were surprised. So was the railway, which ran out of tickets
from Tokyo to Hino-machi, the nearest station. We get a lot of people,
especially on holidays: last year the attendance was something more than
a million and two hundred thousand. Ah, there they are."

A black chauffeur-driven limousine turned into the parking lot and
stopped behind us to let two ladies in kimonos and shawls descend. We
got together with them, but everything had to wait while Mrs. Hayashi
greeted a number of other women who seemed to spring up out of nowhere to bow and smile and pay her polite compliments. Finally the two
ladies got into our car, along with one of the zoo officials, and the gates
were opened. We rolled slowly through and followed a shaded avenue
that rose gently toward the horizon, between wooded enclosures—a pedestrians' path, if the truth were known, but as an ex-director Dr. Hayashi was permitted to take liberties. It was a cold day and we had the
place pretty much to ourselves. Each enclosure stretched far back and up
the rocky hillsides—a pleasant sight with the animals feeding peacefully
or running about. A number of deer browsed behind what looked like
merely a token fence alongside a narrow stream.

"Won't they jump that railing?" I asked. "It doesn't look high enough
to keep them in."

"No fence of any reasonable height can keep a deer from jumping
out if he wants to jump out," said Dr. Hayashi, "but deer don't try to
escape. The mere sight of a fence is enough to deter them."

We had come to the crest of a hill, where the zoo spread out, enclosures distributed according to the hilly terrain. In one rocky space
the arrangement was puzzling—a number of foxes going about their
affairs, completely unperturbed by the huge hulking form of a bear that
sat among them. "It has something to do with a Japanese fairy story
or fable," Dr. Hayashi explained. "We have many stories about animals.

In some zoos they keep a hare in a small cage among raccoon dogs, because all our children have heard about the hare's adventures with other animals. Tama Park gets a lot of schoolchildren as visitors, because of the insectarium. I'd like to show it to you now." We drove along a bumpy road to an approach that was still being constructed, leading to a building set on a steep slope. A truck was drawn up close to the side entrance, men in work clothes forking bales of greenstuff out of it. Climbing over heaps of rubble, we came to the front courtyard, in the middle of which stood the giant figure of a grasshopper on a stand. "There isn't another insectarium like this in the world," said Dr. Hayashi proudly. "Even now, unfinished, it's an important center for education. The government has appropriated three hundred and sixty million yen to maintain it, to be spread through some years to come. That grass and hay they're unloading is food for the insects. They'll eat it all within a few days." With an entomologist's enthusiasm he spoke of the experiments they were making, in order to have lively exhibits throughout the year instead of depending on natural cycles. Butterflies emerging from pupae, moths from cocoons, dragonflies in all their different phases, beetles and spiders and ants—it was going to be tremendous, he assured me. The Japanese ladies stood silent on the hillside and held their shawls tight against a persistent wind, but when he proposed going through the building for a look at the insects, the minister's wife gave a ladylike little shudder and refused, so we got back into the car and went on our way.

From another high point we looked down on the African section of the zoo. One large enclosure held giraffes and another hippos, but I didn't pay close attention to either exhibit because I was absorbed in the chimpanzee archipelago, or isthmus—a long, irregular tongue of land surrounded everywhere but at one end by water. The shelter, an elaborate closed house, blocked up this end, but a low railing ran around the whole area, and this, I understand, was electrified. The chimps didn't go near it. Two were playfully wrestling, and another lay on her back, sunning herself. "It's good," I said, "but isn't it rather bare? A tree or some kind of gymnastic apparatus—"

Yes, Dr. Hayashi said, he agreed, and there would be playthings in time, but the whole exhibit had only lately been completed to the degree where it was feasible to put the apes into it. On the first day one had escaped, through no particular desire of his own, and was badly frightened in the hills until he was recovered and put back with his companions. "And now," he said, "we are going on safari in Kenya."

The car descended from the plateau and went by a roundabout route to a pair of locked gates in the wall of a Moorish-looking edifice, where we waited until attendants inside got them open. Rolling through, we were faced by another pair of gates, this time of iron grillwork, and we waited for a bit in a large, empty chamber that Dr. Hayashi said was destined to serve as a bus station. "The way we came is not the road that will be used when it's all finished," he continued. "The approach is going to be by tunnel. I got the idea of this station when I was in Kenya; I call it Swahili architecture. Moslem, you understand—Arab. All this, the animals as well, comes from Kenya. Now, the surprise." The attendant, with a companion, had unlocked the iron gates and swung them wide, and Dr. Hayashi drove out into an open area, pausing briefly to shut the window on his side of the car. We were driving over red sand and rubble surrounded on all sides by a wall of similar color, made of an adobelike material. Heavily grilled windows looked down on our backs from the Swahili bus station. There were built-up hillocks and banks, and a sketchy, winding road between them. Ten or twelve lions walked about or lay on the ground: one, which had been standing rigidly, his face toward the wind, took an interested look at us and sauntered over. Dr. Hayashi stopped the car, and the minister's wife said something in a squealing voice. The first lion was followed by others. They walked around the car, one of them sniffing it all over like a curious domestic animal examining somebody's shoe. On my side, a lion came up to the glass and looked me in the eye, in which position his face was quite remarkably large. Still, the expression was amiable. When Dr. Hayashi started the car again, all but one of the lions lost interest. That one, however, ran alongside for a bit, frisking. It was a young one, which stayed with us until we came to the exit gate.

The thing wasn't working properly yet, said Dr. Hayashi—when it went into operation, the public would be taken through in large buses. Each bus would go through the area slowly, so that visitors could take photographs, and when the trip was over the bus would circle the wall until it reached the entrance gate again. We compared his lions with the ones on view in the reserve just outside Nairobi. Tama Park's, I commented, were far more lively than the Nairobi cats, which have become so accustomed to sightseeing cars that no matter how many tourists are gawking at them, they are capable of lying down and going to sleep.

At lunch my host directed a curator to sit next to me and answer questions. The curator, a knowledgeable young man, had read a lot of zoological works in English, and had a few questions of his own. Did I know Blank, who had recently published a book on the great apes? If I got the chance, he suggested, I might tell Blank that he had made a grave error in saying that the capped gibbon is of the same species as the white-handed gibbon. The curator knew, because he had recorded the calls of both these apes on a tape-recorder, and the capped gibbon's call is noticeably more resonant, every time. "This week I'm going to tape the siamang," he said. "We have a pair, and they are very vocal. I've got a lot of gelada baboon noises; they have a wide variety. When one gelada baboon calls to another, he sounds exactly like a donkey, but he does it backward—*haw-hee, haw-hee.*" He gave these syllables all the force and value that a baboon would have used, but nobody in the zoo restaurant even looked around.

"There's been a tremendous surge of interest here, in Japan, in monkeys," he said. "I hope you're planning to see the Monkey Center at Inuyama."

"Inuyama? I don't think—"

"If you're going to Nagoya you can visit Inuyama. It's very near. By the way, at the Nagoya Zoo you mustn't miss the gorillas and their trainer, a man named Asai. If possible you should also see Baboon Island in Mikawa Bay, controlled by the Monkey Center. Of course there *are* other monkey centers in Japan. The biggest is on Kyushu, our southern island, you know, on Takasakii Mountain, near the Beipu Hot Springs. More than a thousand Japanese macaques used to live around there. They were nearly wiped out, but now the authorities have started to protect them, and they've increased again to three hundred. The Monkey Center people have divided the group into two. They live in the wild just as they've always done; the Monkey Center people at Inuyama will tell you that they want to keep them like that for purposes of observation. Zoo behavior in wild animals is never quite the same, you see. For instance, monkeys in the wild state warn each other when strangers approach, but in cages they never do. I've taped twenty-three different calls made by Japanese monkeys." But I must not think, he said, that the Monkey Center was interested only in Japanese macaques. They aimed to have a wide variety of species, and had already accumulated sixty at least. At that very moment an expedition of Monkey Center people was in Africa collecting monkeys, at Lake Kivu. Their expenses were being paid by the Asahi Press.

As for Tama Park's breeding record, the curator continued, they were expecting an orangutan baby to be born in May or June, and it would be nice if the delivery was successful. Only one orang had as yet been bred in Japan, at Ueno Zoo. A striped hyena was born at Tama in 1964, and had been successfully bottle-reared. The mother had recently given birth again, and this time was taking such jealous care of the infant that it was still impossible to determine its sex. An adult hyena had escaped in December, but it was a very tame beast and nobody was worried. Its keeper eventually coaxed it back. Only a month earlier, however, a banteng had escaped, perhaps because it was restless and unhappy since its keeper had retired and been replaced. (Bantengs are wild cattle from Burma.) "It jumped a low wall and got into the enclosure of the lesser panda," said the curator. "It jumped that wall easily, and got out into the wild country; and it took us two days to recover it. Looking for a lost animal in these hills is not easy."

At the other end of the table I could see the ladies looking around for their wraps and handbags. I had time, I decided, for one last question. "If you could have one rare animal that the zoo hasn't got," I said, "what would be your choice?"

At the look of intense yearning that came into his eyes, I expected him to say "giant panda," or perhaps "Komodo dragon," but he didn't mention either of these. "A serow," he said.

To my shame, I had to ask what a serow was. He said it's a goat-antelope, found in a very few regions of Asia. One subspecies of serow lives in Japan, but is so rare even on its home ground—Uvaisha Mountain Park in the Mira Prefecture—that the government protects it with vigor. "We have a serow from Taiwan," he said. "If only we had another, for a pair! Nagoya has two and Kyoto has four. Only one serow has been bred in captivity, and there are only twelve Japanese serows in all the zoos of Japan." He was still lost in a dream when we left. As soon as I had the chance I looked up the serow in Walker, and I admit it's an appealing animal, with goatish horns.

Waiting for Dr. Hayashi with the car, the minister's wife teased Mrs. Hayashi, asking her if she didn't miss living at Tama Park. Mrs. Hayashi laughed, and explained to me that she'd lived there for two years while her husband kept an eye on the planning and construction of the new zoo; the sojourn had not, I gathered, been wholly blissful. "Very lonely," she admitted. Still, one good result came of the long exile—she knew the neighborhood like the palm of her hand, and was able to lead us directly to the temple the minister's wife wanted to examine. Picking out the right place to write a poem, I gathered, is a serious business, and the minister's wife treated it with proper gravity. The head priest listened respectfully to her ideas, and led us on a tour through the building, a house of polished wood, mainly one long room of hushed emptiness. Around it ran a veranda, carpeted in soft dark red. There was a little garden of classic type, one or two growing things set among strangely shaped rocks. The minister's wife was pleased with the temple, and made all her arrangements then and there.

Before we returned to Tokyo Mrs. Hayashi reclaimed the chauffeur-driven car and I said good-by to the ladies. Dr. Hayashi didn't take me straight back to the hotel, but persuaded me to stop off at a bar where the mama-san was a special friend of his. He wanted me to try the cuttle-fish.

"You cannot leave Japan without seeing more of the zoos; it would be a great mistake," said Dr. Koga. We had our interview in the office he oc-cupied as head of the Tokyo Zoological Park Society, in the administra-tion building of the zoo. Photographs of zoo men all over the world hung on the walls, with two or three particularly good posters. "You people from abroad never take the necessary time," he said, "and so you miss some very good things we have in other regions. Why be in such a hurry?"

"Well," I began.

"Good, then I shall make out your itinerary," said Dr. Koga. Next day I went to Nagoya.

This town is a seaport—most Japanese cities are ports, come to think of it—and a manufacturing center as well, a big city, but off the tourist route. In the two days I spent there I saw only one other American, a factory-supplies salesman distracted by homesickness. Almost nobody I happened to encounter, even behind the hotel desk, spoke English. But whether or not tourists know it, Nagoya is an important city, and every year its Higashiyama Zoo, a municipal organization, attracts nearly two million visitors. Few Japanese zoos have anything like the area boasted by Tama Park, and Higashiyama Zoo covers less than thirty-five acres, but it is cunningly arranged, and the exhibits don't seem cramped. It was first opened in 1936, and had barely got under way when the war started; thus, like all other zoos of the country, it had to be started over again afterward, but it has caught up in several respects, as I soon found out. Not that the general layout is particularly modern. For example, in a little artificial lagoon several large plaster dinosaurs stand, some rearing as if threatening each other. Somebody had visited Hagenbeck's zoo in Hamburg and had come back to Nagoya determined to copy the Germanic style.

A veterinary officer who was showing me around led me, by one of the byways reserved for the use of employees, to a door in a high curved wall, which he unlocked and opened. Stepping in after him, I was tumultuously greeted by a number of baby orangutans. They were very tame, very de-manding of attention, and I was paying no heed to anything else until, as I exchanged kisses with the boldest of them, I heard a burst of applause that seemed to come from a long way off, and looked up to find that I was in a public enclosure, or monkey house, with hundreds of people over the way, across the moat, staring at what was going on. What with feeling confused by this, and the fact that the vet didn't speak English, I couldn't ask how the zoo happened to have such a lot of rare young animals. Dealing in orangs is simply not supposed to be done nowadays. It will be remembered that the curator at Tama told me that only one orang had been bred in Japan at that time, though they were hoping for another birth soon. Clearly, not all Japanese zoo men were conservationists.

We left the orang enclosure by the little back door and came around to view all the great-apes living quarters from the public side. There were several of these moated areas in a row; the one in the middle was empty, but a crowd had gathered at the railing that commanded a view of it, nevertheless, and the vet plunged into the scrum to make a way for me to the front. I was finally deposited at the rail where I had an uninterrupted view; which was fine as long as there was nothing to look at, but a moment afterward the door into the back wall was opened, and the people around me surged forward so that I was nearly cut in half across the middle. People lifted children to their shoulders, or just pummelled their neighbors in the scramble, as a tall, lanky man in overalls and a floppy hat came through the door, followed by a sort of chain gang of three gorillas, single file, the second and third in line with their hands on the shoulders of the one ahead. What was striking was that they weren't baby gorillas or even toddlers; they were nearly full-grown. Once in a great while some animal trainer will put on an act where he is at close quarters with a gorilla of reasonable size, but it happens very seldom, and I'd never before seen one man on such familiar terms with a trio. Chimpanzees are generally said to be difficult actors after the age of eight, or even six, but gorillas are believed to be difficult at any age. Yet these three went through their paces without any friction at all. Mr. Asai—I remembered now that the Tama curator had told me his name—washed their faces one after the other with a wet towel as they sat in a row. He gave them hats which they put on. They had a tea party at a table, during which Asai swapped food with one of them, almost mouth to mouth—a whole gob of half-chewed lettuce. Though Western audiences might be too squeamish to appreciate this part of the act, it was done with a purpose: gorilla mothers sometimes feed their children in this way, and no doubt Asai maintained a close relationship with the apes through such gestures.

Like chimpanzees and dogs in other animal acts, they put on a show within a show; one gorilla pretended to be disobedient, and when Asai clumsily chased him, the others jumped him from the back. For a while they sat in a row like Occidentals, their feet dangling. For another while they sat on their heels like Japanese. They played musical instruments— a horn, a drum—and as a climax, to the beat of a flat percussion instrument played by Asai, they did the twist. I can't say that they did it very well, but they did it.

It wasn't until trainer and apes had left the enclosure that I became aware once more of the discomfort of being pinned to the fence by large numbers of enthusiastic spectators, but they had been gone a long time, and the marks on my anatomy were fading before I stopped marveling at what I'd seen. Remembering that the superintendent spoke some English I went back to the office to ask him about Mr. Asai, but we couldn't really communicate very well. All I gathered was that Asai is also very good with elephants. There is a sequel to the incident, however. After my visit to Nagoya I bored people to death, talking about the gorilla act. Some of my hearers didn't know anything about the subject and so couldn't appreciate the wonder of it; others just didn't believe me and said that what I'd seen were not gorillas, but chimpanzees—a remark calculated to send me into frenzies of indignation. Only one man, Dr. Ernst Lang of Basel, gave me credit for knowing what I'd seen, because, as he said, for a while his zoo had featured a young performing gorilla—Lang believes firmly in the therapy of animal acts—but had given it up. "He used to ride a tricycle and so on," he said, "but we found that he was taking it too hard. He was overanxious about the performance, and began losing weight, so we put a stop to it."

Apart from Lang, then, nobody believed me. Then, at the AAZPA meeting of early spring 1966, at San Diego, during an evening when some of the members showed their own films, the chairman made an announcement. "We're now going to see something that I won't describe in advance," he said. "You wouldn't believe me if I just told you about it. It's a documentary made by a local company, at the zoo at Nagoya, Japan."

There he was—Asai—getting ready for the day's work. It was early in the morning, and he was waking up his three gorillas, who slept in the same house with him. They all had breakfast together, then set out for the enclosure where they went through the day's first performance. I saw it all again, the tea party, the twist, and the rest of it, while all around me in the audience AAZPA members watched in silent amazement. On the screen, Asai took his gorillas home, put them to bed, and sat down at a desk to write up the day's notes. The End. The lights went up, the audience applauded, and the chairman said,

"Those are the biggest chimpanzees I've ever seen in my life!"

CHAPTER 15

Monkeys

☐

Three passengers were in the car to Inumaya. The municipality had furnished me with a girl to interpret, and we were also accompanied by a veterinarian who worked with the Institute of Primatology at the Japan Monkey Center. Our first stop was at the lower boundary of Inuyama Park, where steep, forest-covered hills rise from a gentler slope. The motor road was bordered by the usual procession of posts carrying wires, and the traffic was fairly heavy all the way until we turned into a driveway that led through a gap in a low brick wall. There was no fence between road and park—not that fences serve to keep monkeys in or out, I reminded myself; in any case, the ground inside the park seemed empty of life except for an old watchman sitting in a small hut. Here the veterinarian, Dr. Kotera, bought two packets of peanuts. We stood there, looking around. There was only bare ground with a few trees and hedges, leafless so early in the spring, and a row of benches. It might have been a rest haven for old people or cripples. Then the watchman put his hands to his mouth and uttered a loud cry, and rang a cowbell.

The land came alive. Down the hillside they streamed, alert and eager —a clan of monkeys large and small, some with babies clinging to their stomachs. They were Japanese macaques, or *Macaca fuscata*, the kind often portrayed by Japanese classical painters and ivory-carvers—stocky animals with long, thick fur, and whiskers, and pink faces. No doubt they recognized Dr. Kotera, but they weren't shy of any of us, demanding peanuts as if they were accustomed to such handouts.

"These are of a subspecies, we call them 'yakui,'" said Dr. Kotera. "In this troop are a hundred and fifty. Every single one is known to us; every one, as you can see, has a tag in its ear, so that we can keep track."

I asked if there was any hidden fencing to keep the animals from straying. "No," he said. "There's no need. These monkeys don't go away from their territory. It's not their habit. Besides, they are fed, and that in itself would keep them from wandering too far. We wouldn't want to fence them in; we don't want them to live like zoo animals. That's not the idea. Our professors wish to observe their way of life in the forest." He broke off to give peanuts to a large monkey that impatiently tugged at his trouser leg. When he had time to speak again he said that every monkey in the troop had a name, the males being called after fruit and the females after flowers.

At last his peanut sacks were empty, and the monkeys, as if knowing this, stopped begging, but as we got into the car and started away, several of the younger, more daring animals got up on the wall to watch our departure. Not one jumped into the road or climbed a telegraph pole; they were too sophisticated for that.

A side road took us by winding ways to the top of the range, where the offices, laboratories, and museum of the Monkey Center command a splendid view. There Dr. Kotera procured some literature for me, and I had time for a read-through before the tour recommenced. I learned that the Japan Monkey Center evolved from two other bodies, the Primate Research Group that two professors at Kyoto University started just after the war, and the Experimental Animal Research Committee, headed by two professors of Tokyo University, at about the same time. These two groups amalgamated, forming the Japan Monkey Center, and in 1956 the Nagoya Railroad Company, rather surprisingly, pledged themselves to furnish financial support for the enterprise. The Railroad Company foots the bills, but the Minister of Education actually controls the Center. The Kyoto group had specialized in ecology and social behavior of primates: Tokyo was more interested in ensuring an adequate supply of monkeys for experimental purposes. In the JMC both objectives remained and proliferated. *Macaca fuscata* is studied ecologically and sociologically, monkeys are bred for research purposes, and the Center serves as a clearing-house for data obtained in all similar institutes in Japan, in order to promote the studies of anthropology, zoology, and medical science generally. The JMC have sent six expeditions abroad for various purposes connected with their work: to observe gorillas in the wild, to study the crab-eating monkeys of Malaya, and, above all, to collect primates for the Center museum as well as the children's zoo. The museum contains a living section where fifty-six species of primate are to be seen; the authorities hope eventually to step up this number to two hundred.

Under JMC auspices a club has been organized among children of high school age—the Monkey Friend Club, associated with the Japan Society for the Protection of Wild Monkeys and the Association of Nature Conservation. A monthly magazine called *Monkey* is issued to all members.

Apart from the living monkeys, the museum exhibits stuffed animals, pictures, diagrams, and any other object that fits into the subject of primates. A much-frequented room houses the "Monkey Doll Collection," the gift of a private benefactor, which consists of ten thousand dolls. Japanese think well of dolls—the annual nationwide Doll Festival is an important occasion—and, furthermore, their tradition is full of primate legends, like the saga of the monkey that made a long pilgrimage and ultimately became a Buddhist.

The children's zoo is separate from the museum monkeys, and includes other animals as well as primates. Of necessity it is large for a Japanese collection—sixty acres—because the JMC has designed a "releasing method" to house the occupants. Each species has plenty of open ground: Spider Monkey Hill, Kangaroo Yard, Penguin Pond. Various methods have been adapted to keep the denizens within bounds: moats for some enclosures, electrified wire for others, and though some of the animals appeared to me to be staying in place purely voluntarily, no doubt this was an illusion. The JMC is particularly proud of its "monkey apartment houses." I saw one community, of spider monkeys, housed in this fashion. I was much struck. Admittedly I can't say what it would look like during the heat of the day, because by the time we got there the short spring afternoon was drawing to a close and the tenants had retired. Still, it gave me a turn just as it was, this little village with nothing outlandishly whimsical or Disneyish about it, just some little houses, sober in design, on stilts, and none more than four feet high. A bamboo curtain covered each doorway. Dr. Kotera stepped into the enclosure and went over to one of the houses and called or knocked at the door; suddenly the curtain was pulled aside and a monkey's face looked out. A moment later the monkey dropped the curtain again, and presumably went back to sleep.

Before we left I heard more about the JMC's project of studying wild colonies of primates. The "free-ranging" macaques in Inuyama Park are not really native to that district, but were transplanted a long time ago from Yakushima Island, south of Kyushu. The brochure telling about the various troops always gives the name of their leaders: Inuyama troop is led by a large male named Nolo, but I couldn't discover if I'd seen him or not. Three little islands at the west end of Mikawa Bay, near Nagoya, support other monkey communities that are not Japanese macaques: one has crab-eating monkeys from Southeast Asia, one (called Baboon Island) is inhabited by an interesting integrated group of Doguera and yellow baboons—the leader is a Doguera named Jiro—and the third is the home of fifty Formosan monkeys. Outside this group is another islet in the same bay where forty-five Japanese macaques of a species slightly different from Inuyama's, *Macaca fuscata fuscata*, were settled in after being moved from Shodoshima Island in the Inland Sea. As a sideline, the JMC control one more islet in the vicinity, Maejima, given over to rabbits, guinea fowls, pheasants, and peacocks. The public is permitted to visit most of these island parks.

But such small troops close to Inuyama are not the whole story. Outside the area are many other monkey communities that JMC people have been observing for years. Much of the Center's work doesn't attract attention except among scientists of similar interests: studies in morphology, neuro-physiology, parasitology and so on seldom make front-page news. But almost everybody wants to know how monkeys behave, and such observations made by sociologists, psychologists and anthropologists will always find an eager audience. Thus it was a big story when two Japanese, an anthropologist named Junichiro Itani and an ecologist named Masao Kawai, released in 1965 a report on a twelve-year study of the Japanese macaques of Kyushu, with special emphasis on one troop that lives on Koshima Island.

There are sixty-one of these monkeys, *Macaca fuscata fuscata*. Formerly they subsisted exclusively on food they found in the forest, and only just survived the long, hard winter when they had to depend on winter buds and bark. The JMC team started their observation work in 1948, when almost nothing was known about the ecology of the macaques; for a long time they found it difficult indeed to watch the beasts, because the monkeys wouldn't stand still or let humans come near them. The men had to walk, or even run, through forest land on steep ground; even then they hardly ever managed to get close to the quarry. At last, in 1952, the monkeys started to take food—sweet potatoes and wheat—that the scientists left regularly on a certain beach, and things became much easier. Little by little the animals turned up in force at feeding time, so that the human watchers got acquainted with them and could follow social changes in the group and the development of individual members. The same methods are now used with all the monkey groups under observation—thirty of them, comprising forty-three hundred individuals in troops of widely varying size, some of the largest numbering about seven hundred members and the smallest four or five. The usual troop, however, can be anything from thirty to a hundred and fifty strong.

In all these communities, the order in rank is well-defined but not, warns Dr. Itani, "rudimentary." There is one supreme rank of leaders, the most dominant males, and a secondary echelon of lesser, or sub-, leaders. Then come the "peripheral" males, or dominated male monkeys, so-called because they literally take peripheral positions when the troop is stationary and feeding. The arrangement is always the same: the monkeys sit in two concentric circles, inner part occupied by females, juveniles, infants, and the leader and sub-leaders, while the second, larger circle is made up of young peripheral males. These dominated young monkeys, incidentally, have their own classes too, with leaders and inferiors.

In a general sense the troop leaders, or elite, have claim to all the females. Nevertheless, a peripheral male may occasionally borrow one, rather like a human bachelor who has affairs from time to time with married women: if the guilty pair are caught out by a dominant male, nothing very terrible seems to happen. In fact, there are few fights as we count them, the leader managing to quell an inferior merely by his intimidating posture. But now and then a peripheral monkey seems to become dissatisfied with his position and walks out on the troop; usually it is a large, vigorous monkey that does this. He may join another troop but usually he lives on his own. Sometimes such an Ishmael attacks his former colony in an attempt to carry off females and set up as a troop-leader on his own. At moments like this, his former colleagues, the peripheral monkeys, join together with the leaders to drive him off. The Japanese observers have never seen a case where Ishmael has been joined by the peripheral monkeys so that the leaders are overthrown: complete revolution seems to be unknown to *Macaca fuscata*.

As has been mentioned, the super-monkey, or leader, doesn't have to fight; his leadership is accepted. At times, however, he does wield his power, when arguments blow up among youngsters or quarrelsome females. He strolls over and puts a stop to the disturbance by sheer strength of personality.

In some troops the leaders and sub-leaders fulfill an interesting function. *Macaca fuscata* has a well-marked breeding season, so that all the babies are born at a certain time of year. This saddles the females with the domestic problem of year-old juveniles interfering with the nursing of the newborn. At such times, the leaders and sub-leaders may take a hand and look after the juveniles, playing with them and distracting their attention until the new babies are older and the females can cope once again with the whole family. But not all troop-leaders do this. At Koshima, for example, they don't. Indeed, one of the most interesting aspects of Japanese monkey life that emerges from these studies is that various troops have developed differing behavior patterns.

The females seem to ignore the considerations of rank that preoccupy their mates and other males, but form "kinship groups"—mother with daughter and granddaughter, sister with sister and so on. These are the factions responsible for the squabbling rows the Old Man sometimes finds it advisable to quell. Females get strength from such numbers: Dr. Itani says that on Koshima, the more female infants a group contains the stronger its position in the group. It was a female monkey that altered the Koshima troop's habits in a striking way.

This part of the report is supplied by Dr. Masuo Kawai. It was 1953, and the female, a juvenile named Imo, was only one and a half years old when she picked up a sweet potato from the communal dole-pile on the beach, intending to eat it. The potato was covered with sand. Imo then did something no Koshima monkey before her had ever done—she washed the potato in a nearby stream, dabbling it in the water with one hand while she brushed off the sand with the fingers of the other. Next day she did the same thing with another potato, and the day after that, and the day after that. About a month later, a male among her age group began to wash his sweet potatoes in the same manner, and, after four months, so did Imo's mother. The behavior spread to other members of the troop through mother-child, brother-sister, playmate and companion relationships, until by 1962 seventy-two percent of the fifty-nine monkeys who then made up the troop were doing it. The ones that didn't were all the males and most of the females that were adult by 1953, as well as six out of seven children borne by a monkey named Nami, who were mentally subnormal. "From these results," says Dr. Kawai, "we concluded that adults are too conservative to adopt a new behavior, while the young ones are very adaptable." Later this conclusion was enlarged. The Koshima males, because they don't help with the children, are not in close relationship with the younger generation, and so are not affected by new developments among the young as the mothers are.

Ten years later, the washing behavior invented by an infant female in 1953 had become part of the troop's normal feeding behavior, and would be passed on to each succeeding generation. Dr. Kawai speculated as to whether it could be called a culture, but finally decided to call it monkey culture, or preculture. In addition, he observed as time went on that the monkeys slightly altered the washing procedure. Imo's first inventive dunking had taken place in a fresh-water stream flowing through the sandy beach, but after a time one of the potato-washers dipped his potato into the sea instead. One after another the other monkeys followed this example, until eventually all the potato-washers were using salt water instead of fresh. The observers concluded that this wasn't only because the monkeys preferred their potatoes salted, but that in the dry season the fresh-water stream dries up. There were also, they noticed, two ways of washing a potato: Imo's, which entailed brushing the sand off with the hands, and a different method, of rolling the vegetable in shallow water. Then somebody in the troop thought of yet a new way of doing it— alternately nibbling the salty potato and dipping it again, as if to refresh the salty taste.

In 1956, when Imo was four years old, she invented another improvement in Koshima eating habits. This time the food involved was wheat grains, always given to the monkeys scattered on the sand. Before Imo thought out her new system her fellows had picked up the wheat grain by grain, but she scooped up a whole handful, sand and wheat together, and threw it into the water where the sand sank, and the wheatgrains, left floating, could be picked up and gobbled without effort. By 1962, six years later, nineteen monkeys were doing this "placer mining," as the Japanese called it. No adults born before 1956 would adopt the new method, but two of these conservative-minded animals, a female named Eba and her eldest daughter, Sango, were not above playing an unworthy trick. They would wait until another monkey had thrown mixed sand and wheat into the sea, then move in, scare off the industrious monkey, and grab the floating grains.

"This kind of behavior, which takes advantage of the results of another monkey's labor, is not found in other troops of Japanese monkeys," Dr. Kawai notes severely.

For some time the observers had noted a fact that is not strange until one thinks about it—that the Koshima monkeys, surrounded though they were by water, had never tried to enter the sea. Even after they took to dipping potatoes into salt water they wet only their hands and feet. Finally, in the summer of 1959, the observers brought in an innovation by throwing peanuts into the sea. After a while a few daring monkeys jumped into the water to get them. The behavior spread. By 1962, all the monkeys but the same conservative adults who hadn't changed their eating habits were paddling in the sea. Dr. Kawai points out that even a simple thing like walking into sea water is "precultural behavior" for the monkeys who introduced it, yet the offspring of these monkeys will jump into the sea as a matter of course. Originally their reason for jumping in was to pick up peanuts, but a few of the young ones enjoyed doing it for its own sake, and after a while, during the hot part of the day, they took to diving in just to enjoy a swim. Today some juveniles plunge to the bottom to bring up seaweed.

The development of another new precultural pattern dawned on Dr.

Kawai one day when he went to feed the monkeys with his pocket full of peanuts. He had just put his hand into his pocket when he noticed that a waiting monkey was sitting in front of him with his arm lifted and bent, the palm of the hand turned upward. Looking about, the doctor saw that about three-quarters of the troop were all doing the same thing: even conservative types that had never adopted food washing or swimming were plainly saying with this gesture, "Give me some." Ten years of peaceful relationship with human observers had completely altered their formerly unfriendly attitude toward people, and, what was more, had changed their attitude toward each other: "they had no need to snatch their food and would wait for it." In short, "Both the friendly attitude and the give-me-some behavior are precultures which had become established in the group."

After such long contact with the animals, Dr. Kawai and his colleagues know a lot about the characters of the individuals they have been watching. For example, there was a great difference between Koshima monkeys of high and those of low intelligence, and these characteristics ran in families. "The acquisition of cultural behaviors necessitates a fairly high ability," he says, and it was obvious that some lineages had a high rate of acquisition, whereas others hadn't. The best family was the Ebas. Imo was an Eba: so was Ego, the first monkey to jump into the sea. There were fifteen Ebas: eight of these acquired all four precultural behaviors: i.e., potato washing, placer mining, swimming, and "give-me-some" gestures, and six acquired three. All members got at least six out of ten marks in intelligence tests. (But wasn't Eba one of the monkeys who learned to profit from others' labor? She's too clever by half, one might think.) The most inferior family, judged by the same standards, were the Namis. Nami had seven children, and six of these acquired two kinds of precultural behavior at most: some didn't acquire any. All six scored two or less marks in the intelligence tests. Two Namis, a twelve-year-old male named Naki and a four-year-old male named Namazu, are weak-minded and have underdeveloped physiques. Everything considered, it surprised Dr. Kawai very much that the seventh Nami, a male called Jugo, turned out to be "a wonderful monkey." He alone of all the Namis acquired all four precultural behaviors, "and, although we could not give him tests because he left the troop to live as a solitary male, he would probably have obtained full marks," writes the doctor. "It is still not clear how such a talented monkey came from such a simple family." Not clear at all, but it does seem fairly obvious why Jugo left home. His siblings must have got terribly on his nerves.

Recently there has been a "sudden increase," says Dr. Kawai, in the number of monkeys maintaining an upright posture. He thinks it a natural development, now that they're carrying their potatoes and wheat into the water to wash: they need their hands for carrying, so of course they stand up straight: it's easier, especially for the distances they sometimes have to go. Some of these upright monkeys walk, or run, as much as thirty yards, and the more they do it the easier it gets . . .

And what comes next?

CHAPTER 16

Brightly Witnessed

□

My introduction to the phenomenon of the hybrid animal in zoos was made years ago when I visited Regent's Park with a date, to fill in time before tea. We were attracted by a strange label in the Lion House—"Tigon" it was, or "Liger," I can't remember which, but I do recollect the animal, the result of crossbreeding between a tiger and a lion. My escort justly described it as a striped beast with a ruff round its neck and a surprised expression. Not so just was his own expression, of marked distaste, but then hybrids do arouse distaste in people who consider them a sort of insult to nature. Oddly enough, it is only wild-animal hybrids that evoke this reaction: the same people do not mind crossbreeds of domesticated animals. We are quite accustomed to mules, even to jokes about them: Disraeli called Conservatism "an unhappy cross-breed, the mule of politics that engenders nothing."

Incidentally and contrary to popular belief, mules aren't invariably sterile, and—as far as is known—neither are wild-animal crosses. As far as is known . . . For obvious reasons mankind can't state with certainty that there is any hybridization at all in the wild. The chances are against it on the grounds of geography if nothing else. Take my Regent's Park tigon or liger; how often do lions meet tigers in the wild? They might possibly coincide in one particular spot of India; nowhere else. Furthermore, in the unlikely event of two such closely related species encountering each other, the result is far more likely to be a territorial fight between males than any crossbreeding. Generally speaking, what leads to crossbreeding—which at best takes place in defiance of deep inhibitions—is hypersexuality, a characteristic of captive rather than free wild animals. Our own inhibitions cause us to regard the subject with mixed horror and fascination, from which come strange legends as well as fresh rumors of "monsters" purported to result from the most unlikely matings. Two good books of reference on the subject are Annie P. Gray's *Mammalian Hybrids* and *Hybrid Birds*, in which all authenticated cases of crossbreeding are described, and the more popular rumors investigated. In his foreword to *Mammalian Hybrids* Osman Hill comments, "In the older literature, the claim that an animal is a hybrid has sometimes had no more solid foundation than that a possibly mutant type happens to have characters which are a mixture of those of two different species, or that an animal of one species is found suckling young which bear a strong resemblance to the young of some other species." The book offers effective correction to many of the wilder fables. A cross between *Homo sapiens* and any other species, for example, has never yet been reliably reported, though few of us have not heard periodic rumors to the effect that the Russians have artificially inseminated a female chimpanzee (or gorilla) with human sperm.

Crosses between lions and tigers like the one in London, though not everyday sights, are not really uncommon. Zebra-donkey crosses have often been effected in zoos: there is a "zebronkey" in Manila today, and Japan can show plenty of equine hybrids. Among the anthropoids, only the gibbon seems to have crossbred; the records show various combinations of gibbon subspecies—agile gibbon with hoolock, agile with lar and so on. Among the monkeys, however, there is a long, verified list of hybrids. Captive subspecies of lemurs have occasionally got mixed up, as have civets and genets. A fox of one subspecies can mate with one of another and produce young. We have verified records of dogs with jackals, dogs with dingos and even one dog with a South American fox, as well as wolf and dingo and possibly—though this is not absolutely proved—dingo and coyote. (It should be remembered, however, that the dingo may quite possibly be a direct descendant of the domestic dog.) Among bears in zoos there has been a lot of crossbreeding, sometimes by accident rather than design on the part of the authorities. The most startling hybrid of this description on record, perhaps, is Willy of the National Zoological Park in Washington, D.C. Willy's father, a polar bear, lived in an enclosure next to that of a female Alaskan brown bear. One night he broke through the wall separating the yards. Willy is one of the cubs that resulted from this romantic interlude—an immense, beautiful creature, his size probably due to what geneticists call "hybrid vigor."

Writes Richard Moore in *The Reporter,*

> *Willy, enormous Saskatchewan grizzly—your blood*
> *partly polar, tranquil your temper,*
> *. . . How did they dare to confine you, those*
> *vermin alive in your shadow?*
> *What is it that makes you endure them, O*
> *swaying and perilous tower,*
> *Touching our day with a second of terror,*
> *our nights with a nasty*
> *Freudian dream? . . .*

It was because of an unusual case of hybridization that Dr. Koga included in my itinerary the zoo at Hanshin Park, Koshien, at Nishinomiya City. He must have told me about it, but I didn't remember, and at my first sight of the zoo I wondered why I was there. It was quite pretty, but it looked bare, new, and raw, nor did there seem to be a great variety of exhibits. However, even before the light broke on me I had found one piquant fact, or at least a fact I considered piquant for a moment—that Hanshin, like the Japan Monkey Center, is supported by a railway. Then I had a second thought, that a tourist attraction may well be very important to the railway that runs to it, as witness opening day at Tama Park. Over tea in the administration office, with the director and veterinarian, I learned about the breeding at Hanshin of "leopons," or hybrid lion-leopards.

Often, as in Willy's case, hybridization in zoos takes place by accident: occasional crossbreedings between similar primates, or ungulates, or equids, are due simply to the fact that the animals involved are living in the same enclosure. These breedings happen. But others are deliberately fostered by zoologists in the cause of scientific investigation, and the leopons of Hanshin are a case in point. Hiroyuki Doi, the director under whose management the first mating and resulting births took place, was no longer at Hanshin when I visited there, so I didn't make his acquaintance, but now that I have read his working reports I feel as if I know him. According to his record there was some question, when the project was first discussed at Hanshin in 1954, as to which big-cat cross they should attempt to accomplish, lion-tiger or lion-leopard. Hanshin had a good breeding record for all three of these species. The deciding factor was that other zoos had already bred tigons or ligers, whereas none, as far as they knew, had produced the cross they were already calling "lipard" or the less confusing "leopon." Therefore, they decided, they would aim for a leopard-lion cross.

It was to be no hit-and-miss preparation: each parent was carefully selected. A male leopard, Kaneo, was born at the zoo in January 1955, and in March of the same year a female lion cub, Sonoko, saw the light of day. They were put together in a cage in December, presumably while they were still young enough not to injure each other in the process of getting acquainted. For three years thereafter, Mr. Doi wrote, their food was carefully chosen and hormones were added. "However," he says of the project, "it was not without difficulties and obstacles. To say the least, it was not on a few occasions that we were tempted to abandon the plan." One of the obvious difficulties was that a male leopard, even at his largest, is far smaller than a lioness. However, the animals ignored this fact, and the director was able to write, "Eventually in March and June, 1959, the copulation was brightly witnessed three times. A specific supervision was then placed in expectations. No sign of pregnancy appeared, however, so far to our disappointment on the one hand but it was vaguely felt on the other hand that the road to success was near." It was. By the end of September they felt safe in confirming that Sonoko the lioness was pregnant.

The anxiously watchful Mr. Doi could not be quite sure when to expect the birth. According to existing records a lioness's parturition period can be anything from a hundred and five to a hundred and ten days—the discrepancy is probably due to incomplete evidence—and for leopards the period is ninety to ninety-five: the logical thing to do was to strike an average, so he and his keepers settled down to wait for events in a hundred and one days. Sonoko jumped the gun by three or four days. Perhaps this is why on that important day the cage was not divided into two chambers as was possible when for one reason or another the leopard and lioness had to be separated. Kaneo was with Sonoko, and this could have been a tragic circumstance. It was on the morning of November 2, 1959, that Mr. Doi got word from the keeper of the animals that Sonoko was behaving in a manner out of the ordinary. For two months the lioness had been carefully observed, with six formal checkups every day. Now her appearance had suddenly altered: the abdomen had dropped, and she was obviously uncomfortable. The director hurried to see for himself, later reporting, ". . . her motion was restless, loitering about in the cage and all the time searching for something. . . . At the time of the third observation it was apparent that she tried to get out of my sight and was very cautious against me. Her eyes and motion told that. She walked around in the cage . . .

She was restlessly sitting, standing and looking around. She tried to get out of my sight as if she felt something unusual at my gaze. When I made observation from outside of the cage, she went to the back section of the cage, and when I went round to the back section of the cage, she ran around to the front section."

That afternoon an urgent summons called Doi to the cage again. Kaneo was carrying around in his mouth a baby animal that made no move and uttered no cry. It must have been a terrifying moment. Finally, however, the little thing was got away from the leopard and handed back to Sonoko. Doi, in despair, assumed that the baby was already dead, and was doubting if he could even get hold of the carcass for examination. Just then the keepers succeeded in coaxing the excited father into the other end of the cage, and the grille was closed. At that moment the little leopon came to life, getting up and actually tottering about for a moment. Outside the cage, rejoicing gave way to caution as the humans hastily concealed themselves to watch "without breath" for what might happen next. They were rewarded when the cub made a noise of reassuring volume.

"This cry or voice," says Doi, "was not of dying one but was a very strong one, however thin and low . . ." Inevitably, misgivings followed. "What would be the wound?" he wondered, listing his afterthoughts:

"Can it survive?

"Can the mother lioness which gave birth for the first time nurse and bring up the baby successfully?

"No more leopons except one?

"Seeing that the average fertility of grandparent of leopard was two head and that of the lion was three, would one more be coming out?

"If the baby ceased to breathe, what should we do to preserve a specimen of it?

"If unfortunately the mother ate up the baby, there would be no trace of the evidence of the birth of the 'leopon.'" Then he rebuked himself for such neurotic imaginings. "Nay, it was going excellently as originally planned. Yes, a successful achievement.

"Such were my thoughts at the moment. Hopelessness and hope mingled at one time, mixed with anxiety and craving. The expense of excitement and deep emotion seemed inmeasurable. I was unable to go to sleep all the night."

Next day he resumed his journal: "Long, long night of impatience was over. At 7:00 a.m. the moment of judgment approached. I peeped into the cage with nervous attitude and feeling a tension. A little sunlight was coming through the clouds. I searched into the inside of the cage. There, I found two 'leopons.' . . . Excitement and strong feeling struck me, struck my whole body heavily. Pulse of my heart could be heard indeed. Eureka!"

There has been another litter since then, and I saw all five of the youngsters. Two are almost mature. All are spotted: the older male has longer hair around his neck, like a rudimentary mane, and all five take after their mother rather than their father in being large. The parents are still together in one cage, small leopard and tall lioness, padding about or resting in the inscrutable way of cats no matter what size they may be.

Mr. Yamamoto, director of the Kobe Oji Zoo, wears a beret, perhaps because he paints pictures. Indeed, he said, he would far rather spend all his time painting than directing a zoo. Before taking the present post he was in the Department of Jurisprudence and Statistics, and specialized in foreign trade, in which capacity he spent two years in Kobe. "In other words, I've been a city official for thirty years," he said. "I've been director here for ten years. I've been painting for ten years, too; I'm president of the Painters' Club of the City Office." He directed my attention to samples of his work that hung on the walls along with animal skins, photographs, and zoo posters from various foreign cities. "It was supposed to be a temporary appointment when the mayor first asked me to take on this job," he went on pensively, "but as you see, I'm still here."

"Then you don't like animals?"

"Oh, I wouldn't say that. The fact is, animals like *me*. Several times I've attempted to resign, but the municipality always tells me to stay on."

Mr. Yamamoto is also a writer, and had recently published a book, *Forty Days Around the World*, about a trip made in company with Dr. Koga, when the two men attended an international zoo directors' conference and visited outstanding zoos on the way there and back. He has written essays, on "The Duties of a Zoo Director," "The Children's Zoo of San Diego," and similar subjects, and, of course, he writes poetry; most Japanese gentlemen do that. It needed only a few hours of his lively, sardonic personality to show me that Mr. Yamamoto didn't mind working at the zoo as much as he professed. He liked it: he was proud of it. The cherry-blossom festival was approaching, and everyone was getting things ready; at cherry-blossom time, I gathered, Japanese people visit zoos in even greater numbers than usual. Before he showed me around his little kingdom, the director told me something of its history—not a long one, for Kobe Oji Zoo is a postwar creation. "This ground used to be the site of the city's university," he said. "After the war it was decided to rebuild the university further out, and this space was bought by the city and used for the Foreign Trade Exhibition. I had a lot to do with that exhibition, as I was then working in foreign trade. Well, after it was over we began constructing the zoo, but, as you see, it isn't yet finished: a good deal remains to be completed. In the meantime, we manage. For example—" He broke off as we approached a building. "Here is the reptile house," he said. We made a tour of the reptiles, including a remarkable monitor from Malaya. "Is it warm enough in here, do you think?" asked Mr. Yamamoto, and when I replied truthfully that it seemed quite tropical, he nodded. "We have to depend on an oil stove for our heating," he said. "It will be replaced by something more efficient, but this takes time and money. We can't use pits for our snakes and reptiles in Kobe: people throw things in when they get the chance. Now we had better look at the first rhino baby ever to be born in Japan, and after that I have a surprise."

The surprise turned out to be a pair of male chimpanzee twins—not a first in Japan; in Enoshima I had recently seen another pair, a little older—but still, fine babies. Like the Enoshima mother, this one had neglected her young, and the wife of a young keeper had taken her place. It was the keeper who showed me the twins, sleeping together in a Moses carry-basket. At seven months old, they were still infantile. The keeper's wife, in an advanced stage of anthropomorphism, had dressed them alike in long white nightgowns and knitted booties, and tucked them in with baby blankets. I'm not at all sure I wouldn't have done the same in her place. Looking down at them, the keeper said, "They live in my house. They were born in the Olympic year, so they are named after the prize medals—Silver and Gold. This is Silver; this Gold." His face shone with love.

Kyoto, city of temples and heart of Japanese Buddhism, has the second oldest zoo in Japan, a municipal undertaking. Apparently Japanese Buddhists have never adopted the attitude of opposition to zoos that makes their Ceylonese co-religionists the scourge of Colombo's zoo director. Since 1903, when the Kyoto Zoo opened its gates for the first time, its blackest hour came during the Second World War, when all the animals were slaughtered or starved to death. When the authorities revived the zoo afterward, there came a certain amount of help from friends abroad. Kyoto is a "sister city" to Boston, Massachusetts, and the director of the Boston Zoo, Walter Stone, has sent them an American beaver: Dr. Wilhelm Windecker of Cologne has contributed a rare Ethiopian bird, and so on. The citizens of Kyoto itself, however, were the true architects of the new zoo, and it does them proud, being exceedingly well kept, with tiny gardens of plants and flowers squeezed in wherever the hilly terrain permits. Though the grounds are small, room has even been found for a pair of elephants.

"Indian elephants," said the director, Dr. Sasaki. "There aren't any African elephants in the whole country, and there are only fifty of these Asians, of which forty-seven are females. Not surprisingly, no elephant babies have yet been bred in Japan." In the eyes of zoologists the prize exhibit Kyoto has to offer is two pairs of the rare serow. There was also yet another baby chimpanzee that had been rejected by its young mother and was being raised by human foster parents. It, too, was clothed and even wore mittens, but the keeper explained that this was not a mere whimsical gesture. Unmittened, the baby had given itself serious scratches, doubtless because its waving hands kept searching for a hairy warm body to cling to.

Osaka Municipal Zoo was the last one on Dr. Koga's list. Mr. Yamamoto accompanied me when I went—Osaka is not far from Kobe. During one leg of the trip we caught a crowded subway train and stood clinging each to a strap as it swung and swayed along at top speed, talking at the tops of our voices in order to be heard above the rumbling of the tunnel. "You know Dr. Ernst Land of Basel?" shouted Mr. Yamamoto. "You know his ten principles for keeping a good breeding zoo?" I shook my head, and he enumerated them: "Healthy pair or group. Well-balanced diet. Well-trained visitors. Good animal houses. Good surroundings. Good appearance of animals—attractive to each other as well as the visitors. Personal care of animals. Good staff. And, most important of all, *big money*."

In Tennoji, a suburban district of Osaka, the zoo is surrounded by an amusement area much frequented by sailors from the ships in port. A museum is connected with the zoo, and all these amenities are jumbled together in a cheerful, noisy way, visitors aiming for the top of the outlook tower pushing past other groups determined to see the animals, or dine out in a seafood bar, or play the slot machines, or look at themselves in distorting mirrors. When you add to this din the noise of carpenters and masons hard at work enlarging the premises, you have an indescribable racket. On top of everything else they go in for sculpture at the zoo: a lagoon possesses in addition to islands, or-

namental bridges, boardwalks, and visiting ducks, a few dinosaurs on
the order of Hagenbeck by way of Nagoya, calculated to strike awe
to the stoutest childish heart. Another statue, on dry land, commem-
orates a famous chimpanzee of Osaka whose death plunged the public
into mourning. The figure is fully clothed and wears glasses.

With the director and his assistant we dined in one of the seafood
places, and, in spite of the fact that I was coming down with a violent
coughing cold, I had a merry time which I remembered weeks later, when
I got a letter from Mr. Yamamoto. "The cherry season has now passed
by so many visitors, chicks of Black Swan having been admired," he
wrote. As an afterthought, he sent a poem:

> One day's tour is one day's comfort.
> Colour of her lipsticks will rub out her sorrow of
>   some sort.
> Moistened throat with Japanese sake-wine,
> For tomorrow's tour fine.
> She disappears by air-line,
>   Singing no sweet song
>   but friendly melody
>   to me.

Not that I did disappear by airline quite right away: I had to return
to Tokyo. The night before I took off once and for all, I went with
Dr. Hayashi for our last trial of unusual food, this time at a restaurant
that specialized in wild boar meat sukiyaki and raw venison. As usual
on such jaunts, we were drinking *sake*. The waiter appeared at the proper
time with bowls of rice, but Dr. Hayashi shook his head and refused
it.

"When I am drinking this wine," he said to me, "I shouldn't eat rice.
It makes me fat, and I have to watch that."

I said, "Oh yes, I know, because I have the same problem. I was
awfully fat when I was a child."

"When I was a child I was enormous," said Dr. Hayashi. "They were
all worried about my being so fat."

I said, "I was the fattest in the family."

"I was the fattest boy in the whole neighborhood," said Dr. Hayashi.

"I was so fat," I said, "the other children used to call me Hippo."

Dr. Hayashi slammed down his *sake* cup in amazement. "They called
me Hippo!" he said.

Both of us cried.

CHAPTER 17

Washington, D.C.

□

Not counting aquariums, roadside zoos, and such special collections as
snake farms, there are one hundred and one zoos in the United States.
I would willingly have visited them all, but I doubt if anybody would
want to read through that many descriptions. I apologize to those excellent institutions I left out, but something had to go. Of those I *am*
writing up, I start off with the National Zoological Park in Washington,
D.C., as seems fitting.

There I sat in an office of the Park, a subdivision of the Smithsonian
Institution, waiting for the director, Dr. Theodore H. Reed, who was elsewhere in the building finding some informative literature to give me. I
didn't care how long the quest took. It was pleasant there, with the floor
spotted by sunlight green from shining through trees in new leaf. The zoo
is located in Rock Creek Park, a sharply cut ravine that has managed to
remain rustic in spite of being close to bustling Washington streets. In
the outer office a woman was talking on the telephone. I heard her hang
up and say to another office worker, "She wanted to know if turtles have
rabies. I don't know how they could, do you?" Then Dr. Reed, a tall, ebullient man, came in at a fast pace, carrying a sheaf of pamphlets which he
handed me. He sat down and crossed his long legs.

"One thing that distinguishes this zoo from others in America is that
we're government employees, all of us," he said. "Everybody working
here is a civil servant; we're answerable straight to the top; no state
legislature or city government comes between the federal government
and us. This position gives us a nice sense of importance, but it also
carries with it extra duties. You see, we're part of the Smithsonian. But

you know this if you've read Bill Mann's book. I was under him when I first came here."

I had read the book. The late William M. Mann, for years a director of the Washington Zoo, published it under the title *Wild Animals In and Out of the Zoo*, in 1930 in the Smithsonian Scientific Series, and tells, among many other things, how the National Zoological Park came to exist. The Smithsonian kept a little group of wild animals in cages behind the Institution building—this was early in the 1880s—for the rather bizarre reason that the society was forming a collection of mounted animal specimens of North American fauna to be exhibited in the National Museum. The living animals were models for the taxidermists involved in the project: when they'd been used, they were either killed and stuffed in their turn, or—if the museum didn't need them—sent to the zoo in Philadelphia. Then the people of Washington discovered the little makeshift menagerie, and began coming, as people will, to look at the animals. More and more they came, until the Secretary of the Smithsonian, Langley, noticed them and grew thoughtful. At the time a lot of large cities in the States had installed zoos: in modern jargon we would say that America was becoming zoo-conscious. Langley wondered if the Smithsonian animals weren't filling a definite need for the city.

Finally he decided that they were, and that the public should have a better deal, and he created a Department of Living Animals as a new subsection of the museum. For curator he chose William T. Hornaday, who was later to be director of the New York Zoological Society's zoo and aquarium. Hornaday, a taxidermist and naturalist, had traveled widely in search of wild animals. He now devoted his energies to enlarging the Smithsonian collection, and by 1889 had amassed two hundred and twenty-five living specimens. By that time, as Dr. Mann dryly observes, something else had happened to the American consciousness. ". . . a few interested and intelligent people were commencing to realize that the destruction of game actually destroyed it, and observers noted that where herds of almost countless numbers of game had roamed, there were now only small and widely scattered groups. So to those interested in wild life, it became evident that unless something was done, important native game animals would follow the great auk and the sea cow to extinction."

Langley reasoned that the Smithsonian could do its part for conservation by creating a zoo not only to exhibit animals to idle visitors, but as a means of breeding and perpetuating some at least of the waning species. The Rock Creek Valley was selected as a good place for the collection, mainly because it was a long way from town and the land didn't cost much. After surveying the proposed tract of a hundred and seventy-six acres, Hornaday reported that though there were certainly precipitous slopes on it with differences of up to two hundred feet in elevation, it was feasible. Next, a bill creating a National Zoological Park had to meet with the approval of Congress, but the first attempt, in 1888, failed to pass. However, a year later a similar bill got through, and in 1890 a more specific act placed the park under the direction of the Smithsonian's Regents. Frederick Law Olmsted, the landscape architect responsible for planning many American parks and estates, was asked to design the garden, with a warning that funds permitted only a limited section to be developed at that time.

While the plans were still mainly on paper, the Regents acquired a head keeper, William H. Blackburne, who had been twelve years with the Barnum & Bailey Circus. It wasn't long before his expert knowledge was called for. Another circus firm, the Adam Forepaugh Shows, presented two elephants to the government, and it was Blackburne's task to march these beasts from the circus grounds in Washington to Rock Creek valley, "followed," as Dr. Mann says, "by all the small boys in Washington who were not at the circus that day. . . . Mr. Blackburne, going ahead, warned the people to look out for their horses. An elderly express driver with an elderly horse. . . . replied that his horse was too old to run away. He was mistaken. Otherwise the journey was uneventful. The elephants were chained to a tree, and the Zoo was a fact."

When there was room for them the reprieved animals were brought from the Smithsonian Institution's back yard. Then the zoo acquired a lion in a roundabout way. A lioness belonging to a small circus touring in West Virginia gave birth to two cubs which the circus couldn't find room for, and they were left with a blacksmith in the village where this had happened. One died, but the other survived and grew until the blacksmith's neighbors objected to it, whereupon he and his wife loaded the young lion into a buckboard and drove it to the National Park. Then a tiger was acquired from yet another circus; he had the mange too badly to be any use to the owners, so they dumped him on the zoo in Washington, where Blackburne cured him. He lived seventeen years in the zoo, and died of old age after at least thirty years in captivity.

Almost as soon as it opened the National Zoological Park faced lean times. The new government wasn't zoo-minded, and the Smithsonians were told that they would have to depend wholly on gifts to increase the collection, or catch their animals solely on government reservations. In spite of this, one way and another they did increase the collection.

Then less tight-fisted legislators got into seats of power, by which time the zoo's reputation had grown enough to insure more generous treatment in any case. Like the zoological gardens of Europe, the National Park felt the effects of the animal boom. On the famous African safari made by "Teddy" Roosevelt with his son Kermit in 1909, the colonel caught or shot so many wild beasts that both the National Zoological Park and New York's Museum of Natural History were embarrassed for want of room to put their new acquisitions.

Mann's book takes the reader through much zoo lore none the less fascinating for being out of date. It comes as a surprise, for instance, when he refers to gorillas as *the* rarity of the zoo world. Gorillas aren't plentiful in captivity today and are far scarcer now in the wild than they were in 1930, but they're not now, as he calls them, "the most spectacular animal that can be secured." He describes the first Washington gorilla, N'Gi, as "nothing less than royalty" in the eyes of the staff. Other observations are not yet dated: he quotes Blackburne on a well-known circus proprietor, overheard one afternoon in the show's menagerie tent, who was "bewailing the public's lack of discretion": "That $12,000 rhino over there—six people in front of the cage. Everybody else in the show hanging around a $45 collection of monkeys." It is a complaint made by every animal man who has ever tried to entertain the public. Mann also touches on another fretful subject among his colleagues—animal performances, of which he strongly disapproved. Jealously holding to the ideal of a zoo as something educational rather than merely amusing, like a circus, he says, "In the Zoo we do not dress (apes) up and teach them to smoke, because we want apes in the collection, not burlesque men." One wonders which director he was sniping at, Hagenbeck or Vierheller of St. Louis. At least, such accusations could not be leveled at Washington then or now.

"Being with the Smithsonian as we are, we have a lot to do on the scientific side," said Dr. Reed. "That goes for the quarantine regulations most especially. They're pretty complex and particularly astringent dealing with ruminants, because of hoof-and-mouth disease. There are also regulations concerning other animals—parrots, bats, and now monkeys. Any member of the dog family is permitted to come straight into the zoo here, but for bats we have to have a special permit each time. Monkeys that come from any place designated as a yellow-fever area are stopped at the border. As for parrots—" he broke off and groaned, then resumed. "Have you ever heard of the Lacey Act? It doesn't matter if you haven't, because after due consideration and plenty of advice from the Smithsonian, it's recently been altered. It deals with 'treaty birds,' which is to say with birds migrating from any country within the treaty concerning this matter. Mainly it was concerned with what the Fish and Wildlife Service calls 'noxious animals' such as starlings, sparrows, mongooses, and mynah birds, all of which used to be stictly prohibited from entering the United States as imports. Now that's been altered. Nowadays the Secretary of the Fish and Wildlife Service can declare any animal noxious according to information he gets through the proper channels, *but*, even so, these animals can still be brought in for certain accredited zoos, or for research purposes. Under this control, the respectable zoos can import controversial animals—that is to say, such zoos as the Secretary is convinced will take the right precautions to protect the public. But your little roadside zoos will fail to get permits, and that's fine with me. They shouldn't be there at all, anyway." He looked around the room as if wondering how best to start saying all that needed saying. Inspiration came. "This house we're in was built in 1805, long before we started; here's a picture of Blackburne, the first head keeper, who might be said to have founded the zoo. He quit the circus where he'd been working, married, gave up drinking and smoking, and moved the first animals to the zoo from the Mall, behind the Smithsonian, all in one day. A dynamic type. Our aim today is pretty much the same as what we started with in 1888 with certain modern additions—to do scientific research, mainly to benefit the animals themselves. If it doesn't benefit the animals I'm not interested in it. Other zoos can take care of the animal-human connection. It's not our specialty. You see, land and space are so tight here that all the work we have room for has simply got to be confined to the zoo inhabitants. Officially, we have a hundred and sixty-nine acres, but twenty-five or thirty of those can't be used at all—the ground's too steep. Then, like almost all zoos nowadays, we're pestered with the parking problem. If you don't provide a place where people can leave their cars, it stands to reason they aren't going to visit the zoo. When Olmsted designed the place space was no problem, added to which nobody had motorcars. Now that they have, and can get out here, space is the real problem, and we're hard at work right now on a modernization and improvement program that we figure will take ten years. Of course Olmsted's original plan has already been much modified; we worked in a parking lot some years ago, but it's not at all sufficient now."

As we went out to look at the latest addition, Dr. Reed talked about their commissary. "It's a special one for our purposes, a modified Ratcliffe diet: we grow a lot of our own grass—have you heard of hydrophonic grass? I'll show you some later. Here's the walk-through flight cage, opened the eighteenth of July, 1965." This is a remarkably original structure that the architect has poised over a steep part of the rocky, precipitous land on which the zoo is built. Like other walk-through cages, it has an entrance and an exit for the visitor, but in this one the path through the cage is hilly to an intense degree. At the lowest point, a pool glittered bluely under a waterfall. "We've got a problem here," said Dr. Reed. "An old problem—how to keep paint under water. This stuff isn't standing up to it, though the contractor swore it would. We'll have to try something else." He pointed out the birds that roosted in the new trees and climbing plants, or flew boldly around our heads. "There's a turaco, a peculiar kind of bird: those feathers are colored with real copper, and when the bird gets wet the color actually runs out. That's a fact. Up here as we go out we can step right into the birdhouse. The flight cage isn't bad, is it? Once you've seen one of these, you'll never be satisfied with bars again. In time we plan to put three hundred birds there."

Standing on one of the highest points of land he expatiated on the difficulties and advantages of the National Park's hilly terrain. "It makes the dry-moat system impossible, but we try hard to minimize the barriers we've got to use, with fine-wire fences and that kind of thing. Another point is that the public might find all this climbing too difficult unless we work out a way to make it easier. We try to maintain a slope of no more than sixteen degrees wherever the paths go, by means of paved ramps like this one—if you've got a long flight of stairs, you'll have a longer ramp. When it's all done, even wheel-chairs will be able to get around everywhere. We also maintain—or, at least, try to maintain— a general eye level of twenty-eight inches. That way, we hope to keep small children away from all the exhibits if they're unassisted; in other words, if an adult isn't there to hold them up so they can see, they just don't see, and that's all right with us. It saves a lot of accidents.

"We want to keep some of the exhibits fairly flexible, with comparative rather than geographic arrangement; here and there a kind of postage-stamp exhibit, with a few of the same or related species on show. Then, when we figure the public's taken it in, we can change it. Down there is going to be our hoofed-stock area, and the elephants. Apart from the postage-stamp exhibits the zoo is actually arranged geographically, but we don't stick too blindly to that rule. The cats of several continents, for instance, make an interesting comparative study."

He looked around with modest pride. "There are only two pens in this whole area where you must look at the animal through wire. We're trying to do the same thing all over the zoo, but it's so up-and-down . . . Still, that's an advantage too, sometimes. Here on this path you can look straight across at the birds in the flight cage, and see them eye to eye—birds usually seen in a zoo only from a long way below."

Inside another walk-through birdhouse, where—as I understood it— the inhabitants are induced to stay within limits by an arrangement of lights, he demonstrated their "selective rainfall" system, in which nozzles are so arranged that the visitor can walk through a tropical rainstorm without himself getting wet. Further on were a Palawan, or Congo, peacock and a number of bird displays in which the birds were separated from us by fine-drawn up-and-down wires, so thin that the view was almost unobstructed. Dr. Reed said, "I like this much better than glass. Glass removes them too much—without the sounds and scents you're not really seeing them. The wires are operated like piano wires, tightened up with a key when they get slack. Notice that the signs are low and angled so that children and adults can all see them. Here are kookaburras— we claim to be the first zoo to breed and raise them naturally, though I believe they've hatched them at Basel and hand-reared them. These are second-generation birds, and they've produced young themselves. Here's another rarity, pileated woodpeckers, largest woodpeckers in the States and seldom seen in zoos. Here is a good arrangement; the cage can slide open when weather permits, allowing the birds to get out of doors."

As we came out from an inspection of the service area we looked downhill at a large, old-fashioned structure, and I cried out, "Oh, look, that's just like the St. Louis birdhouse!"

"That's not surprising," said Dr. Reed indulgently, "considering that the same architect built both of them. The Smithsonian contributed St. Louis's to their new zoo. We're not sure what we're going to do with it—it's not a good house nowadays, but we might keep it as a curiosity." He led me into a large house containing a series of tanks, or swimming pools, and paused before one of them so that I could look at a pygmy hippo half covered by water. Several more of them disported in the other pools. "We've had great success with these animals," he said. "We're attempting to build up a herd, and unless something terrible happens we ought to succeed. So far we have six adult females and two boars, though one of the boars is a non-breeder, I'm afraid. More are growing up and are nearly old enough now for breeding. Over here in the next tank is our best breeder, Matilda. Look down in the water and you'll see her." I peered down and saw the heavy-set little animal strolling unconcernedly along the bottom of the tank toward a rising slope at one end. "Of course that's a characteristic of all hippos, but the big ones usually stir up the water until you can't see them,"

said Dr. Reed. "Actually, these pygmies don't spend as much time submerged as the big ones. And here's where we have what I promised
to show you—the hydrophonic grass."

We entered a room adjoining another commissary department, where
an attendant in uniform was working at a structure that looked like
a skeleton filing-cupboard. Close up, I saw that it was in fact a series
of flat trays, one above the other, holding sheets of turf in various stages
of growth. Water trickled down from the higher trays to the lower.
Dr. Reed explained the process: each crop of this special grass takes
only nine days to mature, from the start to the harvesting. Seeds are
placed on paper and soaked for forty-eight hours, for germination. "It's
a kind of oats really," the attendant explained. "Lee oats." Plant nutrient
is mixed with the water, and as a result the grass when it is harvested
has three percent more protein in it than the seed has.

"This grass has something that's lacking in any of the other material
we use for herbivore feed," said Dr. Reed. "This way, too, you get a lot
of moisture into the animal by way of his food. It takes the water four
hours to leave each tray, dropping down from one to the next. This is a
big unit, the commercial size, but we use every bit of grass it produces;
we couldn't ever get as much as we could use out of it, though your
ordinary farmer wouldn't need even this large a setup—plenty of people
get along all right on the private-concern unit. Incidentally one wouldn't
have to stick to Lee oats. The principle works with other grain—I've
heard that in Germany they use black oats, and some people raise soya
bean and corn on these things. With any luck, in days to come we'll get
two more units like this. Even then, though, we'd never have *quite* enough
grass." He patted the machine affectionately. "This unit saved us a thousand dollars last month."

At the hospital, in the office of a pretty young female radiologist, was
a playpen containing a baby chimpanzee and a young leopard cub which
were in that particular room not because the girl knew much about chimps
or leopards, but because she was a girl and could help out with baby things
as keepers' wives so often do, mothering orphans between more orthodox
tasks. We watched the animals as they wrestled. When the leopard got
bored and tried to move away, the ape clung to his tail. "They play for
hours on end," said the radiologist, "but I'm afraid the struggle will soon
be uneven. The leopard's already stronger than the chimp, and when he's
had enough he knows how to show it."

John Perry, an assistant director, was waiting in the next-door laboratory
to introduce me to the zoo vet, Clinton W. Gray, D.V.M. "Dr. Gray
has recently cured a sick Komodo lizard, the only one to survive out of a

shipment of eight," he said proudly. "Two were ours: the other six went to other zoos. All died but one of our pair."

Modestly, Dr. Gray demurred. It hadn't been a one-man effort by any means, he said—the Armed Forces Institute of Pathology and a Bethesda consultant had both helped, and he went on, "What happened to the male was fairly typical of the many losses of this species in the past. Both of our pair ate all right at first, but after three months the male stopped eating and a little while after that he died. We checked up on the other six that had passed out of our hands—sure enough, they were all dead with the same symptoms within ninety days. We found he'd succumbed to amoebiasis." As I looked blank, Mr. Perry interjected, "A sort of amoebic dysentery." "There were two kinds of organisms, as a matter of fact," continued Dr. Gray, "but the behavior was similar: they encyst in the host animal—in the autopsy we found plenty of them in this phase—and eventually break through into the bloodstream, from which they're distributed from the gut to the liver and other internal organs. Once we knew what we were up against it was a question of getting the right stuff into the surviving lizard, and that was harder than it sounds. It wouldn't have been any use administering it in her food, because she didn't eat often enough for that, and we had to be quick about it, so we used enemas and also intramuscular shots in her tail. We kept that up until the tests for amoebae were negative, and there it is. She's alive and to all appearances well, in the reptile house."

I viewed the animal—she looked as lively as a dragon can look, I suppose—and was also given a glimpse of a Galapagos tortoise with its broken leg in a cast made by the resourceful Dr. Gray. The vet had first pinned the bone with three-inch steel pins. "You're sort of on your own, working with a Galapagos tortoise," he said earnestly. "You can only try, feel your way, but we think this is going to be all right. I plan to leave the cast on fourteen weeks. We had to put him on a mobile dolly until he got the idea of the cast, but now he manages. He's never stopped eating, which is a good sign, and every so often those toes move, so I'm hopeful."

Strolling through the reptile house, Mr. Perry said, "I like it here. This department isn't much bothered by political problems, by which I don't mean what you think I do. Here in the zoo, political problems is our term for unwanted donations from VIPs, things like goldfish for instance. But most VIPs don't collect snakes or lizards. Notice the anacondas: one of them recently gave birth to forty-two babies all in one lot. And over here is the largest salt-water crocodile in captivity, I think—it came from India, but it's been here thirty-three years, and we estimate its age at fifty. They keep growing all their lives, you know. Big beast, isn't it? Nobody can touch it, none of the keepers or anybody; it goes wild when it's touched, and moving it into this pool six years ago was quite a job. Vital statistics? Sixteen feet long, weighing anything from sixteen hundred to two thousand pounds—obviously we can't exactly put it on the scales."

In the ape house I met the head man, Mr. Bernie Gallacher, who asked my opinion, as a woman and a mother, on the state of a female gorilla there. "She's already had two babies, and it seems to me she looks fat again," he said. "Do you think she could possibly be expecting? It's an important question because her mate, the one who sired the two, has gone through a critical experience; he was paralyzed for a while but we managed to cure him. You may have read about the case in the *Yearbook?* He looks fine now, but the test will be if he can continue to breed. Look at him now," he added admiringly. The great animal had stretched out his arms sideways and was running across the enclosure with an oddly graceful sideways step. "Like a ballet dancer," said Mr. Perry approvingly.

In the chimpanzee section we stood for a while gazing at Ham, the most famous chimp, perhaps, in the world as the first ape in space. In reply to my inevitable question, Mr. Gallacher said that he doesn't seem to show any effects whatever of his experience. "That is, not now," he added. "For a while after he got back, though, he seemed to have lost his sense of balance, and couldn't climb at all. Now he can; he's a typical chimp in all ways—gets shook up when strangers are around, has his bouts of temper, the way they all do. There's his mate. They've had one infant. Rules the roost, Ham does."

A young zoologist took me over and we finished the tour without the director, who had to attend a meeting—another meeting—about that fretful matter, the parking lot. The new guide, showing me the prairie-dog colony, remarked that they maintain and control their population numbers. He went on, "All natural colonies do the same, you know; they have their own methods. Man is the only animal that doesn't control his numbers. It used to be thought that prairie dogs hibernate in the cold season, but it isn't quite true, at least here. Sometimes in winter we see their tracks in the snow. These National Park dogs have a perpetual battle with the pigeons. They fight over peanuts, and sometimes a pigeon will be grabbed by a prairie dog and pulled into a hole. It comes out sort of disheveled, and flies away."

A Washington landmark is Willy, the hybrid Polar-Alaskan bear, eleven feet three inches high. My guide was warm in praises of Willy's intelligence. "Once the keeper threw him a fish that landed just out of reach in the corner outside the bars there near the pool," he said. "In his place, *I* wouldn't have been able to get it, but Willy figured a way. He splashed water out of the pool until it floated the fish up and carried it to where he could grab it. A born engineer."

"I didn't have time to tell you half our plans," said Dr. Reed when I took my leave. "We're going to elaborate the aquatic animals' locale, with lots of small pools. We'd like to have a good, comprehensive library for the public, and another for the keepers. We'll give rewards—zoo rewards—for kids with good marks at school. There'll be a sales desk for good zoological literature. We'll have courses in adult education and a higher, or graduate, education course, under Dr. Eisenberg; it'll be on a thesis level. We ought to have a building in which small societies, such as the Mammologists' Society, can have conventions—meet here for dinner and all the doings, with movies or TV and all that. We'll have a Question Room on the order of New York's Answer House. It should be very exciting. And that's not all—souvenirs ought to be really good, not the trash you see around in most places. After all, we're in a special position—we don't have to make money to keep going. I want to do a lion area where you can see the lions as you drive. Transport: trackless rubber-tired trains will take you around and—this is the important thing—stop wherever you want to get off. It'll have to be on separate roads so that the public won't have to be dodging all the time. The hospital and research area ought to be near the main office—well." He sighed. "We're in the fourth year of the ten-year program and three months behind, but one never knows in this game. It might drag out, it might speed up, but when we're finished, I can tell you it's going to be a practically new zoo. If it weren't for that parking space— You know what? I wish they'd built the thing on the flat. You can always put up mountains where you want them."

CHAPTER 18

St. Louis

□

Once I found New York's Seagram Building, unexpectedly, in Baltimore. It gives one an odd feeling thus to stumble over the replica of a familiar building, but it has happened to me at least twice. The other time, of course, was when I saw the St. Louis bird cage in Washington. Perhaps we might make it three, because there's something very like the same thing in the New York Zoo in the Bronx as well, but I believe New York's isn't quite as large. Sentiment apart, all three are pretty bad bird cages, all right for their time but not much good for birds, who need more than a mere hunk of space to live in. I thought about all this when I returned to St. Louis after an absence of nearly a lifetime and looked again at the once dearly loved cage, rising above the trees just as I remembered it, proud and shining like a hangar's skeleton or the X ray of a giant Nissen hut. It has the old-world look of a railway station in some German town, but it reminded me more of something I couldn't put my finger on for a while. Then it burst on me that the bird cage is in fact exactly what it's called, a bird cage, like the ones people keep canaries or budgerigars in, magnified to a tremendous degree. It only needed a monster plastic bath hanging outside by oversized hooks to make the illusion perfect.

My guide, Howard F. Baer, then president of the zoo's Board of Control, deprecated the amount of time I was spending on the bird cage; I could tell that from his glum expression. "Look," he said. "Everything else in this zoo is modern, or being remodeled, so let's go and look at the rest of it. We honestly don't know what to do about this thing. There's a strong feeling among the older citizens that it shouldn't be pulled down: they say it's a kind of public monument, the first building ever to be put up for the zoo, and it was contributed by the Smithsonian—" "—I know,"

"—in honor of the Exposition of 1904. That was the starting-point of this zoo, the World's Fair. I'm pretty sure we'll keep it; we wouldn't dare pull it down, as a matter of fact, but we'll have to adapt it somehow."

A short history written by Howard in the St. Louis Zoo *Album* tells the continued story of the city's zoo. "In 1916, after a series of legal steps, the citizens of St. Louis voted a special mill tax for the development and support of a Zoo. Thus the St. Louis Zoo became the first zoo in the world with no admission charge."

He started up the electric cart in which we were making the tour, and we continued around the premises, through what felt like miles of dug-out earth. A huge reconstruction project was in progress, and the first impression was that the entire eighty-three acres had recently been subjected to volcanic action, with the survivors busily engaged in rescue work. In fact, only seventeen acres were being thus maltreated, and visitors still thronged the place happily just beyond these miniature craters and dust storms. In his later report to the board, the director wrote, "This past spring found the Zoo ready to offer the fruition of several years of planning and construction to visitors . . . A visitor standing at the high level of the Central Plaza sees vistas in all directions. Should he desire more intimate views of the waterfall, he may follow gently-curving ramps to the water's edge. Looking to the north during the warm months, he is able to watch activities on a nearby island where a troop of gibbons swing through the trees with effortless grace. Looking to the south. . . . Heretofore, the central Zoo area had been a bottleneck where nothing happened except congestion. Now the Zoo's equator is an area of activity and a natural transition between the older section of the Zoo to the east and the new development to the west. . . ."

We moved away from the devastated area—"A new miniature railway; see where it's going to take a scenic route?" said Howard, "to the Chimpanzee Arena to the north, just next door, as it should be, to the Ape House, near the Vierheller Station where the zoo line trains start."

The Chimpanzee Arena is something special to St. Louis, though in Germany old people will recall something similar. Similar, but not so remarkable. It was George Vierheller who was responsible for this controversial feature—Vierheller, one of the most remarkable men in American zoo history and the pre-eminent director in the United States, who died in Florida in 1966. "Vierheller was just a clerk in the zoo here to begin with," says the present director, Marlin Perkins, "but he was always zoo- and animal-minded. He was still a clerk when he started to look after the animals in his spare time, and sat up all one night with a sick chimp. He used to say it was during that night that he decided to be a zoo man, and,

of course, we know how well he fulfilled his ambition." Indeed, a large
proportion of today's best directors in America have done their apprentice-
ship with Vierheller, and if—like Conway—they don't approve of his
animal shows, nobody denies his talent, which was all the more remarkable because in those Dark Ages of zoo history he had much to learn for
himself that was never recorded in books or treatises.

That Vierheller was, in Perkins's words, "very show-minded" is evident
in his legacy of animal performances in the St. Louis tradition. Throughout the city's nearly tropical summer, after the middle of May to the end
of September, lions, elephants, and apes perform, sometimes two or three
times a day. We found the chimpanzee troupe rehearsing, and later
watched one of the formal shows, jockeying for position against what
seemed like thousands of children. The chimps rode bicycles, skated,
raced in Dodgem cars, did intelligence tests—it was probably the most
elaborate chimp show I have ever seen, particularly because so many
participated at once, and the stage was always crowded with brightly-clad
apes. Hediger once made a special trip to St. Louis to see this show; as I
have indicated, contrary to many other zoo men he approves of these
features of circus life for captive wild animals, holding that such activity
alleviates the boredom of the enclosure. In Zurich, later, he told me about
an experience he had there: "The trainers insisted that I ride in one of
those little cars with a chimpanzee while he drove it on the stage in the
show. I was incredulous of their claims: 'Surely,' I said, 'the animal doesn't
really direct the car himself?' I was sure there was some backstage mechanism, some illusion, but they said, 'You'll see,' so I got in and off we went.
And do you know, the chimp did do the driving? He did, and he knew
what he was doing. He enjoyed it, too."

We stopped in the Ape House on the way to the administration building, to see a recent zoo-born baby on which the zoo justly prided itself:
Henry, a young orangutan. Perhaps because Henry was his mother's first
baby, or for one of the other reasons that this happens so often in captivity,
she had rejected him after birth, and now he was taking a nap in a baby's
cot with a glassed top firmly fastened down. The keeper took him out to
show him off, an orange-colored infant with big, indignant eyes, who
clutched a piece of cloth with his hands or feet, whichever limb was
handiest.

"He still gets a bath every day," the keeper said. "It's with baby bath
oil, so that his skin won't get dry and crack. Altogether he's on a schedule
that isn't unlike any human baby's. The formula's the same, and recently
we've started him on a little cereal, which he loves to throw around."

"And I suppose, like any baby, he's always hung on to that towel or blanket or whatever it is?" I asked knowingly. The keeper shook his head. "The security blanket's been a recent development," he said crisply. "Just the last two weeks or so."

Howard left me at the office, where I had an appointment with the director, R. Marlin Perkins. Because of his television shows, Mr. Perkins is better known to the public than most zoo directors are ever likely to be. Perhaps it was Vierheller, his old boss, who taught him the value of show business. In any case, Marlin Perkins has spread the name of St. Louis Zoo over the continent and beyond. Every week he can be seen on the goggle-box screen—one day in Africa, another in, perhaps, Alaska: he has recorded animals and zoos from Tucson to Madagascar. I was told that some hard-shelled members of the board once complained that Perkins was an unsatisfactory director because he was never there in the zoo directing: there were dire whispers of a personality cult, but the majority of the board, realizing what Marlin Perkins's program has done for their zoo, shouted down the dissenters. Certainly nobody can fault the place by saying that it has fallen behind: there is no hint of neglect at Forest Park, and Mr. Perkins, between trips, keeps a watchful eye on the collection. He was sitting at his desk correcting proof, a familiar TV face, lean and handsome, with white hair.

"I'm a Missourian, as it happens, though I haven't always lived here," he said. "Born in Carthage, I started here in 1926, just out of the University of Missouri where I'd majored in herpetology, and soon became the curator of reptiles. That isn't as grand as it sounds, because we didn't even have a reptile house until '27. After twelve years here I went on to Buffalo where I was curator through the depression years. The depression helped the zoo: we spent two million WPA dollars there, because it was a public work. It's a nice place, small, compact. We put up five buildings, and managed to do a lot of work on the exhibition grounds, introducing moats in quite a few places like the ones here. You know about our St. Louis moats, I hope? I'm willing to bet you're going to mention Hagenbeck. It's a funny thing, but everybody gives Carl Hagenbeck credit for inventing the moated exhibit. As a matter of fact he didn't: the moat was first used at Berne in the old bear exhibits, where it has been in continuous operation for three hundred years. What we *have* invented is the use of glass instead of bars, with an electric charge to keep the animals from soiling it. The charge isn't very strong, just enough to discourage them without being traumatic. Of course it doesn't work in every case. Orangs can learn to throw stuff at the glass and get it just as dirty as ever. For a few years we thought we had a good thing with an electric fence we had around the elephant yards, but then they learned to cross us up.

A male African elephant we had could break it with his tusk, and an Asian female found out she could break it with her toenail and ground it. Oh, one's constantly matching wits. Well, to get back to Buffalo. It was a nice zoo, but the city was broke, so I moved west again as far as Chicago, to Lincoln Park Zoo, and was director there for a good long time, until '62, when I came back to St. Louis. Have you really *studied* our moats?" I had to admit that to me a moat was just a moat, and he shook his head. There are many different sorts, he assured me, both dry and wet, some symmetrical ditches with vertical sides, others deep and curved, others still with one sudden vertical side and the other a gentle slope. "You've got to take your animal's habits into consideration," he said. "St. Louis is the first zoo in America, with the exception of the bear pit in Denver, that really uses them. We had them first in '21 or '22, I'm not sure, and led the way.

"It was in Chicago that I started the first of my TV shows, under the title 'Zoo Parade.' It was live television then, just a local broadcast direct from the zoo when you never knew what might happen and the animals usually didn't do what you wanted them to when you needed them most. We changed after I came here, to 'Wild Kingdom'; the format's changed— everything's different, and it's much better. The show's filmed, so you avoid the pitfalls of live TV, balky animals and all that. On film you can wait for co-operation. You can tell the story much better, make corrections and so on. And, as I'm very much interested in the cause of conservation, I can generally sign off making a strong pitch for it.

"We do everything we can to breed rare animals. We've got a wild Asian ox, a seladang, the only female of the species in the country. Washington has two males, and they've sent one to try mating, but so far it's no good—she just picks on him and shows no other interest. We've sent male wattled cranes to the Bronx, and they've had better luck than we had with those birds: they're now raising their second clutch, which is heartening. One day we'll get a pair back from New York. In 'Zoo Parade' days, Lincoln Park had a male colobus monkey—you know, don't you, that beautiful black-and-white animal from East Africa? It's never bred well in captivity. Well, while I was doing the show at the Bronx I heard that their male colobus had just died, so I lent ours to them, and the mating was successful; they've got more colobus now at Lincoln Park. I've just sent some rare pheasants to San Antonio, too.

"We have a close connection with the St. Louis educational system: recently we've even appointed an assistant curator of education who's called the educational co-ordinator. We plan an orientation course for teachers, a sort of workshop, and they can help introduce supplementary courses for school children. We're also building a classroom-theatre where films can be shown. The universities of the neighborhood are going to use it for lectures and demonstrations; we've got a course going right now for college students, two for parasitology and others on prairie dogs—the prairie-dog colony is one of our most popular exhibits. We also publish animal-care and general animal information bulletins, because people are always asking for such things.

"As for scientific research, we haven't all the funds we'd like for that. Who has? But I think we *have* got something interesting going. We're instituting a records program. If only we could collate all the autopsies of the rare animals that die in zoos, it would be extremely helpful to everybody. For instance, take Bushman, the famous gorilla. He died of myocarditis; he had a Vitamin B deficiency and heart disease. From a study of his body we learned that gorillas need a higher proportion of Vitamin B than most other animals do. Doctors here make records of sick animals, and they complain that a lot of their difficulty comes from not having any norms. What's the normal temperature for one monkey or another of a different species? For certain ungulates? All these things should be found out. We've instigated a series of X-ray studies. Our radiologist coaxed one of the local manufacturers to make us a permanent loan of an X-ray machine, and we got some out-of-date film that worked all right, and set to work. We just X-rayed everything around; now we're getting some order in the data: we started seven years ago and have all the records taken since then. Of course we're going on with it. At present the equipment's inadequate, but we want to go on until we've established at least a good set of norms. I'd particularly like to get a center for biology started—the Biology of Natural Systems, to determine what other laboratory animals can be used in biological studies. We already use rats, guinea pigs and so on, but there must be others just as useful, perhaps more so. I'd like to have a frozen tissue bank from any of our animals that die. A lot of valuable material in zoos goes to waste through death, and the bank would be a general pool for anybody who needs such stuff. You see, by conservation I mean *general* conservation, not just rare species or nearly extinct plants or soil, but the whole picture."

When I was a small child at school, I saved and collected pennies and brought them to class for the worthy cause many of us worked for, the purchase of an elephant for the St. Louis Zoo. We felt a fine sense of achievement when we actually saw that elephant arrive. We felt as if we ourselves had created it. Now St. Louis children have bought another huge animal, a walrus named Siegfried, obtained from Frankfurt—an imposing beast well on the way to becoming a kind of elephant himself. Mrs. Perkins took me to see him, and as we regarded him she said wistfully, "You should have seen him when he got here. He was the sweetest, cuddliest little thing."

I looked at her skeptically, but couldn't reply, because Siegfried splashed loudly and wetly into his tank and interrupted the conversation. I turned to study a sign hanging outside the moated enclosure, a drawing like those for Christmas fund collections of a large thermometer slowly filling up with red color as the sum rises. This wasn't a money thermometer, but a weight recorder labeled, WATCH SIEGFRIED GROW! At various levels the date was written, with the corresponding poundage. Reading it, I could doubt Mrs. Perkins's word no longer; clearly Siegfried had shot up at an astounding rate, and hadn't even yet got his full growth. I asked how they managed to weigh him.

"Well, that's sort of cute," she replied. "Over there on the opposite bank, there's a scale embedded in the concrete. Do you see the dial? Every time he walks across the scale his weight is recorded. We've made the dial huge so that everybody can see, and he's always back and forth on the platform, so it's no problem."

Siegfried must have cost a packet, I reflected. For all I know, the school children of St. Louis have been saving up for him since I left town, years and years ago. Now, if they could only give a new X-ray machine a name, personalize it, make it attractive somehow . . .

[17]
LEOPARD

[18]

WEST INDIAN FLAMINGO

Young hatched from egg laid in May 1966
in the Bronx Zoo. This chick is the Bronx
Zoo's first and represents the northernmost
breeding in the United States.

[19]

MANDRILL

[20]

LIONS

[21]

DUCK-BILLED PLATYPUS

PANDAS

[23]
PANDA

[24]
WESTERN DIAMONDBACK RATTLESNAKE

CHAPTER 19

Philadelphia

□

The Philadelphia Zoological Garden proudly displays the name *America's First Zoo* on its monthly publication. The number for March 1959 went further and used special nineteenth-century type for the occasion to celebrate the zoo's centennial, devoting the whole issue "to the early history of the Society, and of the Garden itself." Strictly speaking, however, the zoo was only a hope in the hearts of its founders back in 1859, "public-spirited citizens," to use the language of an anniversary brochure, who "joined in common purpose to found the Zoological Society of Philadelphia" in obvious imitation of the London Society. On March 21, 1859, its charter as a non-profit organization was approved by the Commonwealth of Pennsylvania. A site had been set aside and plans were in the making, when the War Between the States interrupted all activity, and the zoo was put into mothballs for the duration and long beyond. Not until March, 1872, was the idea revived. Then a better tract was acquired at one end of Fairmount Park—ten or eleven acres around a pretty little house called Solitude, built in 1785 by John Penn, grandson of William the Founder. The zoo opened its gates on July 1, 1874, "with flags flying and a brass band playing." As the brochure points out, it differed from a lot of other zoos in that it didn't just grow from small beginnings as a private collection or park menagerie; it was a full-fledged institution from the very beginning, with hundreds of specimens. "Transportation was a serious problem in those days, and it was often easier and cheaper to obtain animals from distant ports in India and Africa than to get specimens from sections of our own West where the railroads had not yet penetrated. . . . Visitors to the Zoo in its earlier years were treated to exhibits that would be difficult to duplicate today.

Six giraffes arrived all at once from Africa on August 11, 1874. The kangaroo collection, in point of variety, was particularly outstanding for several seasons. . . . Our Zoo has even had some animals that are now extinct or believed to be on the verge of oblivion. Included among them would be the West Indian monk seal, bubaline antelope, toolache wallaby, Gaimard's rat kangaroo, passenger pigeon, and Carolina paroquet . . . Prickly Pete, the echidna, or spiny anteater, the egg-laying mammal from Australia, lived almost half a century."

The Philadelphia Zoo, like many others, was helped in its hours of need during the great depression by the WPA and similar organizations, which "replaced water and sewer lines, laid walks, and reconstructed many of the outdoor exhibits." That was about it, plus the fact that it now covers forty-two acres, and when I arrived, tipped out by a taxi near a whizzing speedway, I suspected that the Society was not likely to gouge any more land out of the surrounding territory. Similar speedways carried traffic north, south, east, and west. Philadelphia's zoo pays a price for the boast of being the country's first, for the city has grown up all around it.

The bit of land just outside the gate—all that I could see for the moment—was prettily landscaped, with trees and well-barbered grass. It was not yet ten o'clock, opening time, so I read signs and studied a large bronze statue of a dying lioness before I could pay my gate money and walk through. If I hadn't known better I would have supposed that I had entered a newly developed estate: there was a smell of freshly turned earth, and all around were temporary wooden fences and canvas-shrouded structures. This was yet another zoo in the process of revision. In the information office a girl gave me some literature and strongly recommended that I visit the Reptile House until more of the staff should arrive. Feeling like an extra on an otherwise empty stage, I followed her directions through a silent park, around curved pathways and past crisp shrubbery, downhill to a round brick house. Still lower in the valley ran a twisting stream where waterbirds stretched their wings. A raucous cry rang out from the far end.

The reptiles and I were alone together except for a great bruiser of a woman in a blue coverall and boots, who pretended not to see me as she sloshed out floor and cages, carried tin plates about, and prodded an anaconda away from its door so that she might put a plate inside. All the specimens, the snakes and giant frogs and gavials, were motionless. It was a relief when the reticulated python yawned, proving that he wasn't stuffed. I read a long sign headed IF YOU WERE BITTEN?, yawned back at the python, and went out to get a closer look at John Penn's little house, Solitude, which, according to the book, used to be Mr. Penn's residence when he owned the estate. It was a very pretty example of eighteenth-century building, and the vehicle parked nearby, marked SCHOOL BUS FOR ANIMALS, seemed incongruous. The children's zoo, which I tried to visit next, was still closed for the winter, so I headed back to the office by way of a new-looking building labeled RARE MAMMALS. Just inside the entrance hung a series of brightly-colored posters under the heading, MAMMALS IN DANGER, which represented six species: Javan rhino, mountain gorilla, Arabian oryx, Ceylon elephant, sable antelope, giant panda, and cheetah. "What can be done to save them?" demanded the text, self-replying: game laws must be enforced and obeyed, national parks and game preserves must be established where animals can be safe, animals can be transported from danger areas to locations of safety and bred in captivity, and when there are enough they can be released once more in their native habitats. "They are past the point of no return," continued the text. "They must have help to survive."

I was wondering about the giant panda. Nobody really knows if it's on the way out or not, I reflected—nobody, that is, outside of China. Certainly they used to die as soon as they were exported—most of them did, anyway—but how many still live in their own country? Still, I suppose it's better to go on record as being aware of danger than to ignore the possibility that the panda is disappearing. At the other side of the broad panel was another sign of more cheerful burden: "Saved by the Zoo. There is no such thing as a 'wild' European bison or a 'wild' Père David's deer. These animals can be seen only in zoological parks around the world, where they are bred to maintain the species. Were it not for the special care and protection they received in zoos, both would be extinct today." A large center poster portrayed, MAN, PROTECTOR OR DESTROYER?

No "or" about it, I decided. He's both.

The rare mammals are all behind glass. Philadelphia Zoo is known among the interested public for the extreme care it takes to make sure that its animals aren't contaminated by infectious visitors—so much care that one indignant woman told me beforehand that the new apes' quarters are the finest example she has ever seen of Modern Jail architecture—no sunlight, and all gray. "When I mentioned the lack of sun," she added, "they assured me that the animals get all that in their food. Oh, I'm sure they're stuffed with vitamins from A to Z, but surely a gorilla or chimp would like to see a bit of foliage or the sky once in a while, not for aesthetic reasons if you object to that idea, but just because it's their natural way of life." I observed with relief, however, that three young chimps in their antiseptic quarters had a lot of play equipment and seemed to be enjoying themselves. I passed along the gray corridor between compartments. Rare maned wolf, from South America. Two lowland gorillas. Two giant anteaters. A siamang hooting, though I couldn't hear him through the glass: his throat-sac was inflated. Sumatran orangutans, both born in the zoo—the sign added that the Philadelphia Zoo is the first to breed and rear young orangs successfully. Two more of the Bornean sub-species, also born there. I came out at the other side past a panel depicting the most dangerous animal (a rat), the tallest (giraffe), the largest that ever lived (blue whale), and the smallest (pygmy Etruscan shrew). Out of doors where the rare mammals couldn't see it, the day had been transformed by sunlight, and in the clear, chilly air a peacock stood in full display, each feather glittering as if enameled.

The office was humming with activity, and Roger Conant, curator of reptiles and public relations—"snakes and people," he explained cheerfully—was waiting for me. He asked, "What have you seen? You've been appreciating our statues, I hope. Don't miss the impalas, if you haven't looked yet—they're our newest. Then there's the lion house, and you ought to have a good look at the waterfowl down the valley because it's an original kind of exhibit, we think—John Griswold's been working at it for a long time. But let's talk about our problems first. If you drove over you might have gathered that the main difficulty is the shortage of parking space. Our park is very inadequate. Hundreds of cars that would otherwise stop go away because there's simply no place for them. The number that do this on Sundays and holidays would break your heart. Commercial car parks in the vicinity can take care of only five hundred, seven hundred at the most. And it wouldn't pay for us to put up a special one, according to the experts, just for zoo traffic, since it would be used only on Sundays and holidays, so the fees wouldn't meet the outlay. And public transport isn't the answer: we do have trolley cars in Philadelphia, one line running very near the main gate, but not many families would use it nowadays for the zoo. They can carry paraphernalia in a car, or find shelter in it when the weather turns bad, but if they've come in a trolley to the zoo they're stuck. They'd rather go somewhere else in the family car than come here without it." He pondered the problem sadly for another moment, then shelved it. "You've caught us in the midst of rebuilding, but we've been doing that ever since 1938, so it's no wonder. Since the program was outlined we've finished the rare-mammal house, and the small mammals, and the reptiles—not too bad a record. But what you've probably heard of first and foremost about Philadelphia, at least in the zoo circles you've been frequenting, is the Penrose Research Laboratory, isn't it? The director, Dr. Ratcliffe, is also

professor of pathology at the University of Pennsylvania, and he's usually
got some of the university students working here for advanced degrees. It
works well for all concerned. The institution was founded by a former
president of the zoo, Dr. Charles Penrose, in 1901. He was an M.D., and
he started the practice of doing an autopsy on every zoo animal that died
here, since when there has been an unbroken record of these autopsies—it
started far earlier than any other: none of the other zoos can approach it.
Well, a close study of these records revealed certain patterns, or trends, in
causes of death. One of the first problems was the presence of TB
among apes and monkeys. A regimen was worked out at the lab for all
animals—careful quarantine, a TB test, and protection from the public
by glass. We're probably the first big zoo that used glass to such an extent.
Oh yes, Penrose Lab has done many things, but the best one is the diets.
These were worked out by Dr. Ratcliffe and his team when the autopsies
showed that most animals were dying from malnutrition: they got to work
studying dietetics and came up with some basic formulas and foodstuffs
that proved to do very well—a lot of zoos are using the system now.
Death rate went down for some species, and breeding increased dramatically. Admittedly it's not one hundred percent successful—the meat
formulas don't work on big cats, for instance, but elsewhere it's fine,
especially with birds and reptiles, notably turtles. We've got a great
number of longevity records in the zoo, even from way back before the
Ratcliffe diets were started."

Mr. Conant said that he had been at Philadelphia thirty years—"I'm
probably the dean, if you don't count one guard who outranks me in
years"—having been a dropout from the University of Pennsylvania in the
middle of the depression. "It's a lesson to all of us," he added. "I've
never been out of work since." He went to Toledo first, then came to
Philadelphia as curator of reptiles.

"Our cats are outstanding; you don't want to miss them. And, as I said,
you must see the waterfowl, we have more ducks and geese than anybody; we pride ourselves on that collection. The school bus? You've seen
it? Good. It's one of those Volkswagen models, and it's been a tremendous
success. Right now in the fall of 1965 we've got reservation dates up
through March 1967. The team manages two schools a day in the city;
sometimes when they go outside town it isn't that good. But we cover
anywhere up to fifty miles from the town limits. It's fine for education
and for public relations: we're hoping to get Bureau of Education
teachers assigned to the zoo permanently. It started six seasons ago, doing
its tour only Monday and Wednesday mornings, and was immediately
booked solid for three months ahead. Since then it's always booked at

least a year in advance. The animals go in carry-cages except for one young guanaco; they're kept up on the stage behind curtains and exhibited one by one, while the speaker tells about their particular habits and characters. Then there's a film of the zoo, to show the kids bigger animals that can't be carried around. We have a whole series of these films, and we keep careful track of where they've been shown, so as not to repeat. It's a simple operation; you only need the bus, your carry-cages, and gas. For personnel we have girls. The program runs from early April until October. The same girls, when they aren't on the bus, help out in the children's zoo, a splendid one, not new but good anyway. The supervisor there, though, is a man. Mr. Maloney."

Going out to finish the tour, I spoke again to the girl who had sent me to the Reptile House. "As a matter of fact, my husband's in charge there," she said. "I'm awfully glad you paid it a visit. It will be nice for him to know that. You'd be surprised, the people who won't go anywhere near a snake house."

CHAPTER 20

Milwaukee

□

It seems a logical transition to go from America's first zoo to her latest, Milwaukee. A purist might argue that Milwaukee's zoo isn't really all that new; but the original institution has lately been abandoned, and Mr. George Speidel, the director, achieving every zoo director's dream, simply built a completely new zoo instead. It wasn't a question of mere remodeling or any other compromise: the place is six miles from the old grounds. When it seemed feasible to do so, he packed up the animals, loaded them on trucks, and moved them to their new houses. "Zoo still under construction: will be completed in 1967" says the *Yearbook* entry with charming frankness, but that doesn't mean that it is not already open to the public. Almost from the beginning of construction, which began in 1958, outsiders have shown their appreciation by coming to watch the growth of the buildings, and to visit them when they are finished and full, like the first to be completed and occupied, the Monkey House. In 1965 more than a million visitors came to the new zoo. Milwaukee—or, to give it its full title, the Milwaukee County Zoological Park—has mixed but satisfactory financial arrangements. The county pays all operating costs, and the Milwaukee Zoological Society buys most of the animals, but the zoo has other sources of income as well; not gate money—entry is free—but the proceeds from passengers on the miniature railway, refreshment stalls, strollers, talking signs, vending machines, lockers, and the parking fee of fifty cents per car. (The new zoo's spacious parking lot must arouse much envy in Philadelphian bosoms.) None of these money-makers is farmed out to concessionaires: all the profit goes into the zoo treasury.

There in the town's outskirts, on a brilliant autumn day, the trees were red and gold. Mr. Speidel was in Washington, but his assistant, Robert Bullerman, was expecting me, and I announced myself in the anteroom of the administration complex, a pleasing mixture of glass and pale wood around a tiny patio full of flowers and a tree. The wind blew briskly across the grounds with their young trees and even younger structures, to one of which Mr. Bullerman pointed as we left the office. It was a small house in the same wood-and-glass style, the roof slanting down sharply on either side.

"That's an information booth, or it will be next week when it opens. We had no particular architect: you might call all this the result of combined effort. Now, over here are the miniature railway tracks, which we've decided to lengthen for next season. We've got two steam trains and one diesel. I wish you could take a ride, but it's closed down for the winter; perhaps if you come back later in the year—it's a very scenic route and we're proud of it. You can see buffalo from the train, and a few bears, but people who aren't tempted by the railway can get around in one of the zoomobiles—that is, in the summer. The zoomobiles close down the same time the trains do. It's a severe winter here, but I guess you know that. The trees are pretty right now, aren't they? I was here after closing time yesterday until sunset, taking pictures of them. This little tree here is a pepper tree, and you can see how it's gone all gold, it's a special kind. That one over there is still green—that's the kind we see more of. We're lucky, being a county zoo, because it means that we come under the management of the Parks Department, and the two gardeners who work here are paid by that. All the trees are looked after by the Forestry Department. This used to be nothing but a hobo jungle; it was close to a freight yard. Hard to believe now, isn't it?" He indicated a green car with lettering on it, and we climbed in and rode over to look at the bird houses. Few visitors could be seen, but it was still early on a weekday morning, and there was nothing surprising about the small crowd.

Mr. Bullerman parked the car and I followed him into a long room, lined along each side with cage space and full of small birds fluttering about, or perching among the trees and other plants that were growing behind the glass with them. The front of each cage was not a smooth wall of glass, but a series of triangular projections, like boxes arranged with their corners sticking out. The assistant director glanced along the façades and looked thoughtful. "We hardly had this up before we decided to change it," he admitted. "It didn't call for any great alteration, luckily. At first these were broken up into small cages, each with its few birds of one species, but as soon as we saw it we knew that wasn't too good. I believe the original idea was that they'd fight if you put them all together, but lots of other zoos put their birds together, and if they've each got their own space staked out there isn't any trouble. So all we did was to knock out the partitions, and it's much better this way. All the flowers and plants and stuff are real, by the way—you won't find a single plastic flower in this zoo. The gardeners wouldn't stand for it. Now up here is our most popular exhibit. The crowd always stands around staring at the penguins."

The building was T-shaped. One approached the crossbar by way of the two long cages, to be confronted by a very large body of water behind a tremendous sheet of plate glass. This water, deep into which the spectator could look from his vantage point at the side, was contained at the back and sides by artificial land, flat rocks strewn with pebbles in the foreground and tall caves in back. Here and there in the little pond, a rock lifted above the surface. The compartment was full of penguins of several species, waddling or standing about after the dry-land manner of their kind or swimming underwater where we had a perfect view of them, transformed and incredibly graceful. A scattering of visitors had gathered to watch. Mr. Bullerman regarded the layout with what I thought was a special pride.

"Those big ones, of course, are the Kings. There's a little rock-hopper, the one who's just come out of the water. See how wispy the feathers look behind his head? What we've got as a special thing, though, is the Adélie penguins. Our man went down to the Antarctic himself and collected those, and they've bred here—the first time an Adélie has ever bred in captivity, at least in this country. I've got some pictures I'll show you later if you're interested. They build their nests out of rocks and pebbles, so we built one or two in advance, just so they'd get the idea. There's one, over at the entrance to that little cave, see? Just rocks and pebbles, but they're awfully particular where they put the pebbles, and keep moving them around to a better place. We're very careful here about keeping them from infection. The air and water in there are conditioned—we never let it rise above a certain temperature— but we don't filter the water. The men who go in to clean wear surgical masks and high rubber boots, and they're always disinfected first. The results are fine. Only one of our birds has ever been lost through as- pergillosis, and that was at the very beginning before things were running smoothly." Sadness darkened his face when he told me that the baby penguin, after reaching nearly adult size, had died of swallowing a sharp stone. The mother had died the week before, and all the glittering success was over. Still, two other pairs of Adélies were nesting, and they had fresh hope.

We were still among the birds, as I realized when Mr. Bullerman led me into a place I took at first for a yard out of doors. Then I saw that the ceiling, high above us, was of glass, and that the bright sunlight was either filtered or artificial. Two of the yard's walls were of vertical rock almost all the way up, or an imitation of rock, sculptured into little holes and ledges, some near the ground, some almost at the top. The rest of the space was taken up in various ways—vegetation near the cliffs, a pond, and openings among the shrubbery. The birds that lived here moved or flew around unconcernedly, not at all afraid of us. They were of many species and colors and sizes. "We call this the aquatic flight area," said Mr. Bullerman. "We've got two flight areas, east and west; this is the east one. Here's their wading pool, and as you see, that tree is trained to arch over it. There aren't any labels yet so you'll have to take my word for it that we've already hatched a laughing gull this year. This label thing is difficult. We don't want to put them up all over the area; I've seen it in other flight cages and it's hideous. You might as well not make the place pretty if you're going to stick up little tabs in all directions and spoil the effect, and we'd have to have a lot of them here, we have so many species. So what I'm doing, I'm working out a pillar exhibit where we can put pictures and short notices on all the birds, and I'll put the pillar back here, out of the way, near the door. If a visitor's really interested he can step over and look it up, but most people aren't, you know—most people never read a label. I'll keep the messages as short as possible: species, origin and donor, if any. Of course I'll indicate if the birds belong to an endangered species, though. I sincerely feel that the salvation of these endangered animals lies with zoos and game farms. Mr. Lindemann of the Catskill Game Farms is a great man in my book.

"Over here is the west flight area—a slightly different effect, you see, with more trees and less water, more woodsy. Our quail have been breeding here; we incubated some of the eggs but they hatched out a fair proportion themselves. There are crowned pigeons, and those little fellows are sunbirds mostly. We've got one hummingbird, just one, who chases all the others. That one's a bulbul. Bluebirds hatched last year." He led the way into yet another room. "This is mostly macaws and shore birds. That cage at the edge of the room is for native birds, and here are finches and whydahs."

"I notice that in all these flight cages you haven't got the uncaged birds under a particularly bright light," I said. "In fact we're all in the same kind of light. Yet they stay in their own part of the area. I thought you had to keep them the way I've always seen them in other places, all lit up, with darkness in the rest of the room, or they'd wander around."

"No, you don't have to do all that. They stay in their own places, as you say, as long as people are around. At night, though, after the zoo is closed, they wander all over the room. It's our presence that keeps them where they are. Some birds have the freedom of the place completely, wandering around outside—cranes, flamingos, and peafowl. We put them indoors, though, when it gets really cold."

Outside, he drove next to an island in an artificial lagoon not quite like the many other islands I've seen in different zoos, because it was connected to the surrounding land by an arched bridge leading into a small house. "Monkey Island," explained Mr. Bullerman. "We keep rhesus here as long into the fall as possible. It's popular. We had one something like it in the old zoo, but this is much better because of the waterside cage and the bridge. Any time the island needs cleaning we bait the waterside cage with food, the monkeys troop in, we close the door and get on with the cleaning. The house is their winter quarters too so they're never off exhibit. And here's the monkey house." He paused before we went in, to say, "I know this isn't the complete answer to monkey keeping, but it's so much better than the old place we think it's heaven. Automatic flushing system—cages are washed out every twenty minutes. Electrified glass. Plenty of room. Here are spectacled langurs. That contraption they're climbing over with all that bright-colored stuff is in a modernistic design, you'll notice. It's metal, completely metal. One of our men designs a lot of stuff like that to keep the animals amused. We never leave one of these things indefinitely in one cage, because monkeys get used to playthings and neglect them, so we keep swapping them around, and that keeps everybody fresh and interested. We raised all those langurs ourselves—two female, two male. Here are the lar gibbons. That younger one was born here, child of the male there and a female that died recently. The father just took over.

We had drifted along a row of large cages, and now the way led us around the corner, down past even larger ones. A sudden rush of water sounded through the building and made me jump—the automatic flushing system, washing through all the cage floors at once, then subsiding to leave the tiles moist and shining. Bathtub architecture, I said to myself, remembering scathing comments from Bill Conway on this subject. Tile *is* much more sanitary than wood or earth, but it must be cold and uncomforting.

Mr. Bullerman halted me at a very special exhibit. I would have known it was special from the expression on his face, even if it hadn't been for the sign announcing in large letters, FIRST SIAMANG BORN IN CAPTIVITY. NAME MARK. BORN JULY 10, 1962. Behind the bars a young siamang looped about from handhold to handhold, then hung on the front of the cage to look at us steadily with his round dark eyes. Siamangs are usually called gibbons, they look very like gibbons, but they differ to such a degree that some zoologists now argue that they aren't close enough to gibbons to be given the same species name. They are larger than other gibbons, are always of a black color, the hair grows on the head in an ungibbonish way, and two toes on each foot are webbed, but their chief difference is in the throat sac, which swells up when the siamang hoots, so that it looks strangely like a bullfrog. Mr. Bullerman said, "Have you ever heard a recording of a siamang's call? It's got lots more variety than a lar gibbon's, more resonance too. The male siamang has something in his throat that you can feel, even when it isn't distended. Mark, he's just got a little walnut so far and his voice is high; it hasn't changed yet. He was born right here. At first I thought we'd never get the parents together long enough to breed. We had the female first, then the male arrived fully grown from Germany. Had to give him estrogen to start him off, and even so we had a bad time introducing her, he was so violent, but finally she got a good bite on his foot and everything calmed down." He looked fondly at the black shape in the cage and added, "We got an award that year— half of one. We shared with Portland for the most notable birth of the year. Theirs was an Indian elephant. Over here are the most valuable animals in the house, the gorillas. That male, Sammy, was about a year old when he got here in 1950, a present from the Schlitz Breweries. He's fine, isn't he? Once his weight got up to 600, but he's about 596 now, and that's fat enough; we cut back his food on purpose. He outweighs Bushman by 50 pounds, but Bushman was taller; this is a stocky animal. Unfortunately his mate died a while back. We got that young pair—they're between six and seven years old—from Schlitz as well, because of the death of the female. There's a pair of orangs; she's expecting a baby that's due in January."

Discoursing of primate health, we walked toward the door. "One of our patas, the male, is in the hospital; I'm pretty sure he had a broken leg, but I didn't get close enough to examine it, and the treatment seems to be doing the trick because he's getting well. We're firm believers here in the 'don't touch it' theory; you can do a lot of damage, handling a wild animal. With tailed primates you can tell a lot from the condition of the tail; if it doesn't look too good, ten to one there's something wrong with the monkey. Often when new arrivals walk into the cage their tails are mangy or bitten. We feed them up, give them vitamins, all that, and they usually make a good recovery. There's no sunlight in here, as you mentioned; we think vitamins are better."

"Oh," I said.

Mr. Bullerman looked back, down the long dim corridor between wall and cages. He sighed. "It's the limit," he said. "Anybody would say that this is a fine big house, but do you know, it's already crowded."

The Small Mammal House came next. We entered past two engagingly realistic wood-carving decorations, one of a fruit bat, the other of a fennec. The first exhibit was a side view of salt water, some basking rocks, and a harbor seal disporting himself near the bottom of his tank. Past this we entered a red-lit hall in which lived the nocturnal animals. It was effective and simple in arrangement: there seemed no necessity for going down into a tunnel or through a shielding curtain, systems often employed in other zoos for similar animals on display. "No, this works all right," said my guide. "We give them daylight at night so they can fall asleep, and the red lights are turned on when the zoo opens in the morning. You can see for yourself how lively they are." Fruit bats were flying about, palm civets played in the ruddy gloom (more civets than they know what to do with, said Mr. Bullerman), kinkajous, a ferret badger, a vulpine phalanger, a beautiful little pale fox from North Africa, a slow loris, and a Cape pangolin, a large animal that moves slowly into its sleeping quarters once a day to give itself a bath in the rubber tub kept filled for the purpose. At the vampire-bat display Mr. Bullerman told of a doctor who had been fascinated by these animals, coming back again and again to watch them when they were given their daily saucer of cattle blood from the local stockyards. "One day Mr. Speidel was away when he called," said Mr. Bullerman, "so he came to me instead and handed me a bottle full of blood. He said, 'This is for the vampire bats, fresh from a couple of tonsillectomies I did today at the hospital.' Well, you know, I can do just about anything in the way of surgery for animals—I've had lots of experience with that kind of thing—but the fact that it was human blood nearly turned my stomach. I did manage to thank him, though, and I took the bottle away. Of course we didn't give it to the bats. They do fine on cow's blood, and it's a good rule never to change the diet if it's satisfactory. Human blood would have made a change and might have upset them."

The zoo is planned on a geographical basis. Out of doors, we saw the North American fauna first; living in enclosures that were spaced with pleasant irregularity on an artificial mountainside. "You go straight from this lot of brown bears to the bison, then there's the elk, grizzly, raccoons—that is, we're going to put raccoons there—and all that. Over there's the moose. We're the only zoo I know of that can keep moose; they've always been hard to feed in captivity, but we give them nothing but browse, lots of it and plenty of water. In the summer it's fresh of course, no problem; for winter we box a lot of it and thaw the stuff out as it's needed. I'd like you to notice that big bull lying under the tree, because he's the finest moose I've even seen anywhere, in captivity or out. Seven feet high—he was bottle-raised, too. He's not at his best just now, because he's in rut, but have a look." Mr. Bullerman led the way down a path to a strong fence of wire at the side of the exhibit. He called the moose until the animal raised his great head with its branching antlers, gazed in our direction, then wearily clambered to a standing position. He paused as if thinking it over, then crossed the field toward us at a shambling gait, head held down and to one side so that he looked at us out of one eye with a fixed gaze.

Softly my companion said, "He's in rut so he feels like hell. He walks slow, see? and he stumbles. His eyes are sunk. You'd think he could hardly make it. Then all of a sudden he'll start for you at a rate you wouldn't believe, faster than an express train. That's the time to look out for moose."

This beast didn't charge. He came very close to the fence, that small sunken eye fixed on us unwaveringly, lining up his oddly slender hindquarters against the wire while he tried with dull persistence to get his antlers through the fence. "We'd better move off," said Mr. Bullerman, "before he manages to break something, himself or the fence . . . You wouldn't believe that when summer comes he'll be as friendly and bouncy as a collie pup. One thing I always do, though, I always wear zoo clothes when I go into one of these enclosures, and I'm careful not to change the color. They don't like changes. Here are the polar bears, and we've got Steller's sea lions too. That lake's full of birds; this time of year there are more migrants on it than our own stock. We keep the water open all winter—keep it from freezing with an aerating system."

At the edge of the sea-lion pool, where the water was unusually low, several men in boots worked on the draining system. It was stopped up, they told us, but they'd found the trouble and fixed it, and were filling the pool again. From their shallow puddle the sea lions regarded

all these goings on, while my guide told me how careful the men had
to be with them. "They climb pretty fast when they get a chance,
and more than once they've gone right up to the top of the rim there.
They move like inchworms, they're really lively. That day I saw the
male scramble up from the water to the rim of the rocks, and he
fell off it onto the ground. I thought he was a goner; you could hear
the noise he made when he fell—'Oof!' But he didn't break anything,
and as soon as he was back in the water he ate heartily. We've had
to build up the rocks. Stellers are very rare: we've got three of the
only five in captivity. Now we're passing the Australian house; that yard
was designed for kangaroos and emus together, but it doesn't work out
as well as we hoped—even half-grown emus will chase kangaroos sometimes, and we had to separate them. Only one emu travels back and
forth between them. He doesn't make any trouble.

"Now we're looking at a different complex—Africa, India and South
America, depending on which side you're on. These African pens are
arranged in a special way, and the contractor who made them is very
proud of it. Each one is higher than the next, so from the end you can
see all the animals, down to the feet—elephants, white rhinos, tapirs,
kudu—Thomson's gazelle down there, impala, vulture, secretary bird. Up
there are cheetahs, three of them; we're always hoping they might breed.
I've got an idea that cheetahs would breed in captivity if they had
enough space. They're always cooped up; nobody's tried space yet. See
that window at the side? It's arranged so that you can look through the
wall at the big cats, but there's an entry besides, right into the cat house.
The lions have exercise yards in which we give them turns to run, with
stalls underneath." We drove past the South American enclosure as he
explained that all the hoofed stock is taken into quarters at night. Keepers
were driving their charges into their night places, and I saw a tapir chasing an agouti. "Everything here is a pet, as it happens—it's a fascinating
compound," said Mr. Bullerman. "The capybara, the anteaters, everything is tame. Now we come around to the Indian section. The Indian
rhinos have been put to bed already, but there you can see spotted deer
and a blackbuck with his females—he's the king of the castle, I can tell
you; keeps his women in line. There's the Malay tapir."

The tour finished, we went to the restaurant building for a hamburger
and coffee in the board of directors' meeting room, where a handsome
wood carving of an African scene filled one of the walls. "A local artist
did that," said Mr. Bullerman, busy at a projection machine. While he
prepared to show a film that he had made with two other members of
the staff, I examined the carving, tracing out the elephant with his trunk

upraised, the monkeys, the giraffe, the hippo, and the vegetation all twined together in the design.

"All ready," said my host at last. "You don't have to look at this, you know, if you don't want to, but I thought it might interest you because of the hatching of the Adélie penguin. The first part of the picture was shot on the expedition."

There followed some sequences in color of a heavy-looking plane's take-off, then of McMurdo Island. We had close-ups of penguins too, but the most interesting portion of the film, in my estimation, was that made by Mr. Bullerman himself of a nesting Adélie penguin, or pair of penguins: the male takes on half the incubating tasks. When the female had sat for a while, he stood near her. Both birds bowed, twisting their necks in a definite ritual before switching over, and the switch itself was so fast, said Mr. Bullerman, that he almost never caught it: the birds would bow, and then all he saw was the incubating bird off the nest, waddling away to find food, and the other bird solidly in place on the eggs. "They must have developed that speed because the eggs would freeze otherwise," he said. Both penguins accepted food as they sat. We saw the sitting bird arranging and rearranging the pebbles and gravel of the nest, and then, after the keepers realized that a penguin had been hatched, the camera stayed focused on the sitting parent for a long time. Obviously something was going on under her—or his—feathers, for she or he kept twisting around to look down. At last the camera recorded a glimpse of a small dark fuzzy head, moving slightly. As the days went on, Mr. Bullerman continued to take pictures, and the little bird seemed to shoot up, minute by minute. "It really did seem almost that fast," he said. "That little bird was soon eating whole fish for himself." The infant attained almost his parent's height, though he still had his baby plumage, and was walking around like an adult, when the picture came to an abrupt end. Mr. Bullerman said, "Well, there it is: he died. We called him 'Little America,' you know. That was the end of Little America."

I said, "It's a shame."

"Yes, a shame." He looked pensive for a moment, then brightened. "The other pair's nesting," he said. "Maybe next time."

CHAPTER 21

The Bronx

□

It is the fate of the New York Zoological Park to be known to its public as "the Bronx Zoo," simply—and small wonder, since this nickname is less of a mouthful. Besides, as the Bronx Zoo it can hardly be confused with the Central Park Zoo, a much smaller affair in the middle of Manhattan—seven acres to the Bronx's two hundred and fifty. Among the thousands of out-of-town visitors to New York, from America's hinterland and a vast number of foreign countries, a few actually do make the mistake nevertheless, visiting Central Park and wondering why so much fuss is made over New York's zoological garden. Central Park Zoo is not too bad for what it is, and it's much improved lately, since the new Parks Commissioner took it in hand, but it would be much more improved with more space and considerable remodeling, which it is unlikely ever to get, as it is dependent on the municipality, never a good patron. It can't compare with the Bronx, which has other sources of income, chief of which is the city's Zoological Society. In addition there are the city—which must shell out a certain amount no matter how the officials may protest—and yearly perquisites from the usual things. Gate money doesn't add up to much—entry is free four days a week and only twenty-five cents on the other days. But the management pockets fees for buses in the park and the money earned by the talking signs and food shops, which are plowed back into running the place.

The Bronx Zoo is known as one of the outstanding zoos of the world. When plums fall in the zoological orchard, it usually catches them. Though a long way from the center of Manhattan, people beat a path to it, by subway and car. Parking, that bugbear of the city zoo, isn't difficult. In the 1966 *Yearbook* the attendance count for 1964 is given as more than

2,300,000, and this doesn't include visitors to the aquarium, managed by
the same Society: the aquarium attracted nearly 300,000 in the same year.
Even for a New York institution, they are impressively large figures.

In 1895, civic pride in New York could no longer accept the fact
that while other great American cities, even nearby Philadelphia, had
zoos, in New York there was none. In influential circles, discussion of
this lack grew animated. Theodore Roosevelt, a staunch adherent of the
joys of life in the wilderness and hunting, discussed it as much as, if
not more than, anybody else. He was president of the exclusive Boone
and Crockett Club that year, where he led a group that resolved to start
a zoo for New York, and from the club membership he appointed a
committee of three to apply for a state charter to that end. There was
no difficulty, evidently, in obtaining the charter or in collecting $250,000
from the founding members to be expended on the buildings. A site
of some two hundred and fifty acres' extent was selected in Bronx Park,
such a generous slice of land that the staff has never yet had to ask for
more, and when the time comes to accommodate breeding herds in a
conservation program—a project dear to the heart of Dr. William Conway, the present director—there should be no difficulty in finding the
land for it.

The New York Zoological Park opened in 1899, an impressively long-
ago date for our country, but there are disadvantages as well in being an
old zoo, as the Society can testify. The older a zoo building, the more
necessary it becomes to remodel it from time to time. In the Bronx
the original builders did their work too well for the good of the ex-
chequer, as the excellence of their material and workmanship makes this
remodeling painfully costly today. However, in all other respects the Society has reason to be deeply grateful to the zoo's founders. For one
thing, those gentlemen—Elihu Root, C. Grant La Farge, Andrew Car-
negie, Henry Fairfield Osborn, Roosevelt and others—cannily arranged
that those who were to run the zoo in the future should be, in the
words of the guide book, "independent of the inevitable political changes
of the City's administration." In other words, there is no change of
personnel whenever an election takes place. Then, too, costs are arranged, as I have said, so that the city must pay its share without exacting
any pound of flesh. The Society pays the salaries of the scientific staff
and buys the animals; to some extent it is also responsible for the food
bills, but the city meets the expenses for general maintenance, the salaries of the non-scientific employees, and what remains of the food
costs. New York's government must also provide money for capital construction, dollar for dollar to match that which the Society collects

from other sources. The Society was, is, and by charter must continue to be a non-profit-making organization. Apart from income from the original foundation it collects dues from its 6200 members (according to the count in 1965), and such fringe activities as were listed earlier.

"Still, we have to make improvements slowly, one at a time," said Harold C. Palmer of the Society recently, in the Society's offices at Rockefeller Center. "Building takes forever in this town. The new Aquatic Bird House was six years in the making—nobody expected it to take quite that long, but it did, and as a result all other plans are slowed down accordingly. The delay isn't due primarily to labor trouble, though at present the plumbers' strike is certainly not helping. It's due to a variety of things: high cost of material and an outmoded building code that we fervently hope is going to be reformed soon." He did not have to add that the chief enemy is time, that great fashion-changer. In the thirties, when Hagenbeck's ideas were making themselves felt in the United States, the Society became acutely conscious of its shortcomings and was ashamed. Everywhere but in New York, it seemed, young zoo people were installing moated barless enclosures, drastically changing the aspect of their zoos. The Bronx until then had been a pacemaker, and it was felt that it was slipping. Something had to be done. Moats must be constructed and bars abandoned, while the remaining cages must be remodeled and acquire more outdoor space. As the writer of the guidebook feelingly points out, moats aren't easy to dig on the Bronx terrain, which is underlain by rocky ledges: still, it had to be done and it was done. In the doing, the planners hit on the idea of the "continental area," i.e. the presentation of mixed exhibits in the new large enclosures, of animals from the same country or, at least, the same continent. The first one opened at the Bronx was the African Plains area, which was a great triumph and was soon being imitated in many other zoos.

There is one outstanding advantage to being situated near the city of New York, for the immense population and a constant inflow of visitors keeps the attendance record high. But there is also a tremendous disadvantage in the position—vandalism. Ignorant adults and untrained children have long wreaked havoc in the Bronx Zoo, with its far-flung boundaries. People hid themselves in the park until after closing hours, when they were free to do their worst. And in addition, boys climbed the fences after closing time. Even during the day when the park was open, vandals often succeeded in doing grave mischief out of sight of the guards. "Horrible things were happening, and it was getting worse all the time," said Mr. Palmer. "It wasn't only that the keepers kept losing eggs and small animals, but these psychopaths used to break legs, of cranes and such, and leave them there to suffer until we found them in the morning. It got so bad that we finally took a controversial step and introduced our dog patrol of trained German shepherds. We did it in fear and trembling, I can tell you, but the results are great, and we've never looked back. It's the psychological effect, I think, of the knowledge that the dogs are there that keeps people out. The guards haven't had to set the dogs on anybody, not yet, but it works, and the patrol takes a great burden off the night watchmen. Those dogs have made the Bronx a much happier place." Not that all public hostility can be wiped out; it is always the great problem of zoo keeping, and a perverted few continue to hang around the animals, trying to feed them harmful substances. Sometimes it is impossible to tell whether a casualty is the result of deliberate action or accident. Herbert, a walrus that was a great favorite, suddenly died of swallowing a large rubber ball—walruses, unfortunately for themselves, are incurably friendly and trusting. But Herbert's is only one case out of many, some too nasty to describe.

Another phenomenon of the zoo is the public reaction to primates. Something about these near relatives of ours stimulates a special hostility in many people, who seem to take their existence as a personal insult. Children feel this reaction in their elders and are quick to adopt it as their own. A zoologist of my acquaintance has told me of how she was walking in the Bronx Zoo one day and came upon two small colored boys, shouting and whooping at a gorilla that was quite inoffensively sitting in its moated enclosure. "They were yelling, you know the kind of thing," she said, "putting up their fists and shouting, 'Want to fight?' and all that. I said, 'That's a girl gorilla, you know.' The boys were awfully shocked and remorseful. They quieted down immediately, and soon tiptoed away."

"Education helps somewhat," said Mr. Palmer. "Such people as aren't plain nuts can be taught, if only you succeed in getting through to them. We have a tremendous education program, not just here in the city regions but in far-off places as well—the important branch is in East Africa where we teach adult classes as well as schoolchildren. We concentrate on Africa because that's where the greatest reservoir of wild animals still exists—but won't for very long, unless they're taught to take precautions. Among other things we hammer in are the importance of tourism to their country, and how tourism depends on the wild animals they have. That part of our program is tied in with the conservation push we're making. Here, we have in-service courses for New York high school teachers, where they're told how to use the zoo for instruction, and there's a natural history course for children. Then of course there are the class-room lectures in the schools, with wild animals for illustrations: about a hundred thousand children in the area hear that lecture in a year. Organized school groups come to the zoo; about four hundred thousand children came in these groups last year. We also maintain what we consider an excellent educational-film library—we have a contract with an educational-film house that makes them for schools. And there's research: through the years the Society has sponsored at least thirty-six Ph.D.s, and and twenty-four M.A.s work in the labs of the Society and the Aquarium. During the past two seminars, Cornell University has been sending students down to work in the park. Half the day they're busy with curatorial duties, the other half they're researching. Negrelli at the Aquarium has two M.D.s from Yale who come down every week to work in the lab."

Mr. Palmer gave me a book published by the Society in 1961: *To All Who Care About Tomorrow.* "A good deal of it's dated now, I'm glad to say," he commented. "Some of the plans outlined in there have been implemented, but it might give you a fair idea of what we're after."

The reader is reminded that the Society's original charter set forth three principal aims of the proposed zoological garden: First, it was to be a feature of the city's cultural life, letting man see life within nature; second, it should be a focus for education and research, where man can know life with nature; third, it was to be a force for the conservation of wildlife, so that man can conserve life within nature. For sixty years, continues the brochure, the Society has carried out these three purposes.

It was to help man to see life that they built the original zoo, completed in 1911, with later developments including the opening, in 1922, of the Heads and Horns Museum, the completion in 1940 of the first stage of the African Plains exhibit, the post-war building of the new Great Apes House, the Penguin House, the "Jewel Room" Birdhouse, the modernization of the Reptile House, and the addition of a Children's Zoo and a Farm-in-the-Zoo where children can see and fondle domesticated animals. "The Society has always worked to acquire and maintain rarities among its collection. . . . As early as 1912, the first Pygmy Hippopotamus in America was shown in the Zoo. Among the many other notable Zoo 'firsts' have been the Duckbilled Platypus, Vampire Bat, Gorilla, Bongo, Okapi, Congo Peacock, King Penguin and the Komodo 'Dragon.'"

The second point: If the procuring and exhibition of rare animals were the zoo's only functions, it would be vulnerable to the accusation that it is merely a more dignified version of the circus side show. We have seen how anxious the London Zoological Society was in the past century to disprove such an allegation, and how it succeeded in overcoming the more intellectual public's prejudices. Half a century later the New York Zoological Society felt it equally incumbent on them to prove the same thing. A zoo can and should have educational value, the members often announced, and in the 1961 book the case is stated once again: "It is the slow, painstaking work of research, study and observation of natural history and zoology—the organized, concentrated, never-ending attempt of man to know the mysteries of living wild things." They are proud that William Beebe was one of the Society's men: he was curator of birds in 1899 when the zoo opened. They name other famous naturalists who began their work at the Bronx. But the most convincing proof of how the Society keeps the faith lies in the zoo's tie-up with city schools.

If the third purpose named in the charter, to aid Man to protect life, has only lately been widely publicized, this is because the cause itself has waited for recognition by the public. The Society did not wait: it has a long history of activity in conservation. The Wildlife Survival Center, a subsidiary of the Society with offices in the park, was established early in the century; its members are interested in conserving animals in their natural habitat if possible, but where this is not possible —a common contingency today—the aim is to protect and maintain such animals in a habitat as similar to their own as can be managed. It was the Center that set up the American Bison Society in December 1905, when the complete extermination of that animal seemed close at hand. In its day the bison had roamed the American plains in thousands, but for years it had been hunted and displaced and harried until in all the North American continent only about three hundred specimens remained. The American Bison Society rounded up these survivors and put them in a reserve where they could live and breed in peace, and at the same time managed to push through an act that declared bisons protected animals. Since then, twenty thousand bison have been released in Canadian national parks, and an equal number in American reserves. For once at least, Man had reversed his customary procedure by actually saving a species from extinction. It is a classic interlude that belongs with the stories of Père David's deer and the Arabian oryx.

But as time went on it became clear to naturalists that a lot more activity along parallel lines was urgently necessary unless Man was to live in a desert world, devoid of all animal life but his own. Fairfield

Osborn, president of the Zoological Society, said in 1944, "Points of view should and do change with the passing of time. Our thinking regarding the activities of the Society in the field of conservation is gaining a new perspective. It is becoming more and more apparent that if the present rate of injury to the forests, soils, and streams of this country and in other parts of the world continues, the extinction of many lingering populations of wildlife is inevitable. It is time that the Society's future work in the field of conservation be extended, due to the serious threat to these natural resources in this country and in other parts of the world. These living resources are the basis for the protection not only of wild animal life but of Man himself. The Society intends, therefore, to give its active aid toward a better public understanding of these matters."

The range of the organization's efforts in this direction extends to such extramural activities as the educational program in Africa described by Mr. Palmer, including practical help—a gift consisting of three aircraft for Tanzania to be used for spotting poachers, radio equipment for gamekeepers on the ground, and a large truck that transports armed men who defend the game as well as any poachers they catch. Through Dr. Osborn the Society also set up an affiliate, the Conservation Foundation, to study, advise, and educate people on the general conservation of nature, not animals only but water, soil, vegetation, and air.

When conservation at last became a household word, many people quickly pointed out that zoos and zoological societies were hardly convincing proponents of the cause, considering how destructive wild-animal collecting has been. Such criticism might well have been justified in the past, retorted zoo directors in effect, but the bad old days are over now. To carry the refutation further, the leading spirits in the zoo world of the West met to talk it over, and from this symposium came an agreement to cut down the waste of threatened species by refusing to buy from collectors who don't obey certain rules. It all helps, but wild-animal collectors for zoos are only part of the story; the real threat to the wild is neither greed, cruelty, nor stupidity, but Man's proliferation. At the AAZPA meeting in February 1966, the Bronx's Bill Conway suggested that the members of the association take a new look at the situation and ask themselves what more zoos can do for conservation. Admittedly, he continued, the bulk of such work as breeding and protection can hardly be done within the confines of the ordinary zoo. Herds need more space than such collections usually enjoy, and breeding with very small groups might be worse than none. But there was a way in which zoos could make more space for themselves: they could change their standards and lower their sights. Why should every single zoo show a whole long list of animals? Wouldn't fewer species do as well, even better? Each director could concentrate on a restricted collection of such animals as were best accommodated to his particular climate, and the space gained might be used for breeding.

After hearing this talk I decided that it was time for a fresh look at the Bronx itself, which I hadn't visited for two years. With a few companions I went to the park in a car and left it inside, in one of the clearings saved for the purpose. A rough path uphill took us through thick woods of maple and oak. It was a fine Sunday, and the lanes were so full of family groups that making a way to the exhibits was like running interference in football. I dodged a baby carriage only to be overrun by half a dozen small, screaming Puerto Ricans, then narrowly escaped colliding with a crowded bench. It was a relief to step aside and read a sign I hadn't seen before, boldly labeled IDEA No. 3. It turned out to be a foreword on an exhibit not yet ready to be seen: the House of Darkness, or nocturnal animals. When I had caught my breath we moved on our way to the buildings. It would be a mistake to guess from the outside appearance of the older edifices what the interiors will be like. I'm fond of these houses, but their charming old-fashioned exteriors lead to far less charming scenes inside. The zoo's earliest architects didn't know any better, and their ignorance is all too evident as one stands inside one of the dismal damp gray halls. But in some places whatever can be done has been done: the snake and reptile displays are absolutely modern, with attractive, instructive arrangements. One wall, for instance, labeled FEEDING HABITS, represents its subject with text, pictures, diagrams, and, here and there, an actual animal in a small enclosure within the wall. Between such frankly educational panels, the reptiles and amphibians are themselves on view. A big open pool of crocodiles, surrounded by a ring of forbiddingly spiky plants, is further protected by a warning notice that anybody throwing food into the water is liable to a twenty-five-dollar fine. "Please do not strike glass," said another message on a wall that displayed a number of live reptiles: "What would you do if it broke?" Just as I read this a small boy climbed on the railing beside me and heartily thumped the glass.

Outside, a placard put up by the Wildlife Survival Center showed a square shield that depicts a horned head behind the red-lettered words, VANISHING ANIMAL—their special symbol, which decorates every enclosure or cage that holds members of a threatened species. There was one on the fence that protected a pygmy hippo, grazing alongside the pretty old Elephant House, the green dome of which dominates the zoo. "Pretty?" I imagined Conway saying bitterly. He hopes to be able soon to move the elephants out of it, into a rebuilt African Plains area, and no doubt he is right. Still, I like the outside of the house.

Far more to his taste, I know, is the zoo's newest building, the Aquatic Bird House. Near its entrance flamingos graze or stand on one leg in a lagoon. The zoo's first home-bred flamingo got itself hatched there just too early to be accredited to the surroundings of the new house, but there will be more, and inside is a series of displays that is Conway's pride and joy. For that matter, it should be the pride of all Bronx patrons. Imagination, variety, and beauty are evident from "the Tree Tops," where trees grow from a level well below the floor on which the spectator stands, and treetop birds roost happily at eye level. Then there is "a River Bank," with a startling collection of scarlet ibis, black-necked stilt, and African jacana, and a great open-room exhibition of flamingos, plovers, and curlews. On a wall hangs a panel depicting a photograph taken after some shoot, of row on row of dead game birds. Nearby, without direct comment, is listed "extinct or vanishing water birds," and a passage from Beebe's works:

"The beauty and genius of a work of art may be reconceived though its first material expression be destroyed; a vanished harmony may yet inspire the composer; but when the last individual of a race of living things breathes no more, another heaven and another earth must pass before such a one can be again."

Of the same modern school is the Great Apes House. It is not only the apes that deserve to be called large—the interior exhibit-room takes up the whole public part of the building. The Bronx recently acquired six young gorillas more or less of an age, in hopes of starting a breeding program when they have grown old enough. These youngsters were busy that afternoon, playing with each other or throwing themselves around the cage. A woman next to me remarked to her husband, "They're so ugly they're almost pretty, aren't they?" These people had a little boy with them, who shoved up closer for a better look just as two of the gorillas began to wrestle. "Lookit! Lookit! They're fighting!" he cried in ecstasy.

"So they are. Well, I never. Ugly, aren't they?" replied Mom. "Like I said, they're so ugly they're almost pretty."

The little boy tried to roar, shouting, "Waaah!" and the three humans continued to watch, pleasantly horrified, as I moved away. Soon I came to a display I remembered hearing about from Conway. I admired it: it seemed very effective. As you approach it you see a closely-barred cage, ostentatiously and hugely padlocked. There is a large-lettered sign above:

The Most Dangerous Animal in the World.

Coming closer, as in curiosity you are bound to do, you find only a mirror behind the bars. Underneath is another message in smaller letters; "You are looking at the most dangerous animal in the world. It alone of all the animals that ever lived can exterminate (and *has!*) entire species of animals."

As I went to one side to copy it down, a man and his wife approached, the man reading the upper sign aloud. They paused in front of the mirror and stared, and stared. "I don't see nuttin'," he said at last. They walked off.

CHAPTER 22

Aooo, My Brothers

□

Visiting Tucson for the first time makes some people wonder what on earth residents can see in the place that makes them so fond of it. The mood does not last. After a few days, though the ground continues to seem arid and untidy, familiarity brings to light compensating features. The mountains that ring the city are tinted with colors that constantly change. Just breathing the air makes one feel good. In the middle distance new details emerge on the sandy soil—cacti of interesting shapes and variety, pincushion and staghorn and cholla—and there is other life as well, though up until a few weeks ago I didn't realize it. I am not a newcomer to the Southwest. I used to live in New Mexico, and I loved it and thought I knew it, but until lately I believed that all its wild animals had been killed off. Possibly this impression owed itself to the "Coyote Song," a ballad my elder sisters used to sing in the evening after they had practiced their vocal scales, while upstairs, in bed or lingering unlawfully on the landing, I listened to every sorrowful word. I loved the "Coyote Song."

A-oooo, my brothers,

it began, in minor key. (Rose and Dorothy always made it sound exactly like a dog's howl.)

> *The moo-oon is red,*
> *And the antelope leaps from his prairie bed,*
> *Then join ye again in the ancient threne*
> > *For a day that's dead*
> > *And a hunt that's fled,*
> *And the terror of things unseen. . . .*

In the ensuing lines the coyotes lament the passing of the happy times when they were free to kill all the antelope and buffalo they wanted. Now they are not only defrauded of these innocent pleasures, but are occasionally scared to death, they complain, by a fiery comet that tears through the night shrieking and "all ablaze with the White Man's light." To add to their confusion, they sometimes think, mistakenly, that they can still hear the rumbling hoofs of bison. I seethed with indignation and sympathy for the coyotes. A lump rose in my throat as the sisters downstairs wailed the last verse:

> *A-oooo, my brothers,*
> *The stars are red,*
> *And the lean coyote must mourn unfed.*
> *Then join ye again in the ancient croon,*
> > *For the dawn is gray*
> > *And another day*
> > *Has faded the red, red moo-ooooon.*

One night, having finished her stint, Dorothy came upstairs for some reason and was alarmed to find me sitting on the top step, weeping. "Oh, it isn't fair to the coyotes!" I sobbed.

Still in my mind in 1965 was a conviction that the whole situation was unjust—or had been, for all must surely be over for the lean coyote by that time. Then, in Ceylon of all places, I heard from some chance-met tourists from Arizona that at Tucson was a place called the Arizona-Sonora Desert Museum, full of animals of the region. "Every kind of animal we have around there," they said. "Nothing from anywhere else—just desert animals." Desert animals—the very phrase was a contradiction in terms, I thought, unless the collection was of stuffed coyotes and rattlesnakes, but my new friends assured me that the museum was actually a zoo, and that its denizens were alive. Back in New York, I checked up by asking William Conway at the Bronx about it. He said emphatically that the Arizona place should be seen, so I went to Tucson. Having arrived late in the afternoon, I found that the museum, like so many other places in our spacious West, was a long way off from town—fourteen miles. According to the map it took up sixty-six acres of the fourteen-thousand-acre Tucson Mountain Park. I was wondering how early to start out the next morning when I got a telephone call from Harold W. Gras, known as Hal, head of the museum's public relations department.

"If you can come to the Duffy School tomorrow morning at nine, I'll meet you there," he said. "We're having one of our programs for the kids, and that would be a good introduction for you, to our aims in the way of education. Conservation is the watchword—but you'll see for yourself. You can't possibly miss the school because our Ark will be in the parking lot."

Driving to the appointment in the morning with my hostess, I found a lot of my recollections of the desert country refreshed. Air conditioning makes a difference indoors, but outside was much as I remembered—dry. There is little that residents can do with the ground around their houses. A few people cultivate cacti, but cacti go their own ways and are apt to look straggly. However, there are trees and shrubs, and that morning I saw a lot of birds concentrating on them. The Duffy School is one of those new-looking, expensive-looking buildings that strike the European with awe at lavish American habits—an airy, wide-sprawling, one-story edifice surrounding a patio. The grounds swarmed with excited small children. Among the cars in the parking lot was a large white station wagon labeled THE DESERT ARK, from which two men were busily unloading some sort of apparatus. A pattern emerged among the children— teachers were shepherding them into a doorway that led to a large room full of chairs in rows, and as we, too, approached the door we were greeted by the principal, Mr. Rykken. He said that this was a great day for the school, they had been looking forward for months to Hal Gras's visit.

"One must make arrangements a long way ahead, he's so popular," he said. "I put in my request, for example, last March, and now we're in November. It was the first time he had available . . . Good morning, Mrs. Bassett; what have you there?"

"Birds," said the young woman he had addressed. She carried a large cardboard carton and was followed by a boy older than the other children, who kept an anxious eye on the box. Mrs. Bassett entered the auditorium with us and put her burden down on a chair to open it. "What kind do you think they are?" she asked as we peered in. They looked like nothing particular to me, except that one was a good deal older than the other and had a few more feathers. Mr. Rykken said he knew nothing about birds, but they might be road runners. "Where did you get them?" he asked.

"The children picked them up in an alley near the house," said Mrs. Bassett. A likely story, I thought, and I looked suspiciously at her son, but his face was bland and innocent. She continued, "I simply must go to work—I just stopped in to leave these for Mr. Gras." She shut the carton and picked it up again. I saw her weaving her way among the children, the boy behind her, to where a man with a small mustache was busily moving about among the others who were helping him arrange a microphone just short of the platform at the top of the room. Mrs. Bassett talked to him, and he nodded and took possession of the carton, and handed it over to one of the men, who put it out of sight. She and her son vanished through the door. Ranged on the platform behind and above the mike were five green-painted metal cases with air holes in them, like heavy dog carriers. There were also a few other objects, in the line, one of them a Teddy bear lying on its back. The mustached man, Hal Gras, saw us sitting near the door and came over.

"Is it all right if we sit here?" I asked him.

He said, "Fine, sit anywhere you like. There's something I ought to point out to you in advance about this talk. I'm sure you've seen dozens of school programs on the same order, but we think our routine is a little bit special." I started to say, "I've never—" but he swept on. He was in a hurry. "It's not supposed to be all playtime. The kids enjoy it all right, but I try to incorporate lessons all through—practical psychology, you know, to help with character building and so on. The museum's main purpose is to educate people about conservation. Oh well, you're bound to see what I mean—you'll notice the little touches I put in. Here in Arizona we like to claim we're first in everything, but we can honestly claim that this *is* the first time just this sort of thing's been done in schools. People have always taken animals to visit schoolchildren and given little natural-history talks, but—" Again I attempted to say that for my part, I'd never experienced such a lecture at school. In my youth nobody, at least in St. Louis, had ever heard of illustrated animal lectures. If the authorities *had* tried to introduce such a custom, most of our mothers would have objected. Mine certainly would have, because of her fixed idea that furry animals were typhoid carriers. However, Hal Gras wasn't in any position to listen to my memoirs: one of the helpers called, "Ready when you are." "Yes," Hal yelled back. "Hold on." He continued to us, "This particular program is geared to the understanding of very small children, aged five or six. Immediately afterwards I'm going to address an older group, and I'll use more advanced material with them, but this will give you enough of an idea, I hope."

As he went back to the mike I surveyed the audience, twisting my neck to see them—row upon row of round faces of all complexions, head after head of soft hair that was light or dark or woolly. They had settled down to a quiet almost unnatural, all staring at Hal Gras in anticipation. "Good morning," he said. "Do you know what we have in these boxes?"

"Animals!" shouted most of the children, but a small girl behind me yelled, "Bears!"

"Animals, that's right," said Hal. "Now these animals are awfully lazy—as a matter of fact they're sleeping right now. We'll have to wake them up. Think we can do it? Let's shout like this—'Ho!' as loud as we can. Come on; one, two, three—Ho!" The children joined in, rapturously swinging their legs, while the speaker leaned forward, hand cupped to ear. "You didn't even wake *me* up," he said as the echoes died. "Try again." At the shrill noise that followed, he pulled out a handkerchief and waved it, shouting above the hubbub, "I surrender!" The children settled back and looked proud. Among the animals he was going to show them, said Hal, was a snake, at which news the boys cheered but some of the girls looked thoughtful. Here he interrupted himself to administer one of his little moral lessons: "I'm warm and I'd like to take off my jacket, but gentlemen don't remove their jackets just like that, without first asking the permission of whatever ladies are present. Girls, may I take off my coat?" "Yes!" shouted the girls, and he duly pulled off his jacket to reveal a gray shirt piped and cut like a movie cowboy's, which I gathered was the Ark uniform. Hanging the jacket on a chair back, he went on, "Suppose you're out on the desert playing with your little sister Susie, who's only three years old, and you happen to see a wild animal—any wild animal, a raccoon or a squirrel or a snake; the rule's the same no matter what it is. What did I tell you last time about what to do if you see wild animals? Does anybody remember?" Remembering, they chanted in chorus, "Leave —them—alone!" "Exactly. Because wild animals are afraid of you, and there's a reason for that, isn't there? Are all people nice to wild animals?" "No!" "If you were a wild animal, what would you want to do if you saw people?" "Run away!"

Hal approved of this reply, but went on to say that an animal that can't run away might possibly do something else. "Suppose your little sister Susie catches a squirrel because she's too young to know any better, suppose she pets the squirrel and it bites her. It might, you know. Your father and your mother take Susie to the doctor and he says the squirrel might be rabid—it's only one chance out of a hundred, but your parents can't take that chance, and Susie has to have shots to keep her from being sick. Fourteen shots, and you know where most of them are!" Clearly, from the laughter this evoked, the children did. Hal confessed that he'd had the shots himself when a bat once bit him. "So, don't forget, when you see wild animals, to leave—them—alone." People get scared of wild animals in their turn, and do silly things. For example, some girls scream when they see mice. The speaker demonstrated, standing on a chair, holding up imaginary skirts, and squealing. Then suddenly he brought out a small, docile animal which he said was a pack rat, some-

times known as a wood rat. He walked up and down the aisles between
the seat rows, while he put on and took off of the rat's head, in rapid
succession, a series of tiny hats—ten-gallon, fireman's helmet, and mortar-
board—"Woodie wears the college hat because he's a scientist—he digs
things up and brings them home. What kind of a scientist would that be?
It begins with 'Ark' . . . Woodie hopes you'll all be archaeologists like
him; then you can wear this hat. Some people think that all rats are
dirty. They say 'dirty rat' and things like that. But Woodie isn't at all
dirty. Here, smell him." He held the animal under the nose of a nearby
little girl. "Does he smell dirty?"

The little girl blushed and giggled and shook her head.

"Then are all rats dirty?" "No," shouted the children. "But are all rats
clean?" "No." "That teaches us never to say all things are one or the
other." He stowed the rat away and brought out in its place a creature
strange to me, a sharp-nosed, bright-eyed little beast colored black, gray,
and white, with pointed ears and a long fluffy tail that looked bigger
than the body. This was a ring-tailed cat, said the speaker, not really a cat,
but related to the raccoon, the coatimundi, and even the bear. "You
know, Old Smokey," he elucidated, and with his free hand he picked up
the Teddy bear to show us. I now perceived that it was dressed like a
forest ranger. Hal embarked on a little homily about fire prevention, but I
was preoccupied, worrying about that ringtail. I wondered if he wasn't
palming off a foreign animal on us as a native. I'd never heard of ringtails. Later I looked it up in Walker's *Mammals of the World*. Hal Gras
was quite right, after all. The ring-tailed cat, or cacomistle, or *Bassariscus
astutis*, ranges from Oregon, Colorado, and Texas to southern Mexico.
. . . is found in a variety of habitats but seems to prefer rocky, broken
areas . . . good climber . . . eats insects, plant material, rodents, birds . . .
makes a charming pet. "Early settlers of the southwestern United States
sometimes had them about the home as house cats to catch mice, and as
companions," says Walker. I felt humbled.

The children were now lining up to pet the ringtail, while Hal assured
them that she didn't mind who petted her, because she trusted people.
She didn't care if the people were tall or short, if their eyes were green or
brown, because she'd never been hurt. "If you hurt or tease another
living thing, who loses?" He held the little creature on top of a small
boy's head, where with its curled tail it gave an excellent imitation of a
Davy Crockett cap. When released, the boy returned to his seat pink
with pride.

We were shown, in turn, a barn owl, a frightful little doll called John
Q. Litterbug (complete with lecture on litter), and, at last, the promised

snake, the appearance of which was heralded by an impressive talk. "In this sack is a real live snake. You boys must promise not to meddle with him, and you girls must promise not to pass out. My snake is a kind one, but there's one thing you should remember about snakes everywhere. Suppose you're playing with a kind, harmless snake in front of your little sister Susie. Remember, she's only three years old. Suppose then she goes into the desert and plays with a snake that isn't harmless. Now, I've seen people who chase girls just to make them scream. They think it's funny when girls scream. But should we laugh at someone who's afraid of snakes?" "No." "Now you don't have to be afraid of my snake here, Charlie, because he's harmless. You wouldn't believe it, but I've heard children say, 'I don't want to see Charlie!' Is anybody here going to say that?" Nobody did. Charlie, a reptile of respectable length, was at last pulled out of the sack and held high, dangling. He looked blasé. "Charlie is a gopher snake, and I'm showing him because he looks like a rattlesnake. Do we kill him? No, we don't, because farmers like him: he's useful. There are two hundred and thirty different kinds of snake in our country, but only four kinds are bad. Yet people kill every snake they see, because they're afraid of it. Should we do that? No. People should learn what bad snakes look like. Now, I'm going to ask two of you to help me put Charlie back in his sack. Are there any children here who used to be afraid of snakes? I want a girl and a boy." Two children of the proper sexes confessed to having entertained this particular weakness in the past, and came up to the front of the room. Without flinching, they held open the mouth of Charlie's sack while Hal stowed him away. "When this lecture's over, you may all touch one of the animals you've seen," said the speaker. "I'll let you vote as to which. You needn't be afraid of any of them." A porcupine was brought out next, and then there was a bobcat, somewhat larger than an ordinary cat, who snarled a good deal but permitted Hal to put a finger in her mouth. "Diablo lets me do this because she trusts me," Hal explained. He carried her like a baby, sucking a bottle of milk held in her paws and snarling the whole time. Then she, too, went back into her box, and the demonstration was over. Hal put the question of the animal to be touched to a vote, and the snake had it by a vast majority. "You'll be surprised how dry he is," Hal said. "Most people think snakes are wet and slimy, but they aren't. I'm going to stand out there in the patio with Charlie, and you make a nice orderly line, and each one can touch Charlie as he walks back to his room. Of course, those who don't want to touch a snake don't have to. They can wait indoors until it's over." Every child in the room took his place in the line.

The road from Tucson to the Museum drives toward the foothills, past a sign, OLD TUCSON. This points to what resembles in the distance, at the end of a side road, a picturesque cow town of long-ago days, straight out of Western films. This in fact is just what it is—an elaborate stage set built and maintained by, and for the benefit of, various movie makers who use the premises whenever they need them. Residents of the true Tucson have long been accustomed to the sudden arrival of film stars, cameramen, and directors who demand hotel accommodation and transport to the location. Old Tucson is also a tourist attraction. Beyond the signpost the road rises, and after a while swerves and loops among hills. The driver crosses a pass, drives downhill, and again rises until the road leads him, through increasingly thicker stands of tall saguaro cactus, to the museum entrance. Two or three adobe buildings are clustered together; between two of them runs a covered walk. Between the road and the ticket office is a sunken enclosure in which lizards dart about or bask on rocks. A sign warns the public, No DOGS, PLEASE, FOR GOOD REASONS. I went in and found the director, a young, dark-haired man named William H. Woodin. He said, "Good, you've arrived in time to meet Mr. Carr, one of the founders. He doesn't come every day, but this morning he dropped in. He developed the whole idea of this Museum." He collected some literature for me and we went into the staff canteen, where at a refectory table I was introduced to a tall, elderly gentleman, Mr. William H. Carr, and Bill Woodin's associate director, Lewis Wayne Walker. Coffee was fetched.

"This Museum really started on the banks of the Hudson in 1926," said Mr. Carr. "I was with the Museum of Natural History in New York at that time, in the education department, and Dr. Sherwood, the director, told me to do something about Bear Mountain State Park that would give visitors some idea of its living creatures and plants, geology and history. That's how the Bear Mountain Nature Trails and Trailside Museums came to be designed and constructed. After a while, though, it all began to be spoiled. Roads were driven through, the animals were scared away . . . well, never mind that now, but it broke my heart and I moved out West. I've never regretted leaving New York. I'm sorry for everybody who lives east of the Rio Grande." He looked at the high window that framed a piece of clear blue sky.

When Mr. Carr settled down in Tucson, he meant to spend the rest of his life in retirement, but soon it seemed logical to accept an invitation extended by the Pima County Park Advisory Committee, and become one of them. At the time, the group was discussing the problem of what to do with a collection of adobe buildings west of town called the Mountain House. Put up by WPA labor during the depression of the early thirties, the complex had been used for various purposes—youth hostels, camping sites for group outings and so on—but the buildings had to be kept in repair, and mounting expenses scarcely seemed justified for these few and far-between visits. Mr. Carr, always an enthusiastic conservationist, wrote out the suggestion that the Mountain House should become "a leading educational center for the purpose of acquainting the public with their rich but vanishing heritage in wildlife, plantlife and scenic values to the end that, through knowledge, will come appreciation and a better attitude toward all resource conservation." The committee didn't exactly greet this idea with cries of joy, because such a project sounded likely to run into money. They might have hemmed and hawed indefinitely if it had not been for another new member, Arthur N. Pack. Pack was a keen naturalist. He founded and edited *Nature Magazine*, and with his father had founded the American Tree Association and the Charles Lathrop Pack Forestry Foundation. He was naturally familiar with Mr. Carr's work at Bear Mountain Park, and he applauded the scheme and offered to pay out of his own pocket for a preliminary survey, in 1951. He is now listed on the Museum masthead as Founder Emeritus. Both men struggled valiantly, and were joined in the fight by local newspapers, until, in 1952, after a tremendous amount of preparation, building started on the new Museum. William Woodin joined the staff that year. Woodin was born in New York, but his family moved to Tucson when he was five years old, and he took his first degree at Arizona State University, following it with graduate work in California in herpetology. Walker too was born in the East, in Boston. He attended school in New York, where he introduced the idea of a "nature room." An innovation welcomed by leading naturalists of the country, it soon spread to the schools of other states. He served in the summers as nature counselor at various Boy Scout camps, and at one of these he made the acquaintance of young Bill Woodin. Lew Walker's road to Tucson wound far and wide; he was a taxidermist under Carl Akeley, went on to the San Diego Museum of Natural History, joined the Marines during the war, and then took to writing scientific articles. When the Tucson Museum opened he was in Baja California studying birds, but within the following year he joined the staff.

I took a quick look at some of the brochures Woodin had handed me and remarked in surprise on the numbers of species listed. "Well, of course," said Bill. "There's a great variety of wild life in this territory, didn't you know that? Mind you, I don't claim that you could walk out of your front door in Tucson and spot them all immediately. Look at this map and you'll see that the Arizona-Sonora Desert spreads over considerable area, west into California and a long way down into Mexico. Besides, certain groups of animals and birds stick to their particular terrain within the area, some in the foothills, some on the low ground, some in the mountains, but you get quite a number right around here—mule deer and javelina, for instance."

"What's javelina?"

"That's the Spanish word for 'peccary'—wild pig. Strictly speaking they're not really pigs, but they look like pigs, so why argue?"

A chart of the Museum grounds showed that only a part of the area was given over to animal exhibits. There were also a "Watershed Exposition," a Papago Indian House, a cactus garden, a mineral collection, an aquarium, and various other spots. The word "museum" was justified, therefore—it was a museum with living specimens among others—and I suddenly realized that there was a connection between this place and the Jardin des Plantes in Paris, where the first public zoo was opened after the revolution, when lions and tigers and elephants were put on show among the old cabinets of mineral specimens and cases of fossilized plants. After more than a century and a half, the wheel had gone full circle.

"We haven't finished everything yet," said Bill Woodin. "According to Mr. Carr we'll never be finished, because fresh ideas keep cropping up. With the help we get from various trusts and bequests, we just about make out financially—we're supported by our memberships and admission charges. Admission's high—a dollar for adults, twenty-five cents for children from six to fifteen, but the public must think it's worth it, because they keep coming—and of course, we think so ourselves. Our budget for next year is pretty considerable, but I think we'll make it. The attendance last year, including about a fourth of the number free entries—school visits and all that—was two hundred and ten thousand. We have various sorts of membership. Students can join for two dollars, a family membership is ten, and so on. We have two thousand members of all sorts. The great advantage financially is that we're on county property, with maintenance and water included for our dollar a year."

Mr. Carr said, "As you've probably gathered, the objective here is not that of ordinary zoos. We want to teach people to look at a landscape, understand it, and appreciate the environment and surroundings all in one, so we study water and regional vegetation along with our animals and birds. You can't expect children to understand the idea of protection and conservation unless they learn to look around for themselves. We want to *orient* people."

"That's why we stick to our own regional fauna," said Woodin. "Once in a great while we have to make room for some animal that hasn't any real right to be here, but when this happens we're very careful to indicate the facts in the label, and it doesn't often have to be done. Incidentally, this is a very inexpensive way to run a zoo; naturally it costs less per head to educate people when you aren't paying fancy prices for rare exotic animals. I feel sorry for children who have only other zoos to visit. They get the animals without any background, and the sight doesn't mean nearly as much as it should. Of course not everybody understands our approach. I practically had a battle right here the other day with a dealer who was trying to sell me an elephant. He said a zoo without an elephant has no right to call itself a zoo. The more I refused the more he lowered his price, and in the end he was trying to give it to me. When I still turned him down, he went away thinking I was nuts."

"I used to have the same experience at Bear Mountain," said Mr. Carr.

"Another thing—we've always got a good answer for zoo haters," went on the director. "I'd say that fifty percent at least of our animals here are orphans, picked up because they've lost their parents. We hand-raise them. We almost never go out and trap big animals—we don't have to, and practically all of ours are pets. Another beauty of the system is that if we have a lizard or a bird or small animal that doesn't do well in captivity, we simply release it right around here, and it fits into the landscape without having to adapt: this is its natural environment."

We said good-by to Mr. Carr and started to make our rounds, at Bill's request, in another room of the same building. "Everybody's supposed to set out here," he said, "when it's all ready, that is—it's still in construction, but you'll be able to get the general idea. We call it the Orientation Room, and first we try to set up comparisons between our desert and various other large deserts of the world, with reference to the wildlife. Animals in widely separated regions quite often show similarities in their adaptation to similar environments." Above charts, maps or blocks of clear print, the walls asked such questions as WHAT IS A DESERT? and attempted to answer them in simple terms. I noticed particularly a spy-hole in which, when a button was pressed, a scene of the Sonoran Desert blended imperceptibly, by means of hidden reflections and lights, into a different but similar scene in the Sahara, in an adjoining exhibit, and the Sonoran Desert was transformed into the Australian. By the same method a horned lizard turned into a "moloch," or thorny devil, a jerboa dissolved into the very similar guise of a kangaroo rat, and a horned viper became a sidewinder. I was enthusiastic about this display.

Bill said, "Actually, it was invented for use by circuses in side shows—

you know, penny-in-the-slot machines, but the Albany Museum rigged up a weasel that turns into an ermine, to show the color changes, and we figured we could improve on that. Now here, on this wall, we're going to show the seven subdivisions of the Sonoran Desert, and in the center of the room we'll have a relief map of the whole thing. Over there we're planning a living diorama. That's what we call the little displays that Mervin Larson makes up, with artificial background and genuine animals living in it. Here we'll have a sand-dune scene with living lizards and a kangaroo rat, and we'll explain that these rats are able to live without drinking water at all. It's a very interesting adaptation, you know—the animal spends most of the time underground where it's cool, and it has powerful kidneys. With its extremely economical system it lives on its own metabolism product of water, made out of what it eats, even though it may eat only dry food. Next to it we have this diagram of a fringe-toed lizard, much enlarged to show the toes and *its* system for living in the desert. Here we have a cross-section of a desert mountain with the life zones marked out in different colors. In the last panel there'll be a summary and an invitation to move on and look at the actual exhibits themselves."

In the Small Animal Room, thronged with visitors, Bill demonstrated how a "Living Diorama" case could be unhooked and swung out back of the wall, all in one piece, for servicing. I spotted what I thought were chipmunks, and was told that they weren't: they were Harris antelope squirrels, which live in the desert and eat cactus fruit. There was a gaudy lot of invertebrates and reptiles, described in the guidebook in a charmingly tactful manner. Tarantulas in the United States are not dangerous, said the book. The giant hairy scorpion's sting "is very painful but seldom is dangerous," and most snakes in the Southwest are of a more benevolent nature than I had supposed, for the bite of the sidewinder is seldom fatal, and though the bite of the Western diamondback can be dangerous, "the human mortality rate is very low, and it is a valuable rodent exterminator." Privately I made up my mind that I would *not* be reassured about the Gila monster, which I have always considered a remarkably unpleasant animal, but the book managed to say something extenuating even about that. Gila monsters have a true venom, it admitted, but no way of injecting it directly; "poison mixed with saliva enters wounds inflicted by sharp teeth." Even the coral snake, though its venom is potent, has "a usually gentle disposition." Turning my back on all these debatable creatures I looked for some time at the chuckwalla, a lizard that has the habit of hiding in crevices when it is frightened, and puffs up so that it cannot be dislodged save by certain unsporting

Indians, who like to eat chuckwallas. They prick the poor creatures with pins or cactus thorns and thus deflate them to manageable size.

In the middle of the room a lifelike rubber model of a rattlesnake lay coiled on a table, its tail sticking up from the center of the heap. By pressing a button one can make the tail shake and emit a very lifelike rattle, or buzz. Chatting about the commissary for his charges—for which the museum buys sixty-five thousand mealworms and a thousand crickets a month, among other provisions—Bill led the way out of the room, but paused at the entrance, where glass covered a dark hole in the wall. A small revolver was fixed to the pane in such a way that it could be aimed here and there, and when he pulled its trigger it shone a light into the hole, exposing a cave in which hung a cluster of sleeping forms. "Vampire bats," he said. "We had quite a struggle persuading the authorities to let us have this exhibit, because it meant importing them from Mexico. However, as they do live this side of the border as well, the prohibition was sort of pointless, and naturally we keep them segregated from the other animals. I believe there are only two other vampire-bat exhibitions in the United States. Did you know that there aren't any vampire bats at all in the Old World? It's a fact. Nobody knew they existed in real life until explorers went into South America and found them, yet there have been horror stories and legends about vampire bats in Europe for centuries, long before any Europeans had ever heard of Brazil. These animals eat only blood, nothing else. You'll see other bats here—insect eaters, fruit eaters—but blood is the only food these animals here are equipped to digest. We feed them a shallow bowl of it every day. Quite a sight when they cluster around the dish. People love to work that gun and swivel the light around."

Near the building was a low circular wall, inside which tortoises made their lazy way back and forth on the sand. A sign said, "You are welcome inside the enclosure." "People wouldn't believe it until they were told," said Bill, "but we *like* kids to get inside and handle the tortoises. They've never hurt one so far. The animals are weighed and measured every so often; we're trying to get comprehensive records on their growth and longevity."

"Bears!" I cried as we came around the corner. The animals were scratching their claws against a log within an enclosure—big black things. "You can't tell me that bears are native to these parts." But they are: they live in the mountain ranges, a fact that everyone except me seemed to know. After that I accepted, without argument, the other animals: raccoons, porcupines, jaguars, mountain lions, bobcats, jaguarundis—"Very rare here," said Bill, "but they've bred in the zoo, and it's a record; first time in captivity,"—margay cats, ocelots. He was just telling me that the Museum has all the species of cats that occur in the region when I interrupted him with the cry of "Look! Coyotes!"

"Well, of course," he said. "They're one of the most common—" He broke off, because I was raptly reading the label, which said that since the advent of man in their habitat, coyotes have *increased* in number. The author of the message obviously thought this a good thing, as coyotes constitute a valuable check on the rodent and rabbit population. At last I turned away, quite happy. "I had no idea," I explained. Bill looked at me in a puzzled way and led on.

Mexican wolf. North American river otter. Hognose skunk. Striped skunk. Spotted skunk, and a fourth one the name of which I forget. Peccary (or javelina). Whitetail deer. Mule deer. Pronghorn antelope. Coatimundi (or chulo). Prairie dog. Bill said, "Something I didn't know until lately is that a large number of the public can't read straight. Look at the sign on the prairie-dog colony fence; it's clear enough, isn't it? It says that 256 prairie dogs eat as much as one cow, doesn't it? Well, you'd be surprised at the number of people who come and tell me that they'd never realized that prairie dogs eat cows. We'll have to re-write it, that's all."

As we walked along the path (firmly called, by Mr. Carr, the Nature Trail), he pointed out locations for new projects. We paused briefly by a huge palm to see how a new wasp colony was getting on, took a long-distance look at the saguaro ramada, and came to a halt at two large circular edifices, like wheels, with each spoke a cage full of birds. "Lewis Walker designed these," said Bill. "The service areas are in the middles, very convenient. We're proud of our ceramic labels—the tile makes the sketch of the bird stand out, doesn't it? They don't fade, either. We'd like to have Spanish labels everywhere as well as English, and some day we will, but it does cost a lot. I've asked Lew to meet us here—he's our bird expert. There he is now."

According to the guidebook, there are sixty-five species of desert birds in the collection, and I must have seen them all, but I was most struck by the elf owl, a tiny creature no bigger than a sparrow. "It lives on scorpions mostly," said Lew, "or at least forty percent of its diet is scorpion. Look at the horned owls. We get so many of those that we turn a few loose from time to time, but they won't go away. They nest on top of the cage if they can't get in, and naturally we have to go on feeding them. Finally they seem to get enough self-confidence to fly away. Wild birds are always trying to move in on us, too, for the sake of the regular meals. Here are teal—we get a whole lot of different sorts of teal. Pay particular attention to those burrowing owls. They've *bred*, and it's the first recorded instance of burrowing owls breeding in captivity in America. England produced some, though, years ago. Here are jays—lovely color, some of those—and a mottled wood owl here. It's possibly the only mottled owl on show in the world. That spotted owl is rare, too: I don't know if any other zoo's got it."

The Tunnel Exhibit, Bill explained, was invented by Mr. Carr, and has been widely imitated since the public was introduced to it. He said, "Practically all desert life is nocturnal, and we had to adapt our exhibition to that fact, otherwise you'd just have a lot of sleeping animals to look at. This way, the animals wake up because it's dark. The money for it was supplied by the Pack Foundation." We entered a long, slowly descending tunnel, where there was hardly enough light to walk by until we reached the exhibits. There, by pressing a button, one or another little room was lit up, and you could look straight into the face of a pack rat, a kit fox, or a prairie dog, going about his business in his own particular burrow. I came out of the tunnel's other end blinking in bright sunlight. Then, before I knew what had happened, I was in the Watershed Exhibition, with labels everywhere. A relief map of Arizona made clear the state's watershed drainage system. Through telescopes one could study the real thing in the distant mountains. There were working demonstrations of cascades, retention dams, planting and its effect on water catchment, irrigation canals, and glass-covered samples in cross section of different kinds of soil, with the vegetation that went best with it. There was a lot of information, by recorded voice or in print: "Did you know that the average annual rainfall in Arizona provides eleven times as much water as the entire state used during 1957? Or did you know that a very high percentage of that rainfall was carried away to other parts of the world through evaporation and atmospheric action before it could be used by plants, wildlife or man?" One could make rainstorms in miniature by pressing buttons, and watch the water evaporate. Wind erosion. Water erosion. Soil retention or lack of it.

After all this, it seemed natural to be taken to the Demonstration Desert Garden, where native plants and trees that don't require much water were set out attractively, to tempt local householders away from their doomed efforts to grow grass and eastern flowers. From these we went into the first of two walk-in bird cages. "These are really ecology exhibits," said Bill. "This one contains plants and birds from right around here, and that one has the plants and birds of the Mexican side of the desert. They're very different regions really. Here in the Arizona collection we have road runners and jays and vultures and the Gambel quail. The

Mexican cage has macaws and so on. Last winter we had a freak snow-storm, seven inches of precipitation, and we spent a miserable night on top of these cages, keeping them clear of snow. Even so, one of the ramada shelters collapsed. We get quite a few birds from a banker in Texas. He grows a lot of rice, and he's got a permit from the government to go through the fields just before the harvest and pick up whatever eggs he finds. He puts these in incubators and hatches out a lot of them, and supplies a number of zoos."

We returned to the main buildings by way of the Papago bee-house, a part of the Indian Exhibit, where I learned that the Papago reservation, whose limits are near the Museum, is the second largest in the United States. "Now, before you call it a day you'd better look at our new Amphibian Room," said Bill.

"I'll look at the amphibians, but it's not nearly the end of the day for me," I replied. "Lew Walker's going to show me the animal blind to-night."

Bill handed me over to Mervin Larson, who showed me around the Amphibian Room. There he has designed and built four main dioramas, large displays typifying distinct sorts of water habitat in the desert region: canyon stream, river, permanent pond, and temporary rock pool. "The cycles of the creatures you see in any one habitat are geared to that habitat," he said. "Take the temporary rock pool, for instance. No animal with a slow rate of development could survive the changeable conditions you find there. As a result you get tadpoles that develop completely within twenty-four hours, a great acceleration of the ordinary processes." Like the smaller dioramas, these were designed for ease in servicing; the backgrounds can be raised hydraulically when cleaning is necessary—"Like curtains," he said.

I spent the rest of the afternoon reading one of the Museum publi-cations of 1964, a "Special Bulletin" by Lewis Walker with the title "The Return of the Masked Bobwhite." All in all it is a poignant story. This particular bird, the only bobwhite ever seen in Arizona, suddenly disappeared about 1912, presumably because it needs long grass in its habitat. Before that time, parts of Arizona *were* grassy, but the grass disappeared under the feet of the millions of cattle driven from Mexico to the meat markets of the United States, and conditions never permitted it to grow again. In 1927, an American rancher who had property in Mexico saw some of the bobwhites below the border, and captured five of them. Other Americans got interested and kept a lookout. Finally a famous conservationist and bird man named Ligon collected twenty bobwhites, and with Lew Walker developed a scheme to bring back the bobwhite to Arizona by breeding it near the Museum; a fantastically difficult project, involving considerable sums of money and much persuasion. First they had to get the consent of such ranchers as had a claim on the land, persuading them to give up their grazing rights. Then dams had to be constructed and wells sunk so that grass might be persuaded to grow again on the 640 acres they needed, and a whole acre was wired in for the nesting area. They were not friendless. The Allegheny Foundation, the Arizona Game and Fish Department, the Department of the Interior were all interested and helpful, but it was a tremendous task. The weather did not help. After a protracted dry spell came a dangerous flood. But the grass grew, and the birds actually began to lay. So far the pamphlet ended on a high note of hope, but an added sheet had to be slipped in just before it was mailed out, bearing a tragic postscript: ". . . Three Papago Indian boys, ages 7 to 9, entered the cages and by chasing the birds against the wire eliminated over 75% breeding stock. Partially incubated eggs were used as missiles to throw at handy targets and at signs the boys could not read."

It was with some trepidation that I mentioned the matter to Lew Walker, but he was calm about it. "Yes, they ate some of the birds," he said, and added, with admirably scientific detachment, that as the masked bobwhite had always been a sacred bird to the Papagos in the old days, "I daresay those boys are the only Papago Indians ever to have eaten bobwhites. It shows how even an old tradition can die out." The project will be attempted again—if only more birds can be found.

Fortunately, Walker's interest is not exclusively devoted to the masked bobwhite. He has been instrumental in persuading the Mexican authorities to declare as a preserve an island in the Baja California, Isla Rasa, which has long been a roosting and nesting ground for birds. Mrs. Walker, who works as a secretary at the Museum, served us drinks at their house while her husband showed slides of Isla Rasa and the birds, whiling away the minutes we had still to wait before it was time to visit the wildlife blind. "Those birds were being completely wiped out," he said. "Every day during nesting time people would come over in boats, fill their baskets with eggs, and take them back to sell in the market. They knew, though, that it couldn't go on forever—the birds were decreasing—so there wasn't too much resentment at the government's decision." He looked at the clock. "I think it's time to go."

During the short drive he told how the blind had happened to be built. It came of an accident: One morning in 1954 someone noticed that a waterpipe near an old corral was leaking, and that the soft, wet ground beneath it was covered with a variety of animal tracks. The staff improved this artificial waterhole by running pipe from the leak to a hollow under a saguaro, where observers could hide behind piles of brush. It took three days for the animals to find the new pool, though it was only forty feet from the old leak. "So much for the theory that they can smell water," said Lew. But then a deer stumbled into the new waterhole, and the rush was on. After a while, tired of creeping about behind brush piles, the Museum naturalists put up a small cabin close by from which people could survey developments more easily. Four windows overlook the pool, fitted with flashlight cameras. A spotlight has been fixed so that a rather dim light shines on the water—the animals soon got used to that, Lew said, and nowadays seem uneasy if it isn't switched on. Creeping in to my place, I felt delighted with this chance to see wildlife at close quarters. According to photographs the Walkers had shown, deer, javelina, cottontails and even toads visited the hole regularly. Lew, too, was in an anticipatory mood. He spoke in a low tone that was not quite a whisper: "I'm wondering what will turn up to-night. You never know, but it might be especially interesting because last night we had something extraordinary taking place an hour or so after we'd left the blind. A mountain lion killed a deer just about fifteen feet off from here. He was scared away before he'd finished his meal, but we've left the deer just where he dropped it, hoping he'll come back."

We waited. We waited. We waited. "I can't understand it," said Lew. "Every night there's *something* . . . I can't understand it." The only animal we saw that night was a pack rat.

"So the blind was a flop? Bad luck," said Bill Woodin cheerfully. It was next day, at the Woodins' house, which is well outside town, built by the side of a stream. There were other guests, Joseph Wood Krutch and his wife. Krutch, once a well-known New Yorker, has, like Mr. Carr, cast in his lot with the Southwest. He is Secretary of the Museum Board of Trustees. He said to Mrs. Woodin, "Where's my friend?"

Ann Woodin replied, "I've been keeping her out, but she can come in now." She opened a door to admit a fairly large bobcat, with alert, tufted ears, which trotted over to Joe Krutch and leaped up to his knee. There it did not exactly nestle, but stoically accepted his attentions. "Not long ago, some papers published a photograph of me with a young bobcat," he told me. "I had a letter soon afterwards from a woman in

Chicago who said she was glad to see that I have a nice little kitty just like theirs. She and her husband had picked up their kitty while driving from Colorado to Illinois—it was wandering, lost on the road, she said. They loved it but it seemed to be getting wilder and wilder. She wondered if I was having the same experience with mine."

Ann suggested that we go to see the wolves. I followed the party out of the house, where we stopped and looked through wire netting into a large—a very large—pen. For a moment, nothing was to be seen in there but a few worn-out shoes scattered about on the ground, and a structure strangely like one of those jungle gyms in kindergartens. I remembered that the Woodins have four sons, but surely they didn't keep them locked up?

"I've always thought it very proper to keep children's equipment in your wolf pen," Bill explained, and Ann said, "The boys are so fond of the wolves, they'd rather play inside the pen than not. They have full charge of them, you know, though of course Bill oversees things now and then."

Two wolves came lolloping over the ground to the wire to investigate. The larger one came as close to us as he could, but the smaller hung back. "He's named Beowulf," said Ann. "The other's Gwendolyn; she's only half-grown, and she's always been timid, but I do think Beowulf's a splendid creature, don't you? And so friendly." Beowulf rubbed pleadingly against the netting. His enormous eyes, a startlingly beautiful amber color, were almost opaque as he looked up at us. "I do believe he wants to be petted," said Ann. "That's unusual with strangers, isn't it, Bill?" We pushed our fingers through the wire and he went back and forth, rubbing against them, sometimes playfully chewing at mine, like a puppy. Two of the Woodin boys came out of the house to see what was going on, followed by a German shepherd dog. Their father said, "Boys, have you been giving those wolves their vitamins? Beowulf's skin seems to be itching." The boys assured him that they had given the wolves just what they'd been told to. One of them unlocked the gate and went into the enclosure, taking the dog with him. It wasn't until the dog and the wolves began playing together that I realized how big Beowulf was. "He's full-grown, and that's what worries us," said Bill. "If we can't find a good place for him in some acceptable zoo, he's going to dig his way out of the pen one of these nights, and then some hunter will get him. There's no room for him at the Museum, either. We're full up with Mexican wolves."

Ann said, "The boys really ought to clean up that pen. Look at all the worn-out shoes lying around in there. If there's anything Beowulf really loves, it's burying old shoes."

The boy in the pen ran a race with Beowulf, while his dog barked excitedly.

Hal Gras and his wife Natie live in town, in a house with a large back yard that is full of outbuildings. This is the headquarters of the animal nursery, to which waifs and strays, like the birds I had seen at the Duffy School, are brought by their rescuers. The birds were there when I joined the Grases on the porch that overlooks the yard, but they had been put into a cage. "Did they turn out to be road runners?" I asked. Hal said, "Goodness, no. They're pigeons." "And what's this?" I asked, bending over a shallow box in which lay a small animal, its head on a pillow, its body covered to the chin, if the creature could be said to have a chin. Its eyes were closed. "Oh, I see now," I added. "A baby peccary, isn't it?"

Natie said, "That's right. We have five just now, and I'm not at all sure this one is going to pull through. It's awfully small." Her husband said, "Natie won't give up, though. She never gives up. We get a lot of little javelinas around this time of year. Most of the time they're real orphans—hunters have shot the mothers illegally—but sometimes, unfortunately, people find the babies alone and bring them to us when really their mothers are just hiding somewhere. Then, of course, a baby javelina will follow a human if he hasn't got his mother close by to stop him. At that age they follow anybody."

Natie leaned closer to the small animal. She said, "He's trying awfully hard to live. Last night I was sure he was gone, but he rallied."

I asked if one person had brought in all five, but Hal shook his head. "No, separate lots," he said. "Game and Fish Department, Museum workers, and a couple who drove all the way from Salford, a hundred and twenty-five miles away, and arrived at ten o'clock at night." He turned away from the box and pointed to another cage. "There's a hummingbird we've had for quite a long time. His wing's never going to be all right, but he seems happy enough here, and he eats well. You can see by the sign where he came from." I read the tab on the cage:

HUMMINGBIRD, REC.—10/28/65.

FROM—ALICE VAIL JR. HIGH

REMARKS:

TWO WERE FOUND ON STEPS OF SCHOOL. ONE WAS DEAD.

"Out there in the yard is a speckled owl," he continued. "He's not really an Arizona bird, but somebody brought him in, and sometimes I

use him for an Ark animal, though naturally I always explain he's a
foreigner when I do. I've named him Little Nemo. I give all the Ark
animals names. The kids like it, and it sticks in their minds. One of the
Ark javelinas is Gregory Peccary, and another one, a female, I call
Olivia de Javelina. It's corny, of course." He looked at me a trifle
anxiously. "But it does help the kids to remember things. I was proud
when a little boy came up the other day with a name for one of the
gopher snakes—Julius Squeezer, because a gopher snake is a constrictor.
That's really good, isn't it?" We strolled down the yard and looked at
slightly older peccaries running around in pens. Natie began feeding one
from a tiny nursing bottle, as Hal explained, "We had a lot of trouble
finding a nipple they could get into their mouths, but finally Natie found
these dolls' bottles at Woolworth's. They're exactly right." We moved on,
to look at a red-tailed hawk. "A permanent resident," said Hal. "One of
his wings was shot off at the second joint. If an animal takes to captivity, we keep it; if it doesn't, and recovers, or grows old enough to
manage on its own, we release it. Here I've got my office and a lot of
small stuff." He led the way into an elongated shed.

"Where did you train for this work?" I asked, looking through a book
of press clippings.

"I didn't. I took a degree in speech, and I was a TV announcer
here on the local station at first. Actually, I was born and grew up in
New Jersey, a city kid who'd never even had a pet, and I didn't know
one thing about animals except that I was scared to death of them.
The only ones I'd ever seen were cows, when the class went on a trip
to the country . . . Now, here we've got a very nice fellow, a badger."
He brought it out with an expert clutch on the loose skin at the back
of its neck, and held it as he talked. "One day the station needed somebody to run a new children's program, so they put me on it. Then the
Museum sent somebody out with a few animals to go on the air and
get people interested. I was interested too. Natie and I used to smooch
in Bear Mountain Park: we knew all about Carr. But it was the kids,
really, who taught me to like animals. We had a daughter, and she and
her friends started to watch the show, and I had to handle the animals,
and—well, showing animals to kids on TV makes you a sort of hero.
I took to it—first because I had to, and then because I liked it. Two
years later I left the station and went over to the Museum, to their
public relations office, but I found I was missing direct contact with
the animals. Then our girl got me to give a show for the Brownies,
and it caught on. The word spread. I began to be asked to do the
same thing at schools, over and over, and now it's a pretty big operation.

We go to fairs as well. That performance you saw at the Duffy School was the two thousand and sixty-fourth one I've done since I began in 1956. We've just about worn out the Desert Ark car, too, but the Thunderbird Civitan Club—that's a service club here in Tucson—have collected the money to get us a new one."

Leafing through his book I found a stack of letters. There was one particular one from a child: "I liked mostly the way you imitated a lady when a mouse came into a room. . . . About what you said about snakes, I still do not like them and hope not to meet up with one. If I do I will not stop to find out whether it is poisonous or not I will just run and not ask questions."

Hal had put away the badger, and now he suggested that we look at the cages in the shed. We walked down the passage between them and he pointed out this and that inhabitant. "Here's a Gambel's quail, and here are a couple of ringtails, and this next door is a coatimundi. We got those exercise wheels from a chinchilla farm that went out of business; they like playing on them. This bobcat's very affectionate. She bites, but only in play. Did you know a bobcat can turn its back and spray you? It's a sign of affection. Better step back a bit . . . Here are two baby bobcats." He reached in and brought out a small creature much like an ordinary kitten save for its short tail. For a little while it lay quiet in his grasp, until suddenly, for some reason known only to itself, it began struggling and spitting and screaming hysterically. Twisting from Hal's hands it landed on the counter and made for the cage. Very quickly Hal caught it, and while he held it in a firm grip he talked to it in a low, calm voice: "No, no. What's the matter? What's the matter with you? Don't be afraid. Nobody's going to hurt you." The noise subsided as suddenly as it had begun. The little cat's eyes were fixed on Hal's face. Its mouth, still wide open, closed very gradually as he talked. Finally, in a dead hush, he replaced it in the cage and we walked on.

Outside we approached a tall, round cage at the bottom of the yard. "I'd like you to see this because we're proud of it," he said. "It's our young coyote. Its mother, over at the Museum, didn't give birth when she should have done—they keep tabs, and they knew just when it should have been—and she was obviously in trouble, so they did a Caesarian section. Three of the babies were already dead, and this one wasn't in too good a shape, but they sent it over here. For two months we didn't know if we could save it, but Natie never took her eyes off it, kept it warm, all that, and now you'll see a fine strong animal. Tame, too. But you'd better stand here, not too close." I stopped short, while he went into the cage. The coyote greeted him enthusiastically and whisked its tail as he carried it out to the sun where I could see it. Its foxlike mouth hung open as it panted; its eyes sparkled.

"A real coyote," I said in wonder. "Beautiful. But I suppose it howls terribly at night?"

"Coyotes never howl. They yip," said Hal.

CHAPTER 23

Fort Worth

□

"Remember, this is a little zoo. It's a poor boy's zoo," said Lawrence Curtis, who is director of the Fort Worth Zoological Park and James R. Record Aquarium all at once. "We have only twenty-four acres." To hear such disclaimers in Texas was pleasant, especially as there was much that he could have boasted about. His zoo is as prettily placed, for instance, as any I have seen in the States, in rolling, wooded country well outside town, and I liked such buildings as I could see, made of stone and reddish wood. Lawrence continued, "Just the same, we do some things pretty well. To start out with this was just a regular small-town zoo with an elephant and maybe a couple of lions, you know the kind of thing. Then somebody decided it ought to be developed, and that's where I came in. We have a Zoological Association, and people around here have been generous. What with donations and subscriptions I haven't yet had to scrounge around very hard for funds whenever I get a good idea. But we try to be careful. We don't do things wastefully. There are some ideas we're going to carry out in the near future. I have notions of what a zoo ought to be."

He enlarged on these. People who come to a zoo, he said, should be taught by what they see, by indirect method, to appreciate nature. "It's one of the aims I'm writing about, 'Appreciation of Nature' as part of a zoo's function. It oughtn't to be just a special, segregated section of life, something you go to see on Sunday if you can't think of anything better to do to kill the time. A zoo should play its part in the com-munity—after all, this is a park too, and they should be able to use it as such. Concerts, for instance, in the zoo; why not? You see that piece of woodland; it's a swamp, very pretty. We've dredged that lagoon in the

middle. Well, we're going to fix it up so people can enjoy weekend
concerts here. We're putting up an acoustic shell on the island, and we
can set up chairs, folding chairs, around the lagoon every Friday, Saturday, and Sunday evening through the summer, beginning in May. Sometimes the concerts can be live, sometimes taped—water music, *Swan Lake*
maybe, and Handel and Debussy, anything like that. That'll be pretty
good, don't you think? The aquatic bird display is right next to it. That's
one good way of orienting people to animals—getting them used to using
this park. We stay open until eight-thirty on summer nights, so it works
in well, but we could stay open later on weekend evenings on purpose for
the music." We walked toward the lagoon as he talked, halting opposite
a silvery trickle on the bluff opposite. "This waterfall is very pretty in the
right season when the water birds and all the spring flowers are out," he
said. "And I plan to have a few lights in the trees." He turned away.
"Here's the birdhouse, not really a new place—we adapted an old building. Outside there were these cages, and we just used them the way they
were; they're all right. Do you see that green jay? It's a hybrid, the offspring of a jay from Mexico and one of the plain blue ones. Over here we
have tanagers. There's a hyacinthine macaw that laid an egg last year,
which has never before happened in captivity. But come on in; we have
something special here."

We stood in a darkened room, facing a well-lit display of tropical
plants, birds, and water creatures living in what looked very much like a
section of South American swamp. A large log lay half submerged in
the middle of it. No glass separated us from all that tropical life, and
when Lawrence found the right switch and flipped it, there was a vigorous
rainstorm in the middle of the alcove, complete with lightning. "The
Rain Forest," said Lawrence. "This is the first rain forest any zoo has
ever exhibited, though other places are imitating us now. Look closer
and you'll see that we have three kinds of forest here. We used to keep
a sloth—he lived here for three years—but he died. We always have
turtles and amphibians, though, and soon I plan to put in some marine
animals. I'd like to use our manatee—we have a manatee. But I'm
still experimenting; I'd like to develop a proper habitat theme instead
of only a bird exhibit like this. This is just a pilot scheme so far, but
even as it is, as I've said, other people have picked up the idea, and
you'll see rain forests at San Diego, Birmingham, Houston, and Detroit.
Dallas is building one. It's become a fad. And it works; those birds
have nested in the plant roots and we've bred quite a few of them
right here. You know, it's fascinating to see what happens with birds
when they're put back in even an approximation of the right habitat.

Some birds that have been caged all their lives and have never nested before suddenly begin building when they're put in here. They behave like birds in nature. Take that cock of the rock, he's become very territorial. I could watch him all day. Here, let's throw some meal worms in . . . There, that was outside his area and the starling chased him off, did you see?"

I walked around the room reading signs. WHAT KEEPS THE BIRDS IN? was one, followed by an explanation from which I gathered that Mr. Curtis holds by the light-security theory. Another sign above a bench announced that the bench was for sitting and relaxing, and that during the time the reader spent there he would be able to forget such things as hydrogen bombs, high taxes and Cuba, while he looked at the rain forest. WHY NOT GIVE IT A TRY? it ended seductively.

As we left the house, Lawrence said, "We did all this remodeling on very little money; plywood painted black, air-conditioning, electronic music . . . Here are more jays. We have a good collection of jays; over there's an unusual one from Brazil, one of the largest sorts. Here's a motmot. You know anything about the motmot? It pulls out its own tailfeathers to build its nest: during the nesting season a motmot's tail gets awfully ragged. That's a fact. They nest in claybanks, in burrows, and they can sit absolutely motionless. These pygmy falconets are the smallest raptors in the world. They always huddle like that—at night they sleep with their heads together and their tails sticking up. We have one of the best collection of raptorial birds in the country—twenty-five species. Most of those owls were bred right here. Our snowy owl's been here four years and that's a record. Those are road runners, of course—we raised four here, taking the eggs away from the nest and incubating them electrically. Do you notice anything out of the ordinary in the scarlet ibis? The color—our ibis never fade, neither do the flamingos, the way they usually do in captivity in North America. The birdhouse cost us only thirty thousand altogether. Here's an old building we're going to tear down, but for the moment it's used to keep new arrivals in." He undid a large padlock, and ushered me into a round house where in the dusk several big birds of strange aspect sat on high perches and blinked. Their beaks were enormous, spreading back under their ear feathers like beards.

"Boatbill herons," said Lawrence lovingly. "Beautiful, aren't they?"

I liked the two underwater displays, each a small tank enclosed by a glass box. In one a pair of American otters were swimming, and in the other two snakebirds, or anhingas, walked about on shore or dived when they felt like it. They could all be seen as they swam, down to the bottom of their tanks, from three sides of the boxes. It was a simple and striking display.

In a large cage on the hillside was a harpy eagle, which Lawrence called the most spectacular of all eagles: "They live in Mexico and Argentina. Look at those talons. It's such a fierce and ravenous monster that the natives call it Lobo Volante, the flying wolf. Once this one attacked a keeper. It's been here since '56. I want you to see it right: I wonder if we can manage to make it fly." By feigning to enter the cage door, he persuaded the bird to open its great wings and fly threateningly toward him. Then it settled down again and folded the pinions, half closing its eyes.

"Now we'll go to the herpetarium," said Lawrence. "I'm just showing you the more interesting things, but as you can see we also have the usual animals, and they're doing all right too. A pair of our giraffes has supplied babies to plenty of other zoos . . . This is one of the newer buildings, and I coined the word for it—'herpetarium'—that everybody uses now."

I admired a long bas-relief sculptured creature that sprawled in color over the front length of the building. "It looks like one of those lizards that Australian aborigines draw," I said. "Is that what it's supposed to be?"

"No, it's an abstract of a plesiosaur—plesiosaur fossils are frequently found in this area, so I thought it would be fitting. The plates are ceramic and copper, made by a local person who's interested in that kind of art. We keep the display of American alligators over there outdoors, by the way, in all weathers, and they flourish. Sometimes in a severe winter we've even had ice in the pool, but they didn't seem to suffer a bit, I suppose because the water isn't very deep." He paused as we entered, and pointed to an empty case.

"We usually have a big animal right here, a boa—the largest one in the collection, behind slanting glass. Slanting glass because it doesn't reflect the light right back in a visitor's eyes, and he can see the boa just the same as if there was nothing between them. But the other morning we found that glass cracked right across, and we've had to remove the snake until we get another one put in. I don't know how it could have happened. Inside here, I've tried to keep things mixed up. I don't think zoos ought to be arranged the way they so often are, like old-fashioned museums with one specimen after another in the same kind of glass-fronted box, all in straight rows." There was nothing like an old-fashioned museum in this collection. Some of the reptiles were displayed in immense cages, others in tiny spaces the size of cigar boxes. Some were labeled with signs through which the light shone.

"You don't need money so much," went on Lawrence. "You just want to think it out, which kind of space fits your reptile, and where it's most likely to attract the eye. As I said, this is a poor boy's zoo. Detroit spent $800,000 on their herpetarium and Dallas is spending almost $400,000. This only cost $150,000, but I'd back it against those others. We *are* getting to a point where we'll need more money, but on the way we've learned a lot. For one thing, we have a little lab with this building and one with all the others too. That way if anything goes wrong with an animal it can be examined right on the spot, not carried across the zoo to the hospital. Now, this display attracts a lot of notice for some reason." Black glass was inset in the wall, surrounding a brilliant little opening of clear glass, with a sign over it, A Gold Python? Smaller text explained why the snake should have this name. "I call it stamp collecting, the way zoo directors scramble for rarities," said Lawrence. "Here we've got things sorted out geographically, and while you're looking around you can soak up some idea of how these animals are distributed over the world. The problem is to correlate. Take that Indian snake goddess over there, we'll put her somewhere in a little box, perhaps in the king cobra's place, and in the explanatory text we'll mention Crete, where they also had a snake goddess. There ought to be something about snake charming, too, in this room. You see, the interpretation of material in a zoo has only been touched on so far. There's a lot one can do. First, for instance, we ought to teach people just what a reptile *is*. Then we can explain how reptiles live and meet their day-to-day problems of existence, what we call housekeeping, and so on."

After the herpetarium we looked at some of the rarer animals the zoo can boast. Next door to a pair of aardvarks was a huge creature, the remaining one of a pair of giant armadillos that was one of the prides of the zoo. The director said, "These animals are on the endangered list, you know, so it was a blow when we lost the male. Reminds you of a glyptodon, doesn't it? She weighs a hundred pounds, that animal. Giant armadillos live in the Amazonian forest and feed on carrion. Probably they rob graves." In the half-dark he watched the great bulk silently for a moment, dreaming, then said longingly, "Wouldn't it be wonderful if she turned out to be pregnant?"

In the aquarium, on our way to look at the Amazon dolphins, I paused for a while, fascinated by the jewel-box displays of little fish that were ranged up and down a wall. The secretary joined me. "See that one there, the polka-dotted catfish?" she said. Following with my eyes her pointing finger, I soon found it, swimming alone in its little tank. It was a catfish all right—even I, who know nothing of fish, recognized the characteristic projections around the lips, and the shape of the head, though it was smaller than any catfish I had ever seen. It couldn't have been much more than an inch and a quarter long, but it was a puffy little thing. The secretary said, "That fish barks."

I thought she was joking. She said, "Look," and waved her hand close to the glass, and the tiny fish swam furiously at it, mouth wide in threat. Sure enough, a little noise came through the glass—"Yap! Yap!" If you can imagine a doll's-house-sized Peke yapping, that was what it sounded like. The girl and I exchanged glances, hers triumphant, mine amazed, then I, too, angered the fish by making faces at it close to the tank. At this it barked so loudly that the secretary could hear it a good three yards off.

When I had returned to New York, still full of the wonder of it all, I reported on the barking fish to Christopher Coates, who used to direct the New York Aquarium, and he squashed me.

"Lots of catfish bark," he said scornfully.

CHAPTER 24

San Diego

□

As holiday-makers and the United States Navy know, there is a kind of euphoria about San Diego, due to sun, sea, and, on occasion, the fact that one has just got out of Los Angeles. On the morning I was going to visit the San Diego Zoo, I rode back and forth twice, out of sheer high spirits, across the street my hotel was on, by means of what they call a travelator—a horizontal electric moving sidewalk at second-story level. I had reason to feel so well. The air was pellucid and the colors of the town were clear and bright, while the harbor at the bottom of the road glittered, a freshly painted blue. It was preposterous to think that all this was happening in February.

"Exactly," said a staff member of the Bronx Zoo, when, some weeks later in his office, I described the experience. He sighed ruefully. "That's what beats us here in New York, that San Diego climate with weather hardly changing at all the year round. Here, the zoo season averages about three or four months out of twelve. We can't begin to compete with that."

Yet I can remember when San Diego's zoo wasn't much to boast about. It must have been early in the thirties when I was there first, idling away an hour or two on the way to Tia Juana. I have an impression of sandy surroundings, stunted brush, and cages set down here and there like blocks left by a tired child. Two large orangutans, the first I'd ever seen close up, sat together on their cage's cement floor and looked at the infrequent visitors in the supercilious manner of their kind. The only vivid memory I have of the experience is of our brief encounter when I tossed them a peanut. Observe that I didn't throw it—I *tossed* it. I meant well, but one of the orangs evidently misinterpreted my action and resented it. Untangling himself from his companion's arms, he picked up the peanut and threw it back at me, hard. I reflected as I rode in a taxi to the zoo after my travelator trip that the incident must really have hurt my feelings to have stayed in my mind all those years. Yet the ape, in all likelihood, had never given it another thought.

Though I'd been warned that the place has changed considerably since then, no word of mouth could quite prepare me, and my eyes grew bigger and bigger as we passed along an imposing approach, past myriads of parked cars, to the entrance gate of today's San Diego Zoo. I didn't recollect anything of this palatial estate, not even the wooded surroundings of Balboa Park. One reason for my mystification, I later understood, was that there's such a lot of green stuff growing there now. The director, Dr. Schroeder, told me that the zoo's botanical collection, valued at two million dollars and worth more than all the animals put together, does not contain one indigenous species—a fact that comes in handy at times when some exotic animal needs a special herbivorous addition to his diet.

I referred to the guidebook: "The San Diego Zoological Garden is unique among most United States zoos in that it exhibits nearly all animals outdoors the year round. In this city of more than half-a-million people the weather is tempered by the Pacific Ocean, with the result that summers are cooler and winters warmer than the latitude would indicate. Rainfall averages only 10 inches a year, wind velocities are low, and 330 out of 365 days have sunshine! High mesas, cut by deep canyons, give good air drainage. Because of our healthful climate, and our friendly exchange relations with other zoos, the San Diego Zoo contains one of the largest and rarest collections in the world. It exceeds most others in the number of animals and species exhibited. Within the Zoo and Balboa Park we harvest the leaves from many exotic plants relished by our animals."

Much of the zoo's land, a hundred and twenty-eight acres, is mesa country divided by three steep canyons, and it's a good idea to take the bus ride for a preliminary reconnaissance. After that's been done, you know what you want to do and where to find the rain forest or the lions and tigers or whatever you may fancy. The bus driver acts as guide, philosopher, and keeper as well as chauffeur, piloting his large vehicle along pathways thronged with pedestrians, turning sharp corners, all the while keeping up through a loudspeaker a running patter of information and comment. More: as the bus rolls along the high road by the bears' grottoes, he must encourage certain of these animals to dance, and sling pieces of bread to them in reward when they have done their act. Since that first day I have taken more bus rides in San Diego Zoo than I can count, and I've never yet seen a driver throw bread that falls short or otherwise misses its rightful recipient.

"But Dr. Schroeder doesn't really care for animal acts," explained Fred Childress, the director of the public relations department, when I called on him at the administration building. "The zoo used to have chimp shows, but he put a stop to that as soon as he arrived to take over. We haven't anything else in that line except the seal shows five times a day. They're California sea lions really, of course, from this coastline. The bears that dance picked up their acts before they came here, so we just play along with them. There's not much you can do with a bear determined to beg."

The man responsible for the zoo's beginning was Dr. Harry Wegeforth, whose bronze bust decorates one of the office-building halls. Wegeforth, a physician and a San Diego citizen, in 1916 was offended by the presence in his town of several small, unsavory zoos, detritus of the recently closed Panama-California Exposition, which had been there for two years. Many of the fair's exhibitors had gone broke, struck their tents and faded away, and some in so doing had left animals behind to eke out a hungry existence in the places Dr. Harry and other citizens found shameful. The doctor appealed to the municipal authorities to grant land where a respectable zoo could be established and the orphan animals taken care of properly, but the authorities were reluctant to give away any of their choice territory. When popular opinion appeared to force some action, they granted Dr. Wegeforth a patch of difficult terrain, all mesas and canyons, at the edge of Balboa Park. Wegeforth accepted it gladly, and moved in the animals. By this time he had become infected with a passion for the idea of a San Diego Zoo, and thereafter he spent a vigorous life fighting for funds to support his cause. An indefatigable money-raiser, he has inspired a large number of legends.

"Do you know how Harry used to work?" Robert Bean said to a group of reminiscing old-timers, during a conference in San Diego. Knowing that Bean had worked there himself in earlier days, they listened respectfully. "Some rancher gave him a mountain lion, so he put it into an orange crate. Then he went to the city and said, 'I've got a lion up there on the mesa and there's only an orange crate to keep it in. I can't be responsible for what might happen if it breaks out.' Of course everybody got agitated, and they whipped around and raised the money to build a lion cage. Built a fine one, too. Then Harry went to them again and said, 'I've got a fine lion cage, and nothing to keep in it but one measly mountain lion. It looks awful. We'll have to get more animals.' He got away with things like that, Harry did."

Dr. Wegeforth "had single-minded persistence and the fascinating ability to talk anybody out of, or into, anything," says the writer. In twenty-five years he raised over a million dollars in donations, and an uncountable amount of material and service. He would gather animals from ranchers who had kept them as pets and tired of them; he would get other animals from sailors. One story tells how he was presented with his first Kodiak bear by a Navy seaman who had been outgrown by his mascot. The zoo had no truck in which it could be transported, but Dr. Harry pre-empted a board member of the zoo, put the bear into the member's car, and waved it off to Balboa Park. Occasionally the zoo inherited trained animals from Hollywood studios—they got a chimp named Snooky that way, and Jiggs, an orangutan, who for all I know is the same ape that spurned my peanut. Wegeforth built up a thriving swap business with animals born in the zoo: the beneficent effect of the climate soon made itself felt, especially of course with the lions. He also had a good source of supply for swaps in the wild California fauna such as rattlesnakes and sea lions, for these animals were often caught by San Diegans who sold them to Dr. Wegeforth at a fixed price, and he was then able to sell them again at a profit. The writer comments, "In its early years, San Diego Zoo practically was built upon seals and rattlesnakes." When the doctor wasn't making ends meet, he collated records of the animals' health and diet, which interested him very much.

By 1922 the zoo had outgrown its quarters, and the municipality, now convinced of its value as a tourist attraction, willingly arranged to give the Zoological Society the superior tract of park land on which it now stands. Four years later Miss Ellen Browning Scripps, a rich local resident, contributed the funds for Dr. Wegeforth's pet project, a hospital in the zoo. Mrs. Belle Benchley, a former schoolteacher, came to work in the zoo in 1923, as a bookkeeper. She took so readily to the somewhat special sort of jobs Wegeforth kept giving her that the Society promoted her to the post of "executive secretary." In time she became undisputed ruler of the zoo. Readers of animal books will recall her account of the coup that brought her name, and San Diego's, into prominence all over the country when she acquired two baby gorillas for the collection, from the Martin Johnsons. Gorillas were still a great rarity in captivity, and as soon as Mrs. Benchley heard from Charles Schroeder, then in New York, that two were being placed on the market, she leaped into action. Having found a donor willing to pay the huge sum required for such a purpose, she outbid several far more hoary organizations and earned herself some sleepless nights while she wondered if her audacity was justified. Most people believed that the animals could not possibly survive, or that if they did it would be impossible to control them, for they were thought to be very savage beasts with dangerous sexual cravings for human beings. Mrs. Benchley's pair disproved these myths. She was fascinated by them, became their good friend, studied them intelligently, kept them alive a considerable time, and went a long way generally to make life better for captive gorillas everywhere. It was probably her most spectacular success, but in many other respects, too, the zoo made great progress under her management. She retired in 1953, but now and then she appears at zoo functions, always greeted with affectionate applause by old colleagues.

"This chart might interest you," said Mr. Childress. He had set up a large cardboard square with a diagram on it in colors, and I studied it with mounting respect as I understood what it represented, a breakdown of the zoo's income for the year ending July first, 1964: 36.39 percent from admission fees; 40.16 from "public service," i.e. restaurants, souvenirs and all that; 10.49 from bus rides. "Not quite 5½ percent from City and County," I said. "Isn't that unusual? Aren't zoos always asking for more money from the municipality?"

He smiled rather grimly. "That's usually so, but up until 1952 this zoo wasn't getting any regular subsidy at all, and that was the reason for a constant quarrel between the city government and Dr. Wegeforth. In 1932, just about the worst year ever for San Diego Zoo, the county people slapped an assessment demand on us for something under seven thousand dollars which the zoo didn't have. The animals were very nearly auctioned off to pay it, but just in time the townspeople rallied round and stopped the auction. Then Dr. Harry got up a petition and a new arrangement was forced through. The zoo now gets two cents from every hundred dollars collected by the city in property taxes, and quite right too. Take away the zoo and the navy from San Diego and what have you got?"

However limited their specimen list, most zoos have one or two species of which they are particularly proud, for breeding record or longevity or rarity, or, perhaps, general good health. In San Diego, however, so many claims of this sort can be made that to pick out the outstanding department would be impossible. The specialist goes straight to whatever interests him, but the layman is faced with making a choice. I met some of the outstanding men, curators all—Kenton C. Lint (birds), Dr. George

Pournelle (mammals), and Charles E. Shaw (reptiles): Shaw is also assistant director.

"We go in for mixed exhibits here," said Dr. Pournelle. "Animals from the same country, if they get along all right, are put together. As for rarities, it depends on what you consider rare. We're steamed up just now over the fact that we're getting a female for the Indian rhino, but the public probably pays more attention to the Koala Sanctuary than to the rhino anyway. Before Hallstrom sent us the koalas, nobody'd seen any on this side of the world for a long time. It seems to be a question of letting koalas be perfectly quiet after they've arrived, until they settle in. They've had young ones now, but they won't breed up in San Francisco where the Fleischacker Zoo got a similar shipment from Sir Edward—that is, they bred, but they were losing the young, so they asked us if we'd put up their koalas and of course we said we would. They're here now in the sanc-tuary with the others, and if they start reproducing properly, and we all think it's safe, they can go back then to San Francisco. Koalas eat eucalyptus mainly, though they do vary the diet a little sometimes. We have twenty-seven varieties of eucalyptus growing right here, so it's no problem; out of that twenty-seven they've chosen four or five that they eat. This is the sort of work I like—conserving. I realize that zoos can't preserve on a large scale, but they can carry on with a few of the rarest species, and everything helps. I didn't start out as a zoologist, as a matter of fact. I trained as a pre-medic, then went into biology, and so to this work by way of a study I'd made of the local rodents of Florida. During the war I first came and worked here: after the war I came back. It seems to me that one can make a general statement that many animals continually on exhibit show stress, one of the signs of which is a failure to breed. Why this happens is hard to tell. Some might simply be too much interested in the visitors. Others are probably incompatible with their companions. A lot of possibilities enter into it in conservation; as a result we've taken certain measures to forestall some of the difficulties. With the primates, for example, we've changed the routine a little. Formerly they were in and out of their shelters all day, whenever they felt like it, but now we don't keep them on exhibit the whole time; they have rest periods. In the past, failure to reproduce may have been due in large part to dietary deficiencies, but nowadays when it's necessary we can formulate an artificial diet for everything. I think the chief trouble is psychological. And though we have no births yet among the gorillas, there are other factors to account for that. For one thing we've never had many gorillas—you have the percent-age factor there—and for another, we haven't had them long.

"Territory, too, plays an important part in an animal's reactions. I've done some comparisons of animal reactions to territory situations in the wild, and cage behavior. Some people are making observations of the bison in the Oklahoma preserve right now, from the same viewpoint, and there've been some publications on wolves and territory. If you're interested, read Adolph Murie on *The Wolves of Mount McKinley*. It's fascinating."

San Diego's collection, though representative of a large number of different species, is nevertheless incomplete, and some of the gaps in the list are due to quarantine regulations. It was because of these that Dr. Pournelle has had to give up a cherished plan. "Those people are death on certain exotic animals and insects," he said. "I had a vision of a leaf-cutting ant display. It would have been wonderful to show them at work on something, maybe a bouquet of roses. You'd see them filing up, cutting their pieces out of the plants, and parading away carrying the bits of leaf like parasols, the way they do. It would have been very popular, I'm sure of that, but we couldn't get permits to import the ants—it's absolutely forbidden. I settled for a rodentarium." He sighed.

Mr. Lint's birds are fed from a kitchen so elaborately outfitted that it was the first thing he took me to visit. "A continuous process, you see," he commented as we got out of the way of bustling people. "It's got to be continuous, since we have to prepare dozens of different foods—fruit and vegetables and fish, not to mention eucalyptus that we get right here, which is good for parrots. We have the best breeding record in the world for parrots—seventy-five species have been raised here, and three hundred general bird species. One big red-tailed cockatoo raised her thirteenth baby last year; another cockatoo has never missed since 1929, and has a hundred children to her credit. Here, you see, we keep the protein—rats, insects, mice, everything like that."

Approaching another room, he said that they had inoculated eighty-one species during the past year. "Here we're doing some of the zoo's incubation, which is a science in itself. I've been at it thirty years," he continued. "Those are ostrich eggs in there. Here's a condor egg. Then there are the brooders for the second stage. Our birds, because they come from so many parts of the world, don't always settle down to the new round of seasons, and we have hatching the year round, though some do acclimatize. Here's the third stage, with heat lamps. There are Egyptian geese in this one. There's a front yard for each brooder, for sunlight. Five or six hundred birds go through these every year." On the visitors' side of the bird cages we found a square with thirty-five cages given over to parrots alone. "Here's an ocellated turkey from Yucatan. See the peacock effect? It's a bird that's getting very rare, but we've raised a hundred and thirty-eight here. Peacock pheasant . . . that iridescent bird? Lovely, isn't it—it's a Himalayan monal. This Swinhoe pheasant was born in Formosa, where they're now extinct, but we raised twenty-seven last year, and there are enough in the hands of breeders to repopulate Formosa if the people there want them. Satyr tragopan—Himalayan pheasant . . . Some pheasants eat corn, some have to have insects, or fruit, or seed—it all takes time and study. Here's a Great Argus pheasant. This semi-palmated goose, or magpie goose as it's also called, comes from southern New Guinea and is nearly extinct. It perches in trees, and is the most primitive of all the waterfowl. Takes an almost entirely protein diet, but you've got to give it pepsin as well to break down the enzymes; very interesting. Look at this Laysan Island duck. Ten years ago there were only twenty-five of these in the wild. Now there are about seven hundred."

I had an appointment late in the morning with Dr. Schroeder, the director, a stocky dynamo of a man who never seems to get tired or lose his energy. Immediately he set to work filling gaps in the knowledge I had so sketchily acquired. As to the zoo's earned income, he said, during the past year they had spent one and a half million dollars of it on capital improvements, which should certainly prove worth it. Over the weekend of Washington's Birthday, a clear three days, fifty-one thousand people visited the zoo—"a bigger gate, it seems to me, than baseball games would have earned," he said. "We're considering a new venture, a back-country zoo, a sort of natural-habitat place. It will be a part of this zoo, but it'll be thirty miles away. We would keep herds of plains animals there. The Stanford Research Institute is doing an economic study of the possibilities, and whether or not we go ahead will depend on the trustees' decision after they've seen the Stanford report. An alternative would be a game preserve, without people participating; that would be costly, how-ever; an animal farm might be better, *with* people. We might even have an all-out operation, a series of natural habitats with elephants, rhinos, giraffes, birds, a little railway, with regular roads and safari-type travel. The land is the San Pasqual area, two square miles around a battle monument. It rises to a stone bluff with fourteen hundred feet elevation —the road in front is sixteen hundred feet up; a beautiful piece of country with three valleys. It's facing southwest and always has wind from the sea, so it never gets too hot.

"The Stanford people have already finished their report on our attend-ance; it's been climbing steadily, five to seven percent annually, and they say they can see the same rise continuing until 1975 at least. We're always needing more restaurant and parking space, and the budget, too, goes shooting up—our greatest expense is in servicing people. The budget worries the daylight out of the comptroller, but attendance will be nearly three million this year and we'll have to earn it. We're going to have a new education center, thanks to a big donation of half a million—it's to be called an Indoctrination Center, with closed-circuit TV for schools. We could show things like the birth of a camel . . . Of course our education program's pretty well developed right now. We have three or four full-time teachers for the schoolchildren who come; the zoo has its own school bus that visits every school in town during the year, and carries two loads of kids back and forth to the zoo every day, so every second-grade child gets his visit. The conductor isn't trained for it, but does his spiel very well. As for the county schools, it's the same arrangement except that the second-graders are brought in by county bus. The zoo pays the expenses of all this. A teacher will lecture to the third, fourth, fifth, and sixth graders at school, taking animals and slides along. Another teacher takes care of kindergarten kids and special parties of handicapped children in the pavilion at the children's zoo. We have people from the Brereton training school taking lessons in 'zoo science'; it's a preparation for their biology course."

A zoo car was waiting outside the office, and Dr. Schroeder drove it around, not making the grand tour, but showing me several high spots, the hummingbird house for instance. This was extremely beautiful, probably the most successful display of hummingbirds and other small birds that I have ever seen anywhere—a glassed-in chamber full of growing plants and trees and hanging jars of nectar, and birds. Like tiny jewels they flash back and forth, completely at ease with the visitors. One, taking his time as he hovered in the air, pulled a hair from my head, and another perched on my shoulder and pecked at a nubble in the cloth of my dress. Dr. Schroeder smiled calmly at my delight. "Everybody goes crazy about this place," he admitted. "The Foodmaker Company paid for it, and the Perry Turnstile Company at Goshen is going to arrange an improvement of the revolving-door entrance, so we won't have to keep beaded curtains there. It's pretty now, but you ought to see it when the fuchsia blooms."

From birds to lizards is not a far journey, and as we resumed the tour Dr. Schroeder told me of interesting developments among the zoo's Galapagos tortoises, those enormous creatures so often photographed giving rides to children on their backs. "Shaw's discovered that the biggest tortoise isn't necessarily the oldest, at least not when the ones you're comparing live in the temperate zone. It seems to be purely a matter of heat whether they grow fast or not. If they're kept in warmer quarters than temperate, they grow much faster. Now ours are beginning to lay, too, and Chuck has hopes that some of the eggs will hatch."

Zoo Hospital plays host all year round to visiting scientists, many of whom take time off from their ordinary duties at universities or laboratories to conduct research on various exotic animals they could not otherwise procure. One man when I was there was engaged on a study of the contents of seal's milk, and another was doing something obscure about hoofed-animal diseases, but it was the work of a technician that impressed me most vividly, for he had learned to make molds of blood vessels and muscular systems in blue, red, or green material that was all but unbreakable. They looked like the slenderest sorts of plant or coral, delicate beyond description. Back of this building a path led to the San Diego Primate Center, where the government subsidizes research into the breeding of small primates for experimental purposes, to take the place of the Indian rhesus.

"We're waiting for the summer months with considerable interest this year," remarked Dr. Schroeder on the way to the entrance gates. "Did Dr. Pournelle say anything about the female gorilla we're watching?" No, I said. "Perhaps he didn't want to test our luck," said Dr. Schroeder, "but the fact is, we have good reason to believe that she's pregnant. When we first suspected it, we sent a sample of her urine to the Navy Hospital for the usual tests, Ascham-Zondek and hormone, and the report was positive. We were just about to break into a dance when somebody said, 'Now, wait a minute. We don't really know much about gorilla urine. It might not react like a human's. Better have some controls.' So that's what we did—sent samples from our other two female gorillas to the hospital, and the reports on both were negative. Now we're pretty sure."

When I visited San Diego the next spring, the baby had been born and was flourishing in the nursery, and as I write this, the mother is thought to be expecting again.

CHAPTER 25

Dolphins Are Kind

□

The little office was very hot, making more noticeable a strongly fishy smell that pervaded the building. Nobody seemed to mind. Two men in white coats worked with a microscope at a table that filled half the space, one peering into the eyepiece and dictating to the other, who wrote it all down. A small stove, glowing with heat, served as hitching post for a capuchin monkey that bobbed up and down on its rope, chattering as if trying to attract attention. It got none, even from the shaggy little dog that pranced around barking and barking as I opened the door. A third man, in rubber hip boots, shouted at the dog with no effect, then greeted me. The men at the table glanced up and went back to their work. They looked like adolescents, and from his appearance the man in boots could have been a schoolboy, but this was Enoshima, in Japan, so I wasn't startled to learn that he was Masayuki Nakajima, curator of "Marineland," and—presumably—quite grown up. It was the Marineland basement we were in, next door to the aquarium. Japanese are very big on sea life.

Mr. Nakajima offered me the only spare chair in the place, and I sat down while he read the letter of introduction I had brought from Tokyo. My seat was almost on top of the stove. I mopped my face. Softly the monkey wrapped itself around my leg, its hands feather-light, its imploring face turned up to me. "From England and America," read Mr. Nakajima aloud. He put the letter down and smiled. "Good. I have been to America, you know, several times, and I have seen Marineland in California. Do you know it? Very fine. Everybody thought I was a very young man. Do you think I look so young?"

"Nineteen at most," I replied. He was delighted.

"I am thirty-three. Americans are always surprised. And England—I should like one day to go to England. Well, I think you want to see our dolphin show? It starts in a few minutes: we will have time to look around." He pulled the monkey off me and led the way out.

A cold, briny wind whistled down the wet steps I had just descended, reminding me of the winter weather outside. Instead of going up these steps Mr. Nakajima turned the other way along a descending ramp, to a door which he unlocked. We stepped through, into freezing atmosphere. The floor was covered with hunks of something white and slippery, with occasional streaks of blood. Evidently we were in some kind of giant refrigerating plant. I stubbed my toe on a frozen hummock. "Careful," said my guide. "You really need boots here. Most of this is pieces of a whale I am doing an autopsy on. I took a trip to the Antarctic on a whaler and brought back much material. Look, there is the head, cut through for a cross section, and here I have bottled the ovaries."

"Yes, I see." My teeth chattered, but Mr. Nakajima, clad only in the sweater and trousers he had worn in the warm office, was quite at ease. He clambered as easily over and between the lumps of whaleflesh as if he were mountaineering, but I slid rather than walked to the door opposite. As he opened it we were nearly swamped in a flood of water. I thought at first we had come out into the sea, but we were still indoors: the water had cascaded down a concrete slope ahead of a cleaning man in dungarees, who now sloshed more water out of a bucket and brushed it toward us. Mr. Nakajima ignored the water, so I did too. With soaking shoes and stockings I continued in his track, coming out on a wide, oval-shaped balcony that was roofed over. It surrounded the largest swimming pool, or tank, that I had ever seen. The water lay open to the sky, which on that day was pale gray, a color reflected in the ripples in darker and lighter shades. The balcony was railed, and a few family groups stood against the railing, peering down. Music played over a loudspeaker.

Mr. Nakajima led me into a small enclosure like a theatre box that jutted out from the side, over the water. Here, he explained, I would have an excellent view. It was near a similar protuberance that was built to look like the bow of a ship. Back of me somebody blew a piercing whistle and the water became agitated as a number of glistening gray bodies leaped part way out of it, looped like segments of a sea serpent, then splashed back out of sight. This was the first time I had ever seen trained dolphins, and I couldn't have happened on a more spectacular show, because of the great number of animals involved. I've visited many other dolphin exhibitions since then, but it was the largest I was ever to see. The tank was forty-five meters long, Mr. Nakajima told me, twenty-five meters wide, and seven deep.

A man stepped out to the end of the boat's prow and pulled a rope, setting the ship's bell overhead to clanging. Promptly, below him there appeared a half-circle of dolphin heads staring up at him, like the fish heads in a stargazie pudding. The trainer blew his whistle. One dolphin began to swim in a circle faster and faster, as if gathering steam, until he leaped up and took a fish from the man's hand. The show was on. The trainer climbed a ladder to a higher position: dolphins leaped accordingly higher, ten feet, fifteen feet and more. They jumped through hoops. They stood on their tails almost out of the water and "walked" upright, backward, to catch fish that he threw. They played basketball, bunting the ball with their heads into a basket rigged beneath the trainer's outpost. They rose from invisible depths unerringly to bright-colored hats he threw on the water's surface, and wore these hats while they swam around the pool. They caught rubber rings and threw them back. A small boat was pushed out from the side: my friend the barking dog from the basement office stood in it, stiff-legged and silent at last as two dolphins, working in unison, steered the vessel across the tank.

Mr. Nakajima had disappeared during the early part of the performance. Now he came back with an attendant who carried a pail of fish. I greeted him enthusiastically: "This is great. They're so big, I never realized. How many are there, anyway?"

"You like it?" he asked. The attendant was fixing a fish in a pair of wooden tongs, which he handed to me. "I don't know exactly how many there are just now," continued Mr. Nakajima, "but it's something between seventy and seventy-five. In 1957 when Marineland opened we had ninety-nine, but we lose some now and then. Wouldn't you like to feed one? Hold it out, like this." He stretched out his arm, holding the fish in the tongs over the water. Immediately a huge animal rose in the air in front of us. It seemed to hover at the top of its leap, as Nijinsky is said to have done, while with its beaklike mouth it picked the fish from the tongs, then it dropped back with a huge splash. Another fish was got ready—they were frozen stiff, I discovered—and I held it out as Mr. Nakajima had done. The dolphin that leaped for it was so close to me that I looked into its eye, a pleasant eye unexpectedly low on the side of the head, barely higher than the mouth. Splash. I was left with the impression people always get of these dolphins, that it had been smiling. It is a built-in smile that means no more than a crocodile's, but you can't help responding to it.

"That's fun," I said.

"Then here's another fish," said Mr. Nakajima.

When we had emptied the pail he showed me around the tank. One end of it was walled off, if that is the word—actually the material was a net—for a group of dolphins that were ailing, he explained. Some, in an inner enclosure, were pregnant and close to their time. He said, "Our greatest loss is from pneumonia. In the winter we have to heat the water: wild dolphins go south as soon as the sea gets cold around here. The ones you see are *Tursiops*: I think you call them bottle-nosed dolphins; you have a lot of a slightly different kind, *Tursiops truncatus*, in the Atlantic. These are the Pacific sort, very much the same but a bit larger. There are many kinds of dolphin, you know. We have another sort right here—Risso's dolphin. Come and see." We went to the other end of the pool, which I now perceived to be netted off in much the same way as the hospital. Beyond the line frolicked a number of beasts of different appearance—a dark, blue-gray where the *Tursiops* were paler, with rounded profiles and no beak. In mannerisms, however, they seemed similar. I asked if they did the same things.

"Oh yes, you can train them the same way," said Mr. Nakajima. "They perform just like *Tursiops*. The way we arrange it, they take turns, and in a minute they'll do their show."

Again I heard the whistle, and the trainer appeared, but this time he was not alone. Running at the side were two animals I had not expected to see in any Marineland—young chimpanzees. I looked inquiringly at Mr. Nakajima, and he smiled with pride. "They are twins," he explained. "Twin babies. A friend gave them to us because their mother didn't take care of them. We call them Summer and Winter. Watching the show so often, they got interested and learned how to do it. Just see." By this time the chimps were all over the false prow. One rang the bell, and when the dolphins stuck up their heads as usual the other dropped fish to them, carefully going all around the ring, missing none but playing no favorites. Then they were led off, and the show proceeded according to the *Tursiops* pattern. Between whistles and splashes, Mr. Nakajima told me that a particular Risso's dolphin was once the most famous of his kind in all the world, a well-known character of the sea who lived off the coast of New Zealand, meeting and escorting nearly all the ships that crossed between North and South Island. My understanding of what Mr. Nakajima said was that this animal's name was "Perilous Jack," and it pleased me. When, later, I read Antony Alpers' book about dolphins, I was disappointed to find that the dolphin's name was "Pelorus Jack," because the region in which he cavorted was Pelorus Sound.

"And haven't they been known to save drowning people?" I asked. Nakajima nodded. "Dolphins are *kind*," he said.

I thought it over. The boat was crossing again, with two young Risso's dolphins pushing it this time. "That rope, or net, or whatever it is that you use to divide the tank," I said. "It's only at water level. Doesn't a bottlenose ever jump over onto the Risso's side, or vice versa? Don't they fight?"

"They don't jump, but sometimes they slither. They don't stay very long on the wrong side. I've never seen a Risso's fight with a bottlenose, but they do fight within their own communities, especially in the mating season. See those whitish scratches on the Risso's? If a dolphin fights too much we put him back into the sea."

Reluctant to leave the tank, I strolled back to the bottlenose side, asking more questions of Mr. Nakajima. A bottlenose emerged close to the side and made a noise at us, like a Bronx cheer. It also whistled. Mr. Nakajima found a fish somewhere nearby and directed me to pat the animal's head before he fed it. The dolphin remained quiet as I did so. The skin felt slippery and movable. Just at the top of the head was the blowhole, crescent-shaped when he closed it.

"He breathes through that hole," said Mr. Nakajima, handing over the fish. "He talks through it, too. His mouth is used only for eating."

"Just like a whale," I said. Mr. Nakajima replied,

"Of course. A dolphin *is* a whale—a little whale."

Nothing else that I saw that day at Enoshima made such an impression, though it was altogether a fascinating visit. I went up to see Summer and Winter again, in their cages. When I gave food to one, the other would slap me. Marineland also featured a display of marine animals in a row of outdoor pools all along the sea—walruses, seals of many sorts, sea lions, sea elephants, otters, penguins. The aquarium was beautiful. But, after I left, it was the rising, leaping, glistening bodies of the dolphins that I remembered. Afterward, anywhere I happened to be in the world, I sought out and watched one porpoise show after another—an interest, as I found out, shared with many fellow humans.

For centuries mankind has been familiar with dolphins. Though the last few years have seen a fresh explosion of interest in them, they are not news—not at all. Aesop tells a fable about a dolphin, and one of Aesop's contemporaries, if we can believe the legend, had an important personal experience with one. This was Arion, a famous singer, who was threatened by sailors aboard a ship bound for Corinth. In what he meant to be a swan song he sang his best. Then he leaped overboard, only to be rescued by a dolphin enthralled by his voice, and carried by it safely to land before ever the ship got there. Greeks and Romans loved to portray the animal: ancient coins, pottery and architecture show pictures of dolphins. They look rather like our Atlantic porpoises, *Tursiops truncatus*, but at least one writer on the subject, Winthrop H. Kellogg, thinks that these classic mammals are, rather, the common dolphin of the Mediterranean, *Delphinus delphis*. It doesn't really matter, he says; *Delphinus* etc. behaves very much like *Tursiops*, or the bottle-nosed dolphin. (Incidentally, the name "bottle-nosed dolphin" was bestowed because people saw a resemblance between *Tursiops'* beak and the top of an old-style gin bottle.) Aristotle wrote at some length of dolphins, and knew a lot about them. He was aware that they are mammals, not fish, and that they are closely related to whales. A special passage in his writings appeals to me for reasons that will shortly be evident: "The porpoise. . . . resembles the dolphin, and, by the way, is in form like a little dolphin, and is found in the Black Sea. . . . Many people are of the opinion that the porpoise is a variety of the dolphin. . . ."

Many people indeed. Invariably those who discuss dolphins find themselves in an argument about the distinction between these and porpoises, and I am no exception. The difference boils down, in the end, to a semantic one, but it's a fretful subject nonetheless. I tend to say "dolphin" because in England, where I live, that is what people call them, but—as I am all too well aware—people in America tend with equal stubbornness to say "porpoise" for the same thing. In the standard field book *Giant Fishes, Whales, and Dolphins*, by the British scientists J. R. Norman and F. C. Fraser, twenty-one genera of these—uh—cetaceans are listed, and subdivided into forty-six species. The distinction? As Norman and Fraser so aptly say, it is a question that must have been asked hundreds of times. They continue, "It is unfortunate that it is one which involves the difficulties associated with the use of popular terms," which boils down to the awkward fact that there is also a fish called "dolphin." Now cetaceans—i.e., dolphins and porpoises as well as whales—are not fish, but warm-blooded mammals, like us. They live in the water, but they are mammals, the ancestors of which, like those of seals, sea lions, manatees and so on, re-adapted themselves to a watery life after a period when they were at home on dry land. At first glance, dolphins/porpoises do resemble fish, but they aren't fish. Like us, they must breathe air: if they can't get it, they drown. And they don't really look all that much like fish after all. Apart from less noticeable differences, their tails are set on their bodies in a horizontal plane, whereas fish-tails are always set on in an up-and-down, vertical plane. The dolphin-fish doesn't even look like a cetacean—it's the one that turns different colors as it dies—but the confusion in nomenclature is admittedly an annoying thing, and no matter what I call the animal I can see some virtue in the American use of the word "porpoise." As it is, I often have to interrupt myself when I mention dolphins, to interject the words, "I refer, of course, to *Tursiops truncatus*, not to *Coryphaena*, the fish." It is enough to discourage the most patient listener. However, Americans are wrong, I feel, when they go beyond the use of their chosen term and call *Tursiops* "the *common* porpoise," because there are two other animals with a better claim to that name—the common porpoise of British waters, and another common porpoise that swims around New Zealand. Norman and Fraser don't quite throw in the sponge, however. They summarize: ". . . it may be said . . . that 'porpoise' refers to those members of the family *Delphinidae* that are small in size, are beakless, have a triangular dorsal fin and spade-shaped teeth; and that 'dolphin' embraces the remaining members of the family except the larger forms, as for instance the Killer, dignified by the name of 'whale.'" A likely story. What, then, is the meaning of Risso's dolphin's nomenclature? Risso's is beakless. Moreover, if you're still looking for trouble in nomenclature, he is also, scientifically speaking, *Grampus griseus*, not to be confused with the killer whale, which is also called Grampus. "A point to be borne in mind," say Norman and Fraser about this, "is that the two animals are by no means closely related, and neither in their external appearance nor in their habits do they in the least resemble one another."

If you think all this is confusing, hold on. The United States Department of the Interior has made matters much worse by issuing, in their Fish and Wildlife Series, a leaflet that divides dolphins and porpoises its own way. They have created a whole new family, so now we have two families, the *Delphinidae*, or dolphins—"Snout usually long, beaklike. Teeth large or small, rounded in cross section, pointed. No dermal ossicles (small bony protuberances) in forward edge of dorsal fin (some species lack a dorsal fin),"—and Phocoenidae, or Porpoises: "Snout short, blunt. Teeth small, flattened in cross section, spade shaped. Dermal ossicles usually present in forward portion of dorsal fin (some species lack a dorsal fin)."

These animals, whichever one calls them, eat fish and squid and—probably—nothing else except by accident (some of the grubbing sort do swallow sand and seaweed, inadvertently). They swim fast, though their average rate is another bone of contention: some observers think they go thirty miles an hour, others say forty. They communicate, very likely, by sound as well as other methods. Descended as they are from land mammals, they are most closely, withal still distantly, related to horses, tapirs, and rhinoceroses. The skeleton shows vestigial pelvic bones, also indications of hind leg bones, and digital bones in the flippers. In most species the vertebrae of the neck are fused, and the head's movements are somewhat limited as a result. As the term mammal indicates, the infant animal is nourished by mother's milk, but the process of feeding cannot accurately be called suckling: the baby nuzzles the region of the mother's teats, which are hidden on either side of her anus, until she projects the teat and squirts milk, by a voluntary contraction of the muscles, into the baby's mouth. This is done so quickly that the milk—a rich concentrate, full of protein—is not contaminated by surrounding water. Dolphin young are weaned very slowly, sometimes not until they are eighteen months old or even more. The females produce infants only once—probably—in three years, and the gestation period is twelve months. There is no definite breeding season. Nobody can be sure, as yet, how long dolphins live, but "Pelorus Jack" swam his beat for twenty-three years. In Florida it is claimed that *Tursiops truncatus* can achieve the age of forty.

It is the custom of dolphins to sport around ships, and they are often observed riding the wave that boils up about the bow of a vessel in motion, as if the animals were enjoying a continuous toboggan ride, or, rather, skiing on one of those upward-sliding slopes used by teachers in department-store sport sections. The water keeps moving: the dolphin stays in place. Sometimes, instead of reclining stomach down, he even rolls over sideways and lies like that, evidently quite at ease. This trick was one of Pelorus Jack's: he also used to rub himself against the vessels or simply frolic alongside, appearing to the passengers for as long as twenty minutes at a time. From the day he was first sighted, in 1888, until he vanished in 1911, he was faithful to his self-imposed task, patrolling the beat, and so became the most famous Risso's dolphin—or any dolphin, for that matter—in the world. In 1904 the government of New Zealand issued an Order in Council prohibiting the taking of Risso's dolphins in Cook Strait, just to protect him.

People easily fall in love with dolphins, and, unless we reject most of the stories about them, dolphins like people, too. Antony Alpers has collected these stories, or some of them, in his book *Dolphins, the Myth and the Mammal*. He talks of Arion, and of Koiranos of Miletos, who, pitying a dolphin caught in a fisherman's net, bought it and set it free. Later, shipwrecked off Mykonos, he saw all his companions drown, but a dolphin saved Koiranos and carried him to shore. When in the fullness of time he died, a school of dolphins swam in the harbor and watched the burning of his funeral pyre. And there is the story of the boy Dionysios, who went swimming with other schoolboys every afternoon. One day a dolphin joined the group and played with them, taking a great fancy to Dionysios. Every day these two played in the water, Dionysios often going for rides on his friend's back, until the sad day when the dolphin stranded himself high on the beach—as dolphins still do at times—and died. Something very like this situation actually existed lately—in 1955—at the little seaside town of Opononi, New Zealand. There in the bay a young female *Tursiops* appeared again and again, playing around the holiday launches and fishers' boats. People discovered that she liked being stroked with a mop—dolphins do like to be stroked, as if they feel a perpetual itch—and after a while they began patting her too, by hand. She grew braver, and joined the bathers near the beach, becoming particularly friendly with a thirteen-year-old girl. Every day this girl, Jill Baker, went into the water and was greeted by "Opo," who learned to bounce a beach ball and to give small children short rides. People came from miles around to watch these games, until one sad day Opo was found dead in a shallow basin, where she had evidently been left stranded by the receding tide.

Another voice from the past adds evidence to Aristotle: Pliny the Elder gives an eyewitness account of dolphins that helped fishermen at Nîmes, in the province of Narbonne. He calls the dolphins by the generic name of "Snubnose." Swimming in when needed, Snubnose would drive shoals of mullet into the fishermen's nets at the rivermouth, receiving as reward a share of the catch. Even today certain natives of Queensland avail themselves of dolphin help in fishing.

Today, too, people—quite reputable people—tell stories of dolphin rescues. *Natural History*, in 1949, printed the account of a woman who, six years before this, went swimming alone off a Florida beach and was swept off her feet by the undertow. She nearly drowned, but suddenly, she said, "someone gave me a terrific shove" that landed her face down on the beach. Weak, and naturally assuming that her rescuer was a human being, she lay there for a few moments before rolling over to sit up and thank him. When she did sit up she found herself quite alone on the beach, with a porpoise out in the water, about eighteen feet away, leaping and playing. She was wondering what had happened when an excited man rushed up to tell her that he had seen "a shark" push her ashore, and had thought she was dead.

In 1960 another American woman had an adventure with a dolphin when she fell overboard one night, near Grand Bahama Island. Nobody had seen the accident, and she was left alone in the water while the ship steamed away. For a long time she swam blindly, now and then floating for a rest. Then, feeling a touch on her left hip, she was terrified by the indistinct sight of what she took to be a shark, swimming along with her. She dodged to the right. Now she was moving more easily, for she had been nudged out of the main tide. Soon, to her relief, she saw that her companion was a porpoise, not a shark. It stayed with her, nudging her occasionally, now to the right, now to the left, until she felt land beneath her feet and waded ashore.

There is a reasonable explanation for these so-called acts of kindness. Dolphins are very social animals—that is, they move in groups, and help each other when necessary. Two of them will support another that is injured, helping him to the surface to breathe. In a way this is the same thing one sees with baboons, who are so assiduous with each other that they carry away dead bodies shot by human hunters. Dolphin babies are born tail first: otherwise they might well drown before they can get up to breathe. Occasionally a newborn dolphin will be too weak to swim for a while. When this happens the mother lifts her infant to the surface, or lets it ride on her back. She is aided by a friend during the baby's early days: another female dolphin accompanies her as they swim, the infant between them, to guard it from attack from sharks. If a baby dolphin dies the mother does not seem to realize it, and continues to carry the corpse around at the water's surface for some time. Perhaps, then, humans in distress in the water simply appeal to the dolphin's instinct to help. Another explanation is that the dolphin is simply amusing himself with a drowning person, as if he were bouncing a ball in to shore. If this is so, dolphins must surely from time to time have pushed drowning people out into deeper water—but of course we never hear that side of the story.

It has often been said that dolphins have no real enemies in the marine world except sharks. This depends on what you mean by "dolphin"— and here we are again. If killer whales are included in the family, the saying doesn't hold water. If we leave them out, we still have to qualify the statement: dolphins are inimical to killer whales as well as to sharks. An embattled dolphin will run head on into a shark, aiming for his tenderest spot, just at the gills. The dolphin turns himself into a battering-ram, driving at the enemy again and again until the shark swims away or is killed. Men, however, he leaves unattacked. It goes without saying that men have not usually been as kind as that, in return, to dolphins. Sir Arthur Grimble has given a vivid account of how, among the Gilbert Islanders, there are hereditary "porpoise-callers" who lead their tribes, with much ceremony, down to the beach and summon whole schools of the gentle animals. (Dolphins can hear very well; probably better than we can.) Decked in garlands, the islanders wait. The animals swim in to be betrayed and massacred, and a feast follows. Queensland aboriginals, however, believe that it is very bad luck to kill a porpoise. Tribes of ancient Greece caught dolphins in the Black Sea; they used to pickle the flesh. The leavings of bones show that Nordic tribes ate porpoises from the North Sea. The Minoan Cretans harpooned the animals. The Tudor English ate porpoise pudding. (All these misdeeds are cited by Alpers.) American Indians hunted dolphins. In some Catholic countries porpoise meat has been classed as fish so that Catholics may eat it on Fridays. Scandinavians and Japanese eat porpoise meat, and until very recently the Russians, like the ancient Greeks, caught them in the Black Sea in thousands, and used them for food. However, there has been a change in the Russian attitude: the New York *Herald-Tribune* for March 13, 1966, carried a United Press dispatch reporting that the Soviet Government has banned the catching and killing of dolphins because their brains are "so strikingly close to our own. . . . Fisheries Minister Alexander Ishkov said the decision was taken after extensive research both here and abroad showed that the dolphins' brain power makes them 'marine brothers of man.' Mr. Ishkov indicated he accepted theories that dolphins can talk and may eventually be able to teach their languages to man. 'We hope other governments will follow our example," he said in the government newspaper, Izvestia. 'The catch of dolphins should be stopped in all the seas and oceans of the globe.' Izvestia said dolphins have a 'comradely spirit.' They are selfless and brave, and have been known to save drowning people or play with children."

United States citizens other than Indians can preen themselves on never having eaten very much dolphin flesh, but there used to be a certain amount of catching and killing them nonetheless, for profit. The fine oil from porpoise jaws was in great demand among the makers of clocks and watches: in the early days of this century, such artisans paid twenty dollars a gallon for the stuff. There was a regular porpoise "fishery" at Cape Hatteras, North Carolina, which had been established almost a hundred years earlier. During their best year the Hatteras workers hauled in fifteen hundred *Tursiops truncatus*. Most of the profit was made from their jaw oil, but the hides and blubber also found a market. The animals were rounded up with nets. One, the "out net," which might be as long as half a mile, was carried out to sea by boats, one at each end, until it encircled a school of porpoises, which were then pulled ashore in the "sweep net." Similar methods are used today, but things go more quickly with speed launches.

When Dr. Charles Haskins Townsend, director of the New York Aquarium at the Battery, resolved to add a dolphin exhibition to his collection, he naturally applied to Cape Hatteras. After several false starts he was able to report in June 1914, in the New York Zoological Society's magazine *Zoologica,* on "The Porpoise in Captivity." The New York Aquarium had a school of porpoises (*Tursiops*), "and lays claim," he wrote, "to the world's best single exhibit of captive wild animals . . . They are the same 'jolly porpoises' that make high speed dashes under the bows of ships. No more popular exhibition of wild life has ever been made anywhere. . . . There are five of them and their playful splashing throws showers of water over visitors who dare to venture too close. The exhibit is unique, as there is no other Aquarium in America or Europe equipped with pools large enough to accommodate such animals." Dr. Townsend went on to a general discussion of the dolphin family, mentioning in passing "the strictly fresh-water species inhabiting the Amazon, Ganges and other rivers," and the little white whale, or beluga: the Aquarium had once exhibited two specimens of beluga. He said, too, that small porpoises, of a different species from the bottlenoses, had been denizens of the Aquarium for a short time, but they'd been cast ashore in an injured condition and didn't live long.

His establishment of the school of *Tursiops,* he said, had not been easy. Twice earlier he had made attempts to bring specimens north from Hatteras, but each attempt failed because his instructions for their transportation were not carried out. On the first occasion, eight porpoises were loaded into tanks without water, and had—not surprisingly—died on the way. Almost the same error in judgment was repeated in April 1913, though this time the shippers covered the six animals involved with wet burlap: by the time they arrived in Norfolk, four were dead, but Dr. Townsend, who had come that far to meet them, quickly filled the tank that held the two survivors, and they got to New York alive. One, however, died shortly afterward and the other, blistered by heat, lived only two and a half months more because the blisters festered. When he tried for the third time the director wisely didn't trust anybody else to make the arrangements, but went himself to Cape Hatteras. Ten more dolphins were presented to him, as the gift of the owner of the fishery, a Mr. Joseph K. Nye of New Bedford. Five of these animals were fully grown, the rest half grown. Under Dr. Townsend's supervision all ten arrived at the Battery still alive, but the young ones died soon after arrival. The director explained this circumstance: "The adults, each about eight feet long, gave no trouble during shipment, while the young were exceedingly restless and continually bruised themselves by their

struggles in the shipping tanks." He warned prospective porpoise-ship-
pers that the animals give off much heat, so the tank water must be
cooled off every five or six hours of travel. Since Dr. Townsend's day it
has been ascertained that the greatest danger to a porpoise out of water
is that his internal organs are likely to suffer from pressure, because his
bulk is not supported by the buoyancy of surrounding water. Today
dolphins when shipped are put into slings and in cradles lined with foam
rubber or fiber glass. If they are kept moist and cool, they can travel
considerable distances like this without injury.

Dr. Townsend said that the longest bottle-nosed porpoise ever measured
at Cape Hatteras was twelve feet, and many measured nine, but he
thought that his eight-foot specimens, which weighed on an average of
three hundred pounds apiece, were about the usual size. Roving bands of
Tursiops might number anything from a dozen to several hundred. According to the men at Cape Hatteras they frequented that region from
early October to early May, after which they headed north.

The Battery exhibition of porpoises was popular, though there was
no particular dolphin craze like the one we have today. Dr. Townsend's
animals did not live long, but he replaced them without fanfare as they
died off, this being the customary procedure in zoos and aquariums.
Many people came down to the Battery to look at the fishes and watch
the dolphins at play. When a lot of them complained that their clothes
were ruined because the animals splashed them, the management put up
glass around the tank. Thus things went for the Battery porpoises, fairly
quietly on the whole, until the twenties. Then, the ex-director Dr. Christopher Coates recalls, suddenly there came a flood of complaints that
the animals were misbehaving. Indubitably dolphins are sexy animals,
but then, they always had been, and why the public made up its mind
to protest against the facts of Nature at this particular period instead of
another is a mystery. At any rate parents said that they couldn't bring
their children to the Aquarium any more, if that was the way things
were run. Husbands complained that their wives' sensibilities were griev-
ously shocked by porpoises at the Battery. The chorus swelled until the
authorities could not ignore it, and the bottle-nosed dolphins were banished.

Condemned for immoral practices, dolphins were forgotten until 1938,
and then they came back on the scene by accident. In that year two
friends, Douglas Burden and Ilya Tolstoy, embarked on a commercial
venture that promised to give them considerable amusement as well as
profit—the establishment of large tanks representing life at the bottom
of the sea, to be hired by Hollywood firms whenever they needed background for dramas with marine settings. The studios would be glad to

have such amenities, the partners reasoned. A favorable reaction from Paramount assured them that they were on the right track, so they acquired land near St. Augustine, Florida, and prepared some glass tanks. They went to the Battery and worked for two months learning the techniques of maintaining and exhibiting marine life. Then they moved down to Florida and set to work filling their own tanks with salt water, anemones, shells, fishes large and small, and seaweed.

"Somehow some porpoises got in too," Chris Coates said. "It was purely by chance, but there they were, playing around, and people got wind of it and came along to watch. It got to be quite an attraction."

Like so many good business ideas, that of "Marine Studios," as the venture was called, didn't live up to expectations. At least it didn't make the grade as an adjunct of Hollywood. The owners of the company found they were losing money, so they sold out. The company that bought it also sold out. Marine Studios moved from hand to hand for some years. Yet always the dolphins attracted people. No matter who was running the place, no matter who refused to rent it for movie purposes, the public came to watch the big animals play, until their exhibitors faced facts and decided to build their show around them. Now under the management of Marineland of Florida, Marine Studios is hugely successful, and is known far and wide as the porpoise show. The training and exhibiting of porpoises has become really big show business, as witness not only the parent company of Florida but Marineland of the Pacific and its subsidiary in Hawaii, "Sea Life," Sea World in San Diego, Brookfield's porpoises in Illinois—the first inland show of the sort—and a number of smaller companies. Abroad the idea is catching on everywhere. Japan, naturally, was the first to adopt it, but Europe is taking it up too. Spain has succeeded in keeping alive some that were imported from Florida. Italy tried to, but the animals died. Amsterdam is talking about doing it; England has done it. One wonders about China. One of the great authorities on cetacea, David H. Brown, recently left Marineland of the Pacific to establish a similar place near Melbourne, in Australia, while farther down the coast Sir Edward Hallstrom, moving spirit of Sydney's Zoo at Taronga Park, plans a Marineland of his own.

I have witnessed much of this activity for myself. Having learned that the seaside resort of Morecambe, on the west coast of England north of Blackpool, now boasted a dolphin show, I went to see how it was proceeding. I found that it was getting on fine. I visited it on a nasty wet day in August, when all the holiday booths and stalls were deserted, but the aquarium and especially the dolphin-show auditorium were crowded. "We weren't at all sure we could keep them properly," confessed the director. "Other places have tried, you know. Some dolphins died off not long ago at Plymouth, and they hadn't been there very long. But we've kept ours going. They seem quite at home now, and our trainer's getting results. He went all the way to Florida to learn the business and help with the animals' transportation. We brought them over by plane, and there were no accidents. Shall we go and have a look?"

The pool, somewhat higher than the sea outside, looked uninviting enough, but I could see now-familiar gray shapes swooping around it in the old carefree fashion. I met the trainer, and we stood at the brink of the pool to talk things over. Back of us, the seats were filling in expectation of the next show, though it was not due to start for another twenty-five minutes. A dolphin surfaced and spotted the trainer, and recognized him. It clapped its jaws.

"He wants a fish," I said, and the trainer nodded.

"Yes, but I'm not giving him any until the show starts. I don't want to take the edge off his appetite." He went on to tell me that they were taping their animals' noises at the special request of a nearby university. The basketball practice was coming along well, he said. At that moment we were inundated by a splash from the pool, and as we gasped and choked, there came another splash, and another. Every dolphin as it swam past splashed us as hard as it could.

"They're angry," said the trainer. I said, "Here they come again."

Splash, splash, splash, splash, splash. We refused to show that we noticed. As if unaware that our faces and clothes were running with water, we continued our conversation for a time, and then—slowly—we withdrew. Honor had been maintained.

I visited the Miami Seaquarium in 1966, just a year after I'd seen Enoshima. It is a beautiful place. One approaches it by causeway, looking ahead at a marine palace that shines in the sun. Inside the grounds we went straight to the dolphin house. I was being shown around by a Miami resident familiar with the place, who told me, "This is supposed to be the largest tank in the world. Let's go up to the top deck first."

Looking at the bright blue water I refrained from comment, but it certainly wasn't as big around as the Enoshima tank. But possibly, I told myself, it outdid the Japanese structure in cubic content, and one's got to allow show people to play with their superlatives. A moment later, after the show had started, a *Tursiops* proved one superlative by leaping twenty-one feet in the air to pick a fish from the hand of Jimmy Kline, the chief trainer. "Highest porpoise jumper in the world," said my friend. "She works up a speed of forty miles an hour to do that."

We moved on to a training pool, where a pretty girl in a bathing suit, referred to by the loudspeaker as a lovely aquamaid, sported with a young *Tursiops* that was identified by the same source as "Flipper's understudy." The chatty machine added that seven million gallons of seawater were pumped into the tank every twenty-four hours. Musing on these statistics I watched the lovely aquamaid as she swam with the dolphin underwater, her hair streaming behind her. They rose together, glistening with wetness, and she kissed his forehead just on the bump of intellect, called "the melon," that jutted over his nose.

"When the Seaquarium opened there was a little added excitement," said my guide, as he led the way to the offices. "That was nine years ago. A dolphin baby was born in the tank just the night before, and of course everybody said the management had planned it that way, but actually people aren't sure yet just when a mother's going to give birth. I believe they've had quite a few young born here. Let's ask the Captain."

We found Captain William Gray, Director of Collections and Exhibits, in his office. My friend had told me that Captain Gray is an old hand with dolphins, having been with Marine Studios before he joined the Seaquarium. I asked the Director about it. "Yes," he said, "I've been in this business one way and another for sixty years. I've collected for museums as well as aquariums. Mostly sea creatures, but I've been collecting everything but money all my life." The happy event in the dolphin pool nine years earlier was mentioned, and he said, "Oh yes, that was Clown who was the mother. She was a great dolphin, Clown. Of course we've had a lot of young ones come along since then; we've got three young ones right now that were born here. Not that we have to depend on the birth rate in the tanks: we get new ones. Newly caught adults seem to learn just as quickly as the young ones. They're amazing animals. Even when they're fifteen or sixteen years old, they catch on. I'll show you around a bit."

Walking with him at a smart clip, I wondered how to bring up an awkward question I'd had in mind ever since starting out for Florida. It concerned something disturbing that I'd heard from a New York acquaintance about performing porpoises, something I wanted to check up on. She had said, "They die quickly, you know; those porpoises that do the high jumps, standing up on their tails, dancing and so on. Their life span after they start performing is about four months. It has something to do with nervous reaction. They spend so much energy that they just wear out. Naturally the trainers and owners never admit this: whenever a porpoise dies they just give his name to the animal that takes his place. Try to find out the truth while you're there. Make them admit it."

That was all very well for her to say, but how was I to word the question?

"Only the other day we had a birth here," said the Captain. "It was early in the morning, about seven-fifteen, and nobody was around but the watchman, but he saw it. He said a whole lot of them went wild when the baby swam up to the surface—jumped all over and whistled and rattled. It was a regular party. By the way, we still have that first one, you know—Clown's baby."

No, I couldn't ask that question.

The Captain went on to tell the story of Lalla and Palooza, which is to be found in his book *Porpoise Tales*. In 1959 the Seaquarium received a letter from the mayor of an Italian town, Cesenatico, on the Adriatic. The letter asked for help. In their town canal, said the mayor, lived a female dolphin named Lalla, a great favorite of the people. But Lalla needed a mate. Could the Seaquarium oblige? The request was welcomed by the Seaquarium's public relations office, and as soon as a photograph showed that Lalla was indeed a *Tursiops*, the boys went into action. They were so well along in their preparations that it seemed relatively unimportant when the Cesenatico mayor wrote again to say that Lalla had died, and the P.R. boys were justified when they heard that more dolphins had been obtained by Cesenatico soon afterward, among which was a female named Lalla, after the first one. In Florida, the local press played up the story with all the whimsy papers usually exhibit over zoo news. The *Miami News* inaugurated a naming contest among schoolchildren for the dolphin destined as Lalla's bridegroom. Fifty-nine of them came up with "Palooza," and this name was adopted. Escorted by Captain Gray and his wife, the dolphin was flown to New York and put aboard an Italian Line steamer. Palooza started out in a rubber swimming-pool on deck, but halfway across this article broke, and the dolphin was placed in the passengers' pool instead. The captain made an announcement to the effect that this didn't mean that passengers who wanted to swim would have to forego that pleasure: anyone wishing to swim with the dolphin was welcome to do so. Captain Gray remembers that only two people availed themselves of the offer, a woman and her son. To the sound of cheers from onlookers they got into the pool, emerging again "in just about a quarter of a minute." Palooza landed safely in the Cesenatico canal and was warmly greeted by Lalla.

They did well for three years, but the freak cold snap that descended on Europe in 1963 froze the canal over, drowning all the dolphins in it.

"I've taken porpoises to Duisburg too, and four that I took to Barcelona are still flourishing," said the Captain. "We've had queries from everywhere you can imagine, even from behind the Iron Curtain." He paused and pointed to the nearby shoreline. "There's our Flipper pool. You know all the Flipper pictures are made here? Yes, right here, except when they've got a scene that must be out in the open sea. A big piece of water's enclosed here, and the ranger's cabin, which you must have seen many times on television, is built there on the dock. Ivan Torr is the director; they're MGM pictures. The first one was *Flipper*, and the second was *Flipper's New Adventure*. Those were full-length pictures in color, that turned out to be so popular that they started the TV series. Now I'm going to let you in on a secret—we have *five* Flippers here." He stopped talking and looked at me for suitable signs of surprise, which were not hard to show because I really hadn't known about it. At the same time I wrestled with, and downed, the impulse to ask if he had to hold reserves of animals in this way because the turnover was so vast. But it seemed that this was not the reason. The Captain continued, "Sometimes they're shooting two or three at once, you see, when the sun's right and all. Doing it that way you might save as much as ten thousand dollars a day. Once we had to sacrifice a porpoise for the series, in a deep-sea sequence. The story went something like: there was this fellow sick and helpless out in a boat, and he'd lost his oars, and he needed blood plasma and I don't know what, so a helicopter brought out the stuff wrapped in waterproof material, and dropped it to the sick fellow, only it missed the boat and the fellow's too weak to catch it before it sinks. What can they do? Why, bring in good old Flipper, of course. The helicopter flies back to the bay and hoists up Flipper, and flies out and drops him into the sea near the boat, and Flipper dives down and picks up the package of blood plasma and things, and swims up and hands it to the man in the boat and saves his life. It worked. The only catch was that we had to drop the animal into deep water outside the pool, and when he saw he was free he kept on going and we never saw him again. Still, MGM wanted the scene shot, and they paid."

I said, "They tried something at Oahu with a porpoise trained to come to an electric signal. They took him out into the deep sea and let him go, and went out a week later and signaled, and he came back."

"Is that so!" Captain Gray was deeply impressed.

"But the next time they tried it, it didn't work," I had to confess.

"The second dolphin swam away and stayed away, like your Flipper the Sixth."

"That sounds more like it," said the Captain.

He told us something of the training of porpoises. The only way to keep newly captured animals up to snuff, he said, is to work consistently with them and, above all, to stick to schedule. It takes some new animals as long as two weeks to learn to eat dead—that is, frozen—fish, though with most this period lasts only two or three days. The next thing to do, he said, is to break them in to accepting cut-up fish, for in freedom porpoises scorn all but the whole creature. Captain Gray said, "In confinement, they worry for a while, and they're stand-offish. Then all of a sudden they seem to come to the conclusion that you aren't going to harm them. After that, everything's all right."

In the cafeteria the chief trainer, Jimmy Kline, had coffee with us. I gave him news of the dolphins at Morecambe, which he remembered well, and he suggested that we watch him conduct a rehearsal. He led the way to a working tank behind the scenes. "These animals are the ones we had up at the World's Fair in New York last summer," he said. "We keep up the training because if you don't keep on, four or five times a day, they forget the routine."

With the high-mortality story still in mind, I asked, "*Are* these the same ones that were at the World's Fair? It's been almost a year since that closed down."

"All but one," said Jimmy. "We lost one and we've put another in her place. But the new one had a baby not long ago, so I'm not working her much."

Near us, halfway up a small stand at the edge of the tank, was the familiar basketball net, and it was this trick that Jimmy seemed to be working on with the porpoises. As he tossed the ball in and watched them butt it out, he kept talking to the animals in a low tone—"There, see what you can do over there. Not so high. Now, again. That's better." Over his shoulder he told us, "I'm only talking to myself. They work by gesture, not sound—they don't listen to what I'm saying."

All but one of the dolphins scored pretty well at getting the ball into the net. The odd man out, however, repeatedly bunted the ball in the wrong direction, toward a wooden structure halfway down the tank wall where a trainer could stand high up to conduct leaping practice. Time after time the ball rose and hit this stand's underpinnings, though there was no net anywhere near it. Time after time Jimmy had to retrieve it.

"We had the basket hanging there last year," he said, "and this animal's never forgotten. The others learned to change around, but he's dumb, I guess. Hey you, come on over here and look where the others are putting it. *Look*."

Again, very patiently, the dolphin pushed the ball over to the trainer's stand. There, at least, was one that had survived from the previous year, I said to myself.

We paid a call on the mother and her baby, who lived with another animal in a smaller tank nearby. The mother accepted several fish but seemed reluctant to lift her head clear of the water, even to take our offerings. "Come on, now," admonished Jimmy. He added to us, "She doesn't like to get her eyes out into the air. They none of them do at first, but she'll learn."

But all this entertainment and show business is merely one aspect of the dolphin situation. Close behind the inflation of public enthusiasm for porpoises that play basketball, leap for fish and wear funny hats came the scientific men, seeking explanations for these phenomena and others not so readily perceptible in a Marineland tank. In 1951 two scientists, Winthrop N. Kellogg and R. Kohler, instituted a research program aimed at finding out how porpoises navigate, as they seemed to do, "without the use of vision, smell, taste, or touch." Evidence indicated strongly that they depend on echo-ranging, a possibility that interested naval officials, as Kellogg explains in his introduction to the book *Porpoises and Sonar*: "What these animals can do has a definite bearing on our national defense, as a means of improving man-made sonar. For this reason the project was sponsored by the Office of Naval Research and the National Science Foundation." There followed a strange and fascinating period for Kellogg and Kohler, visiting one collection after another of captive dolphins in their efforts to establish, without any reasonable doubt, the existence of porpoise sonar. The problem resolved itself in the three basic questions: (1) Do the animal's noises meet the requirements for echo-ranging in water? (2) Is his acoustic sense adequate for the decoding and analysis of reflected echoes? (3) Is the sonar system of a porpoise actually used for orientation and navigation? That is, do they employ it to find food, and to avoid obstacles while swimming?

To some extent the field had already been explored. During and after the Second World War much work was done on underwater noises of biological origin, when it was found that underwater in the ocean is a very noisy place, what with snapping shrimp, crabs that make cracking or popping noises, and fish that thump, tick, grind their teeth, or scrape coral rock. But it is safe to say that none of these creatures outdoes in noise and variety of sounds the row made by cetaceans, both underwater and at the surface. A record compiled at Woods Hole, "Whale and Porpoise Voices," is almost deafening. In an article by the Dutch W. H. Dudok van Heel is a striking list of the sounds made by the bottle-nosed dolphin, the pilot whale and the common dolphin, as reported by American scientists: "whistling, shrieking, creaking, groaning, mooing, rasping, snapping, clicks and the sounds produced by a rusty hinge."

It was the clicks that particularly interested Kellogg and Kohler. "In the case of the dolphin," wrote Kellogg, "there is an obvious similarity—which can be recognized merely by listening—between the rapid succession of pulses, or the 'sputtering' sound, and the signals or pings sent out in mechanical sonar." The whistling noise might be some sort of a call—perhaps a cry of alarm. How does a dolphin produce these sounds, as it has no vocal cords in our sense of the phrase? The breathing apparatus ends at the top of the head in the blowhole, a complicated structure with "tongue-like" projections within the air passage. The anatomy of the blowhole has been investigated by other scientists (Thomas Schevill and Barbara Lawrence) who found an overlapping and close-fitting-together of the lips and walls that form a series of check valves. Through this mechanism, the dolphin issues his varied sounds. It takes an effort to think of an animal producing speech in a fashion so unlike ours. Kellogg even argues, half seriously, that we should not refer to a dolphin's "vocalization," but to its "phonation."

The source of the noises, therefore, has been explained. What of the dolphin's reception ability? The cetacean's ear is described as a triumph of special adaptation, the middle and inner ears being together in "a single osseous complex" built to withstand varying pressures. Moreover, a porpoise's acoustic nerve is unusually large, much larger than his optic nerve, reversing the rule of most mammals, and cetaceans in general are known to be extremely sensitive to sound. In the wild, porpoises flee from rifle shots or any other unusual noise, though fishes in the same area are undisturbed. Whales leap in alarm as ships approach. Kellogg and Kohler made tests of the dolphin's acoustic sensitivity—its response to high-frequency tones—that placed the animal third highest in the list, exceeded only by the mouse and the bat.

A large pool was dug in soft marl, where the water was turbid and the walls did not reflect echoes, and there Kellogg and Kohler set up their laboratory. Hydrophones and other equipment in the water listened to the underwater sounds made by the porpoises, recording and photographing them so that the animals' ability to locate, approach or avoid submerged targets could be recorded. The researchers found that the underwater sounds made by porpoises are most often a successive series of rapidly repeated clicks or pings.

In their conclusions, Kellogg says, they found that the porpoise ear and brain, being highly advanced in development, possess important adaptations for perception and analysis of underwater sounds. A porpoise's acoustic receptor is able to compensate for changes in external pressure due to water depth. Porpoises have a much greater range of hearing than human beings do, and consequently respond to many vibrations in the field of ultra-sound. The unusual sonar pulses they send out, and the excellent receptor they possess, constitute an acute transmitting-receiving medium. The porpoise's brain appears to be well equipped to act as decoder and computer for the neural impulses that reach it. Furthermore, experiments made in darkness proved that porpoises can tell the location of strange obstacles at night, such as sheets of plate glass or transparent Plexiglas, and are able to avoid them. The noise of a splash invariably triggered a series of sound pulses: the animals seemed to be "looking with their ears" to find out if some foreign object had entered the water. If the splash was made without anything actually being dropped into the pool, the sputtering signals stopped after a few minutes. But when the splash was followed by the presence of some new object in the water, these exploratory sound signals continued, presumably until the size and distance of the object had been determined. Moreover, even an object introduced soundlessly was soon discovered, because of the animal's habit, every twenty seconds or so, of emitting short bursts of sound signals, which can be compared to a visual animal's glancing about or peering. And so delicate is the porpoise's perception by ear that he can even differentiate between fish of different sizes, just from listening to echoes.

News of such experiments and the conclusions drawn from them naturally reached the columns of the press and caused a stir of interest among laymen, but the public did not get really excited until Dr. Lilly came on the scene. John C. Lilly, M.D., began releasing notices of his work on dolphins in 1957. His popular book, *Man and Dolphin: Adventures on a New Scientific Frontier*, published in 1961, generated tremendous excitement. The preface starts out, "Within the next decade or two the human species will establish communication with another species: nonhuman, alien, possibly extraterrestrial, more probably marine; but definitely highly intelligent, and perhaps even intellectual." More probably marine? Could Dr. Lilly possibly mean that we might be able to talk with porpoises? Certainly he seemed to think so. "In a way this is a crude, elementary handbook for those humans who are interested in the realization of such communication," he had written. "If no one among us pursues the matter before interspecies communication is forced upon *Homo sapiens* by an alien species, this book will have failed in its purpose." It was heady stuff, considering the source—not a science-fiction writer nor a comic-strip artist, but a serious, genuine doctor. No wonder that there was a tremendous reaction.

Yet the story of Dr. Lilly and the dolphins began quite by chance. An assistant professor with special interest in medical physics and experimental neurology, he was visiting friends in Woods Hole during the summer of 1949; they all went together to view a pilot whale stranded on a beach in Maine. Lilly said that he would like to study the brain of such an animal, and one of the other members of the party told him that it would be more practical to work with miniature whales—i.e., porpoises. The idea stuck in Lilly's own brain. Six years later he had organized a group of eight men to spend two weeks at Marine Studios in Florida, studying the brain of the bottle-nosed dolphin. By prearrangement with the Studios staff they acquired five animals and set to work. Nobody had done this sort of thing before, and they behaved with the first dolphin much as if it had been a land mammal—a dog, or a chimpanzee—strapping it down out of the water and injecting anesthetic. To their horror and mystification its breathing immediately slowed down as it fell asleep, and very speedily it died. The men decided they had made an error in their calculations, and on the second dolphin they used a much smaller dose of Nembutal, but it, too, slipped away. Its respiration simply "fell apart," says Lilly. With the third animal, they were ready to apply artificial breathing. To be sure, this dolphin revived, but when they saw how he behaved back in the tank they knew that his brain was damaged, and he, too, had to be destroyed. They used paraldehyde on the next animal, but . . .

By this time, as Lilly admits, the visitors had become markedly unpopular around the Studios. The keepers and curator implied that "these animals were extremely intelligent, playful, and friendly toward man," and that this was a pretty rotten way to treat them. Five dolphins had been sacrificed, and five, the curator felt, was more than enough. The doctors decided to call it a day. They had not accomplished their end, mapping the dolphin's brain, but they had acquired some valuable information, and now felt that they understood why the calamities had occurred. It seems that dolphins do not inhale and exhale unconsciously, as we do: their breathing is voluntary. When a dolphin goes into a state of deep unconsciousness, his breathing stops. In nature, cetaceans don't sleep deeply, but refresh themselves with cat naps as they float near the surface of the water, always alert to danger. The adult dolphin's brain, as the doctors found when they analyzed the specimens they had brought from Florida, is extremely large and complex, but it was the behavior of the animal that interested Lilly most of all. Evidently dolphins, even when painfully treated, do not attack human beings. They will attack and kill sharks, and they fight with one another during the mating season, but they don't attack people. Lilly says, "Physically they are quite capable of tearing or biting an arm or a leg off a man or of damaging him internally by ramming, but there is no record of these animals ever having damaged a human, even when the human has mistreated them." To be sure, later he seems to contradict himself, reporting that one of the Marineland dolphins, after much teasing, took to charging and biting his keeper.

Another manifestation of dolphin behavior: when the doctors returned the brain-damaged dolphin to the pool—the one they managed to resuscitate, but had later to kill—a hydrophone made it possible to hear what was certainly a phonal exchange between this animal and the others. "He emitted a very short, sharp, high-pitched whistle . . . The effect of the distress call was immediate. The other two animals swam rapidly over . . . swam under his head, and pushed him to the surface so that he could breathe. He breathed and submerged. Immediately a twittering, whistling exchange took place among the three animals." Visiting Woods Hole a year later, Dr. Lilly learned all he could about dolphin sounds and dolphin sonar, and when he was back at work he thought things over and resolved to try another method of mapping the brain of the living dolphin, by discovering its "electric potentials." He had already experimented with monkeys, placing electrodes in the brain in certain areas, and stimulating the cells by passing electrical currents through them. A monkey was "rewarded" when he barked by receiving a pleasurable sensation. He learned to push a switch when this action resulted in pleasure, and to pull another when he wanted to "turn off" unpleasant sensations. Ultimately Lilly applied these methods to dolphins, after conquering certain difficulties that arose in dealing with water animals, and the dolphins were induced to "vocalize." In the course of this phase of experimentation, Lilly found out other things. For example, he discovered in one of the animals what he thought was certainly an amiable desire to remain in communication with himself. This animal, while whistling, went higher and higher until it reached a pitch that Lilly could not hear. The man could see the blowhole contracting, but his ears couldn't register the high note. When it understood the situation—and Lilly had no doubt the dolphin did understand—it obligingly dropped its pitch to a level audible to Lilly, and after that, for forty-five minutes, kept its sounds within Dr. Lilly's frame of hearing. Then came the exciting day when Lilly, slowing down and analyzing the recording of a dolphin's sounds, detected in them a definite pattern: the animal seemed to be imitating the speech of the humans who had worked around the pool. Another dolphin copied Lilly's speech so well that his attendants could hear the mimicking.

It was this passage in Lilly's book that most excited people. It is not quite clear why they should have read into the imitation incidents the meaning that the animals were thus trying to communicate. After all, parrots and other birds imitate man's speech. Some other elements of Lilly's report seem, on consideration, more suggestive than his descriptions of dolphins emitting Donald Duck human speech, but so it was: the imagination of the American public had been fired. Nor was the excitement to be found only on the "Flipper" level, among children or the childish. Like science fiction, Lilly's theories were received by intelligent people as well. For a while everybody seemed intoxicated by the prospect of communicating with dolphins. Everybody recalled what he had heard of the dolphin's kindness and tractability: these qualities were now seen to be linked to vast intellectual powers. We had been entertaining angels unawares, and entertaining them shabbily at that. It was time to utilize this good will and intellect. Linked in friendship with *Homo sapiens,* what might not the dolphin accomplish? Leo Szilard's satire, "The Voice of the Dolphin," pictures a world where commonsense reigns over mankind and peace is established forever, all through the agency of a committee of dolphins that act as secret advisers to the United Nations. Loren Eiseley tried to account for the public's reaction to Lilly's book: man, he says, is the loneliest creature in the universe because he is cut off from animals by his intellectual capacity, his "social memory," or history. Children try to talk with animals, but as they mature they give up the attempt. "It is with a feeling of startlement, therefore, and eager interest touching the lost child in every one of us, that the public has received the recent accounts . . . of one of our brother animals—the sea-dwelling, bottlenosed porpoise or dolphin."

As one example of the eager interest of the lost child in every one of us, a 1966 sequence of Al Capp's comic strip "Li'l Abner" featured a dolphin named Dripper who goes on TV and gives imitations of television stars.

Dr. Lilly's ideas interested the National Aeronautic and Space Administration. On the theory that U.S. astronauts might find his language studies useful when they land on inhabited planets, NASA gave a contract to his newly formed Communications Research Institute.

Then the Office of Naval Research and the National Science Foundation contributed their bit, as did the National Institute of Health. Dr. Lilly has continued to pursue his investigations, at laboratories in St. Thomas in the Virgin Islands and in Miami. His latest paper, as of the date of writing, appeared in 1965, and is entitled "Vocal Mimicry in *Tursiops:* Ability to Match Numbers and Durations of Human Vocal Bursts." "These results," says the summary, "show quantitatively something of the ability of *Tursiops* to mimic certain aspects of human vocal emissions. This ability seems to be one of many functions of the large brain (1700 g) of this mammal and entails severe modification of the naturally occurring complex vocalizations of *Tursiops.* . . . Differences from observations of other animals are striking: even parrots and mynah birds apparently do not give such large numbers of replies and such sustained and accurate performances. To date, only dolphins and humans share this ability."

It is interesting, but it hasn't the same old impact. Perhaps the inevitable reaction has set in after the public's early dazzlement. There are scientists who feel that Dr. Lilly, in the preface to *Man and Dolphin*, overreached himself. "He's shot his bolt," said one of these dissenters not long ago. "I don't think dolphins talk, and I don't think they imitate. He'll never be able to prove it." Some other people have grown impatient as the months and years slip past without a sudden incursion of Martians who call upon porpoises to act as their interpreters.

"My husband's going to be late," said a woman I met at a party in Miami. Across the room, Dr. Lilly and his wife were chatting with friends, and her eyes followed them as she continued, "My husband's awfully busy these days. He's teaching our parrakeet to say, 'Dr. Lilly can talk.'"

Two white whales, or belugas, swim about their tank at the New York Aquarium at Coney Island. They are evidently happy creatures, and have great attraction for the public. As a pair they behave as Nature intends pairs to behave, but no complaints have yet forced the curator to send them into exile as was done to poor *Tursiops* in the old days. White whales are dolphins, and they look like dolphins: they smile, and their foreheads bulge in the same intellectual way.

"They have one particular game," said Dr. Christopher Coates, who was showing me around the aquarium. "Sometimes a keeper gets into the tank and plays it with one or the other. They like to push heads. The whale will shove his melon against the keeper's forehead and see which one can push harder. Of course the whale really can, but most of the time he pretends he's just about as strong as the man, no stronger. Once in a great while he gets mischievous, though, and bumps so hard he pushes the keeper off his feet. Notice how much lighter the male is. That's because he's older than the female; they start out grayish and lighten as they mature."

"They're almost exactly like porpoises," I mused aloud, watching the graceful, huge shapes. "A lot bigger, of course. And there's something else—the way they move their necks. Look at that one, up and down like a polar bear. It looks wrong, somehow."

Chris said, "They have flexible necks, and most dolphins haven't. I agree, it does look different."

A few days later I heard more about dolphins and flexible necks. In San Diego at a zoo meeting, I spent a morning watching a young killer whale, Shamu, in her tank at the marine park, Sea World. Then I went to lunch with the zoo people, and spoke about the whale and my quest for dolphins generally. "I ought to take the time to go up and visit Marineland of the Pacific," I said, "but I can't manage it."

The man on my right, who was Lawrence Curtis, director of the Fort Worth Zoo, dissented. "If you've seen the porpoise shows in Florida you've seen just about all of them," he said. "But we've got something in Fort Worth I bet you haven't seen—fresh-water dolphins. Did you ever hear of them?" I said that I had, vaguely. There had been one at the Crandon Park Zoo in the children's section, but for one reason or another I'd missed it. "That's right," said Curtis promptly. "They did have one, but it got drowned or something in the hurricane, and they've just replaced it. But I have a *pair*; they've been doing all right now for several years. Come on down to Texas and see our pink porpoises if you want to see something really interesting. They're *Inia geoffrensis*, from the Amazon—a much more primitive form of dolphin than *Tursiops*. All fresh-water dolphins are primitive. There are four species—but come along and see ours for yourself. You can read up on them in our library."

The first literature he handed me when I arrived in Forth Worth was a paper by James N. Layne and David K. Caldwell, published in *Zoologica*, in the summer number of 1964—"Behavior of the Amazon Dolphin, *Inia geoffrensis* (Blainville), in Captivity." Freshwater dolphins, it seems, do not belong to the family Delphinidae, but to Platanistidae, and appear to be among the more primitive of living cetaceans. "The family includes only four recent species," said the article, "which have typically relict distributions." These are the Ganges dolphin, found in the Ganges, Indus and Brahmaputra rivers, the white-flag dolphin that lives in the Tung Ting Lake of central China and in adjacent parts of the Yangtsze River, the La Plata dolphin of the La Plata River and adjacent coastal waters—the only platanistid that isn't entirely confined to fresh water—and Lawrence Curtis's kind, *Inia geoffrensis*, which "ranges throughout much of the Amazon River system and also occurs in the Orinoco drainage." *Inia* and the white-flag dolphin of China are surprisingly similar in appearance. "Yet they developed so far from each other!" I said when Lawrence showed me comparative photographs. "Yes," he said in tones of satisfaction. "Nice example of parallel evolution."

There is another partially freshwater dolphin that is not mentioned in Layne and Caldwell's paper, probably because it isn't a platanistid. This is *sotalia*, one species of which is known as the Guiana River dolphin and inhabits streams in Surinam and Guiana, and the coastal waters around their mouths. A dozen species of *sotalia* occur in coastal waters off Africa, India and the lands around the China Sea.

Platanistidae, said the article, first appear in the Miocene. The marine deposits of this period, and those of the Pliocene and Pleistocene, are fairly full of their fossils, indicating that at one time they were "a widespread and relatively successful marine group." They were probably crowded back into the rivers by more advanced delphonoids, the odontocetes (toothed whales) that crop up in late Miocene and Pliocene times. The writers point out that a similar thing—"this apparent replacement of one adaptive level of organization by a more advanced type—" happened in the fish world when the teleosts of the Tertiary replaced more primitive bony fishes. Remnants of these archaic bony fishes, like the river dolphins, are now to be found in freshwater habitats.

Layne and Caldwell based their study on two specimens of *Inia* that lived at Silver Springs, Florida, brought there from the Amazon in 1956 by an expedition in which Layne participated. Two more of the same species, and one *sotalia*, failed to survive the first few days of captivity in Silver Springs. Under the heading "White Whales of the Amazon," another member of the expedition described their adventures while collecting, in *Natural History* for June 1957. The common name for *Inia* in South America is *bouto*, but locally, at the Leticia where the Americans did their hunting, it is called *bufeo*. The Indians, said the writer, had some weird and wonderful tales about the *bufeo*. Sometimes, they said, these animals would come out of the water and sing such sweet songs that humans were lured to the river banks. And it must be admitted, he went on, that the dolphin is of such strange appearance that it was only natural it should give rise to odd rumors: "Some of the larger specimens were at least 9 feet long and must have weighed close to 300 pounds. They resembled the familiar marine dolphins but were more slender, with a long tooth-studded beak. The adults were pale-whitish, faintly tinged with bluish-gray above and pinkish below. From time to time, several would poke their ghostly heads out of the Amazon water, exhale with a loud 'Whoosh!' and then roll out of sight. When blowing, they send a misty jet at least eight feet into the air." On one occasion a large one rose almost half its length out of the water and glided straight at their dugout. "It approached so close that its bulging forehead, small eyes and cylindrical beak could be seen plainly. Its speed and silence and the power and directness of its approach—within fifteen feet of the boat— would frighten anyone not familiar with the species."

Layne and Caldwell had the help of our friends William Schevill and Barbara Lawrence, who recorded the underwater sounds of the *Inia* and supplied information about marine dolphins for purposes of comparison. Some suggestions that arose from these comparisons were that *Inia* swims slower than *Tursiops*. In breathing he also behaves somewhat differently, rising and lying under the surface of the water in a horizontal position, with only his blowhole exposed. Sometimes he releases air before he reaches the top—about a foot below the surface—and it comes up in a large bubble. Though it used to be assumed that they were blind— probably because their eyes are so small—*Inias* see well, probably as well as *Tursiops*. They are extremely sensitive to underwater sounds, and the observers suspected, without having time to prove it, that they use echolocation much as marine dolphins do. Like marine dolphins, too, they like to rub themselves against other animals or inanimate objects. The long, thin beak has a few hairs of stubble on it, which are perhaps of use when it grubs along the river bottom.

Unfortunately for the study, both *Inias* died after a year in captivity. One, suffering from a respiratory ailment, died under ether, Dr. Lilly's mishap with *Tursiops* not yet having been publicized. The other died of acute bronchial pneumonia. During their short time in Silver Springs, Schevill and Lawrence managed to record only two sounds, a loud rasping "Bronx cheer" and a faint plaintive yelping, much lower in pitch than that of the "odontocete vocalizations" collected by the same couple. Later observers, swimming underwater, heard two other sounds: a high-pitched squeal and a loud "pow, pow, pow" made by snapping the jaws together. *Tursiops*, too, snaps his jaws, it is thought as an intimidation display, though from what I have seen I think it might be merely an attention-getting device.

Fortified now with a lot of book-knowledge, I went with Lawrence to look at the animals. He told me that Pinky, the female, was his first acquisition. She had arrived so soon after they heard she was coming that the tank wasn't ready, so she was housed for a while in the hippo's pool. Paddles, the male, was a later arrival, but he was older and bigger than Pinky. The tank is indoors at the aquarium, a large affair with a railing along the front, at the entrance. At either end of the railing and the corners of the tank the ground slopes down, and at the lower end of the slope one is at the same level as the tank's bottom. Three wide windows look into the water along the back wall. Overhead the ceiling was stippled, white and not so white. It was late afternoon, and the aquarium was closed to the public, but two people were still there, a young couple introduced as Nancy and Mike Lobb.

"How are they behaving today?" asked Lawrence.

"Pretty good," said Mike, "but he's getting sort of pesky again with Pinky; he's been chewing her up."

"Again?" Lawrence looked disturbed.

Nancy said, "She's got a nasty spot near the tail where he bit her. There, you can see it as she comes by."

Looking down, I discerned a whitish torpedo-shaped creature swimming past. On the far side of the tank a head emerged briefly, said "Whoosh!" and submerged again just as I caught a glimpse of a very prominent melon, a remarkably long thin beak, and a tiny eye. It did not look at all like the porpoises I had grown used to. It was more like some kind of primeval creature, perhaps that bird with teeth, the pterodactyl. Lawrence Curtis took a fish from a nearby bucket and held it up where the tank's denizens could see it. Nearer this time, the bulging-browed animal rose and took it. The beak was really extraordinary, far longer than any dolphin's I had ever seen, but in the animals' movements and their fixed smiles there was something familiar. I could see that they were indeed faintly pink. Lawrence watched them proudly.

"Funny-looking, aren't they?" he said. "Notice the bristles on their beaks? And look how they can turn their heads, a lot more easily than marine dolphins; that's because the neckbones aren't fused. The skeleton shows a lot of differences. There's a more primitive arrangement of the ribs, for one thing. Mike here is working with Paddles's intelligence tests, doing the work for his degree at Arlington, aren't you, Mike?"

"A B.Sc.," assented Mike. "Nancy's helping me, she's got her B.Sc. already."

It was Nancy who explained to me why only the male dolphin was being tested. "He won't let Pinky do anything," she said, a tinge of indignation in her voice. "It was that way when they were learning tricks; he never let her even try. If you give her a fish you've got to slip it to her when he isn't looking, or he might beat her up, and he'll splash you for doing it. We're just going to run a series of the horizontal-vertical tests, to prove that these animals can see the difference between black and white. Want to watch?" He told me that Dr. James Philips, assistant professor of psychology at Arlington, had started the tests a year earlier, using all-black and all-white objects, Paddles remembered the distinction even after a year's rest. By this time another girl, named Phyllis, had joined the Lobbs, and Lawrence Curtis retired to his office to catch up on correspondence. We three women went down to the window side of the tank, and both dolphins immediately swam over to peer at us inquisitively through the glass. Mike remained at the front railing, a bucket of fish at his feet and a whistle in his hand. The girls stood ready, each holding a large square white placard in her hand, painted boldly with a black bar. I went up to see the proceedings from Mike's side. The dolphins had swum over and were bobbing about near him. "Okay," he shouted. "Go!"

Through the rippling water two black bars appeared as the girls held them to the windows, horizontal on the extreme left window, vertical at the extreme right. "He's supposed to go to the horizontal bar," Mike explained. "Now let's see." The male porpoise took a little dash toward the right window, hesitated, then swam in a wide curve around the tank, pausing briefly at the vertical bar but finally pointing his beak definitely at the horizontal. Mike blew the whistle and threw him a fish, to show him that he had hit on the right answer. "But I don't like his going to the right first," he said.

Several more tests worked out exactly the same way. The three trainers were dissatisfied. "He's never drifted to the right so persistently before," said Mike. "I don't know . . . think he's got something wrong with the other eye?"

Phyllis argued that the signs were too wide apart. "He can't get them both into his vision at once," she said. "Last time we were much closer together. Let's try that again, and see if it makes a difference."

I went back to the downstairs side, fascinated by the head-on view I got there of the animals' birdlike faces and the bodies behind them that looked so large and bulky, yet moved so lightly through the green water. The whistle blew; again Paddles had hesitated.

"Let's try Phyllis's idea," called Nancy. "Another thing, Paddles is

[25]

KODIAK BEAR

[26]

EMPEROR PENGUIN

[27]

POLAR BEAR

[28]
WHITE-HANDED GIBBON

[29]

ROOSEVELT'S OR OLYMPIC ELK

[30]

FISHING OWL

[31]

PROBOSCIS MONKEY

[32]

FLAT-HEADED CAT

beginning to jump the gun. I think he can hear you tell us to get ready, and he understands it."

Mike didn't want to follow the suggestion, but at last he consented to try once, at least. "But I still think he'll go to the right," he grumbled. "Okay, unbeliever," said Phyllis. "We'll try, anyway." The girls moved closer toward each other, to one side of the windows. They put up their placards, and Paddles at once, with perfect ease, swam to the horizontal bar and nosed the glass. Everybody cheered. "He's learning, he's learning!" cried Mike. "Phyllis was right." Even when the girls reversed their cards, so that Phyllis's was horizontal and Nancy's was vertical, Paddles picked the right one. I said, "That's remarkable."

"Isn't it?" asked Nancy. "And when you think that up until twenty years ago people thought they were blind! When we finish this series we're going to try him on color. You know, if a leaf or something falls into the pool, no matter how small it is, Pinky gets it and takes it over to that waste pipe over there."

"Did you ever train them to do the things marine porpoises do at the shows?" I asked. Nancy said,

"Oh yes, and they used to do them all right—Paddles did, that is. But I think he's too smart for all that. After a while he got bored and refused to perform any more."

The day's lesson was over, but it seemed that the Lobbs couldn't simply walk out with their books and papers, because the pool had to be cleaned up. Debris from half-eaten fish lay on top of the water, and more fragments rested at the bottom of the pool. Mike scrubbed the bottom with a long-handled broom, then angled for the stuff on the surface, using a net with a long, jointed handle. To distract the dolphins' attention Nancy threw a beach ball at them, but only Pinky reacted and played with the ball. Paddles preferred to bother Mike, playfully catching at the net with his teeth. Lawrence came in to help, brandishing the broom at the pink porpoise to keep him away. "He could rip that net in no time," he explained. Paddles caught the net again, shaking and worrying it like a terrier. "Mischievous," said Mike in fond tones. "After the visual tests we're starting on echolocation. We'll run them through obstacles in the dark."

"And we can really darken this tank," added Lawrence. "It's much better than an outdoor pool as far as that's concerned. But you never know everything in a zoo until you've built a place and made mistakes. This roof is too low—notice that spotty pattern on the ceiling? People ask me seriously what modern artist I got to paint it, but it's what the porpoises do when they blow. The ceiling ought to be at least three feet higher. Better luck next time."

I took a last look at the porpoises, ready to follow the Lobbs and Phyllis out. Lawrence said, "You'll see them again tomorrow. I hope you brought a bathing-suit with you?"

"Why, no. I never thought—"

"Oh, you'll have to go in swimming with the porpoises," said Lawrence. "You can't come all this way and not do that. It's a lot of fun. I often go in."

"I suppose I could buy a suit," I said uncertainly.

I returned to the aquarium next afternoon, a bundle under my arm, to find the director's office unusually busy and crowded. The secretary showed me to an empty office where I could change. By the time I reached the tank room, the crowd had transferred itself to the waterside. I paused. "Oh no!" I said. Newspaper cameramen were there, and a television crew, all ready to shoot. "No!" I said again. "Listen, this is all a mistake. I'm not even a good swimmer, for God's sake—I can't dive or go under water or anything like that. I can't even *dive*. I'll have to go in by ladder."

"Oh, that's all right," said Lawrence cheerfully. "We've got a ladder." Somebody fetched it. Two men knelt down to hold it in place for me. It was like that nightmare when you are up onstage and forget your lines, and all of a sudden realize you have no clothes on. Accepting that it *was* only a nightmare, since there was nothing else to do, I stepped on the top rung of the ladder and started down. Flashlights popped. One of the men holding the ladder said that the floor of the pool seemed mighty slippery, and just as I clambered down to the fourth rung the whole thing slid out from under. More flashlights popped as I fell in. "Whoosh!" I said, surfacing.

At least I was down in the water with the dolphins, but I couldn't see into the middle of things as I had from up above. Lawrence leaned over the edge and said, "They're looking you over. Just swim around for a while." Obeying, I began to discern the animals at last, swimming around below me, crisscrossing the pool, circling me, watching. After a long time going back and forth on top of the water while they went in the opposite direction beneath, I paused at the railing side, and Lawrence handed me a fish. "Now slap the top of the water with it," he directed me, "and then hold it in the water at arm's length. They're still studying you. They can't be pushed." I slapped the water with the fish and waited. Paddles circled the tank, giving me a wide berth but coming very slightly closer with each round. In his trail, as always, came Pinky, staying even farther away from me. From his observation post Lawrence kept up a commentary: "He's getting nearer. It won't be too long now. Next time . . . if he gets your finger by mistake, just wiggle it a little." At this point Paddles made a grab that fell short. Next time around, very delicately, the long, toothed beak removed the fish from my fingers. Lawrence promptly lowered another. "Hold it nearer to you this time," he said. Paddles took that fish right away. "Now, swim on out into the middle and see if he comes," said Lawrence.

He didn't, for a while. I swam and floated, and had just about given up when something tickled my foot. I yelled, giggling, "Quit that!" and whirled around in time to see Paddles's long nose tickle the other foot. All of a sudden, as if he had made up his mind once and for all, he swam up to me, under me, around me, behaving like a rollicking puppy. He would swim beneath and rise up to bump me. When I held his dorsal fin he swam around the tank and gave me a ride. It was as if he knew I didn't want to go underwater; he, too, stayed on top at these moments. Remembering the Greek boy, I rode him for a short minute. I petted him and he rolled over on his back so that I could rub his pink stomach. He was smoother, I thought, than *Tursiops*. Pinky stayed outside the circle, wistfully peering at us sideways and plunging about us as close as she dared.

It is hard to describe adequately how all this romping made me feel. I can say, of course, that it was great fun. I can say I was delighted. This is true, but it isn't all. I don't want to sound sentimental because it wasn't a sentimental feeling, but throughout the game I had an impression, crazy as it may sound, that Paddles and I were friends. It wasn't at all like the relationship one has with a domesticated animal however close the animal may be in one's life or however fond one may be of the dog, cat or horse. This was on an entirely different plane. Paddles was a personality to which you couldn't condescend. Paddles could laugh with me and at me . . . I *liked* him.

"Are you ever coming out?" someone called.

CHAPTER 26

The Private Zoo

☐

"Besides myself, various private persons in different parts of the world have achieved considerable success in acclimatisation," wrote Carl Hagenbeck. "The famous Falz-Fein keeps all the animals on his estate in the Crimea out in the open. The Duke of Bedford similarly keeps his fine collection roaming at large about the great park at Woburn. Lord Rothschild also has in his park very fine collections. What greater pleasure can there be for a private gentleman than that of maintaining and establishing personal friendships with a large collection of foreign animals?"

What indeed? Mystifying as the taste may seem to most of the world, it existed and still exists today, though many modern people who keep private menageries bankrupt themselves for the cause. Even in the most favorable circumstances, keeping wild animals in private establishments is not a simple thing. For this reason, some persons control their appetites and concentrate on one species only: Leonard Williams is one of these, as I used to be when I kept gibbons in the Far East—then, unwisely, I branched out for a while and kept rhesus as well, and it led to trouble. I know a woman who manages to co-exist with a husband and a variegated lot of wild as well as domesticated animals in a New York house, but hers is not exactly a private zoo: she rents the animals out for photographic or dramatic purposes. I've had tea with Mr. and Mrs. d'Essen in company with a lar gibbon, two litters of puppies, a kangaroo, a cat, and a large white llama. We managed splendidly, but Mrs. d'Essen admitted that her life is sometimes complicated. "The worst moment I've ever had was with our lion," she said. "He was just a cub at first, but lions grow awfully fast. One day I happened to look out of the window, and saw that he'd slipped through the front door. He was playing in that little garden. You see, he thought he was a cat—well, of course he *is* a cat, but he thought he was a house cat, and just as I looked he jumped up on the fence and stalked along it, just the way our house cat does. Luckily, nothing terrible happened, but the neighbors could have made a lot of trouble. We keep him in the country now."

Zoos are always being presented with monkeys that until then have been pets. A privately owned monkey becomes troublesome, because monkeys need a lot of attention to keep their egos happy, and after a while the owner usually carts it off to the zoo, where he expects to meet with a glad reception and many thanks for his bounty. In fact, as zoo men have told me, such donations are not at all welcome. "A pet monkey just doesn't realize that he's a monkey," explained one curator. "He doesn't settle down with others of his kind: how could he be expected to know they're his kind? Most pet monkeys never meet another one. He's identified himself with the humans he grew up with, and it's hard on him, suddenly throwing him in with a lot of strange animals. Sometimes the others pick on him and we have to put him somewhere else, give him a lot of special attention. Pet monkeys are more trouble than they're worth."

At the other end of the scale are collectors who do things in the grand manner. It may not be exactly eighteenth-century style, but it's grand enough. A young man in London quietly keeps quite a lot of gorillas. He had nine at one time: at the moment he still owns seven. There was Hearst's Zoo at San Simeon, and there used to be many in England, a number of which are now open to the public. In London not long ago a friend told me about a man he sometimes encountered at the local pub, whose flat was evidently full of unusual animals which he'd seen looking out of the windows. "I don't know what he hasn't got in there," continued my friend. "I've identified a baboon and what I'm sure is some kind of bear, and sometimes I see birds. If you're interested I'll ask him to let you go and see them." Later he sent me the man's telephone number, with the advice that I should call him up, and I did. A harried, fluttering voice replied. I said, "Hello, is that Mr. Blank? I'm told that you keep animals, is that true?"

"Oh yes, yes. You were the photographer, were you? . . . Forgive me, I'm muddled about things today because I'm in the most appalling mess—my man has suddenly left me, and you've no idea what this place looks like. What did you say you wanted?"

A shrill scream in the background, not quite human, sounded out as I explained.

"Yes, yes, I remember now," he said, "but I'm afraid it's out of the question, quite out of the question. With my assistant gone there's nobody to clean up, and everything, even the window glass is— I'm sure you understand. I couldn't dream of letting a lady—mind you, some of my animals are very interesting. My favorite just now is a baboon, an olive baboon. A very interesting creature she is, but I often wonder if I have the right to keep her as I do, without a mate of her own sort. There is another baboon available, not exactly the same species, but I wonder if he wouldn't do. I'm thinking about it. Really, living in London is so distracting that I feel I must move to the country. Cumberland. That's what I'll do. Tell me, Miss Uh, you've obviously had a good deal of experience—do you think one's *right?*"

"Right to do what?" I asked in bewildered tones.

"Oh, you know. To give these animals a home, to—oh well, as long as they seem happy and healthy I don't have to ask myself that question. Cumberland will make them happy. Good-by, Miss Uh. I've so enjoyed our chat. And thank you for helping me to come to a decision."

He is an extreme case, perhaps, but it's an illustration. Of quite another type was the eleventh Duke of Bedford and his Woburn Park, which have cropped up so often in these pages. This is a zoo book, not a discussion of the stately homes of England, so we won't talk much about the present, thirteenth, Duke and his background, which he has written about in A *Silver Plated Spoon*. It was his grandfather who built up the animal collection that still flourishes at Woburn: one could not discuss the earlier days of the London Zoological Society without referring to him, and often. He must have been Carl Hagenbeck's most valued client. According to his grandson, he was passionately interested only in this hobby. He did his duty by his tenants, was icily polite to his wife, quarreled with his son, treated his grandson with extraordinary coldness, but when it came to the animals, particularly the deer, nothing was too good for them. Woburn's three thousand acres were stocked with splendid herds. He raised pheasants and cattle, the usual things, but the rarities of the animal kingdom were what attracted him, and it was this taste—or quirk, as the present Duke might call it—that saved for the world two species, Père David's deer and the Przewalski horse.

Père David's deer is a strange-looking animal, large for a deer, with a long tail that is tufted at the end. When the young French Jesuit missionary, Père Armand David, first saw them in 1865 or 1866, enclosed in the Imperial Hunting Park near Peking—behind a wall forty-five miles long—they were already extinct in the wild, and had been for perhaps two or three thousand years. What happened next is obscure. According to one story, Père David brought out a skull and a skin of the animal, not a live specimen. But certainly, through some mysterious means, a few of these deer were later transported alive to England and the Continent, where they entered various collections. The Duke of Bedford was determined to get hold of all of them, and ultimately did so. He kept them at Woburn, where they did well and began to breed. Back in China, in 1895, a flood breached the forty-five-mile wall, and all but twenty of the deer escaped through the gap and were promptly killed by the peasants. Then in 1900, during the Boxer rebellion, the rest were slaughtered, so the only Père David's deer left in the world were at Woburn in England. Then the Duke, always a sensible man where animals were concerned, began to think that he should not keep them all together. If the hoof-and-mouth disease should hit the herd, the government would undoubtedly insist on killing them all off. Therefore he dispersed them, entrusting one pair to Regent's Park, another to Paris, and so on. Today many leading zoos have specimens of this deer, and a stud book, maintained at Woburn, is carefully kept up to date. In *Yearbook* Number 6, 436 Père David's deer are listed, in forty-six collections, and Woburn possesses by far the largest number. The animals are difficult to catch without inflicting injury, and whenever one is to be sent to another collection from Woburn, an infant is taken from its mother at birth and bottle-fed, so that it is tame enough to handle when the time comes.

"Yes, those deer," said His Grace the thirteenth Duke without marked enthusiasm. "You'll want to see the herd, won't you? I'll ask my animal man to take you around if you like."

It was an overcast day at Woburn, and only a few cars were parked under the enormous trees outside the gate. But almost never is there a complete absence of visitors, not since the Duke put his estate on the "Stately Homes" list and opened it to the public so that he could collect money to keep the place. More than any other of the noble houseowners he has tried to give people their money's worth, scandalizing more conservative colleagues with the innovations he is prepared to make —a children's playground, teas, a fruit-barrow, water-scooters on the lake, a nudist camp, and large helpings of himself, as guide and signer of guidebooks. He has willingly gone on television and embraced any other opportunity that offered to publicize Woburn still further. He works hard and has been successful—so far—in keeping the house and grounds that he loves so much. And of course he keeps up the animals too, though his enthusiasm for them is distinctly limited, as he explained: "You see, my grandfather and father were so keen on that sort of thing that I've rather turned against it. The animals bore me—but they do well, oh yes, they do well. We have excellent people looking after them."

His head animal man, Mr. Talbot, who indeed showed far more enthusiasm than his employer, drove me around the grounds in his car to find the Père David's deer. On the way he spoke of other animals they have at Woburn—three sarus cranes ("We have one extra hen that keeps flying off; we're going to pinion her today"), and the pheasantry, which raises ten thousand common pheasants a year for shooting. Woburn supports a nice little herd of European bison and another of American bison. At a distance we saw a large number of sika deer. "That's the public's idea of a deer," said Mr. Talbot approvingly, "the sika. Exactly like that."

We were driving over grass near a hedgerow, with a great wave of leaping rabbits being stirred up every few minutes as we rolled along. Mr. Talbot went over the list for me: twenty-four axis deer—a very rare species nowadays—red fallow, muntjac, Chinese water deer, Indian swamp, Bennett's wallabies, the Old English Chartley cattle, which are now rated as wild animals, though they started out as a domesticated breed. He put on the brake and shouted to the driver of another car passing us, "Where are the Père David, do you know?" The man shouted directions, and we drove on. "It's a pity you can't see the golden carp in the pond by the dairy," he continued. "We lost them all, unfortunately, in the severe winter of 1963. There was one that must have been nearly a hundred years old. The Duke's father used to call them to be fed with a series of bells, one for each, the largest bell for the biggest carp and so on down. What's this, I wonder?" Again he put on the brakes. We were now on a road that ran between straight rows of trees. Ahead of us was a parked car with a man and woman standing near it. A dog was running around, sniffing. "Signs everywhere, saying no dogs must run loose," muttered Mr. Talbot as he got out of the car and advanced on the offenders. There was a short conversation, and then the strangers called their dog, piled into the car and drove away, looking angry.

" 'We just thought we'd let him have a run,' " quoted Mr. Talbot as he got back behind the wheel. "Really, people! You'd think they were *trying* to kill themselves or the animals. They'll drive off the road right into the herds during the season when the deer are dropping fawns, though we have signs everywhere warning them . . . There they are, the Père David." Ahead of us the great animals cropped the grass or stood with antlered heads held high against the horizon, as if posing. The park stretched on all sides, so large that no boundaries were visible. Grass and trees were softly green in a faint mist. The deer looked at the car as we started up again, and showed no obvious concern, but moved away easily, so that for a while we followed a shifting wall of long legs, powerful bodies, and proud necks. "There must be about three hundred here," said Mr. Talbot, turning the car around at last. We headed back to the Abbey.

In the spring of 1965 another stately-home owner, Lord Bath of Longleat in Wiltshire, announced a plan to attract the public that for sheer daring and originality, many declared, outdid the Duke of Bedford. He would have a lion park, he said. Other people had deer parks, but his would be a lion park. As a matter of fact it sounded very much like the "Kenya" exhibition featured at Tama Park in Japan, drive-in entrance for cars, enclosure with free-ranging lions and all, but to read the protests in the correspondence columns of the press one would have thought that the whole thing had been freshly dreamed up by Satan himself. The danger of it! The cruelty of it! The degradation, the bad taste, and all to earn mere money to maintain the idle aristocracy! Protests were made to MPs, and the RSPCA investigated, but Lord Bath built his park in the wilds of Wiltshire and put his lions in, behind walls of officially-declared height and thickness. To date they have hurt nobody, and tourists find them delightful. For some reason, a lot of zoo people do not. "I won't go to look at that place," declared one, passionately. "I want no part of it." I wondered why. Surely, lions comparatively at large are better off than lions in a cage.

The eleventh Duke of Bedford's name crops up again in the history of the Przewalski horse, that wild Mongolian quadruped whose already uncertain survival was gravely imperiled in the Second World War. It was the Duke who commissioned Hagenbeck to go to Mongolia and capture specimens from the wild herds that were still, if scantily, extant at the time. Such horses by now are probably completely extinct in the wild, but at that time Hagenbeck's men were able to bring back a number of them. The pick of the lot went to Woburn, though several others were bought by Continental zoos. Later the Duke rounded up as many as he could find in those zoos, and set to work building up a breeding herd. Then again, as in the case of the deer, he had second thoughts and distributed his animals among various collections. Woburn has none any more. The horses' stud book shows that there are at least one hundred twenty-one of these animals in twenty-nine zoos, not counting the herd at Askaniya Nova, where the authorities won't tell how many they have. No private zoo has Przewalskis any more, but it was the Duke of Bedford in Britain and Falz-Fein in the Crimea, private collectors both, who were responsible for saving the breed.

Many a public zoo, as I have indicated, started out as a private one. Chester in England is a notable example, but there are many more. The Jersey Zoological Park is one, as readers of Gerald Durrell's books already know—he collected the animals and then couldn't find anywhere to exhibit them until Jersey gave him shelter. During the span of my researches I myself have witnessed the translation of a private zoo, or at any rate a privately owned one, into a respectable institution of *Yearbook* status. It was Caroline Jarvis who told me of it. There was an interesting little zoo, she said, up in Warwickshire or perhaps Leicestershire—on the border, anyway—run by two women who were very good at primates, and the matter of putting it on the approved list had just about been settled. She was correct, as always: the next issue of the *Yearbook* carried an entry about Zoo Park, Twycross, at Atherstone, Warwickshire, directors Miss M. W. Badham and Miss S. N. Evans. Thirty-two acres . . . Special Exhibits: apes, South American primates.

I arrived in the early afternoon, to find a new-looking park spread out over flat, fertile-looking land. Having become wise about the terrain of zoos, I decided that it had formerly been a farm, and that the old-looking stone house near the gate was the original farmhouse. I was probably right, but there never seemed time to ask, once I had announced myself and been led upstairs in the gray house to the office of Miss Badham, a tall woman in jodhpurs. She gave me the freedom of the place to look around, and invited me for tea afterward. A smaller woman also in jodhpurs, introduced as the head keeper, took me under her wing, and we visited it all, seeing, among other animals, gibbons in a splendidly large enclosure, ring-tailed lemurs with a new baby, a pair of lions, a leopard, tapirs, orangutans, and an impressive number of chimpanzees. "All this started with one chimp," said the head keeper as we walked over a grassy stretch toward the new sea-lion pool. "Miss Badham will tell you. We only moved here lately from Leicestershire . . . This flamingo pool isn't bad, I think, considering it was just a mud patch when we started . . . At this zoo we don't *cater* to the public. We just want to have the animals we like, and if people aren't satisfied, let them stay away." It was new hearing a zoo keeper talk like that, and I found her stimulating.

"I used to breed dogs before we got into this," said Miss Badham over the teacups. Her partner was there too, but insisted on letting Miss

Badham do most of the talking. "I bred dachs and Scotties, and we had a pet shop in Sutton Coldfield. One day at Olympia, at a dog and caged-bird show, we noticed a great crowd up at the other end of the place, and when we investigated we found they were looking at two young chimpanzees. We bought them then and there, and it changed our entire lives." They had not enjoyed the company of these new acquaintances very long, she continued, before they had bought yet another chimp, sight unseen. As things turned out, the new ape wasn't as pleasant a character as the first two, but the girls persevered and got a fourth one about a year later, and she turned out to be the most intelligent of all.

"We were still living over the pet shop in a small flat," said Miss Badham, "but the place was coming down around our ears, and people kept asking if they couldn't have just a look at the chimps, so we moved to the country, to a house on an acre of ground where we could build onto it for a chimp-room and a large run."

The expense of this more ambitious establishment was met by training the chimps to pose in various costumes for photographs which were then made into colored postcards and sold at gift shops and department stores all over England. Then a national tea company's advertising agent hired the apes and began making short films of them engaged in various activities—boiling water in teakettles, pouring tea, relishing tea parties—which in that zoophilic country rapidly became very successful in television commercials. The chimps became better and better known, and so did the tea they advertised. Misses Badham and Evans took them around the country on personal-appearance tours, and very soon they were a British institution. "Our chimps' earnings still underwrite the whole zoo," said Miss Badham proudly.

Inevitably the Badham-Evans collection proliferated and grew more variegated, until the ladies realized that they would have to enlarge the premises once again. A factor that made it urgently necessary, explained Miss Badham, was that their favorite chimpanzee had grown old and was too large to keep in the act, let alone keep around the house as a pet. What was one to do with her? "We couldn't bear to sell her to a circus or a zoo for the few years she had left, though a lot of people in our position do that sort of thing. One might as well sell one's own relative. So we decided to have a proper zoo once and for all, where there would be space for her, and company. In any case we were already running a zoo in everything but name. People were visiting us in such numbers we'd started charging them admission . . . The origin of the zoo, then, was that we wanted to provide a home for retired chimps so that circus people needn't shoot them, as had always been done until now. But our place has grown tremendously since the days when we first got our permit. We've had to move twice—the first place wasn't big enough, so we came here two years ago and opened on a shoestring. We have the best record in the country for South American monkeys, though woollies are difficult; we've bred three and never managed to rear them. I think we need a better female woolly. In general it's going very well, though the public are a great trial. We don't put up with any nonsense, but it's hard to watch them every minute; not long ago I caught a boy shooting at our little gray seal with a slingshot. I took him by the nape of the neck and threw him straight out the gate. Oh, I'm willing to admit that a few visitors are good for the animals—to keep them interested, in the same way that taking the chimps around for personal appearances keeps them healthy and lengthens their lives. Chimps need a lot of attention: you can't afford to ignore them. But the public . . ." She broke off and shook her head. Tea over, Miss Evans left the room for a moment and returned with three small apes scampering ahead of her—two chimps and a gibbon.

"This is their playtime," explained Miss Badham.

Because the Catskill Game Farm, the president of which is Roland Lindemann, is called in its entry in the *Yearbook* "Private Zoo," I am including it in this chapter. In fact, however, Lindemann and his Game Farm belong in a separate category. He is a breeder who sells his animals, so one could call him a dealer. He is an active conservationist as well. The zoo is maintained on part of the nine hundred plus acres of the Farm, making the place eligible for the *Yearbook* list, but whether or not it is included hardly matters: zoo people everywhere in the world know Roland Lindemann. With his director and general curator, Heinz Heck, nephew of the Munich director, he had gone to a meeting in Milwaukee on the day I visited the Game Farm, but the assistant curator Frank Dovigh took care of me. The wooded grounds, in the foothills of the Catskills, are quiet and seem so remote that it is hard to believe one of the state's biggest and busiest roads runs close by.

"Specialty; large breeding herds of rare ungulates, animal nursery, educational facilities for staff," says the entry, explaining why most of the farm's land is out of bounds to the public. Within these private compounds the animals are left to get on with their breeding. Before Mr. Dovigh took me into the forbidden area, we walked around the exhibition pens and read the signs, which at Catskill Game Farm are explicit and businesslike, as witness the one at the gate:

"Well-meaning visitors killed Jerry, our prize giraffe. Please understand. No candy, potato chips, pretzels or crackers of any kind. Limited quantity animal food available inside."

I had found Mr. Dovigh in his office in a large farmhouse that was furnished like a Black Forest shooting box. But it is a breeding farm, not a shooting box, and the labels on the exhibit cages leave no doubt of that. "ONAGER—BABY JUNE 14, '65, PRZEWALSKI—BABY JUNE 24, '65. A few go further and are distinctly chatty, as for instance the one on the Poitou ass enclosure: "This stately donkey, at one time raised extensively in Poitou, France, and seldom seen in captivity, was previously used for breeding purposes in order to obtain large mules. With the advance of the motor age they have practically vanished. This trio is the only exhibit in the U.S. Arrived July 19, 1961." Another message announced that Catskill has sent to the new zoo in Los Angeles one pair of tarpan, one pair of Mrs. Hartman's mountain zebra, one pair of Przewalski, one pair of onagers and one of yak. Wandering among the pens, I began to feel confused. Lechwi water buck, a herd of twenty yak, Congo buffalo— "Three point three down here, five point five up in the breeding area," said Mr. Dovigh proudly—and any number of other unfamiliar animals as well as some old friends. "We've had one hundred percent breeding success with our dromedaries the past two years. The trick is to stay right there with the newborn animal for at least forty-eight hours. Yes, we had sixteen young without one loss. Here the contact area begins," he said. "It's a feeding area. That male king vulture we hatched out here in 1960; he hasn't got his adult plumage yet. I believe only four others have been bred in captivity. That pair of pumas were raised on the bottle. Those are hyrax. When we got them in '63, we also got a lot of advice on how to make them breed. We disregarded all of it, and they've bred very well—we have forty-five in there now. As you see, we have lots of lambs; you want about a hundred in the contact area. People like them. You probably recognize those dwarf goats. They come from the Cameroons originally, but we weren't allowed to bring them in from Africa because they're hoofed stock, so we waited until the people in Sweden had imported some and bred them, and then we imported them —genuine Swedish Cameroonian goats. They breed very well, sometimes even have triplets. That little train is going to take people over to the bird section, which we're developing and enlarging this year. Here's the animal nursery, so-called: those little houses—they're popular with the kids. We're keeping a young pronghorn antelope here until he's big enough to go up the hill. Do you know what that animal is? It's a hog deer, found in India and Indo-China and not seen very often in captivity, but it's doing well here. Attractive, isn't it? That's a male. We started with 2.3, now we have 5.4 and that male baby. Here is a banteng, with a baby born a week ago. We just sent a pair to Brookfield. As you see, we have a lot of rare animals. Some of our acquisitions are three Père David's deer, which haven't started breeding here yet in the Catskills, though she gave birth to a female baby in quarantine. There's an anoa, that little kind of cow, from the Celebes—one of the threatened species. We haven't had good luck with the breed. Pittsburgh sent us a female for breeding, but she died. There's another female in Cincinnati and we're trying to arrange something there."

Then we drove up the road to a gate which he had to unlock, and arrived at the breeding grounds which were also, he explained, a quarantine area and general retiring-place for animals distressed by visitors. Here, everything was strictly plain and utilitarian, each group living in its own roomy paddock. Mr. Dovigh drove slowly along, pointing out animals in such profusion that my mind began to swim again, Przewalski, blesbok, Persian onager, nilgai, white-tailed gnu, Osborn caribou, Siberian roe deer, Congo buffalo, scimitar-horned oryx. "Those oryx are the only ones of their kind in the States," he said. "And there, look. A pair of white rhino. It's a species that has never yet bred in captivity, but we have hopes. They're still young, and there's nothing to bother them here."

The car's noise was the only man-made disturbance in the whole quiet, waiting area.

CHAPTER 27

The Dealers

☐

The *International Zoo News* of Holland is a trade paper primarily, and so, between articles on special animals born in zoos and other news from abroad—"Vampire Bat Expedition," "New Guinea Fauna for Chester Zoo." "Crowned Cranes at Kumasi"—there are advertisements. I save my *Internationals* because it is a good magazine, so I had a wide choice recently when I reached out and picked up a copy at random to look at the ads. It turned out to be the July 1966 number, where I noted a full-page spread on behalf of G. van den Brink N.V., Soest, in Holland: "We are preparing a New Expedition to Africa and expect to be able to deliver the following species within a couple of months: sable antelopes, nyalas, Cape hartebeests. . . . The animals will (be) quarantined in our own quarantine station in Bremen, West Germany, approved by the Bremen and USA authorities; or acclimatized in our compounds at Soest."

Next comes a notice from the International Animal Exchange of Ferndale, Michigan, and Nairobi, Kenya: "Invitation to all Zoological Parks," cordially inviting "surplus and wants on all specimens; whether buying, selling or exchanging, you will find our excellent services a pleasing experience. Actively involved in the procurement of many rare African animals, we offer:

CHOICE SPECIALITIES IN STOCK

1.1 Dibatag (*The notation means one male, one female*)
1.2 Black Back Duiker

ALSO: Cheetah, Chimps, African Elephants, Aldabra Tortoises, Bengal Tigers, Caracal Cats, Serval Cats, Jaguars, Pumas, Wild Caught African Lions

R.S.V.P.

The Tyseley Pet Stores Ltd. of Birmingham offer "The Largest Display of Birds and Animals in England," and there were smaller notices from Bazizoo of Cros-de-Cagnes, Nice (Large Collection of Lemurs from Madagascar). "Pets Exotiques" of Nairobi, and P. N. Das & Sons of Calcutta. Then another Hollander. Then Chop Jin Seng of Singapore (Cable: Finches). Trefflich's, New York. Portsmouth, Meerut, Nairobi again, Belgium, Vienna, Constantia Valley in South Africa, Ethiopia, Florida—a lot from Florida—and a full-page spread about F. J. Zeehandelaar Inc., New Rochelle.

Clearly the animal trade is not moribund, I reflected. What kind of people engage in it nowadays? No doubt everybody my age remembers Frank Buck and the Martin Johnsons, and all those films they made of charging rhino, pygmies, chimps, and snakes—collectors for middlemen rather than middlemen themselves. I can recall an early contact with a middleman, a wild animal dealer, not a cat-and-dog man, that took place when I first came to New York and lived in a bed-sitting room. One day, wandering for some reason down to Fulton Street, I found Trefflich's store and went in, and half an hour later, when I came out, I was the owner of a small bear cub with an endearing bowlegged stance. I'd got it at a bargain price, but my landlady didn't appreciate that fact. She told me to take the bear straight back where I'd got it, and it was no use arguing with her. The cub went back. Another, later venture into the world of dealers turned out better, when in London, in the thirties, I wanted to buy an olive baboon as a present for the Oxford Department of Anthropology. Oddly enough this transaction, complicated as it sounds, was perfectly simple. I found the name of a dealer in Camden Town in the telephone book, went there to investigate, and found the baboon straight off. Those were the days, I said to myself as I put down the *International News*, and I wondered if it would be easy today to buy a baboon in London. Did the shop itself still exist?

It was there, all right, when I went to look for it. Nothing in its outward appearance was much altered, but a lot of the interior had been given over to budgerigar food, bird cages, and the like, and in the rest of the place, where they keep the livestock, there was not an olive baboon in sight—the only primates visible were a few Javanese macaques and a capuchin. The proprietor said that he was called on now and then to supply small pythons for debutantes, pythons being fashionable at the time, but his customers for the most part wanted dogs, cats, or birds. Sometimes, though infrequently, he receives in a shipment some rare mammal or bird, and when this happens he gets in touch with the Zoological Society and gives them first refusal. For the rest it's pretty

dull, just dogs, cats, and birds. "Though I do negotiate now and then
for a gorilla," he added as an afterthought. "For a London gentleman."
The London Zoological Society, like the other societies and zoos of
Britain, get most of their animals direct from abroad, he said, or by
swapping among themselves.

When I came to New York I resumed the study of the modern dealer.
Not only because I had fond memories of my lost bear, but because a
curator at the Bronx Zoo gave me the name of Trefflich's as an outstanding dealer, coupled with that of Zeehandelaar of New Rochelle, I
retraced my steps to Fulton Street. Here, too, time seems to have stopped
still, at least for Trefflich's building, though other, newer houses stand
nearby. Famous to two or three generations of animal buyers, it is an old
red-brick four-story structure, a thin rectangular building with the name

T
R
E
F
F
L
I
C
H

painted on it from the attic to the bottom of the third floor, in the
style of a younger, more ebullient day. The sign was designed for people
riding in the El, and though the El is long since gone, there it is. At a
distance, and disregarding it, the place looks like my idea of an O. Henry
boardinghouse, and gives me the same puzzled nostalgia that is stirred up
by the dreaming restaurants of Coney Island in winter. At close quarters,
however, nobody could mistake it for anything but a depot and supply
house for animals. That day the ground-floor shop windows were heaped
with birdseed boxes and puppies, the ensemble seen with difficulty between the many hand-written signs stuck on the inner side of the glass:
"RED-SPOTTED NEWTS, $.35 EACH," "HORNED TOADS 99¢," "WE BOARD DOGS."

Indoors was a scene that for confusion and profusion compared with
the bazaar of Istanbul. There were the noises, for one thing; the barks and
bird-calls. For another, there were the boxes and sacks all over the place.
The counter in front was heaped with prepared animal foods and miniature coats for dogs. Out of a hidden recess behind it, a salesgirl had just
fished a small animal, perhaps a horned toad, for the critical inspection
of a boy with a runny nose. In the rear of the room an alcove was lined

with cages of varying sizes holding birds, garter snakes, tortoises, a fairly
large anaconda, a half-grown Airedale, pugs, small alligatorlike lizards, a
pair of toads mating, and an assortment of hamsters labeled "$1.50 EACH."
I asked a boy who was sweeping the floor where I might find Mr. Trefflich,
at which he stopped sweeping, leaned on the broom, and stared at me
suspiciously.

"You from the municipality?" he demanded. "Sanitary inspector or
something?" When reassured, he pointed to a steep staircase behind him,
and resumed his work.

Upstairs I found a huge room like a barn, filled with cages that
stretched nearly all the way from the rear of the house to the front, but
there gave way to a few partitions. Bearded Mr. Henry Trefflich sat in
one of these, talking into a telephone, and invited me by a gesture to sit
down. Waiting, I looked around and was given a mild shock as my eyes
met the beady false ones of a young stuffed chimpanzee on top of a
whatnot in a corner. Not far from this animal was another stuffed primate,
with moth-eaten tail, clinging to an artificial tree trunk. Everything was
very dusty.

"Looking at the chimp?" asked Mr. Trefflich as he put down the telephone. "I keep it there as an object-lesson. It died from careless handling
—needn't have happened. Excuse me a minute." He turned to the telephone again, dialed a number, and started to talk into the instrument
without salutation: "Listen, Judy, you got any ring-tailed monkeys? You
know what I mean, white-faced, *you* know, with white front and brown
elsewhere. They call 'em capuchin. Colombian, aren't they? Export's prohibited now, so you don't see many around. Let me know." Again he put
down the telephone. "I'm from Hamburg—landed here in 1923," he said.
"I'd always been close to the animal trade. My father had a connection
with the Hagenbecks, used to trap little animals and train them. He was
in the Navy for a while, but in 1906 he started a regular business in
animals, going to India to catch and send them back for Hagenbeck. Later
he had a zoo of his own at Hamburg. As a boy I used to go out collecting
with him. He was good at training police dogs: he did some of that for
the British Army, but when the war came he refused to train any more
unless it was for the Red Cross, and he was locked up for six years on that
account.

"The fact is, I ran away from home and landed here illegally. I worked
in restaurants and all that, and saved up money so that I could go into
business for myself. It's fascinating what you can do in this country—or,
anyway, used to be able to do. I set up in business here in 1930, and
though I've done related work all over the place from time to time, this

has been headquarters ever since. For a long time monkeys were my main import—they called me the Monkey King of America. In 1939 I brought in eight baby gorillas at once. I've introduced a lot of gorillas into this country all in all, but African animals are only a part of it. There was that fellow in Ceylon, a Hagenbeck cousin with a tea plantation—you've heard of him? He got into the animal business because of me, really. All that retail stuff downstairs isn't the backbone of the trade, but I keep it up because people are used to it. Of course I do a lot of trade with zoos all over the world, but it isn't the same as it used to be. Today, a zoo is too much like a department store, and the man who really runs it is the business manager. He's absorbed in a lot of sidelines, and doesn't concentrate on the animals as he ought to. He puts in too many devices for getting revenue out of the public. It isn't good for the collection. Besides—" He sighed. "It's not the same world it used to be. Everybody stocking up on arms, everybody threatening war—what's the matter with the world? In my business you run into national barriers every way you turn, and I often think of old Hagenbeck, the way he did things. He used to keep people from all nations to look after the Hagenbeck animals, paid their way to Hamburg and took good care of them. If we'd all done that we wouldn't be having all this trouble today. We're strangers."

The telephone rang, and he answered it. A woman's voice crackled for a bit. Mr. Trefflich said, "Dead? Are you sure?" The voice, replying, sounded sure. "Well, put it in the icebox, and when you have time bring it back here and we'll see what was the matter . . . No? Well now, let's see. What did you pay for the lizard? . . . All right, bring it in and we'll give you back your two dollars."

"One of the most important things we do is supply rhesus monkeys to laboratories," he continued to me. "You know, for polio research and that kind of thing. This firm supplied ninety percent of the rhesus they used to find out about the RH factor in pregnant women, and we have lots of calls for squirrel monkeys for hepatitis research. It's easier to get squirrels now than it is rhesus: I just had news that the Indians have stopped shipping out rhesus. Stopped completely. What's going on there, have you any idea?"

"There's always been some opposition to sending them," I said. "Religious scruples."

Mr. Trefflich shook his head. Then he delegated one of his assistants to take me around the floor and look at the animals—chimpanzees, African monkeys, a skunk, and an Alsatian puppy were in the front row. As I left, Mr. Trefflich gave me a Xerox copy of two pages about himself in Current Biography 1953, where he is quoted as saying, "Monkeys can teach human beings a lot. They rarely fight among themselves in the jungle." On May 11, 1945, the article says, a hundred or so rhesus escaped from the building and ran wild in the Washington Market area. Neighbors, police, and firemen helped the SPCA to round them up. Mr. Trefflich was called to court to answer a charge that he had failed to safeguard wild animal life and caused injury to the public. He weathered the storm, though more monkeys made their escape the next year, this time at the docks when they were being unloaded. In 1950, at a country place in Virginia, the dealer established a "monkey conditioning" project able to handle a thousand animals at once, where the monkeys could get a chance to settle down a little before being sent on to their purchasers.

I thanked Mr. Trefflich and left. Two little girls came into the downstairs store as I passed through, and before the door swung shut I heard one asking, "Do hamsters eat meat?"

The establishment of Fred J. Zeehandelaar is in complete contrast to Trefflich's. Seeing one straight after the other, I wondered if I had not made a mistake in supposing they were in the same business at all. Mr. Zeehandelaar lives in New Rochelle and keeps an office in the downtown district of that peaceful place. Walking up from the station I looked in vain for any signs of wild animals in back yards. None of the office buildings seemed to have back yards, however. Even a cat would have found it hard to get a foothold in Mr. Zeehandelaar's office, upstairs in one of the newest buildings. He is a man full of vitality, which rings in his loud voice and pushes him into constant activity. Apart from the fact that the walls were covered with photographs of animals, his surroundings were like a stockbroker's, full of electronic gadgets. He had the most accomplished telephones I have ever seen, one with that arrangement through which the person on the other end of the line can hear whatever is said anywhere in Mr. Zeehandelaar's office. Before demonstrating this, however, he showed me his library, dealing almost exclusively with animals and animal-collecting. He had obviously read all the books and could quote from most of them, from *Untruths About Animals* (Orville A. Lindquist) to the latest *International Zoo Yearbook*.

"As you can hear from my accent, I am from the Netherlands," he said. "Born in Amsterdam. Like every other able-bodied man in the country I was in the war. I was in the Army from 1939–40 until the country was invaded and taken. They put us into a POW camp in Germany, but in 1942 I escaped and got to England where I rejoined the Army, the Free Dutch Army of course. I was in the 21st Army group. Our brigade landed at Bayeux with the Canadians, and afterward stayed on the continent, stuck in the South Netherlands for six months. In May

1945, after the liberation they sent me north where I stayed for a few months and then was transferred back to London for six months more before I was discharged. Immediately afterward I emigrated to the United States. That was 1946, and the first time I'd seen America. I arrived with five hundred dollars, which I spent fast. I got a job with an import-export firm downtown, and they put me to handling the export of industrial chemicals and the import of spices from India, Indochina, Madagascar—we also had a sideline in copper-mining. Well, about 1950 the pound was devalued, and thirty-five other countries promptly followed, devaluating their currency too. Overnight the United States changed into an impossibly expensive country for all the exporters we did business with, and our firm was badly hit. We had to export—mostly spices, until we'd used up what there was—but we knew we had to do something else as well. A clove shipper in Madagascar wrote to me suggesting that he send us monkeys for medical research and snakes for the making of antivenin. He said he had a lot of both commodities, and would be glad to send samples.

"It was a good idea, and I thought I'd try it. The trouble was I didn't know anything about animals. I wrote to all the zoos in the States that I'd ever heard of, offering them monkeys, and I didn't know how to spell the monkeys' names or where they'd come from. For instance, I said I had rhesus from Africa, beautiful specimens. Well, there can't possibly be a zoo man anywhere in the country that wouldn't know rhesus are Indian. Besides, I didn't know what price to quote—I didn't know anything. Among the jeering replies I got was one that corrected the price I'd quoted for rhesus, which I'd listed at $98 apiece—a figure I'd simply picked out of the air. This correspondent said I was nuts, and that the regular selling price for a rhesus was $38. I wrote back to him excusing myself for my typographical error and offering him rhesus for $36 apiece. He didn't answer that one. In fact, no orders came, but I got a letter from Lindemann of the Catskill Game Farms, asking, 'Who are you, what are you doing, and what do you know about animals?' I replied that I dealt in rare animals of exceptionally beautiful quality.

"The outfit I was with was located at 39 Broadway, and by coincidence Lindemann had worked in the same building long before. One day he showed up. Waiting for me, he heard people all around him talking about ingots, textiles, sheet metal, all the things the firm dealt in, and he got more and more puzzled. Still, he waited until I came in, and we had a talk. He told me about his game farm: I told him what I could about the animal aspect of my business. Finally he said, 'Apparently, as far as I can see, you know absolutely nothing about animals.' I said, 'Yes, that's true.'

He said, 'But you understand business, I suppose. How would I go about getting hold of forty zebras?'

"Now, at the time I was sending out those letters to zoos I had also written to all the U.S. embassies, asking them to put me in touch with animal dealers in their countries. I wrote one hundred and ten of these letters and sent them via Washington, and I'd had ten or fifteen replies from Africa. I figured that if I sent cables to those ten or fifteen people, I could get those zebras, so I said to Lindemann, 'I'll send a telegram to Africa.' He said, 'You know nothing about animals: do you understand international affairs? Anyway, try to get the zebras.' I said, 'How much?' and he said, 'How do I know?' We talked it over and agreed that he would pay all the costs of transport—freight, insurance, import duty, quarantine—plus twenty-five percent over. Then I sent the cables and got a reply from Mombasa the next day, saying they had the zebras at $202 each. By the time we got them here it would work out at about $700 plus twenty-five percent. I signed the contract, and three months later thirty-nine zebras arrived—one had died on the way. It worked out at more than I'd figured—$787 each, plus the twenty-five percent, which went to the firm, of course, because I was only an employee." Mr. Zeehandelaar rattled off these details and prices as if the transaction had taken place a day earlier, instead of more than twenty years ago. "When the war was over," he resumed, "zoos all began asking who the fellow was who had rounded up so many zebras right away, and I was launched. I made the rounds of the zoos regularly, taking orders. A year after that first deal, Lindemann came back and asked me to get him one hundred and forty-six great red kangaroos. I must have got in touch with every farm in Australia. I got them for $315 each plus thirty percent. At that time such kangaroos were worth $600, and Lindemann made a fantastic deal, which I didn't realize at the time. Then I woke up a little. His orders went on, growing bigger—twenty-six camels, a lot of wallabies—until I said to myself, 'He's passing these on to zoos. Why don't I do it myself?' I went to the zoos and told them that I could supply anything they needed. They pooh-poohed me, so I said, 'All right, what do you want? Give me a list of animals you say I can't get: they're the only ones that interest me.' I got my list, and I admit it included some I couldn't get then and can't today. But I supplied ninety percent of them. Every time I delivered, I would say, 'Now, what about some animals I can't get?' until a fantastic story began going the rounds. It wasn't true, but it was interesting. They were saying I could do all this because I was using blocked currency: it's a story that has lasted through my life, and I wish it hadn't.

"I stayed with the firm until 1957. I traveled for them for four years,

making seventy or eighty thousand a year for them, but we quarreled because they complained that I was losing them lots of money, and I never
got credit or commission for what I earned for them. We had arguments,
and in 1957 I broke away, buying myself out at considerable expense.
It was March, and I was living in an attic room here in New Rochelle.
Since then—" He broke off, with an expressive gesture. Clearly he no
longer lived in an attic room.

But, I asked in puzzled tones, what of the animals? Didn't he ever
have direct contact with them?

"Oh yes. I go down to them on arrival at the docks or the airport,
to oversee the formalities. Certainly I see them. I must make sure
they are fit, according to contract, and I take a vet with me," he
said. "But they don't come to New Rochelle. My hobby is communications. I'm communications crazy. My whole business is done
by phone, cable, wire, and teletype. That's a Western Union tape machine. Zoo people like the setup, because in their business personal
relations are very important, and remember, in the animal business
you're dealing, both ways, with people who are, ninety percent of
them, totally ignorant, uneducated people. That's one bad feature about
it—they can't sign checks, don't even know how to write them. They're
ignorant about everything but animals. The other ten percent are
the business people, bankers and such, and if you have them behind
you you're all right. Mind you, there are exceptions, especially among
the directors, and you have an educated crowd in the Zoological Society
officials, who are commercial people and so on. Well, I capitalized on
the ninety percent: I said to myself that personal contact is necessary. I
tell them, 'Zeehandelaar will take care of you. No Wall Street mongers
are in on this.' They like that. There's nobody in the business who doesn't
know me. They don't all like me—some hate me—but that's all right as
long as they speak about me. I've never received a complaint yet about
animals I've delivered. Of course, if a cat is sick or wrong or something
like that I take care of the complaint. I've had two lawsuits opened by
suppliers—one African fellow started making trouble, and when he lost
the case he went to the Court of Appeals and they threw it out. The second fellow—he's dead now—preferred to withdraw on a settlement. I've
never yet had a legal case with a supplier, and that's unique. Because I
want to be reachable day and night, even in my car," he said, "I've got
a car phone.

"You know, there are three sorts of client in this business; zoos make
seventy-five percent of it, research fifteen, and commercial publicity
ten. By commercial publicity I mean the supply of animals for advertising,

photographs and films. I don't operate like d'Essen, who keeps animals for hire; I sell and repurchase them outright—tigers for the Esso commercials, elephants for Tetley's Tea, all that. Some zoos hire out animals for the same kind of thing, but don't publicize it."

He sorted out a number of newspaper clippings and leaflets to give me. Mr. Zeehandelaar believes in speaking his mind in public print, and the selection was large. I looked through it while he talked to his wife and made arrangements for us to meet for lunch. "City a Babe in Woods When Buying Gorillas," was the headline for one story in the *Herald Tribune* for January 29, 1964. "The city may know how to buy fuel oil, lamb chops, and typewriter ribbons, but it doesn't know its way around the gorilla market," went on the reporter. "This, in effect, was how one animal dealer reacted yesterday when told the city was turning down his bid to supply the Central Park Zoo with two gorillas for $13,000 . . . The department had hoped to get a pair for $5000 . . . The bidder, F. J. Zeehandelaar, a wild animal importer from New Rochelle, said, 'What the city budgets is one thing, and what they'll have to pay is another.' Then he gave this explanation for the high cost of gorillas. The city had specified the animals must be guaranteed to be in good health for ten days after delivery to the zoo. The animal dealer said that would require his taking out special insurance that would add thirty per cent to the cost. 'No wonder I was the only bidder. Suppose a keeper leaves a door open, and the gorilla catches cold. Suppose a kid feeds him something that makes him sick?' he asked. 'We're being asked to insure the management of the zoo as well as the health of the gorilla . . . I can tell they don't know much about gorillas down there.' He noted that the specifications called for a male sixteen to seventeen months old and not less than thirty-two pounds, and a female of fourteen or fifteen months not less than twenty-nine pounds. 'The female should be 10 pounds heavier than the male,' the dealer said. 'The male will grow bigger, but at that age the female has to be big enough to say "No!"'"

In August 1963, in the *Daily Oklahoman*, Mr. Zeehandelaar was complimenting the Oklahoma City Zoo: "'There are only two zoos in the country preparing properly for the future,' a noted wild animal importer said Tuesday. Fred J. Zeehandelaar, New Rochelle, N.Y., said Oklahoma City's Lincoln Park Zoo and the Bronx New York Zoo are the only ones looking progressively toward the future. . . . 'they are making the right selection of animals and are willing to pay the right kind of prices.' Zeehandelaar said zoos that are not obtaining proper breeding herds will not have replacement animals. And what will be the result? . . . they will be coming to Oklahoma City trying to obtain the animals because they will be unable to get them from the animals' native land."

On the other hand, in February 1964, he was "rapping" the New Mexican Game and Fish Department, to quote the *Albuquerque Journal*: "Rio Grande Zoo needs a wider variety of animals, according to Zeehandelaar, who suggested cheetahs, black leopards, giraffes, polar bears and either rhinoceroses or hippopotamuses. . . . Zeehandelaar said the zoo here greatly needs public support."

The *Standard-Star* of New Rochelle, in August 1963, ran a photograph of Mr. Zeehandelaar actually standing side by side with a baby elephant, with the caption, "Importer Fred J. Zeehandelaar with one of his 'grandchildren.' The New Rochelle wild animal fancier says he considers all off-spring of animals he has imported as if they were his own grandchildren," which was news to me as well as to the New Rochelle readers.

Mr. Zeehandelaar plonked down more paper on top of my pile. "I send these out once in a while," he said. Each was a mimeographed sheet decorated with colored pictures that illustrated the text. A yellow and blue rocket, for instance, hitting a green moon surface, accompanied the headline, "They said it couldn't be done!" Underneath Mr. Zeehandelaar's business address were paragraphs of which the following is a sample:

> Topis could not be obtained. . . . We have obtained 3.7—lost 0.1— sold 1.3—have 2.3 for sale, *now isolated* in Hamburg-Germany, ready for shipment to USA end of July (USDA approved zoos only). Other items were a U.S.-born giraffe, six orangutans with legal documents, and mongoose lemurs.
> P.S.: Stock (subject unsold) 1/1 AARDVARK—1/0 CLOUDED LEOPARD— 1/1 MALAYA TAPIR—1/1 POLAR BEAR born 1965—1/1 BROWN HYENA —1/1 RINGTAILED LEMUR

"I like this one," he said, picking out a caricature of a brown gnu with a yellow hairpiece, eating yellow hay. The heading was "What's Gnu!" and the page consisted of quizzes. "Did you know that. . . . Orangutans are strictly protected by the International Union for Conservation of Nature due to smuggling from Borneo and Sumatra? Zebras are divided into different species, each differently striped or even partly colored? Giant Pandas are not only nearly-extinct but also prohibited for import into USA due to native habitat Communist China (forbidden trade)? Cheetahs run faster than antelopes (70 mph)? . . ." Unanswered questions

followed: "Why don't you test your knowledge? Is a Lesser Panda a bear?
. . . How many species of hyenas? . . . What is the most dangerous
bear? . . . What is the anteater's diet? . . . What is a cuscus? . . .
dikdik? . . . wowwow? . . . roulroul? . . ."

According to my informant at the Bronx Zoo, Florida has the largest
concentration of animal dealers in the United States. She gave me
names of a number of these, with addresses all over the state, but
I confined my researches to the Miami area. Dr. and Mrs. Henry Field,
the couple who had given me a letter to the Zoocentre in Moscow,
live much of the year there, in Coconut Grove, and on most days,
in their house, Julia Field and I talked about zoos. Julie is a remarkable
woman, fair and beautiful, with a soft voice and the gentlest manners,
I am willing to bet, that any of my readers is likely to encounter in
a lion tamer, which is what she used to be. She started working with
animals when she was just out of her Massachusetts high school, at
Benson's Animal Farm in New Hampshire. There she showed such aptitude
that in a short time, while still only eighteen, she was in complete
charge of the animals. Then she worked in several other establishments
around the country. It was at the World Jungle Compound in California
that she discovered her special talent for training lions. A lion tamer
worked there, and Julie, watching him, became fascinated, and sometimes
asked him if she could try her hand. He merely laughed at her. But
one day he was drunk, and before she realized it he had playfully
shoved her into the training cage and slammed the door behind her,
just as the cats were released into the same place through a chute.
She had seen the routine so often, however, that she did the right
things and came through unscathed. After that she studied under the
best man she could find, and became thoroughly accomplished in the
whipless method, directing the animals with hand gestures. Henry Trefflich, in an "as-told-to" book written with Baynard Kendrick, recounts
the first time he met Julie, who was then working as director of Miami's
Crandon Park Zoo and giving twice-weekly shows with her lions on a
nearby lot. He and a companion, the Captain, went to watch the
lion act. "Dressed for her act in black riding breeches, short riding
boots of soft leather and a white blouse open at the throat, she looked
even younger than the Captain's description had led me to believe. It
seemed incredible that this exquisite blond child with her delicate pro-
file, shining yellow hair, and slight figure could already have a top
reputation as a trainer and directress of a big city zoo. Slender as a
reed, straight as a young pine, I would have expected to find her a

valedictorian of a senior class in high school. Yet when she spoke there was a dignity and maturity in her voice that belied her youthful appearance." "But she's so young," the Captain protested when she started the act. "She works the lions without anything, not even a whip—no chair, no gun—and just one helper."

As luck would have it, on that day Julie's biggest lion, Rudy, played rough. She was scratching his stomach with her foot when he grabbed it and held on with "those crunching jaws" until she reached down and said, "Rudy!" as if to a naughty child. Rudy let go.

But by the time she came to work in Miami she had begun to question the structure of the zoo world and its attendant traffic in wild animals. Many aspects of these disturbed her, until finally she decided to finish forever with zoos and all their works. "No more animals," she said to her husband. In proof of this decision she signed up for a course in architecture and park planning at Cambridge. But it wasn't easy, after all, to forget everything she had devoted much of her life to, and when the time came to write a thesis she chose as her subject, "The Animal in Art." Since then, Julie has done a lot of thinking about zoos. She feels that the animals in them have a formidable array of enemies—political ramps in administration, the hostility and cruelty humans often show to animals, and hideous surroundings. She would like to abolish most zoos and replace them with parks that she envisions as small reserves.

I protested, "Surely not all zoos are bad. Don't you like the Monkey Jungle?" Yes, Julie admitted; Gould's Monkey Jungle is different. I had seen it only that morning, and was full of admiration. It is an establishment about twenty miles south of Miami, past the Serpentarium and the Parrot Jungle: the founders had exactly the right surroundings for their project in a locality where trees and vines grow in profusion. There are a few sideline exhibits, i.e., a chimp show and a collection of primates in cages, but the two outstanding features of the establishment are the free-ranging colony of Javanese macaques and the "Amazonian Rain Forest." This latter is simply a portion of the Jungle's fifteen acres where South American primates, squirrel monkeys, and uakaris mainly, live in a free state. The owners were hopeful that the uakaris, usually difficult to take care of in captivity, would soon breed. None of these animals are timid, though visitors walk close to their favorite haunts. The macaque colony has been there longer and is very interesting. The public can see it only by following a passageway inside a cage, which leads them to various places where the monkeys choose to gather. It is the humans who are restrained, and the animals are free. Signs warn the visitors that anyone teasing or feeding the monkeys will be thrown out—though it would tax the ingenuity even of a small boy to tease or feed anything through the wire. Another sign says briefly, ALL MONKEYS BITE. The macaques frolic about unconcernedly and never roam very far, for they are territorial animals and are fed on their home ground. At one point along the way is a rocky pool into which they dive for food thrown by an attendant, and play about at the edge of the water. During this period the attendant gives a little lecture about the social structure of the group and points out various individuals. "Early in 1933 a small band of monkeys was imported from Singapore and liberated in this natural jungle more or less as an experiment," says the guide leaflet. "Not only did this little band of immigrants from far off Asia decide the jungle was satisfactory, but they set up their own government, ruled by a chief, and took over the jungle so completely that it was soon found necessary to construct a cage to protect visitors from the jealous monkey inhabitants . . . The little band of pioneers has greatly increased so that native born animals have practically replaced the original immigrants."

The Parrot Jungle, run by another group, is half aviary, half botanical garden. It, too, maintains a free-ranging group, of macaws that fly where they will—never too far—and always come back to the home perch at feeding time. Both jungles owe their existence to Florida's mild climate, but at the time I was there that same climate had not been equally kind to the Crandon Park Zoo, Miami's zoological garden. Situated as it is on a reef, the fact that a recent hurricane had inundated it is not really surprising, but the effect was none the less disastrous. Water that had been three feet deep in places had subsided at last, and repairs were under way when I paid a visit, but much damage was still evident.

Julie steadfastly refused to visit any of these places with me, but we talked them over afterwards. My main reason for having come, of course, was not to look at zoos but to see dealers, and she thought this a good idea. "I won't take you myself because I can't bear to go," she said, "but I know somebody who'll make a good guide. And before you start out, I thought it might be interesting for you to talk to a man who used to do collecting for the dealers, in Central America. He doesn't do it any more—he's a sculptor now. I've asked him for tea this afternoon."

Her guest was very ready to talk about the bad old days, and his reasons for having suffered a change of heart. "I gave it up," he said.

"I couldn't stomach the emotional strain. These poor small animals . . . It seemed all right when I started—I got into the trade by accident, you see; I'd gone out to Nicaragua on an engineering job, but after several years it folded up, so I turned to collecting animals. There was a lot of graft in the trade. Most of the men who are hired to do the work are peasants who turn to catching now and then in the slack season—not that life isn't always slack there: everybody has a low-grade malaria. I had it myself. Well, I organized the catching and paid the men honest wages, and soon I was doing better than anybody else. But little by little I got so I was having bad dreams. Do you know anything about what it's like? You go out and wait for a troop of monkeys to come feeding in the trees, then you shoot the ones with babies, hoping they will fall right, so that the baby isn't killed. Usually, of course, it *is* dead when it lands. You shoot about five monkeys for one good baby. Then twenty-five percent die in quarantine and ten percent die en route to America. Some of the dealers who were careless sometimes used to lose whole shipments. No, I couldn't stomach it."

I was not exactly in a receptive mood, therefore, when my guide, Tim, came to take me on a round of the animal shops. Tim, who was about twenty-two but looked younger, explained as we drove briskly through the town's outskirts—wide, flat, sparsely built over—that he had in the past worked at one of the stores, looking after the animals. "I know most of the fellows that do the same kind of thing," he continued, "and they keep dead specimens for me, because I collect skulls and other bones; I prepare stuff for schools. I generally make the rounds at least once a week." He drove up to the curb near a rambling building with plenty of outhouses, and shut off the engine. "This isn't one of the better places," he said apologetically. We went in through a back door, past a medley of packing cases and other containers piled up in an anteroom, and into a dark chamber so full of built-in cages that space was hardly left for a narrow path between. The place was hot, and the air reeked. Tim was greeted by a stubbly-faced youth in overalls, and they chatted while I stared around. On one side my dress brushed against cages full of birds with bright feathers; on the other side my elbow jutted into a tiny square pen that contained a baby elephant.

"Toucanets," said Tim of the birds. "I've got a lot of nice skulls of those. Over there beyond are squirrel monkeys, but I guess you know that. Have they just arrived?" he asked his friend.

"Last week," said the youth. "It was a bad shipment—six hundred, and forty percent of them dead."

I exclaimed at this, and even Tim was startled. "That's worse than usual," he assured me. "It's usually about ten percent dead. The main thing is that the shippers don't feed them; sometimes they're all living when they start out, but they haven't been fed, so some die before they get here. The shippers don't care because they make a profit anyway. Got any stuff for me?" he asked his friend.

"Yeah, there's some stuff and I put 'em in the icebox for you, but I can't do it any more. Bill was swearing about it this morning—says there's so much dead stuff in there he hasn't got any room for the meat."

Tim shrugged philosophically. We looked at the little elephant, which the other youth said was sold and would probably be shipped off soon. Tim said to me, "They won't neglect an animal like this, you see, there's too much money sunk in it. They'll feed and water him all right, you bet."

We sidled on toward the end of the room, past more birds and monkeys, and up shaky wooden stairs to a loft in which chicken-wire boxes of lizards were stacked up like cordwood. "Look at that," said Tim angrily, pointing to a box near the floor. "Look at the way they're treating them. They're very rare skinks from Australia; there's supposed to be an embargo on them, but they get smuggled out just the same. I've seen some arrive packed in with pottery. Yet I bet you anything you like they haven't been fed since they started out." He pulled one out and examined it where it lay stiff in his hand. "Dead," he said, and dropped it back. "Sometimes it's even worse, when they give them an egg or something and then never clean out the box. They arrive all stuck up with dried egg, and egg all over the box so they can hardly breathe. Let's see what they've got over on the other loft."

To reach this we had to descend and ascend again, to a large enclosure in which torpid-looking snakes, quite large ones, lay heaped inches deep. Tim told me not to step inside, as the place would be full of lice that get into one's shoes. He called downstairs, "Anybody been up here lately?"

"No," was the answer. "Bill's supposed to look after it, but you know how he is. He doesn't like snakes."

Tim waded into the enclosure and shifted the bodies around, handling them like so many lengths of rope, searching out dead snakes. Sometimes, he told me, they die from the weight of other bodies on top of them. As he brought out the dead ones he threw them over the edge of the loft: there was a heap of tangled serpent when we descended. At that moment another man came in.

"Hi, Bill," said Tim. "I've got about six snakes I'd like to take away. Okay?"

"Okay," said Bill. They counted the bodies—two boa constrictors, one five and one six feet long, and four slightly shorter anacondas. Bill said, "Better get them off the premises right away. An inspector was around yesterday, raising hell about keeping dead stuff outside."

Tim said he'd put them into the rear of his car then and there. A few frozen bird bodies were taken from the refrigerator and these, too, we carried off.

At the next place things were tidier, with plenty of room between cages and more space altogether. Here Tim garnered two dead baby woolly monkeys and a small bird. He said the monkeys had been caught too young and couldn't possibly have survived. This shop specialized in what it called Florida alligators, which are really baby caymans, for Florida alligators have long been too scarce to waste in this lavish manner. At the next establishment, Tim was greeted with the news that the proprietor wouldn't save dead animals any more for him—it was too much trouble.

"Throwing all the dead animals away now, eh?" asked Tim.

"Yeah," was the answer. There seemed little to say about that, so we merely looked around a bit. This was another place with fixed cages, two ranks of them back to back. In one of the lower cages a lot of baby chicks were running around. They would be food for those animals that simply had to be fed, said Tim. He glanced at them. "What's that they've got in there, a spider?" he demanded. Then, as he reached in and picked it up, "No, it's a baby white-lip!" he said. The tiny marmoset lay in his hand, stirring faintly. An assistant came and peered at it, and said, "Well, I'll be darned. I didn't know that marmoset was expecting. They always have twins. Guess she's still got the other one—wait a minute . . . Yep, the father's got it. Well, I'll be darned."

"Tim," I said, "I guess I'll go home."

CHAPTER 28

Conservation

□

"Noah's work is not done," was the heading of a brochure that announced a conference to be held in San Diego on October 4–6, 1966,
on the role of zoos in the international conservation of wild animals.
"During the last 150 years," it continued, "some 40 species of birds
and animals in the U.S. are in danger of extinction. All over the
world hundreds of others are on the verge of joining the same society.
Since the time of Christ, it is estimated that 100 kinds of birds and
animals have become extinct. About 65% of these losses have occurred
within the past century; 38% within the last 50 years. Appallingly,
1000 species are on the waiting list today. . . . While most conservationists
recognize the need for game preserves, little thought has been given to
the role of zoos in conservation. . . ."

Nevertheless, some thought has been given, I reflected. In 1964, the
International Union of Directors of Zoological Gardens held a symposium
in London and there resolved to form, through the IUCN—the International Union for the Conservation of Nature, etc.—an organization
of zoos, animal collections, experimental research institutions and animal
traders to develop a method of distribution of rare animals for exhibition,
in co-operation with IUCN's Survival Service Commission. This sounds
complicated, but simply means that the delegates want to round up
everybody in the world connected with the exploitation of wild animals
and persuade these people, or if necessary force them, to obey certain
rules aimed at preserving threatened species. Quite a job, one would
say, but the commission's efforts have met with some success. Recently,
for example, the British authorities confiscated three young siamangs at
the customs barrier because the little apes were not accompanied by

the proper documents. The Chester Zoo was the lucky recipient of the siamangs, and no dealer is likely to send uncertificated apes to England again. Whenever a similar offense is discovered, its description is published in periodicals read by zoo people, and the publicity is not good for the offender's trade. Even earlier than the symposium, in 1962, AAZPA at one of their conventions formed the Wild Animal Propagation Trust to preserve vanishing species, and United States zoo directors naturally expressed approval of the London resolution of 1964, but not all of them really like it.

"You've got to look at it from the animal's point of view," said the director of a small West Coast zoo in earnest tones. "Natives catch orang babies, right? These babies wait for purchasers in Palembang or some other southeastern port, right? They stockpile if nobody buys them. Well, the dealer's going to neglect them if they stay on his hands, right? No food, nothing. Finally they die. Putting restrictions on the import of orangs is simply condemning those little orangs to death. What's so conservational about that?"

Unmoved by such arguments, Dr. Schroeder of San Diego published a paper on the subject in the 1965 Transactions of the Pacific Coast Oto-Ophthalmological Society. "What role can zoos play in the conservation effort?" he asked in this, and replied, "They can stop traffic in rare animals, the bootlegging and falsification of legal documents. This can be done by encouraging legislation here prohibiting the entry of rarities from around the world unless the shipment is approved by the country of origin. Those zoos which do acquire and exhibit rarities can make every effort to have pairs and attempt to bring about reproduction. In this way, zoos can become the source of rarities for other zoos, rather than depleting numbers in their native habitats." He goes on to say that the zoo has the opportunity to show the public what it is they are being asked to preserve, and to publicize the entire matter of conservation, not only through all news media but first-hand. American zoos alone have an attendance of more than sixty million a year. "If we are able to overcome our greatest and first problem—human over-production—all other problems will soon dissolve. . . . The achievement of freedom from hunger and that of conservation have to do with the same thing: the proper use of land and its priceless treasures."

San Diego was chosen for the conference because the zoo was celebrating its fiftieth anniversary in 1966. Besides, zoo people always like an excuse to go there. It is the zoo man's zoo.

On the plane to California I looked at the additional literature that had been sent, finding a number of familiar names and some not so familiar in the list of speakers. Commander Peter Scott and Caroline Jarvis were two of the lot that represented Britain. Bill Conway of the Bronx, Charles Shaw of San Diego, Dr. Lee Talbot from the Smithsonian and other Americans took care of our side of it, but there were others, too, from South America and the Far East and Africa. It should be a good meeting, I thought. Like most of the others I arrived on Monday, October 3, in order to get the registration and all that out of the way. In accordance with custom, the delegates were housed in the hotel where most of the talks were to be held: this time the choice had fallen on the Hanalei, one of the most recently opened inns in Mission Valley. A glorified motel, it is built in a rectangle around a huge patio, or park, which contains a swimming pool and a lot of lawn scattered with tables and deck chairs, and crisscrossed with winding walks. At a table to one side, two busy young women in dark but lightweight dresses registered the delegates and gave us our name pins and folders. The Indian summer of the East Coast was only a memory. Here we were in southern California where the tweediest-looking autumn costume must not be too warm, and the skies are not cloudy all day. The old euphoria stole over me as I stood around on the grass and chatted with acquaintances, and watched the newcomers drive up to the door of the glass box that was the reception office. More and more arrived, and the name pins proliferated. At the stipulated hour we climbed into waiting buses and were taken to the zoo, where the staff had invited us for a reception. There, on the restaurant terrace covered and lit up for the occasion, we ate and drank and met old friends. Later I returned to the hotel with a number of these boon companions, and by some arrangement I didn't notice we were soon having more drinks in a grand ground-floor room. We were still on the first round when a new man came in and paused as if surprised at sight of us. He was Dr. Eric Guiler from Tasmania, one of the speakers on next day's agenda, and we were in his room.

"No, no, do stay," he protested, when some of the more conscientious among us apologized and offered to go. I didn't even offer to go, because I had a question. The Tasmanian wolf, to give its popular name to the thylacine, a large marsupial beast with transverse stripes and a canine head, used to be known as the greatest threat Tasmania offered to European sheep ranchers. Most Antipodean fauna are noted for their gentle characters, but the thylacine was rumored to be ferocious. Settlers went after it with dogs and guns, until it was said to have disappeared. I asked Dr. Guiler point-blank, "Is the Tasmanian wolf extinct?"

"No," he said, in just as point-blank a manner. "I'm discussing the thylacine in tomorrow's talk. If you're interested, here's a picture. I didn't take it myself, but it's authenticated. Look at the way the mouth opens, much wider than your non-marsupial carnivore's. The jaw is tremendously long—this animal can kill that way, with one clean bite. I'm happy to say that some thylacines are still in circulation."

After that I departed, because I wanted to see the films I had heard were being shown in a banquet room upstairs. By the time I got there the room was nearly full, and half the first picture, dealing with the capture of white rhinos, was over. I got a seat, however, in ample time for the second offering, which dealt with Jane Goodall and the chimpanzees she watched so long in Africa. Soon Dr. Guiler came in and joined me.

"I wanted to see this picture again," he said. "I've watched it once on television, and liked it very much."

Miss Goodall was shown looking through her binoculars at a troop of chimps, and, as the months went by, getting closer and closer to them until they had learned not to flee at her approach. Before the picture was over, they were making free of her camp and playing a game with her that looked like ring-around-a-rosy. Dr. Guiler said, "Here comes a bit I find very touching, very touching indeed." On the screen a stranger chimp had arrived, a female carrying a small baby. She was clearly tired and would like to join the group but was not sure of her reception. The camera showed her sitting at the periphery of the party, hesitant and worrying. At last the leader of the locals approached to look her over, and the tired mother timidly held out a hand, evidently as an offer of fealty. The leader chimp accepted the hand, taking it in his. With eyes watchfully fixed on his face, the female leaned over and kissed his hand. All was well. From the audience around me, of hard-bitten zoo people, rose a murmur of approbation and relief.

We were nearly all there on time next morning at nine o'clock, in the Golden Empire Room. There was a certain amount of woffle to get through first, of course—introductions, polite little speeches and all that, before the dignitaries were sorted out and proceedings could begin, but the presiding officer, a San Diego man named Sheldon Campbell, soon got down to business. Among us, he said, were students of San Diego, one from each high school, who were deputed to take notes of proceedings and carry the word back to their mates. Then he spoke about the conservation of wild life, and held up, where we could all see it, a stuffed bird, Martha, the very last of the passenger pigeons whose flights used to darken American skies before they were slaughtered in their thousands. Clothed in buff and black plumage, neck iridescent, Martha sits with cocked head and alert expression. She died in 1914. "We have her here on loan by courtesy of the Smithsonian," said Mr. Campbell. Robert Bean, who was sitting in the row ahead of me, turned around to whisper that he used to see Martha when she was still alive in the old Milwaukee Zoo. Concluding his remarks, Mr. Campbell reminded us that any money taken in at the conference was earmarked for the World Wildlife Fund. Then he introduced Commander Peter Markham Scott, who was to be our general chairman.

Residents of Britain and anybody almost anywhere else who has some connection with natural science need no information on Peter Scott, but it is the custom at such affairs to furnish the printed biography of every speaker among their brochures. Here, Scott's biography took up a page and a half. Son of Captain Robert Falcon Scott of the Antarctic, internationally respected conservationist, author, lecturer, illustrator, yachtsman, ornithologist, Chairman of the British Appeal of the World Wildlife Fund, President of the Wildlife Youth Service, Chairman of the Survival Service Commission of the IUCN, President of the International Yacht Racing Union, the Gloucestershire Association of Youth Clubs and the Newport Wildfowlers' Association, Vice President of the Inland Waterways Association, the Charles Darwin Foundation for the Galapagos Islands, the Camping Club of Great Britain and Ireland, the Council for Nature, the Royal Society for the Protection of Birds, the International Cadet Class and the Bristol Gliding Club. Founder and director of The Wildfowl Trust at Slimbridge, Glos. In the war, in the navy, won the MBE and the DSC. Has also been in politics. I should add on my own account that it is a rare week on British television that Commander Scott is not heard from. Still, I had never before seen him in the flesh, and it was good to have the chance.

Not unexpectedly, he is a practiced speaker, and started out with an anecdote illustrating, as he said, the difficulties inherent in communication.

Driving along a typical winding road in the English countryside one day, he saw another car approaching and realized that—as is often necessary on a typical English country road—one or the other would have to give way. He therefore drew up close to the side of the road and stopped so that the other car could get by. As it passed, the woman driving it leaned out of her window and said, "Pig!" Commander Scott was outraged, since he had been very courteous. Resuming his way, pondering the horrid ways of other drivers, especially woman drivers, he rounded the next curve and ran into a pig.

After that, however, his talk was grave. "Anyone who looks ahead must be alarmed at the fate of the earth," he declared. The biosphere is a terribly thin layer covering our planet, and—he emphasized the words—*it is finite*. The two main problems we are facing today are population and pollution. Commander Scott says that he has no doubt we'll settle the population problem, for mankind is adaptable and finds an answer to such problems as he recognizes. It may take time and patience to do this, it may take even one more generation, but the answer will be found. And the louder we shout, the sooner it will be found. "Already," he continued, "we have a Noah's Ark operation to undertake, in the interim." The problems of population and pollution extend beyond our immediate concerns, however, to the conservation of animals and plants. In twenty million centuries of evolution, Man's own history probably accounts for less than two million years. Here he broke off to say, "It has been less than a million days, you know, since the birth of Christ. Yet during this comparatively short span, Man has accelerated the rate of extinction by at least a factor of four; some hold that it is a factor of sixteen. One vertebrate has disappeared every year since I was born." Since the First World War, eight species of fish have disappeared in the United States alone. Man the predator is the first to realize what he is doing, and the first to blush; as Mark Twain said, Man is the only animal that blushes, or needs to. Is Man, when he behaves thus, only obeying the laws of evolution? No doubt, said Commander Scott, but he has also evolved this congress . . . "At least one thousand vertebrates are threatened," he went on. "We might ask ourselves, how threatened is threatened? It is better to put an animal on record as such too early than too late." He spoke of the Red Data Book, an IUCN publication which has, at the present reading, 210 mammals and 259 birds on its "threatened" list. Later publications in the series will deal with reptiles, amphibia, fish, and vertebrates. Finally, there will be plant volumes. The colors of the pages are significant: for very rare animals the paper is red; for those which have been saved, it is green. "The intention," said Commander Scott, "is to make the whole book green before we're through."

How can zoos fit into the pattern of the conservation campaign? In six ways, he said, and listed them: by educating people in natural history, ecology and conservation; by giving visitors a general increase of aesthetic appreciation; by making a scientific study of threatened species as is done in San Diego; by breeding threatened species, as has been done with the Arabian oryx in Phoenix and Galapagos tortoises in San Diego, and by helping with translocated problems; by fund-raising with wishing wells or other methods—at Slimbridge they manage to extract about $2000 a year just in small change, and model "Panda" collecting boxes here and there in England have also been effective; by maintaining an acute sense of responsibility in all these matters and refraining from acquiring rare animals that have no prospect of breeding in captivity. He went on, "Two years ago in London the question of quotas was discussed at the symposium, what numbers of certain rare animals can safely be taken into captivity and to which zoos they should be awarded. Fortunately, we got away from the dangerous notion that no rare animals whatever should be exhibited in zoos. A round-robin letter to this effect was circulated, but I am totally opposed to extreme ideas like this, holding that such exhibits are educational for the public and good for breeding knowledge. Some day it should be possible to breed everything in captive or semi-captive conditions."

In time, too, it should be equally possible to sweep away bars and all other suggestions of imprisonment. Bars, etc., are not so bad for the animals, he declared, because he's sure they don't mind, but he objects to them because of what they do to the spectator. They're bad for the whole movement. So are bad conditions in small zoos, and often this statement goes for some of the big zoos too. If the offending zoo authorities argue that they haven't enough money to maintain proper standards, they should be told to sweep away their old cages and get rid of the animals rather than keep them there as a constant reproach.

"I believe conservation is gaining ground," he said in closing. There was to be a great conference on the subject in 1968, an international quinquennium. In the meantime, as always, they needed the co-operation of zoos.

Richard S. Fitter, honorary secretary of the Fauna Preservation Society of London, followed with a "General Survey of Captive Breeding in Zoos and Zoological Parks as a Method of Conserving Rare Species." First, he said, he wished to go on record as agreeing with Commander Scott on the round-robin matter. "I don't see how one can expect people to support creatures they can't see," he declared. "A blanket ban would be wholly unrealistic." Then, swinging into his prepared piece, he recited more unhappy statistics of waste and catastrophe. Each year, on an average, one bird and one mammal becomes extinct, and this isn't counting other forms of life. Mostly because of Man there is a perpetual drain on the globe. Man kills directly for sport, food, or to rid himself of pests, but indirectly he kills just about as much again. Some people throw up their hands and say "You can't obstruct the march of progress," but he, Mr. Fitter, believes that there are ways to prevent these losses, and of them all, the most effective is the park. He cited famous cases; Père David's deer and the wild cattle of Chillingham. Both are now unknown in the wild, as are Przewalski's horse and the wisent. The wisent, or European bison, is a good case in point; not only has it been saved from extinction, but there are enough animals now for both breeding stock *and* release in its former habitat. At the end of the nineteenth century it was known to exist only in two places. The First World War almost wiped it out. In 1923 the International Society for the Protection of European Bison took over, and in 1932 started a stud book on the animal, in which thirty were counted in the whole world. Now there are about 800, with 58 in a wild state again in Poland. Some have been born in the wild, but nowhere else except in Russia will there be enough land available to set many more free. It's up to such places as Askaniya-Nova or the Catskills Game Farm to take care of the bison. Then there is his own society and its interest in the Arabian oryx—but we would hear more about that from Major Grimwood: Mr. Fitter would only give us the following figures; 16 animals at Phoenix, 8 of which have been born there. It would now be a good thing to disperse them to different centers: perhaps first they should be re-established in the National Park in Jordan.

All animals he had mentioned, he continued, are ungulates, which are easiest to save in such a way, and he talked about more ungulate species he hopes to see rescued in the near future. But, he continued, it is not so simple to work with the other endangered mammals. Certainly it is essential to save the large apes; the big zoos must club together, so that in nine or ten years they can breed all their own specimens, as the present methods of capture are too utterly wasteful. Breeding colonies of monkeys and apes of every species should be established. Rodents can be notably successful at breeding in captivity— look at the hamster, every single one of which, as far as anybody can tell, is descended from that one pair caught in the Lebanon not long ago. Birds? Well, the nei-nei goose has been re-established on Maui. The Laysan teal needs to be tackled, but this bird's story is somewhat different: its native habitat is too small now to accommodate any reasonable number of individuals. It is doing well at the Ornamental Pheasant Trust in England. The Swinhoe pheasant is soon to be released in its original environment, and also at Poole in Dorset.

Of parallel importance with all these rare animals are the commoner species, and these too the zoos must breed, for if they don't, many animals now common will soon be rare in the wild. He had asked Lang of Zurich which animals, in his opinion, might soon again be self-supporting after being conserved in zoos, and Lang, offhand, had named the great gray kangaroo, marmot, spiny mouse, brown bear, spectacled bear, Malay and South American tapir—"A wonderful list," said Mr. Fitter enthusiastically. "I would feel enormously happy if other directors could add to it, and confident of success."

At the end of his talk, the speaker gave a warning about capture methods. Some people, he said, are gun-happy with their tranquilizers. For many species the drug-darting technique is still nonexistent. You need an expert in such matters if you want to avoid certain recent disasters. (Here I put a note commanding myself to investigate this subject, but as things turned out it was done for me, when another speaker examined the question in detail.)

Our next lecturer, Dr. Guiler, described as chairman of the Animals and Birds Protection Board at Hobart, talked on "Tasmanian Conservation Problems in Relation to Land Development." He showed us on a map where the land in Tasmania remains wild enough, with hills and rain forest, to support much of the island's original fauna. Even in the cultivated plains where sheep graze, wallabies would be able to live side by side with the stock, because they don't eat the same kind of grass and so don't compete. But wallabies, like rabbits, are bitterly hated. Tasmanians put down poison, hoping to kill them, thus endangering all other wild life as well. Still, Dr. Guiler doubts if this poison affects the surviving thylacines, since some have been seen on a certain road where it runs into the forest—just the sort of habitat these animals have always preferred, and other animals, too, are doing well. One hundred and thirty-four Tasmanian devils live in an area two miles square which he keeps as a reserve. "We ought to remove some, I suppose," he said, "but they're very difficult to raise in captivity. There's bound to be a population crash there in the near future. Devils nearly disappeared in 1900, but have recovered very well. I don't visualize the devil becoming extinct; recently one was killed by a car very near my house, six miles outside Hobart."

Birds, too, are dependent on the forest. Many of their dead bodies, when autopsied, have shown poison residue that evidently killed them, even if indirectly. Fortunately, some Tasmanians are at last waking up to the danger of using poison so recklessly, but teaching is a slow process. "Through this use of poison by farmers and stockbreeders, not to mention land-hungry speculators, the greatest possible pressure is exerted on our most valuable habitat," said Dr. Guiler. "When I took this job I asked myself what I could do about it. The main thing is to avoid enmity or clashes, and hope that education and publicity will bring the public around to a right way of thinking. We need sanctuaries, habitat reserves, and recently we've got the land. My board owns one sixth of our state, which means all of the southeast; it was granted to us only six months ago. It contains at least one pair of thylacines. We want to develop Maria, an island off the east coast 23,000 acres in extent, as a combined sanctuary and tourist attraction—we've got to have some tourist facilities I suppose, but it can be kept within bounds, and at least on an island we can really control the population. The big problem in Tasmania is always rabbits and wallabies, which farmers don't like; there is an inevitable clash between our aims. I foresee some difficulty with carrying our ideas through, but we'll do it, given enough time. Another thing: I should like very much to recreate the Tasmanian emu on Maria. This dwarf variety of the emu died out in the Twenties; only a few skins are left. There's the water problem too. As water decreases, the rain-forest habitat vanishes. I'm not interested so much in now as in the future, in fifty years or so. We ought to take out our insurance policies now. We don't need all that land we've got as yet, but we have to be watchful. Now and then we can grab a water hole surrounded by farmland, which makes the farmer cross, but not all agriculture is necessarily bad for wild life. The coreopsis goose has been helped by it; it now breeds in twenty-four islands where before they were on only four, and this is due completely to agricultural activity, clearing the land, irrigating it and so on. In sum: in Tasmania we are not desperately fighting for our wrecked fauna, because it hasn't been wrecked—yet. We are fighting for conservation against newly felt pressures already familiar to older countries. We have gazetted large tracts of land for reserves, but we also want to work in other ways, with nature-strips here and there in settled country. Our main object is to maintain our present hold and develop co-existence and peace with agriculture. It's a bit of a struggle. We have only four wild life officers of our own; we have to depend on regular police officers, and they're reasonably good. Conservation is part of a p.c.'s training program. Even the traffic cops have been known to catch duck poachers."

Tasmania's worst transplanted-species problem is the rabbit, but the kookaburra is another one—this bird was brought over from the mainland —and a third is the European fallow deer which some sport-loving settler established there. If Dr. Guiler could have his way he would exterminate the bird and the deer, but he can't. The deer is a good game animal, and people want to keep it. "At least we haven't the mad situation they face on the mainland," he said, "where they have hedgehogs and all that."

At the question period, somebody asked how Dr. Guiler intended to set about recreating the dwarf emu. "We'd probably simply cull out the big birds," he answered. Another delegate asked how many thylacines survive, and the speaker replied that he didn't know: "I think there are certainly twenty pairs, maybe fifty, maybe a hundred, but this is only guess, based on reliable reports. I myself know of one den, but it's in difficult country. I know of twenty localities, and we get constant reports. A sheep was killed about thirty miles from Hobart, probably by a thylacine. In the old days there were a lot of the animals in that locality. They never lived right in the rain forest, but at the edge. There's no evidence that they feed on rabbits. Devils do, but seem to be immune to poison. Possum-cats die of the poison, but many of our animals and birds aren't damaged. It kills off feral cats, of course, and that's fine as far as I'm concerned."

As it was somewhat past noon, the meeting adjourned. Most of us followed the set plan for the rest of the day—a boat tour to Los Coronados Islands, where sea lions, hair seals and elephant seals abound. Partly because it would take too much time for us to get off at these rocky specks in the Pacific, but mainly because of the red tape such action would involve, since Los Coronados belong to Mexico, we only chugged out to look, and circled the islands, now and then moving in close to observe the animals that lay on their rocky ledges, some of them piled up like playing cards, others moving languidly from one spot to another, or diving in to sport in the shallows. There seemed to be no segregation, either on grounds of race or color. Elephant seals lay uncomplaining beneath the weight of two or three smaller animals, which ranged in tint from dark brown to pale silvery gray.

Wednesday morning, October 5, started out at 8:15 with an address on the subject "Colombian Zoos and Their Influence on Conservation," given by Dr. Carlos Lehmann, director general of the Vale State Museum of Natural History in Cali, Colombia. Dr. Lehmann, after a short apology for his English, plunged straight into a harrowing talk. There is only one zoo in Colombia, he said, and in that all the signs are wrong; one of Colombia's characteristic birds is labeled GOLDEN EAGLE, and the jaguar is called, simply, CATTLE KILLER. This is no good, said Dr. Lehmann, and he ventured to hope that San Diego and other zoos might help, through their various chambers of commerce, to reform conditions there. Some other reforms, too, were urgently needed, mainly in an industry that gives work to poor peasants, the export of Colombian birds and mammals. It is a cruel, wasteful procedure, he said: "Many avifauna die before shipping, even rare birds—the scarlet cock of the rock, the quetzal—for each one exported, no less than fifty die before reaching their destination. Thousands of tanagers die in the hunters' cages. Something should be done short of stopping the trade altogether, because this is a terrible thing. At the museum we rescue hundreds of birds every week that have been kept utterly devoid of nutrition, without food or water, for more than three or four days. It is a serious problem. Our turtles, too, are being exterminated—one exporter sends tens of thousands a year, and the hunters also collect the eggs. They will do anything to sell things. One of the worst trades is in skins of peccary and deer, and thousands of cayman skins go out also. Half a million lovebirds, not counting those killed, with more than a hundred thousand monkeys and two hundred thousand snakes, were sent last year from Barranquilla alone. I try to persuade those in charge to let the hunters at least send these animals alive instead of dead, but it's hard. To help with the economy in another way, I want to persuade bird watchers to come, instead of depending on this slaughter. I've already arranged a lot of tours from the United States for bird watchers. The worst record of all is the capybara's. These animals live on fish and so their flesh has a fishy taste: hunters kill them and sell the flesh as 'salmonet,' for fresh meat, which our people need. In Venezuela, a conservationist has succeeded in getting the capybara onto the protected list, but only recently we in Colombia had a request from one of our ministers to slaughter three hundred thousand a year. I refused, but now another very influential ministry has asked for seventy thousand. Nobody can control this kind of thing. The capybara are herded into corrals and clubbed to death for the sake of the meat, and the skins are wasted.

"Only an international body can handle the situation," he told the hushed room. "Our beautiful cloud forests are being burned down to make clearings for corn, yet one hectare of corn is not worth one tenth of this destruction of Nature. After the trees are gone, rains wash away the soil. We must establish parks and reserves and encourage the tourist bird watchers. Twenty-seven hundred different birds can be observed in Colombia, yet more than six hundred species are now vanished. There is a museum I started at the University at Papoyan in 1936; I can't find some species for it, and there are many beautiful butterflies we no longer have. The same holds true for other places in Central and South America. In Colombia we have the beginning of a movement, at least, for national parks—one mountain has been set aside, and will be included in a park. Then there is an island on the Caribbean coast. Other associations have established a little park of only 700 hectares; it isn't much. Oil birds live inside this area, in caves full of marine fossils. However, these birds fly more than fifty kilometers, and such a small park is no good for them. I've been pressing the Ministry about this."

Dr. Lehmann showed some colored moving pictures of Colombian mountains and a condor that lives in that area, a wonderful great bird that hung in the sky and for a long time refused to be tempted down to the ground where the camera could get close-ups. "One could get to Cali by direct flight from New York, and it would be well worth coming, just to see the condors," said Dr. Lehmann. "It's easier to reach than Peru. That isn't white on the wings, but silver."

"His figures were grossly exaggerated," Bill Conway protested during an interval. "They must have been." Delegates were talking hard to Dr. Lehmann and making notes. I talked to nobody, but thought about the Florida dealers.

Caroline Jarvis gave the next talk, "The Importance of the Zoo in Wild Animal Conservation—as a Fund of Wild Animal Data and as a Bank for Endangered Species." She had told me that she was very nervous, this being the first time she had ever addressed such a large gathering, but she concealed her feelings well and within a few minutes, I was sure, forgot them.

In 1965 Miss Jarvis went to China on a routine tour and managed to concentrate on the zoos of the country, a trip that held much interest for Western zoo people, who are almost completely ignorant of the subject. In Nationalist China the tradition of Parks of Intelligence had all but died out, but since the Communist takeover the whole zoo situation has been revitalized, and there are flourishing gardens in most large cities. Caroline has brought back photographs of these, and information of rare animals, including details of the breeding of giant pandas that has so far produced three young animals in captivity. She is also firmly convinced that Chinese claims to have found live elephants in their western territories are true. She told us that she would show a film at the end of her talk, with pictures from Peking of the first giant panda to give birth in captivity.

"Those organizations most closely concerned with conservation," she began crisply, "are the zoos, universities and research establishments. We must all fight together or the battle is lost. The two most serious problems we face are the aggression and expansion of the human species. Our continued existence is at stake, and whether or not we survive may well depend upon Nature."

In the more than five hundred top-ranking zoos of the world, she continued, are half a million living things, yet zoos are too often unaware of their responsibilities as custodians. In that way we are inferior to the Chinese, who with their Parks of Intelligence anticipated the situation some four thousand years ago. Our museums and botanical gardens have fostered a far more intelligent attitude than zoos have done; people don't go to botanical gardens to laugh. Today when zoos are coming of age, the audience should remember that it is not enough to establish a connection with research: we must lead the way. The influence that zoos could have in the conservation movement could be enormous—millions of people visit zoos annually, and if only a fraction of this number came away excited and stimulated by what they have seen, it would be tremendous for conservation. In other ways zoos are invaluable; they can record data and breed against extinction.

"It is astonishing how little is known, for example about wild animals' behavior patterns," she said, "yet a mass of data can be obtained in captivity. Until lately, zoos were unaware of the value of these things. They kept a few records, but this was nothing compared with the information that could have been noted down and preserved." A case in point was the way they reacted to the Yearbook. As editor of this book, she sends out questionnaires every year to all the zoos on the list. In 1960, when the Yearbook was just beginning, there were three hundred zoos listed, of which 170 returned the questionnaires properly filled in, but 130 did not even reply. But in 1966, when the number of listed zoos is far larger, only 23 failed to reply. More than 500 sent them back filled in. The quality of replies, too, had improved. Such a response would never have occurred seven years ago. The Yearbook is now selling to universities and laboratories all over the world.

In a zoo, for example, the gestation behavior of mother animals can be observed closely. With the panda in Peking the keepers were aware of everything about their female, her estrus, gestation, behavior—and all this was absolutely new material. In London, the zoo has a tie-up with the Nuffield laboratory similar to San Diego's with the virus center. Zoos can and must be of value to researchers everywhere. We must know more about wild animals' behavior and biology, since we are going to have to look after them absolutely some day soon. Every zoo must have a good efficient record system, not haphazard as so many still are. There must be basic data in the records: when and where the animal has been caught, its weight on arrival, all sorts of items. At the London zoo they are preparing guides for such study of wild animals in captivity.

Then there are the wild animal banks. It should be possible to maintain a gene pool for future breeding. At Askaniya-Nova the eland has been maintained since around 1892. The animals started breeding in 1897, and no new blood has been introduced into the herd since. Findings on these animals at Askaniya-Nova, therefore, are extremely important—what the meat and milk are like, to name only two points. There is still no difference, evidently, between these animals and elands in the wild in Africa.

"Rare animals are bred in captivity despite zoos rather than because of them," she said bluntly. "Until recently they were bred only for exhibition, and zoos refused to cull the stock, because they could sell everything surplus that was born. Under this mismanagement and with such small numbers, stocks were not infrequently wiped out. This whole attitude should change, and breeding must be managed as a racing stud is, with large enough groups so that herds can be scattered as they ought to be for the health of the new animals. Of course exhibition is important, but it must take second place. Small zoos should concentrate on only one or two rare animals. And we must not ignore stud books, which should be kept for every rare species as they are for a few today. With the stud book program we would, of course, include a proper marking or other identification system.

"Every zoo can do research on nutrition and ethology. If you say that you haven't funds for such a purpose, then pay an outside research worker to do it.

"Zoos, universities, game departments and governments will have to co-operate if we are to save the animals. There should be an international federation devoted to the study of all this, with regular meetings and methods and card systems. The whole concept of the zoo's function is changing, and ought to change. A zoo can be a center for education, learning and research. Zoos are the trustees of the wild animals of the world, and as trustees they have grave responsibilities. They have the power to see that wild animals do not become extinct.

"It is too late, and the situation is too serious, for us merely to pay lip service to conservation."

The room was darkened for the picture from Peking. In another moment we looked into the face of a female panda standing on her hind legs and holding in the front legs, or arms, a small panda. Caroline commented, standing on the podium and silhouetted in the gloom, "This is the first panda to breed in captivity, and she has had another baby since this picture was made. The panda is the only carnivore that takes a primate position in holding the baby." "Not so," growled Robert Bean in an undertone. "I've seen bears do the same thing." "There are about twenty pandas in all in Chinese zoos," said Caroline. "They're not particularly rare in the wild, but they are scattered in difficult country where field workers can't easily observe them. In the wild they are scavengers. In zoos they will eat meat as well as bamboo. In China they are fed meat regularly."

Now the mother, having decided to lie on her back, lowered herself slowly to the ground until she was maintaining a half-sitting, half-lying posture with the baby clutched to her breast, and then gave a little heave of her fat Teddy-bear body to make herself comfortable. It was endearing, and there was a ripple of laughter over the audience before the lights went up and Caroline, to sustained applause, retired to give way to Perez M. Olindo of Kenya, who talked on "Conservation Problems and the Role of the Nairobi Animal Orphanage in Wildlife Education and Research in Kenya."

According to the biographical notes Mr. Olindo is responsible for the Kenya parks system, including the Animal Orphanage in Nairobi Park, opened in 1963. First scholarship student in the African Wildlife Leadership Foundation. Attended a course in national parks administration at the University of Michigan. He is a good-looking young man, too. He said that three problems face them in Kenya: poaching, the rarity of the black rhino, and recent overpopulation of the elephant. He thinks they are getting poaching under control. They are carefully watching the rhino. The elephants will have to be culled before they eat the country out and endanger the whole reservation. We saw moving pictures of the orphanage, where care and temporary sanctuary are given to young animals found without their mothers, and others whose human foster parents cannot cope with them any longer. The animals stay only a short time and then go back to the wild or, if they seem unfitted for that life, to zoos, the final decision on this matter resting with Mr. Olindo and the Keeper of National Parks. The orphanage is open to the public and school parties. It maintains a film library, from which five films are shown without charge every weekend. In three months they entertained 17,000 people in this manner. In a year, 25,000 schoolchildren visited them in parties. The African Wildlife Association of Washington, D.C., has contributed an education center. In all, the orphanage not only takes care of animals but gives the local people a chance to study them in almost wild conditions, for, as Mr. Olindo rather surprisingly reminded us, many of those people would otherwise have no chance to see such

animals at all. "The people of our villages," he said, "have no experience
with any wild life other than the few animals immediately around
them." It was a fairly obvious fact if one stops to think about it, but one
always assumes, however erroneously, that natives know everything about
their own countries.

Breeding animals for zoos is an important part of the orphanage's
work, he continued; the more animals produced in this way, the fewer
will be caught in the wild. Professor Leakey has established a private
center in Nairobi to study the adaptation of wild animals to captivity.
Adjustments are easier there on the ground, and his studies are expected
to be very helpful, especially in the matters of food and care. Even now
very little is known about many animals' habits and their preferences in
food. As for the pathological problems, they are enormous. It has been
observed, for instance, that animals from the wild are immune, or at least
resistant, to many of the diseases that affect the same species in captivity.
"But this is still an observation only," added Mr. Olindo, "not a proved
fact. We have to do more work on it."

He retired and Dr. Boonsong Lakagul took his place to speak on
"Threatened Species in Southeast Asia and the Role of Zoos." A Thai, he
is secretary general of the Association for the Conservation of Wildlife in
Bangkok and a member of the executive board of the IUCN. He
apologized for having no slides with the lecture; it was the war in
Vietnam, he said, that had prevented him from getting any, since the
wildlife in the north is that which is particularly threatened and conditions
there are not helpful just now to the art of photography.

"I used to consider all you people enemies," he said. "Let me tell you
why. We have, or used to have, many unusual species in our area, which
lived fairly untroubled lives until war came. Now, jeeps and other
vehicles have penetrated our forest. Hunting and collecting of these
species goes on day and night, and even more at night since they have
taken to slaughtering the animals with the aid of lights. Within these few
years many animals have been almost wiped out. They are really facing
extinction. We have preserve and park laws, but in many cases it's
difficult, impossible, to enforce them because of our shortages of funds
and trained personnel. At the same time, Thailand is undergoing a
population explosion. Not all the destruction can be blamed on foreigners;
many of our own hill tribes are responsible too. They go out to slash
and burn off forests so that they can raise food, grow their crops for one
or two years on this ruined land, and then move on, leaving it a desert.
Such action is a main cause of destruction of much of our habitat.
Added to this we have a heavy demand from dealers for rare animals

wanted by zoos. Often to capture a young animal the hunter shoots the mother; this is usually done, for instance, with the gibbon. Sometimes both mother and baby die from the shot or the fall. That is why I used to consider zoos my enemy. Then there are the demands of research— hundreds and thousands of monkeys are exported to the United States to be killed and used for polio vaccine, and the gibbons are wanted for anthropological studies. Two years ago one American university ordered eight hundred monkeys a year from Thailand to be used for behavior research. This wipes out such monkeys in many places. As they grow rarer the price goes up, until our people see the animals only as so many dollars, and it is most difficult to stop the poor villagers from destroying the wildlife. Southeast Asia understands the value of conservation, but we are powerless, and now, with the infiltration by Viet Cong, we may succumb to chaos in this matter. Then it will be Malaysia, then In- donesia . . . However, we try; we do our best. But dealers and poachers will always have their dirty tricks, and the situation is almost hopeless if the demand is not stopped.

"In Hawaii, in 1962, as many of you must know, a conservationist conference from Southeast Asia met privately in a hotel and discussed forming a special body to handle this matter. Another meeting was held a year later, in Java. It was resolved to form a group from Southeast Asia, to hold meetings every two years; this conference was last held in Bangkok. Another meeting, of the IUCN with the Wildlife Fund, Unesco and other organizations, took place in Bangkok in November of 1965, urging more alertness and more nature reserves and national parks. To protect the habitat is the best system of conservation, but it's not easy to do so because of political and financial problems. Soon, I hope, old enemies will become friends. Perhaps we are friends even now, since zoos are becoming conservationist at last."

The speaker gave some blood-chilling figures on threatened species, chief of which is the Javan rhino: one or two of this rare animal are killed every year in Thailand, for the people use every part of the animal, even the dung. Then there is an ungulate, the last big game animal in this area known to science—its biggest concentration is now in Cambodia, where eight years ago there were eight hundred. Today there are about two hundred. The anoa and the wild buffalo are rapidly decreasing, though there are many still in a sanctuary in India. The list went on and on. "We would like to ask zoos to raise these animals in captivity, so that there will be a source of supply forever," he said.

After this account of wanton destruction it was a relief to hear from Major I. R. Grimwood of the British Embassy at Lima, on "The

Attempt to Re-establish the Arabian Oryx." The biography part of my notebook explained that Major Grimwood served in conservation positions in Northern Rhodesia, Kenya, and Ethiopia before going to South America. He spent fifteen years in the Indian Army before joining the Northern Rhodesia Game Department in 1948, later becoming chief game warden in Kenya and a Unesco adviser to the Ethiopian Government. "In 1962 he led 'Operation Oryx' in Arabia, an expedition to capture a breeding nucleus of Arabian Oryx to save the species from extinction."

The most effective conservation reserve you can have, began the Major, is in the wild. If this is impossible a reserve must be found outside the animal's normal range, yet as like it as can be managed. If hunting and capture can be controlled, that's fine. If not, one must undertake a breeding program, though this entails the risks and dangers of capture, and the creation of the right conditions. The captive breeding of Arabian oryx in 1961 presented such a case. "Getting the animals together was the first stage. The second was breeding. The third, which we haven't yet achieved, is replacing, without which the operation can't be called a success," he said. The Arabian oryx is found, or was found, in the Sinai Peninsula, where it could, and often did, travel fifty or sixty miles a day in search of food. Because it was so fleet, and could avoid the Bedouin on foot or camel, among these tribesmen it became a distinction to kill an oryx. Unfortunately, killing the oryx retained its social-prestige-giving power even after the advent of the motorcar, though the possession of a car made it unsportingly easy. The animal was nearly exterminated by rich car owners, including Americans. In 1961 the only oryx left were living in one corner of their former area. The little-known eastern district of this country was in Muscat, the Oman Sultan's area, but the west part was in Aden, at the Sand Sea, in better-known country. In the west, small parties of five to ten animals were occasionally seen emerging in the hot summer weather for water. Each time they appeared, of course, three or four were killed, but things didn't get too bad until early in 1960, when a motorized party raided the region and killed forty at once, half of the known population of Arabian oryx in the whole world. (At this point in the narrative, Major Grimwood's voice, usually carefully noncommittal, took on a distinctly steely tone.)

For some time the Fauna Preservation Society, in collaboration with the IUCN, had been keeping an eye on what was happening to the Arabian oryx, and now they decided that the time had come—if it wasn't past—to step into the matter. Grimwood was asked to take charge. He and his advisers planned to start activities in April or early May of 1961, but in

February they got word that the same raiders had returned and killed every remaining oryx, at least in that part of the country. Nevertheless they went ahead, in the hope that the report wasn't quite accurate, and they stepped up their plans. It was in March that they arrived at a so-called water hole, a former haunt of the oryx even though it contained more gypsum and other minerals than water itself. This was in the center of a hundred-mile fringe along the Sand Sea. Here they found tracks of hunting vehicles, mostly Cadillacs, but no oryx. After a week's search, however, one was seen and captured. "It was a wonderful sight," said Major Grimwood fervently. By the end of the tour, when they had explored the entire area, it looked as if only eleven animals had survived. Five had gone into Muscat and Oman where hunting princelings could not follow. Four others, including one male, had been caught by the Society party. Their spotter plane had seen three others; two male and one female. The captured animals were flown to Nairobi and thence, by way of England and quarantine headquarters, to the Phoenix Zoo in Arizona, Arizona having been selected because the country there is something like the desert the oryx is used to. On the way, in New York, one more female oryx joined the group—a lone specimen chipped in by Regent's Park, London, for the cause.

"It was something to have the animals safe, but they couldn't be considered a viable breeding nucleus," said the Major. "We had hoped to get more from other zoos, but all the animals we'd planned on turned out to be either the wrong species or crosses. We did find two more, however, in Yemen, tame but wandering around without owners; they were probably cast-off pets. Abdullah of Kuwait was known to have two in his private zoo, and Sa'ud of Saudi Arabia had more—six, it was rumored. Britain and Yemen were not on speaking terms, but the American government had a go at Sa'ud, requesting him to let us have his oryx. It was no good—in fact, he had strong objections. Abdullah of Kuwait, on the other hand, freely gave his two, and refused to take a present in return. One died in childbirth before it set out on the journey. We got the other. Sa'ud was a much more difficult old man, but after he went into a mental hospital our contact agreed to give two pairs of his oryx to the World Herd. Feisal had eight males and five females in his private zoo, which is a good one; some of these oryx had been born there, and even after giving us two pairs he had some left.

"At least we now had five females and four males. It wasn't a really viable group even then, and we were lucky in having this particular species to deal with, because oryx are easy to catch, and even if they attack, they do so half-heartedly. Once caught, an oryx is extraordinarily phlegmatic, and never tries to escape from the crate. Nor do they panic. From the start they seem resigned. The chief difficulty is in getting them to start feeding, but they are robust and can survive some days of not eating. Ours had to be robust to survive the journey, because it was rugged. Two of them were in transit for thirteen hours. They also withstood well the change of climate and altitude, unlike many other antelopes that die even under ideal conditions of capture and transport. Our one young male that died had been wounded by some hunter before capture, and died of a ruptured liver within one hour.

"In another way too we were lucky: we had a lot of help. The Air Ministry permitted us to carry the animals, and the officers of Arabia, Kenya, and Britain did all they could for us. Some animals had to be flown straight to Aden, and troop transport was delayed so that this could be done immediately. Then there was the money many people sent to the World Wildlife Fund for the oryx. The Safari Club paid the costs of the first five via London to New York, and shared the cost with the United States and the World Wildlife Fund for others. For the last four, quartered at Naples, Pan-American lent a special chartered plane to get them to New York. Five zoos, many societies and chambers of commerce, and thousands of private people helped. It really deserves to be called a World Herd."

He cautioned his hearers, however, that the work of conservation in this way has only begun. "We must maintain enthusiasm for other operations." The Survival Service of the IUCN needs a strong unit for governing and pooling people in the field of animals, especially the dealers. The London symposium of 1964 was more than a step in the right direction and their resolutions should bear fruit, but a dealer who lately acquired two more Arabian oryx independently has been offered high prices for them from lots of zoos. To buy these animals would not be illegal, but it is against the good of the species and encourages such dealing outside the World Herd, and such action should be deplored. Glancing around, I saw as nice a collection of frozen faces as I have ever witnessed in my life. Like myself, all my neighbors were well aware of the identity of the zoo that had offered the highest price for the Naples oryx.

Major Grimwood now came to Stage Two, or Breeding. In this respect the oryx are doing very well, he said. One female from Kuwait died, but the others are all right, and there had to date been eight births. The first seven were all males, a fact that plunged their guardians into despair and set them to wondering, as one does, if some maleficent force in Nature has not determined that a species will die out no matter what efforts are made. But the eighth and most recent oryx baby is a female, and everybody is happy again. The little female was sired by a young male who until then had not bred. Might this fact be significant? There are still only five males in the first herd, not a satisfactory situation as yet. One wants at least ten times as many animals before one can be sure the Arabian oryx is safe. They are maintaining a stud book at Phoenix. They will want several other herds before they can embark on Stage Three, but still the prospects are much better for the oryx than they were in 1960.

"Israel and Jordan offer the only terrain suitable for natural parks," said the Major, "and introducing them into Israel would be sticky, politically." But it will be a long time before they have enough stock to try it, he added: one need not cross that bridge as yet. Meanwhile, in the original country of Muscat-Oman, some British officers have spotted more wild oryx, perhaps as many as two hundred. The Sultan has now prohibited hunting them from motorcars, but there is still the danger of raids or some prince's idiotic idea of what hospitality requires, and chances of survival for these animals are small. However, the Bedouin regard themselves as the Sultan's trustees, and they may protect the oryx even though they allow themselves to hunt them in small numbers.

The Naples oryx are still there, and have bred two young, one male and one female, while waiting to have their fate decided. The Sultan has offered another oryx and her expected offspring to the World Herd, and the prince who led the worst raid in that disastrous year has at last undergone a change of heart, and now keeps a fairly large herd of his own. Sometimes his people go out to capture more, but they have slap-happy methods, and kill almost as many as they used to when they were trying. Still, the prince means well, which is something.

"Tinker of Phoenix is the man to talk to now, if you want to know about oryx," said the Major in conclusion.

On this comparatively happy note the meeting adjourned for lunch. Most of us spent the afternoon at the zoo, checking up on things we had seen before and looking at new arrivals, and before we dispersed visited a special conservation exhibit displayed in a temporary canvas structure— a few cases containing stuffed animals, and long messages attached to each. Pride of place, naturally, was given to the Smithsonian loan, Martha the passenger pigeon, but of equal interest was a California condor. From his label I learned that this nearly extinct bird has a wing spread of nine feet and can weigh up to twenty pounds. There has been a steady decline in condor numbers, with an average of three flying birds lost to every two young ones mating, statistics that indicate total extinction within a few years. In another case, containing a southern sea otter—a surprisingly large animal—I learned something less gloomy. "From near extinction—a slow recovery," the label was headed. For a long time these animals were killed at sight for the sake of their fur. The greatest slaughter of sea otters on record took place when two Russian sailors on St. George Island killed 5000 in a single year, all by themselves, about the middle of the nineteenth century. Next year hunters bagged only 1000 in all, a circumstance that startled and alarmed furrier circles and resulted in Russia's making rigorous restrictions on killing the animal. Unfortunately, when by virtue of the treaty of Sitka, 1867, the United States bought Alaska, Russia's restrictions automatically lapsed, and the resultant killing brought the southern sea otter so close to being wiped out that in 1910 one skin fetched $1,703.33 in the London market. The publicity given to this incident shocked the authorities into doing something about it, and by international agreement, in 1911, Russia, Japan, Great Britain and the United States ordered a stop to all sea-otter killing whatsoever. The animal's comeback was hearteningly prompt. Today there are about 3000 sea otters around the Aleutians and 900 along the California coast between Monterey and Point Conception.

Before the group at the exhibit broke up, I had a little talk with Al Oeming, director of the well-known Alberta Game Farm in Canada. Mr. Oeming, who holds a record for breeding the musk ox, was pleased and excited by the prospect of travels he plans to make in the Far East. When I asked his opinion of the Chinese claim to have recently discovered herds of elephants alive and flourishing in the wilds of Yunnan, he shook his head. "Look, the Chinese can say anything they like and who's there to check up on it? They'll never convince me that a country with their resources and their record in intelligence and spying would have been ignorant all these years that they had elephants—elephants, mind you, one of the biggest species—tramping around in there. No. They got hold of some pictures of elephants in Thailand or Cambodia, and that's what they're showing. I don't believe what they told Caroline Jarvis about the panda in the wild, either. I bet they've got all their pandas counted, with somebody watching."

Next I paid a quick visit to the children's zoo with Dr. Lang of Basel, who was draped with heavy necklaces of cameras on straps. The chief object of our attention was the little Bonobo, or pygmy chimp, born the preceding August. John Muth, an ex-marine who looks after the children's zoo and brooks no nonsense from small humans, was in the nursery kitchen, behind the exhibition-case that holds young creatures, with the medical man who had officiated at the birth of the little animal. I said to the latter, "Well, this *is* a surprise. I saw Kakowet and Linda fooling around last February, but I hadn't the slightest idea . . . How long was the gestation, then?"

"We don't know any more than you do," he said. "We were surprised too. But she isn't a premature baby. Linda seemed willing enough to be a good mother, carried the infant around in the right position and all that, but we could see it wasn't nursing and we kept an eye on it. Finally, after about twenty-four hours, we tranquillized Linda and took the baby out and fed it. It fed fine: it was hungry. We expressed some of Linda's milk, but didn't get much—not enough to fill a teaspoon. Still, on the chance that she'd start up later, we gave the baby back for another twelve hours, but no luck. Now it's feeding fine on the bottle here, and Linda's in estrus once more, so we moved her back with Kakowet."

Dr. Lang wanted photographs of the baby, and took them through the front window—Dr. Schroeder is very strict about antisepsis. A nursery attendant picked up the tiny creature from its crib and held it so that the photographer could see it from top to toe, while it wailed and scrabbled wildly in the air. Back on its stomach in the crib it stopped crying and "swam" in the manner of human babies trying to crawl. Ten minutes later John Muth came out and found me still crouched at the cage, enraptured. He sighed. "You women!" he said. "I'll swear you're as bad as any of my nursery girls. I can never get them away from here. Judy, who looks after that chimp, won't even go home when it's time. I have to chase her out."

On Thursday, the last day of the conference, Charles Shaw, curator of reptiles at San Diego, opened the proceedings with an account of his success in hatching out Galapagos tortoises. At the end of the nineteenth century, naturalists had begun to despair for the future of these great animals. They estimated that ten million had been taken by ships that stopped at the Galapagos islands for the express purpose of providing fresh protein food for their crews, and they would load up on live animals. There used to be fifteen sorts of tortoise, each having evolved on its own island. Females were easiest to catch because of their habit of coming down from the mountains when it was time to lay their eggs, and no doubt the wholesale capture and slaughter of the females rather than the males hastened the decline in their numbers. On the other hand, because of what Dr. Shaw described as a pronounced sexual dimorphism in size, animal collectors tended to grab the males because they were bigger and more spectacular, a circumstance that naturally resulted in very little mating in zoos. Then came the white man's improvements on the islands, with dogs and other predators that he brought with him. Goats and cattle were left there for future victualing, and they competed with the tortoises for food, tortoises being grazers too. As if all this were not enough, hunters began killing the tortoises for their oil, which is believed by some women to have rare cosmetic qualities.

Seeing the danger of all this, Dr. Townsend of the New York Aquarium brought 150 young tortoises back to America for conservation purposes, and dispersed them in about fifteen places, among them Bermuda. In Bermuda, five out of eight eggs actually hatched, but there were no reports of such success from the other recipients. Miami, San Diego, and Honolulu had a lot of the tortoises, now and then replenishing their collection by additional trips to the islands, and sometimes the females laid eggs, but these all proved to be infertile. Finally Shaw and a laboratory partner decided that their tortoises didn't have enough room to mate. Accordingly, they enlarged the enclosure and replaced its floor with a more yielding substance. They were right, because, as they soon had a chance to observe, the male tortoise in the act of copulation must dig his shell a short way into the ground. In 1958, one of the San Diego tortoises laid 15 eggs of which one or two were broken—a common accident with tortoise eggs, due to the female's habit of dropping them, when she is laying into a hole, from a considerable height. Five of the remaining eggs hatched, and one got out but was dead on arrival. The other eggs were infertile. "Fifty per cent fertility, in other words," said Shaw. From 1958 to 1961 there were no eggs, and that was an anxious time at San Diego. Then, in '61, the curator sorted out the fertile egg-layers from his twenty-three adult tortoises, of which only seven were female. Of this seven, one laid that year; 258 eggs were laid in 1962, with a total fertility of 10.2, and 6 of these hatched.

"We have to put the animals to bed every night in the winter," said Shaw. "The greatest egg-depositing activity takes place from November to April, usually at night, so we leave them out of doors then if they seem to want to stay there, but they can come in at will, into the barn. They may lay twice in a year. The eggs are hard-shelled. The mother digs a hole that widens at the bottom, so that in cross section it looks like a bottle. Then she lays, breaking some in the process, and after she's finished laying she breaks more by sorting them around, stirring them up, and finally covering them by digging backward with her back legs. After that she tamps the ground down hard, and that helps to break the ones that are left. They weigh on the average 106.86 grams. We incubate them in heated quarters, above 82 degrees temperature, maximum 90, average 82.5 to 84. The period of incubation varies. We've had hatchings after 173 days, 174, 191, 198, 204, 232, and, once, 160. As the time approaches the shell becomes friable. The little tortoises have sharp claws and seem to use them rather than the egg tooth to tear down the shell. The fertility rate is low here, and in Bermuda and Miami as well. This may be an inherent failure to reproduce many at a time, as a self-limiting factor; it stands to reason that if all the eggs hatched, there wouldn't be enough food for the tortoises in the Galapagos."

From moving pictures of various phases in tortoise breeding, we saw how the male tortoise's shell digs into the ground during pairing. As we watched a close-up of a female tortoise dropping her eggs into the hole she had dug, the curator's voice sounded genuinely cross as he said, "Now look at that, what a crack the egg gets." Some of the eggs are caught by attendants in a net as they emerge, an activity of which the female seems unaware. "Here's the thirty-first youngster we ever hatched," said Shaw, of a picture of a tiny tortoise scrambling across the ground. "He was only two and a half inches long and weighed under two ounces. Now he weighs more than a hundred pounds."

Next on the agenda was a lecture by Ian Player, chief conservator of Zululand in South Africa, on "The Translocation of the White Rhinoceros—a Success in Wildlife Conservation in Southern Africa." Mr. Player, a sturdy-looking man who served with the U. S. Army in Italy during the Second World War, "is credited with a successful breeding program," as the biography said, "bringing the white rhinoceros population up from 20 to 812 during the past 12 years. He became chief conservator of Zululand in 1964 and has charge of 14 game reserves there. . . . Gary Player, the professional golfer, is his brother."

Mr. Player and his colleagues experienced great difficulty in the early days, arguing with farmers and natives and convincing them that good land should be used for such a crackpot scheme as bringing back the white rhino. Even though this animal is believed by Zulus to have got its name because it has a tractable temper—because in the Zulu language "white" means "good" in some connotations—it was a struggle. Without his former superior, Colonel Vincent, said Mr. Player, it couldn't have been done. Today the government controls the project through its parks department, and the conservation of the white rhino is respectable, but the battle isn't quite won and never will be. "We couldn't have done what we did without international co-operation," he assured us, "and we must have the same co-operation to continue."

There was a time, in 1896, when the white rhino was presumed extinct—and small wonder, considering how vigorously Europeans had hunted and shot it. Then it was refound, and a few people attempted to push through protection laws. Sometimes they seemed to have won, sometimes they lost; the process was a seesaw, said Mr. Player, with at least one weird result when all the other animals in the Mfalozi Reserve had been killed off, and the rhino, with no competition, came back with a bang. Resulting overpopulation of rhino was disastrous to the countryside, for they grazed everywhere, leaving the ground naked to the forces of erosion. For a while the farmers had their way, hunters were permitted to do their worst against the rhino, and conservationists were powerless against indignant public opinion.

"It gave our opponents a political weapon," admitted Mr. Player.

Not until 1949 was order brought into the situation and protective game laws put in force. The conservationists began to catch rhino alive and move them to national parks, out of the farmer's way, but it was slow, arduous work until the introduction, in 1960, of "darting," or shooting with tranquilizers. Even with darting, I realized as I watched some of Mr. Player's illustrative films, it's fairly arduous work. A darted animal doesn't fall down insensible the minute the missile hits him, but takes off into the bush, and if he isn't followed at his own formidable rate of speed he might well disappear in some hidden spot and die when the dose takes full effect, for administration of the tranquilizer must be followed up with a neutralizing drug within a very few minutes. For this reason, two or three men always accompany the hunter on horseback. As soon as the rhino has been shot the horsemen tear off after him, following him through the thickest growth. When he has been found and properly dosed, he lies there insensible, an immense weight. A truck is backed up and the rhino is winched aboard it, and carted off to the pens in deep slumber. He wakes up in a pen to the strains of music. This is no dream: the hunters keep transistors playing to soothe the rhino. "Rhinos are very responsive to noise," explained Mr. Player. "We play the transistors for about seventy-two hours."

Dazed and terrified, the animal refuses for a day or two to eat. Then, little by little, he will accept food if the captors are lucky, but sometimes they get a stouthearted subject who stubbornly continues to turn away from the proffered greenstuff. It is an odd fact, said Mr. Player, that the white rhino, a timid animal at large, becomes very aggressive in the pen, whereas the black rhino is just the opposite, aggressive at large but very tractable in captivity. "When we get one of the white rhinos that won't settle down no matter how long we keep him, we set him loose again. Here's a picture of one of those, taken, you see, at large. He lived near the camp so we scooped him in, but in the pen he wouldn't eat, wouldn't settle down at all, and we let him go. And there he is, living where he lived before, not far from the camp."

When the animals have been pacified, the next stage of the objective is to move them to other areas—reserves on the continent for the most part, though some go to zoos abroad. Kruger National Park is a particularly suitable place, because it used to be a haunt of the white rhino before hunters cleared them out. When the animals are released, they immediately come up against the hard facts of life in the wild all over again. A rhino just released in Kruger fought an elephant fiercely over possession of a water hole. The battle continued for twenty-two hours and ended with the death of the rhino. Lions lie in wait for them, too.

Transporting the animals is another headache for the men. Recently, after much time and talk had been expended, the Rhodesian authorities agreed that they would take a hundred white rhinos into their reserve at the Matopos Mountains, which was fine. But then another question arose, as to how the South Africans were to get them there. Mr. Player's young men decided to transport them, two at a time, in trucks. From Zululand to the Matopos is a thirty-six-hour drive over bad roads. Carrying two huge rhinos in this way, arguing with suspicious policemen every so often, and coping with the animals when they tried, as they often did, to get out, was not exactly as easy chore. Nevertheless, said Mr. Player, one load and sometimes two went off every day until the operation was concluded. "The staff were magnificent. They did more than a thousand miles on that job," he said.

In addition to such work, the staff has embarked on a marking program so that they can study the rhinos further and measure their growth and habits of moving about. "We've swapped some for other rare animals," said Mr. Player. "The cheetah was believed extinct in 1927, but luckily it wasn't. We can now get a cheetah and a giraffe for one white rhino."

In conclusion, he said, "Remember, we are all brothers in the same cause. I'd like to say to Dr. Lehmann that Colombia is not alone—we're all in this together. Zoos can play a very important part in conservation; indeed, their importance can't be exaggerated. The key lies with the United States in international co-operation. Don't let's delude ourselves: conservation is politics, and you hold the power right now."

What he had said about darting gave the next speaker, Dr. Lee Talbot, exactly the opening he wanted for his talk on "The Problems of Capture." Dr. Talbot has served as an ecologist for Unesco, and has been on the South and East Asian Land Use and Wildlife Survival project. He is a consultant to Kenya and Tanzania, has lectured in Southeast Asia and served as a field biologist for the U. S. Forest Service and the University of California. That afternoon he was also an angry man, or a least a very emphatic one, as he talked about darting and the activity springing up around this invention. "Two months ago we got news of a Malaysian plan to capture one lone Sumatran rhino for a reserve, or zoo. The animal would then be protected, and the people involved planned to use a 'new mercy gun'—but what gun exactly? Nobody could find out. I mentioned this to a prominent conservationist in Washington, D.C.," he went on, his voice almost trembling with rage, "and he just shrugged and said, 'Well, you can't blame them for wanting to try: with that gun *it's so easy.*' Lots of people are planning to use capture-guns for rare species, but"—and here Dr. Talbot leaned over to emphasize his remarks—"*it is not easy.*" At the Survival Service they get on an average one request every week for instructions as to how to use it. Many an expedition is going out right now, equipped with these guns because "it's so easy." The problem of survival is critical, with two hundred species now gravely threatened in the wild. In years to come an increase in this number is inevitable. The question is, how to get the stock safely into the zoos? "Let's consider the normal capture of wild animals. Have we any idea of the measures taken and the mortality involved? Very little. Some people simply don't want to know: they assume that the animals they buy have been bred in captivity, or they say 'If we don't buy it, somebody else will.' It's a business deal. But to carry this deal through you need a capture team, with expensive equipment and people trained in their work. Economic deals call for efficiency, and to have a high mortality rate in a capture operation is not efficient." He quoted some figures from an article in the magazine *Oryx*, from one capture in Africa: Giraffe, three captured, one dead. Wildebeest, nine captured, six dead. Topi, five captured, five dead. Buffalo, five captured, one dead. Ostrich, ten captured, eight dead. Zebra, eleven captured, eight dead. Zebra yearlings, eight captured, six dead. "Rather sobering, perhaps?" said Dr. Talbot. "I've heard worse. A man who deals in animals told us that in the first three months this year in East Africa, one animal reached the zoos for every eight killed. Of course one can't generalize, but the mortality in carriers is known to be very high. And what of the rare species? This is an entirely different problem. They are uncommon and less known and so is the area where they are found. Catching them is not an economic proposition—you have an unknown area that calls for equipment and personnel not easily available, and we can't afford a high mortality." So far, he asked, what is the record on the capture of rare animals? There are two methods: one is the commercial trapper, who is usually unavailable or, if he can be found, he increases the mortality rate, as witness what has happened with the bongo. There was an attempt by the

Survival Center several years ago to capture some threatened Sumatran rhino. They caught a few females and only one male—which the trapper let go so as to prolong his job. Three of the females went singly to zoos and two of these died very soon. But mercy-gun capture, on the other hand, calls for a special team, and the complications are immense—one must have expertise, training equipment, the lot.

"Expertise on certain animals must be built up over a long period. Not all species react in the same way to these drugs; indeed, we are not sure that individuals within the same species necessarily react in the same way. I should say that there *is* another method, a special emergency team like that that caught the Arabian oryx, who, after they have done the job, disperse. Major Grimwood said that they succeeded through luck, but his organization too was splendid. That was an amazingly successful operation; they lined up the politics and everything. Contrast it with an organization I won't identify, composed of a leader and his gun men, who killed 100 percent of the rare bovines they sought and caught. There were political repercussions from that fiasco—terrible results. Yet two of that number were supposed to be experts."

The capture gun, he said, offers a grave threat to conservation. Introduced at a wildlife meeting in 1957, it was then hailed as a wonderful advance, but when, in 1959, Dr. Talbot visited East Africa, he never met a man who didn't curse those guns. Only one, Dr. Helmuth Buechner, had managed to capture thirty-six Uganda Kob with them. One man. With other people there was sometimes 100 percent mortality with the same make of gun. Talbot and his wife once tried to use it, because they were in a hurry, but the try didn't succeed. They killed twelve animals and wasted time. Later, the Forestry, Game and Parks people finally got hold of new drugs that worked, and have since collected lots of animals with an overall loss of only 2.5 percent. But they had to train hard first.

Dr. Talbot talked for a while of the different effects of drugging on wild animals. There are two sorts. One affects the central nervous system, the other paralyzes the muscles, but in either case administration gives a severe shock to the animal. A human in a hospital, before such drugs are administered, is tested first for allergy and reactions. His size and weight are known, as are the times he last ate or drank. He is relaxed. The drug is administered into the bloodstream very slowly, with an anesthetist watching to make any necessary adjustments. Oxygen is close by. Yet sometimes the patient dies, and insurance companies regard anesthesia as the most dangerous part of surgery. Animals in zoos are taken care of almost as well, but what of the animal in the wild? We don't know his weight, or his condition, or when he ate. There is the stress factor too.

We just shoot and count ourselves lucky if we hit him at all. Mr. Player had said they have to get to the shot rhino within a minute or he dies. Many other animals die within two or three minutes at most. You have the predator factor to contend with; the hyena will attack a lion speared by a human within five minutes. A deer may die in a gulley and you only know where he is by the vultures that gather. In darting, a massive dose is usually lethal. The same drug varies greatly with the environment, the temperature and humidity. There is no one all-purpose drug. "The wonder is that so many animals survive," he said bitterly.

A delegation from Burma had just left, he continued, with some information they asked for about the capture gun. Obviously Dr. Talbot had no confidence in the future of the animals they meant to catch. A polar-bear expedition, using the same dosage that had been successful with the grizzly, shot six from the plane, of which five died immediately and the sixth was shot the next day by a hunter. The incident caused an international outcry. On a fallow-deer expedition the hunters failed to find any animals, so they turned over their drugs to the helpers and said, "Go and shoot them."

"The problem of capture is still a problem, and we must realize this," said the speaker in conclusion. "So when we talk of the Survival Center, remember that we can't afford the continued abuse of drug methods and still less can we afford the loss of rare animals—not to mention bad publicity. We need a capture code of ethics, and a pooling of information and of experts. No one person is expert in all animals and all conditions; therefore we must get people who are most expert in each particular case. We should do something internationally, as Peter Scott suggests. It is *not so easy.*"

After every talk, naturally, there had been a question-and-answer period, and from the way this one started out it was immediately apparent that Dr. Talbot's talk was the most controversial yet. Al Oeming plunged in by declaring that he, personally, found the capture gun a boon. He had suffered no losses when he used it. Others chimed in with similar statements, until Dr. Talbot said that he was not denying that there have been 100 percent successes as well. All he wanted was that people should realize the use of the capture gun requires a greater investment in expertise. "You shouldn't just buy a gun in a drugstore and set out," he declared.

"This has been a hot subject ever since 1957," said Robert Bean in the coffee break. "When the stuff first came in I used it on some Guinea baboons, twelve of them, all sired by the same animal and all more or less the same age. Three died immediately, three reacted right, and the rest showed no effect whatever, good or bad. I suggested then that we all pool our information, and sent out questionnaires, but I never got any replies. People were afraid to talk about it."

After Dr. Talbot, the talk on "The Need for Underwater Parks" and the accompanying movies of Dr. Eugenie Clark of the Cape Haze Marine Laboratory seemed far away indeed. A member of the Society of Ichthyologists and Herpetologists, Dr. Clark seemed too young to have done as much as the biography credited her with. We had talked chiefly of land animals, she pointed out, but in this question of conservation it is good to consider the sea too. In 1962 Marine Park Sanctuaries were suggested, and a year later there was more talk at a symposium in Washington, D.C., when Dr. Luke Hoffman, Mr. Harold Coolidge, and some others proposed a series of "wet lands" adjacent to the sea. But it is high time something is done in the sea itself, said Dr. Clark, and quoted statistics to support her statement. The largest animal that ever lived in pelagic waters, the blue whale, faces extinction very soon, what with modern methods of hunting him—exploding-head missiles, drugs, air spotters and so on. Yet there are countries that refuse to control the hunting of whales. "More than 630,000 finback whales were killed in this century alone, and many other species, all large animals, are threatened. The International Whaling Commission has set for 1966–67 a much smaller quota than they have ever set before. They are obviously concerned."

Another danger lies in uncontrolled "long-line" fishing, which threatens the big-game fishes. From Japan alone, long-lining in 1965 took in 459,000 blue marlin, 436,000 striped marlin, and so on. Long lines can be set twelve miles from the coast, as far out as the limit permits, and they are a grave threat to all countries that depend on fish. Some, like Chile, propose a two-hundred-mile limit, but this isn't recognized by other countries. Each country might perhaps control its own continental shelf.

"Skin and scuba divers are aware of the wide destruction along the coastal waters. The American Littoral Society and similar organizations are promoting conservation programs. One thing we can do that is non-political—protect our own waters by the formation of state-controlled marine parks. If you have any ideas as to how to do this, please send them to the Department of the Interior, the National Park Service. There are pitifully few natural areas left along the coast, so we must hurry to preserve the marine life of our coastal waters. Buck Island near St. Croix has recently been declared a National Park, and at Key Largo, Penny Camp, there is another, not as complete as we'd like because commercial fishers are still allowed in, and this is wrong. One of the most beautiful is Fort Jefferson at the Dry Tortugas, which is our first area that has proved really effective in preserving marine life—it's hard to get to the Dry Tortugas. But will somebody build a hotel there one of these days? We hope not." She mentioned other marine areas that have been, or ought to be, declared national parks—Channel Island at Santa Barbara and the Pallas Islands in Micronesia are two of them—and then she showed a film about Buck Island.

"It has a barrier reef around a coral reef, which makes it unusual and very interesting for divers. This film had a strong influence on President Kennedy, who in 1961 proclaimed Buck Island a national monument," said the doctor, and proceeded to describe the wildlife there, both above and below the water's surface. I was impressed by her story about mongooses. It seems that frigate birds that used to nest in numbers on the island were discouraged by the many rats that also flourished there and had learned to depend on frigate-bird eggs for their food. (Dr. Clark didn't say where the rats came from originally.) To counteract the rats, a well-meaning naturalist imported mongooses, expecting them to kill the rodents. It didn't work out that way. The mongooses and the rats joined forces, and the consumption of bird and turtle eggs went up enormously. Now they even attack the birds and lizards, and the main problem at Duck Island is to stamp out the mongooses.

The talk ended with a few discouraging reminders of pollution in sea water and a rather haunting comment on the coral-eating starfish of Australia. The only effective enemy of this starfish, it seems, is the gastropod. Australians are fond of gathering conches, which are gastropods, and at certain places they have taken away so many that nothing remains to hinder the starfish, which forthwith wreaks havoc.

Last speaker on the agenda was Dr. Conway of the Bronx, on the subject "Zoo Opportunities in the Propagation of Endangered Species." Parks and reservations are of first importance in conservation, he said, but we should remember that they are not inviolate. Thus zoos may become even more important than they are now. The human population is increasing so fast that our globe will soon be crowded, and the parks will suffer accordingly. We have already seen water starvation in the Everglades and encroachment on the Grand Canyon. "Parks are not sacrosanct. Indeed, the time may come when men like cities and dislike the open country. The United States, though it is not nearly so crowded as some other places and though it is richer than most, yet has to struggle to maintain her parks and reserves. In any case there are too many visitors in our parks already, and the animals there are bound to disappear. Bird preservation will prove impractical even where mammals can be preserved.

Lizards lack immunity to contamination. The time may not be far distant when we use antelopes for food. In domestication, not parks, is the only safety for animals, but the zoo is the one widespread organization that can work, even with too many people, on conservation. The time is past when the zoo was attacked by the conservationist: today, serious conservationists must seek positions in zoos."

To propagate is a zoo's first obligation; the parks themselves depend on the zoos for replenishment. In fact, the zoo is the *only* place for captive propagation. On this subject Dr. Conway, growing fanciful, talked of the possibility of bringing back some species of birds now extinct, simply by working in the protected environs of the zoo. Why not breed the great auk again? "Seriously," he continued, "to propagate living rarities can be fascinating, though one is hampered by the usual lack of zoo data through all these years."

The major zoo responsibilities are capture, care, and propagation. Ecological studies of lizards and other neglected species should be undertaken. Some rarities should not be taken for exhibition purposes, and zoos should prohibit their purchase. One example he had in mind, he said, was the monkey-eating eagle, which is being exported from the Philippines at a ruinous rate. ("Hear, hear!" said a voice behind me.) We need a truly representative international organization. Until such a body exists, the effectiveness of the council is problematical. It is only since the Second World War that zoos have been interested in such breeding programs; since then some animals in zoo-breeding groups have done well but others, like cheetahs and orangs, haven't done well at all. "Each project must begin with a large sample," he continued. "Small differences in species may have to be agreed on. Zoos must show a smaller list of exhibition species. We must have dispersal as a precaution against natural calamities and accidents. And we must use careful selection. Some people fear that this is merely domestication, but I think not: survival features may be the same in the zoo as outside. At any rate, captivity itself is selective, since the parents have been subjected already to the greatest possible stress. However, even if we grant that zoo-bred animals will change slightly, propagation in captivity should not be discouraged. I hope that we will soon see special breeding centers for rare animals. The great gap now is between the desire and the space for this."

There was a last meeting that afternoon for what the agenda called a summation, at which the delegates talked informally back and forth, through Commander Scott in the chair, about plans, signs, future meetings, collecting for the Wildlife Fund, enforcement of rare-animal agree-

ments, the possibility that Russian delegates might attend the next meeting as they have done before in Europe—a whole lot of divergent
subjects, but however much the talk circled, it was brought back every
so often by Peter Scott, who with a light but firm hand headed the
delegates toward their main purpose of formulating resolutions to be
published the next day. The meeting was about to close when a tall
young man in the back of the room—I learned later that he was Richard
Warner, a zoologist at Berkeley—jumped up to say, "We ought to do
something about the over-exploitation of primates for university research
in this country. I've been growing increasingly concerned about it. Let's
get the research groups together and try to bring them to some realization
of the danger of what's happening." He talked feelingly of the waste of
the proceedings, of experiments needlessly repeated again and again.
Monkey species all over the world are in danger of being wiped out, he
said, and all for nothing.

"Yes," said Scott thoughtfully. "It's a problem of communication
mainly, don't you think?"

No, said someone nearer the front: he feared it was something worse
than that—the system. The government is subsidizing this research,
and when you have subsidies the same thing always happens; each
department feels bound to use up the appropriation for the current year
so that next year's won't be cut down. Hence, more and more primates
are bought . . . "Another thing is that it's such a tremendous program,"
said a third speaker. "That means they've taken in a lot of laboratory
technicians who are really not awfully good. You just can't find that many
skilled men."

By the close of the meeting they had hammered out the following
resolutions:

1) That the International Union for the Conservation of Nature and
Natural Resources be requested to review, through the Survival Service
Commission, the urgent necessity for closer liaison between zoological
parks and other organizations that use wild animals, with a view to averting
the threat to wildlife and especially to endangered species.

2) That the United States Government (which, through its federally
financed research and pharmaceutical production, uses large numbers of
wild primates) be requested to consider closer evaluation of research
grants in terms of the number of primates and the merits of the
individual projects, to reduce primate movement in order to reduce their
mortality and to support the captive breeding of primates for research
purposes.

3) That the IUCN be requested to set up a translocation unit to

collect and codify information in collaboration with the FAO on future schemes for animal capture, transport and wild release, especially of endangered species. It also asked that the IUCN organize a symposium on immobilization and other capture techniques.

4) That thought be given and action taken to implement the need for underwater parks and their full protection.

We trickled through the doors of the banquet room, and somebody turned out the lights. I don't know what the others did—most likely they just continued to talk somewhere, but I went up to my room and packed.